Lindow Man
The Body in the Bog

I. M. Stead   J. B. Bourke   Don Brothwell

Published for the Trustees of the British Museum
by British Museum Publications

Cornell University Press
Ithaca, New York

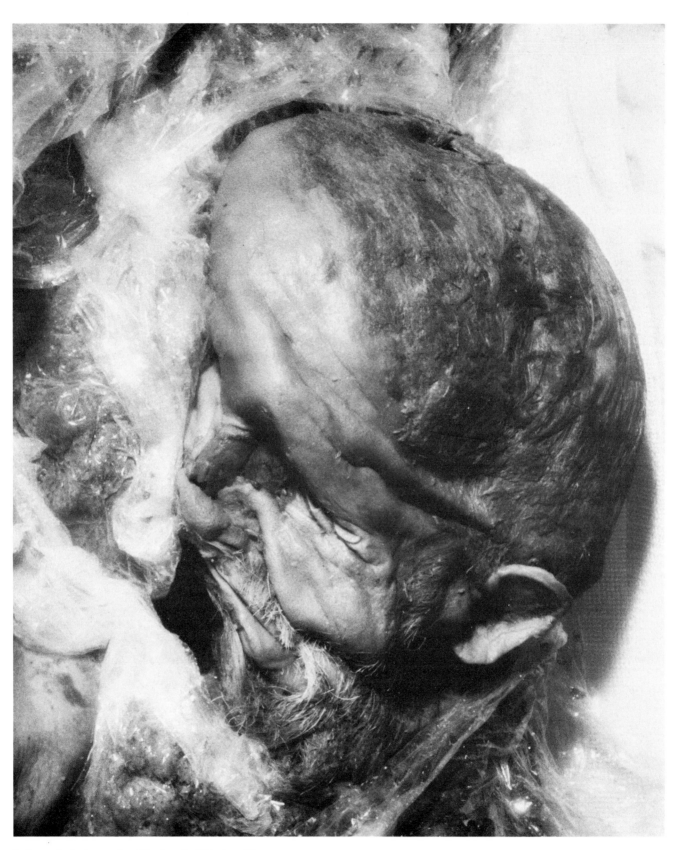

Infra-red photograph of the head of Lindow Man.

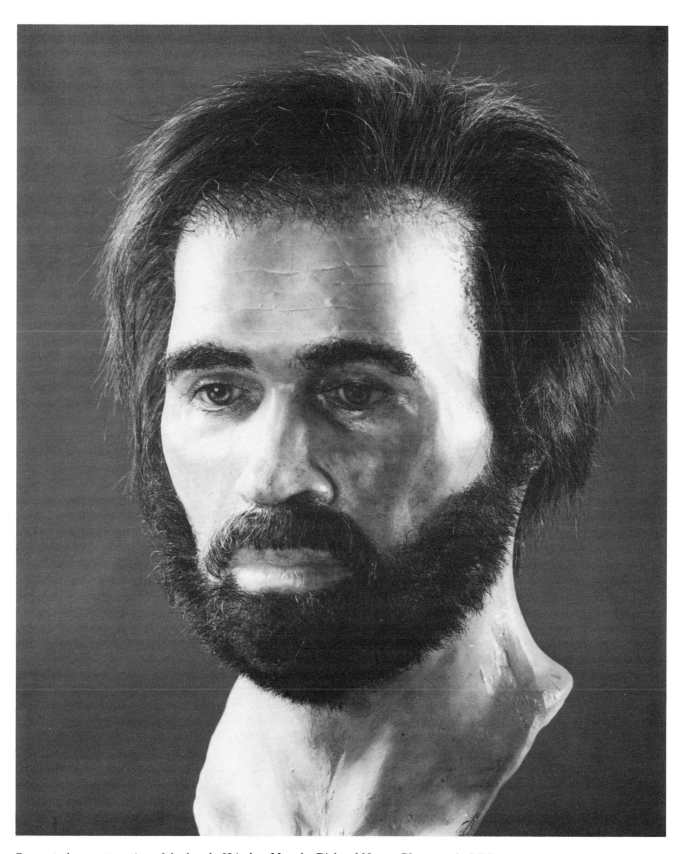

Suggested reconstruction of the head of Lindow Man, by Richard Neave. Photograph: BBC.

For information address Cornell University Press
124 Roberts Place, Ithaca, New York 14851

First published 1986 by Cornell University Press

International Standard Book Number 0-8014-1998-0
Library of Congress Catalog Card Number 86-47720

Printed in Great Britain
at the Bath Press, Avon

Contents

List of Contributors

J. C. Ambers British Museum Research Laboratory, London   WC1B 3DG.

Keith Barber Department of Geography, University of Southampton, Southampton   SO9 5NH.

P. Beahan Department of Materials Science, University of Liverpool, P.O. Box 147, Liverpool   L69 3BX.

J. B. Bourke Department of Surgery, University Hospital, Nottingham   N67 2UH.

S. G. E. Bowman British Museum Research Laboratory, London   WC1B 3DG.

C. S. Briggs Royal Commission on Ancient and Historical Monuments (Wales), Edleston House, Queen's Road, Aberystwyth, Dyfed.

Don Brothwell Institute of Archaeology, 31–34 Gordon Square, London   WC1H 0PY.

G. Budworth (Secretary, International Guild of Knot Tyers) 45 Stambourne Way, Upper Norwood, London   SE19 2PY.

M. Charlesworth Department of Diagnostic Radiology, St Bartholomew's Hospital, London   EC1A 7BE.

R. C. Connolly Department of Anatomy, University of Liverpool, P.O. Box 147, Liverpool   L69 3BX.

S. M. Dadson Isotope Measurements Laboratory, AERE, Harwell, Oxon   OX11 0RA.

Judith Dayton Department of Geological Sciences, University of Birmingham, P.O. Box 363, Birmingham   B15 2TT.

Keith Dobney Institute of Archaeology, 31–34 Gordon Square, London   WC1H 0PY.

G. Embery Department of Dental Sciences, University of Liverpool, P.O. Box 147, Liverpool   L69 3BX.

R. P. Evershed Department of Biochemistry, University of Liverpool, P.O. Box 147, Liverpool   L69 3BX.

R. Gillespie Research Laboratory for Archaeology and the History of Art, 6 Keble Road, Oxford   OX1 3QJ.

Maureen Girling Ancient Monuments Laboratory, English Heritage, Fortress House, 23 Savile Row, London   W1X 2HE.

J. A. J. Gowlett Research Laboratory for Archaeology and the History of Art, 6 Keble Road, Oxford   OX1 3QJ.

D. A. Green Department of Dental Sciences, University of Liverpool, P.O. Box 147, Liverpool   L69 3BX.

E. T. Hall Research Laboratory for Archaeology and the History of Art, 6 Keble Road, Oxford   OX1 3QJ.

Marion Hallett Department of Diagnostic Radiology, St Bartholomew's Hospital, London   EC1A 7BE.

R. E. M. Hedges Research Laboratory for Archaeology and the History of Art, 6 Keble Road, Oxford   OX1 3QJ.

S. R. Higgitt Department of Geography, University of Liverpool, Roxby Building, P.O. Box 147, Liverpool   L69 3BX.

Gordon Hillman Institute of Archaeology, 31–34 Gordon Square, London   WC1H 0PY.

Timothy Holden Institute of Archaeology, 31–34 Gordon Square, London   WC1H 0PY.

Andrew K. G. Jones Environmental Archaeology Unit, University of York, Heslington, York   YO1 5DD.

Norman Lindsey Terrestrial Photogrammetry Unit, The City University, Northampton Square, London   EC1V 0BH.

K. J. Matthews British Museum Research Laboratory, London   WC1 3DG.

Margaret McCord Department of Conservation, British Museum, Franks House, 38–46 Orsman Road, London   N1.

N. Mirza Department of Clinical Microbiology, University College Hospital, Grafton Way, London   WC1E 6AU.

Richard Neave Department of Medical Illustration, University of Manchester, The Royal Infirmary, Manchester   M13 9WL.

Duro Oduwole Department of Chemistry, Queen Mary College, University of London, Mile End Road, London   E1 4NS.

Frank Oldfield Department of Geography, University of Liverpool, Roxby Building, P.O. Box 147, Liverpool   L69 3BX.

Sherif Omar Department of Conservation, British Museum, Franks House, 38–46 Orsman Road, London   N1.

R. L. Otlet Isotope Measurements Laboratory, AERE, Harwell, Oxon   OX11 0RA.

M. Powell Department of Clinical Microbiology, University College Hospital, Grafton Way, London   WC1E 6AU.

A. V. Priston The Metropolitan Police Forensic Science Laboratory, 109 Lambeth Road, London   SW1 7LP.

Ruth Quinn Make-up Department, Granada Television, Manchester.

R. H. Reznek Department of Diagnostic Radiology, St Bartholomew's Hospital, London   EC1A 7BE.

N. Richardson Department of Geography, University of Liverpool, Roxby Building, P.O. Box 147, Liverpool   L69 3BX.

G. L. Ridgway Department of Clinical Microbiology, University College Hospital, Grafton Way, London WC1E 6AU.

Don Robins Sciencewright Ltd., 26 Elms Lane, Sudbury, Middlesex HA0 2NN.

Anne Ross 8 Rose Road, Southampton SO2 1AE.

Keith Sales Department of Chemistry, Queen Mary College, University of London, Mile End Road, London E1 4NS.

J. B. Shortall Department of Materials Science, University of Liverpool, P.O. Box 147, Liverpool L69 3BX.

P Skidmore Museum and Art Gallery, Chequer Road, Doncaster DN1 2AE.

J. B. Stanbury Department of Dental Sciences, University of Liverpool, P.O. Box 147, Liverpool L69 3BX.

I. M. Stead Department of Prehistoric and Romano-British Antiquities, British Museum, London WC1B 3DG.

G. W. Taylor York Archaeological Trust, Conservation Laboratories, Galmanhoe Lane, Marygate, York YO3 7DZ.

R. C. Turner County Archaeologist, County Planning Department, Commerce House, Hunter Street, Chester CH1 1SN.

A. J. Walker Isotope Measurements Laboratory, AERE, Harwell, Oxon OX11 0RA.

I. E. West Department of Forensic Medicine, Guy's Hospital, St Thomas Street, London SE1 9ET.

G. Yates Department of Geography, University of Liverpool, Roxby Building, P.O. Box 147, Liverpool L69 3BX.

Acknowledgements

The large number of contributors to this volume is only the beginning of a long list of those involved in the discovery, recording and researching of Lindow Man. Other specialists, including Denys Goose (formerly Department of Operative Dental Surgery, University of Liverpool), Rod Hay (St. John's Hospital for Diseases of the Skin, London), George Mann (formerly Addenbrookes Hospital, Cambridge) and Juliet Rogers (Department of Rheumatology, Bristol Royal Infirmary) have submitted reports incorporated in papers published here; and many more, notably Paul Buckland (Department of Geography, University of Birmingham), have given advice and help.

Joan Taylor and Robina McNeil-Sale (Department of Archaeology, University of Liverpool), Colin Shell (Department of Archaeology and Anthropology, University of Cambridge) and Helen Lockwood helped with the excavation, while Velson Horie (The Manchester Museum) worked on the excavation and dealt with initial conservation problems. Supt. Neville Jones and his colleagues in the police at Macclesfield, Alan Williams (Chief Pathologist, Macclesfield District General Hospital) and Ken Harewood, manager of the peat workings, gave invaluable assistance. The finds from the site were presented to the British Museum by A. P. Bingham, on behalf of the landowners, and by the Chief Constable, Cheshire Constabulary.

In addition to the contributors, radiographic and other facilities were generously provided by David Thompson and Jean Harvey (The Middlesex Hospital, London), Reg Davis (The Royal Marsden Hospital, London) and Picker International, Ltd. Research Assistants were employed for two aspects of the work: Sandra Higgitt processed the peat samples and was financed by the Historic Buildings and Monuments Commission, while Tim Holden dealt with the stomach contents and was paid by the British Museum; the Museum also financed the initial sorting of the beetle remains. Most of the excavating at the British Museum was carried out by Valery Rigby and Gill Varndell, while David Wraight and Kay Collins dealt with boxing, transporting, crowd-control, and many other problems. The freeze-drying was carried out at the Ancient Monuments Laboratory, by courtesy of Clifford Price and with the assistance of Jacqueline Watson.

Writers of individual Chapters wish to thank the following organisations and colleagues: A. D. Bowles, J. F. Foreman, M. J. Humm, I. Law, C. Perry, A. R. T. Stoker, E. Hendy, and research grants from SERC (Chapter 5); J. Clarke, J. N. Hooker and R. Bebei-Mahani (Chapter 8); R. Brammar, Roz Carter, George Rogers, John Storey and Carol Waugh (Chapter 11); the Special Trustees of St. Bartholomews Hospital, Ian Kelsey Fry and Jullie Jessop (Chapter 15); A. Moss and B. Wilkinson (Chapter 22); Vaughan Bryant, Sally Davis, James Greig, Pat Hinton, Karl-Heinz Knörzer, Professor Körber-Grohne and Patty-Jo Watson (Chapter 25); Stephen Carter, Camilla and Jim Dickson, Jill Dunstan, Dawn Holmes and Mark Nesbitt (Chapter 26); Nick Balaam, Vaughan Bryant, Cheryl Haldane and Wendy Scaife (Chapter 27); D. J. Burden and Mrs E. Harris (Chapter 28).

The photograph on page 2 and figures 4–6, 11, 13–20, 24, 35 and 39 are British Museum photographs taken by Tony Cowell; Figures 34, 36 and 46–9 are photographs taken at the Institute of Archaeology, University of London; and the sources of other illustrations are acknowledged in the captions.

I
Excavation, Recording, Conservation and Dating

Fig. 1 The excavation of Lindow Man at Lindow Moss on 6 August 1984. Photo: R. C. Turner.

1 Discovery and Excavation of the Lindow Bodies

R. C. Turner

Of all the unusual stories and circumstances surrounding bog burials, the finding of a female skull at Lindow Moss and the police investigation which followed is the most bizarre. Its repercussions were to affect the subsequent discovery of Lindow Man and the period immediately after his excavation.

On 13 May 1983, two men (Andy Mould and Stephen Dooley) were at work on the elevator at the depot of a peat company on the edge of Lindow Moss. The peat is brought to the depot from the diggings on the moss by narrow gauge railway, then put through a shredding mill before despatch. Any obstructions which may block the mill such as branches or pieces of wood have to be cleared from the elevator. On that day, a round peat covered object about 20 to 22 cm long was discovered. It was soft and pliable and, jokingly, it was called a dinosaur's egg. The manager thought it might have been a burst football and gave orders for its disposal. However, the curiosity of the men had been aroused and they hosed off the peat in the yard. It became obvious that it was a human skull (Fig. 20) and the manager Ken Harewood, immediately took it to the police.

The skull was examined by Mr J. G. Benstead of the North West Home Office Forensic Science Laboratory at Southport, at the request of H.M. Coroner. His description reads:

'In my opinion, this is the skull of a European female, most probably in the age group 30/50 years. Some hairs were still adherent to the outer surface and membrane was still attached to bone to the right side of the vault and the left side of the base. The left eyeball was still identifiable and a little pultaceous matter was present inside the brain pan. The vault and the base are now separate and along the bone edges and the natural lines of cleavage, damage present is consistent with rough treatment before or after burial. No specific identifying features are apparent, since the cheek bones and both jaws were missing.'

At the time of this discovery, the Macclesfield Police were investigating reports of a long unsolved crime. Whilst interviewing two suspects about another crime, they were told a story of a man with whom these two had shared a cell. This man, Peter Reyn-Bardt, had claimed to have murdered his wife over twenty years before, dismembered and burnt her body and buried her remains in the garden. He had met his wife in 1958 and within two hours had proposed; three days later they married. They set up home in a cottage, whose garden backed on to Lindow Moss, where they lived together for a few weeks. After that she was seen by the neighbours making only brief visits, the last of which took place in 1960.

The police had first interviewed Reyn-Bardt in January 1983. A thorough search of the garden was made and large parts of it were excavated, but nothing was found. Reyn-Bardt firmly denied the accusations of murder and there was no evidence against him. Now in the middle of May, a woman's skull, of the right age, with tissue and hair adhering was brought in from Lindow Moss. It had come from a spot about 300 m from the cottage where they had lived.

On being told of this discovery, Reyn-Bardt made a full confession, confirming the information given and saying his wife was killed in a fight over blackmail demands. The police continued their search for evidence on the site and volumes of peat were dug and carefully sieved. A lorry load of peat, dispatched to Somerset on the morning the skull was found, was also traced and sieved. No more human remains were discovered, and the only object found was an unusual pin (see p. 40).

However, the police were suspicious of the skull and sought an archaeological opinion on its date. Professor Hall and Dr Gowlett of Oxford University's Research Laboratory for Archaeology and the History of Art came to their aid. Their results are discussed below (p. 22). They provided a radiocarbon date for the skull of 1740 ± 80BP, so it was clearly not connected with the case. Subsequently, on the strength of his confession, Reyn-Bardt was tried at Chester Crown Court in December 1983 and convicted of his wife's murder, even though no trace of her body had been found.

Lindow Moss (NGR SJ 820 805) was formerly very extensive, once covering some 600 hectares, and was formed in two shallow hollows within the boulder clay and glacial gravels. By the time of the publication of the Tithe Maps in 1843, it had shrunk in size to about 300 hectares, and today it is only about a tenth its original area, half of which is worked commercially for peat extraction. The remainder is covered in birch scrub.

It is divided between two parishes, Mobberley and Wilmslow in Cheshire, and since medieval times has been common land, where freeholders of the two parishes once had the right to cut peat for fuel. The first documentary reference to the moss is in 1421 when the right of turbary was confirmed. Samuel Finney, writing in the 1780s, mentions the occurrence of disastrous fires on the common in the dry summer weather and that both men and cattle had sometimes been drowned in the treacherous bog. He also records that vipers were so common that a viper catcher came annually to catch them, and relates the story of a boy bitten whilst collecting cranberries. (Earwaker 1877).

The first description of any antiquities coming from the bog and speculations on its long history were made by Norbury (1884). He comments that he should record his observations because 'Lindow is fast being cultivated, and in a few more years all that can be said will be – "This once was Lindow"'. After describing the size and appearance of the moss and the fallen trees to be found at the bottom, he remarks on the only two archaeological finds that have come from the site up to the present day. Firstly he mentions 'a decomposed skeleton of a boar found on the Lower Moss at Mobberley', and secondly 'what appeared to be a roadway made of logs of timber placed end to end, with sleepers across, laid close together, and this I am told continued for some length up the moss'.

Norbury ends his paper with some rather prejudiced remarks on the people who lived around the moss in past years. 'From actual observation of their physical characteristics and habits during the last fifty years, I am of the opinion that they are of a very ancient race, totally different from the surrounding people. The physical peculiarities were

very marked.' Their lifestyle, which made use of the full resources of the peat bog and its fringes, may not have been very different to that at the end of the prehistoric period. They were seen as separated and were clearly mistrusted. 'I may add that they in a general way shunned society, and appeared to be almost destitute of religious instincts'. It would have been interesting to have had Norbury's reaction to the two finds from the moss in the 1980s.

The modern appearance of the moss is very different. The commercial workings are divided into long rooms, 7 m wide and up to 200 m long, on either side of a central roadway. Alternate rooms are excavated by a large Hy-Mac excavator to a depth of up to 1 m, and the peat is stacked alongside to dry out for 6 months or more. The first skull (Lindow Woman) and the first part of Lindow Man came from these stacks.

On 1 August 1984, one of the men who had found the head of Lindow Woman pulled a long object off the elevator and, thinking it to be a piece of wood, threw it towards his companion. On hitting the ground, the peat fell away from the object to reveal a well preserved human foot and a ragged piece of skin from the lower leg. The police were immediately informed and they came to take the foot away for examination. The writer was telephoned that afternoon by Rachel Pugh from the local paper, the *Wilmslow World*, who asked for comments on this discovery. Visiting the site the next morning he was shown where the peat stack which produced the foot had been and walking along the adjacent uncut section edge, he noticed a flap of skin protruding. About 0.7 m below the present surface (itself some 2 m below the surface in 1962 when commercial operations began) it was about 250 m SW of the spot where the head had been found (Fig. 2). It was coffee-coloured and flexible, with the pores clearly visible on the underside. The tip had become blackened and hard, having been exposed for at least six months. The section was repacked with wet peat and this new discovery was reported to the police.

In discussion with the police, it was decided to arrange to excavate whatever this flap of skin represented. It must be remembered that the body of the murdered woman had never been recovered and here were remains, even better preserved than the first skull. Also the site was now known and stood close to a footpath which crossed the moss; it was feared that what was either a remarkable archaeological find or evidence of a modern crime might be disturbed. The excavation would have to be carried out in a day for the same reasons. By Monday 6 August people, equipment and permissions were all ready.

Because of the limited time available, a trench only 3 m square was laid out, so that the exposed portions of the body were central to its eastern side (Fig. 1). Water pressure from inside the peat had caused a serious crack to develop along the site, and the side containing the body was in danger of collapsing. The reason for this became apparent during the excavation. The upper levels consisted of loosely packed and recently redeposited peat, the remains of the stack left by the workmen. This was removed to reveal a layer of bleached vegetation, which had regenerated after the previous cutting of this area, probably some 20 years previously. A baulk was found, standing some 40 cm high and running along the line of the present section. This baulk, left by the earlier peat diggers, proved to contain the body. This is another remarkable circumstance in the preservation of Lindow Man, for its context would have been lost if the peat diggers of the 1960s had moved 1 m further east. The serious crack had developed along the line of this baulk and had not affected the body.

As this preliminary work was being done, Gill Yates and Nigel Richardson drew the complex peat section (Fig. 41). This well weathered section showed considerable variation at the level of the body and above. Some few centimetres below the body, however, there was a marked change to a more uniform humified layer. The more friable rust coloured peat which contained the body has the qualities the company is specifically interested in. Its nature and probably its date is the same as the peat from which the recent Danish finds have come. The Danes vividly describe it as 'dog's meat' as it has the consistency, colour and something of the smell of cheap pet food. Two soil monoliths were taken, one immediately alongside the protruding flap of skin, and one some 1.5 m further south, to act as a control.

Having removing the level of regenerated vegetation, a consistent layer of the rust coloured sphagnum peat, with bundles of *phragmites* and *eriophorum* leaves and roots, was revealed. Along the inside edge of the baulk, two small pits were discovered, slightly undercutting the baulk and containing humidified grey peat. No explanation was found for these pits and they could have been caused by the recent peat diggers. Though neither reached the body, it is tantalising to think how close to it someone must have come.

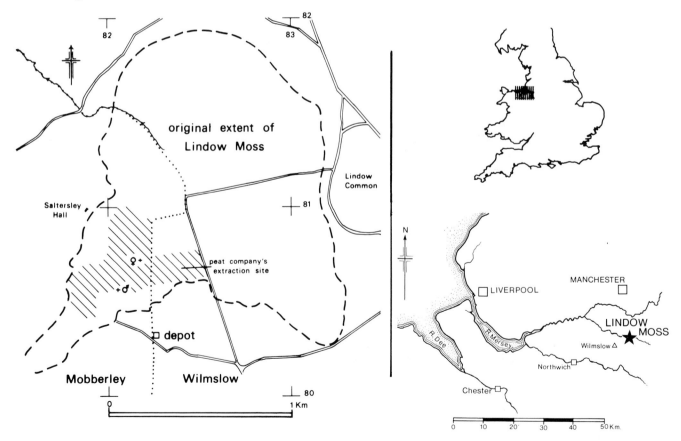

Fig. 2   Site plan, showing the relative positions of the remains of Lindow Man and Lindow Woman.

Work was concentrated on the area above what was hoped would contain the body. It was decided that only the edges of the find would be revealed and an attempt would be made to lift it in a block. Its context both above and below would be intact, and more leisurely excavation could then take place under laboratory conditions. As the rust coloured peat was removed, an uneven and thin layer of fine silt was uncovered. This layer had formed in an open pool of water in the bog, (p. 84) and proved to be associated with the body. During the excavation, no other artefacts were discovered and no wood or stone was found in association with the body. As the afternoon was drawing on, all efforts were turned to cutting out and lifting the body. When the edges were revealed it occupied a surprisingly small space, about 0.7 m by 0.55 m in plan. At the time it was feared only a small part of the body had survived, but the task of lifting was made much easier.

A block was isolated by cutting down around the body on three sides and introducing a heavy plywood sheet underneath. This was then slid back onto scaffolding and six people were needed to lift the block out of the trench and down to the narrow gauge railway which runs across the site. It was hauled back to the depot on an open bogey and was wrapped in water-soaked foam and heavy plastic sheeting. The block, on its board, was then driven about seven miles, by van, to the mortuary at Macclesfield District General Hospital.

Work continued on the block the next day. It was heavy and cumbersome and in danger of breaking up. All the excess peat was cut away from around the body and a wooden box was constructed to fit around it. The block was then wrapped in cling film and the cavities filled with expanding polyurethane foam. This froze the position of the body, allowed the box to be inverted and further peat removed and so reduced the block sufficiently in size to fit into the mortuary's cold store.

The body was now in the hands of the coroner and his officers. Because of the circumstances of the previous discovery and the police search for a murder victim, it had to be shown beyond all doubt that the body was ancient. On the other hand, it seemed very probable that the body was an archaeological find of the greatest importance. Every effort had to be made to keep the body in its original position, its context undisturbed, both above and below, and free from contamination from bacterial or fungal agents of decay. A number of arguments for its antiquity were presented. The body had come from below at least 2.5 m of undisturbed peat, since modern digging

had begun. The bone was highly decalcified and the condition of the tissues was comparable to that of the famous Danish bog burials. X-rays through the box showed there to be no metal objects associated with the body and nearly all modern bodies have fillings in the teeth. To make absolutely certain, the coroner asked the British Museum to arrange for a C14 date to be carried out before he would release it.

2 Excavation and Examination

I. M. Stead

Alerted by a telephone call requesting help with conservation, Sherif Omar and the writer travelled to Wilmslow on 7 August 1984 but arrived too late to see the body at Lindow Moss. It had already been boxed and removed to the mortuary at Macclesfield District General Hospital where it was in the custody of the coroner. Over the next few days the box was opened twice by the coroner's advisers, Dr Alan Williams, the hospital's pathologist, and Robert Connolly acting on behalf of the Home Office Pathologist, but after discussions with the excavators, landowners, police and coroner it was decided that all further excavation should take place at the British Museum. However, before the box could be moved the coroner had to be certain beyond any shadow of doubt that the find was indeed ancient: he decided to keep the remains until a C14 date had been produced. This could have been done by the British Museum Research Laboratory, but an extremely large sample would have been needed; the Oxford University Laboratory for Archaeology and the History of Art – already involved in dating the severed head from Lindow Moss (Lindow Woman) – was then approached, but their specialists were on vacation; Bob Otlet of the Atomic Energy Research Establishment at Harwell came to the rescue and the samples were duly delivered by the police. Two suitable samples were received: some small bones from one of the hands, collected on site by Connolly; and the detached leg which had been kept in formalin since its discovery. Priority was given to the hand bones but the sample was small (6.5 g) so the remaining piece of tibia (30 g) was removed from the detached leg and also submitted to Harwell. On 17 August Otlet reported that the first sample was at least 1,000 years old, the coroner released the body, and on 21 August the wooden box was taken to London.

Many of the problems posed were well outside the range normally met by the British Museum, so one of the first tasks was to recruit a team to investigate the body. In fact the formation of the team had already started at Wilmslow: Rick Turner was keen to continue with the job he had started, Robert Connolly had also been involved from the beginning, and Frank Oldfield's students (Department of Geography, Liverpool University) had played a major role in the field. At an early stage Don Brothwell (Institute of Archaeology, London University) was invited to join the project and he in turn introduced and coordinated a wide range of specialists. Offers of help and advice came from far and wide; such was the enthusiasm that several distinguished scientists had to be turned away because their fields of interest were already covered. At a seminar in January 1985, arranged at very short notice and restricted to those actively working on the project, no fewer than 31 people attended. But interest in the discovery was not restricted to specialists, and publicity could not be ignored. Initially it was possible to keep a low profile, which was surprising because the press had known of the discovery before the archaeologists, but gradually interest increased. One of the first in the field was David Richardson, producer of a series of television programmes on 'The Celts', who was keen to film the forthcoming excavation and persuasively countered all objections. Having said that he would be happy with a remote-controlled camera and using daylight only, he ended with a film-crew and powerful lights – but cold lights which in fact helped the excavators. Oliver Gillie, medical correspondent of *The Sunday Times*, also booked a place to observe the excavation.

The prime consideration was to preserve the body – to excavate, record, investigate and display, but essentially to preserve it. Conservation was in the very capable hands of Sherif Omar and Margaret McCord; their detailed report follows, but as preservation was the first concern and set limits on the excavation, it cannot be ignored in the present account. It was vital that a low temperature (about

4°C) should be maintained at all times, and the body was far too large to go into a normal refrigerator. The immediate problem was solved by the Middlesex Hospital, which provided space in the mortuary, and the long-term solution was a purpose-built refrigerator capable of accommodating a full-length body just in case Lindow Moss provided further finds. As an interim measure, pending the arrival of the refrigerator, a coffin-cooler was borrowed. This was a normal coffin-lid with a refrigerating unit attached, and it was fixed to a large wooden box with demountable sides bolted in position. The smaller box made in Macclesfield Hospital fitted comfortably inside. The excavation was to take place at Franks House, a British Museum out-station at Hackney, and a large corner-room was emptied for the purpose. The demountable wooden box with its coffin-cooler lid was set on a desk at one end and a barrier of tables divided the room and separated excavators from observers.

On 24 September the body was removed from the mortuary and taken to Franks House. The excavation was carried out by Frank Oldfield, Valery Rigby, Gill Varndell and the writer, with Margaret McCord on hand to keep a strict eye on progress, to monitor the temperature of the remains and to ensure that they were kept damp. Temperature was the controlling factor, and excavation was restricted to short sessions; it soon became apparent that too many bodies were warming the room so the observers, press and television personnel had to be evicted and were allowed back only for brief visits.

The lid was removed to reveal a mass of peat, much of it re-deposited as packing, but there was no difficulty in distinguishing this disturbed material from that stratified around the body. The peat was removed with wooden and plastic implements, and by hand, whilst brushes and jets of water were most effective when working close to the skin. A dental vacuum was used to remove excess water. At one edge was the darkened flap of skin which Rick Turner had seen in the section at Lindow Moss: that was the obvious starting point, and the excavators then moved towards the centre of the box and uncovered the skin of an arm. At the Middlesex Hospital Dr David Thompson had arranged for radiographs to be taken: one humerus showed prominently and some vertebrae, ribs and the outline of the skull were also discernible. The radiographs were a useful guide, but because they had been taken through a thickness of peat they lacked clarity: the humerus was the only long-bone visible, but others could have been obscured by the peat or virtually destroyed by decalcification. One leg had been detached, but it was not

at all clear how much of the rest of the body had survived. All the stratified peat was kept and carefully labelled – there was a particularly deep deposit over the chest – and Oldfield took a series of spot samples each recorded by photography. The body was now resting on its back (it had been turned over since being found in the bog) and the humerus visible on the X-rays was that of the left arm whose skin was now uncovered on top of the body. The left forearm was in worse condition, coming to a frayed end before the wrist and with the skin broken to reveal bone at the elbow. Two loose fingernails, and another still attached to a phalange, were found near the end of the arm. The flattened right arm with outstretched elbow was then excavated, and a full column of peat was taken from below as well as above the body near the right shoulder. Finally the head was excavated and found to be downturned, facing in to the right shoulder. Only the upper part of the body was in the box, sliced at the waist, and it was quite naked but for a piece of fur on the left arm. Part of the fur band had been disturbed and replaced in the excavation at Wilmslow, and more of it was now visible around the upper part of the arm. At this stage the first side of the body was cleaned and thoroughly recorded. Throughout the excavation Tony Cowell was on hand to photograph every stage of the work (Cowell 1984), and the BBC teams (in the middle of the first week David Richardson gave way to Simon Campbell-Jones who produced a programme for the 'Q.E.D.' series) paid frequent visits to make a film of the proceedings. Finally, a team from the Terrestrial Photogrammetry Unit, The City University, took a series of accurately-measured stereo-pairs.

The body was then prepared to be turned over. It was covered with cling-film followed by bandages of fibreglass impregnated with resin, which rapidly cured and set hard when sprayed with water. The mount thus made was then removed, backed and strengthened, and replaced on the body. The box was tightly packed with polystyrene pellets, the lid screwed in position, and then it was turned over. The side now exposed had been filled with expanding polyurethane foam which was cut away to reveal only a thin layer of peat. The back of the body was cleaned, and then examined by Dr Paul Buckland (Department of Geography, Birmingham University) and Maureen Girling who stayed to supervise the washing of the hair and the collection of samples to be searched for parasites. But the most significant discovery at this stage was the thin 'cord' encircling the neck – the body had been garrotted. After preliminary cleaning the back was thoroughly recorded

Fig. 3 Cartoon which appeared in the Sunday Telegraph on 7 October 1984. Opposition leader Neil Kinnock, in the guise of Lindow Man, is viewed by his Front Bench colleagues.

like the front, including another visit from The City University team, and then a second mount was made. The basic excavation had lasted from Monday to Friday.

In the second week a Press Conference was called and news of the discovery was given world-wide publicity. One outcome was that the body acquired a name. Indeed, the Middlesex Hospital had discovered the need of a name when they recorded the radiography: there they called him Pete Marsh, and that obviously appealed to the journalists. Lindow Man will be used for scientific purposes, but it seems likely that Pete Marsh will remain his common name. The body became so well-known in the next few days that it even appeared in the *Sunday Telegraph*'s political cartoon (Fig. 3). Subsequently the main publicity feature was the 'Q.E.D.' film, viewed by more than 10 million people in April 1985 and given an award by the British Association for the Advancement of Science for the best scientific film shown on television in 1985. This film was shown again on 7 May 1986, and a follow-up Q.E.D. film produced by Bob Bootle was screened on 14 May.

The press coverage undoubtedly helped to attract both individuals and institutions to join the research, and a steady stream of specialists descended on Franks House. Early in October the body was examined by Dr G. L. Ridgway, a microbiologist from University College Hospital, and his colleague Dr C. K. Campbell, a mycologist. Thereafter its condi-

tion was monitored at frequent intervals, mainly by another University College microbiologist, Dr M. Powell. Jim Bourke, a surgeon from Nottingham University, agreed to explore the contents of the body, but before this could begin attempts were made to record any internal features. First, it was taken back to the Middlesex Hospital for further X-rays, now that the peat had been removed. Then it went to St Bartholomews Hospital where Dr Rodney Reznek and Marion Hallett scanned it with a CT 9800 body-scanner – a fifth generation model, one of only five in the country, which had a larger aperture than that of the corresponding machine (second generation) at the Middlesex Hospital and was big enough to take the entire body without disturbing its unorthodox position. Magnetic resonance imaging (MRI) was also deemed worthwhile, so the body was again taken from Franks House – this time to Wembley where the very latest machine was made available by the manufacturers, Picker International. A fourth outing, to The Royal Marsden Hospital, for xeroradiography was not particularly successful because details were obscured by the fabric of the mount. Six months later a second attempt with a different support produced excellent results.

Throughout October and November the body was available for specialist examination and the removal of samples, and then in the second week in December it was passed to Sherif Omar for conservation.

3 The Handling and Conservation of Lindow Man

Sherif Omar   Margaret McCord

Cleaning and Excavation

Between the end of September 1984, when Lindow Man arrived in the British Museum, and the middle of December when he was handed over to the Department of Conservation for preservation, the body was subjected to numerous periods of excavation and examination. In order to minimise deterioration it was important to keep it cool and wet which was achieved by intermittent spraying with freshly boiled distilled water during the course of the excavation, covering parts of the body not being worked on with cling film to prevent evaporation, and by returning the body to the cool-box once the temperature had risen to 10–12°C. In general it was found that this temperature (which was measured by a thermocouple connected to a digital thermometer) was reached in approximately two hours, inspite of turning off the room heating, keeping windows open, limiting the number of people in the room to those essential for whatever operation was required and fitting an air cooler to the window nearest the body so that a cool draught passed over the working area. In addition, polythene bags were filled with wet paper towelling, chilled in a refrigerator and put on top of the body. These packs were removed to expose appropriate areas during cleaning, excavation or examination.

One of the factors contributing to the fairly rapid temperature rise in the room during the excavation and examination was the presence of a BBC film crew. However the effect of filming was minimised by using 'cold' lamps.

One of the first tasks carried out by conservation staff after the excavation of the front of the body was to make a mount both for ease of handling and to allow the body to be turned over to excavate the back. The mount was made from Delta Lite strips, a fibreglass casting tape, now used by hospitals as a substitute for plaster bandages when applying splints to broken limbs. The body was covered with cling film and then strips (127 mm in width) were cut into squares and moulded to the body and overlapped to give strength. When all the body was thus covered, it was sprayed with water which caused the Delta Lite to become rigid in a few minutes (Fig. 4). The mould was removed and strengthened further by painting on Tiranti Rigid Laminate, a polyester resin thickened with glass beads over reinforcing strips of coarse and fine fibreglass.

The mould was then replaced over the body and packed with peat in areas where it did not fit accurately. The work, as explained on p. 15, was undertaken while the body was in its original box. Polystyrene pellets contained in a polythene bag were used to pack the box as a replacement for excavated peat; then the wooden lid was fixed in position and the whole turned over. After excavation, the back of the body was again covered with cling film and the same process of mould making was repeated except that, in this case, strips of Scotch Flex casting tape were used for the initial moulding. This had a larger weave and, accordingly, more flexibility for taking the contoured shapes of the body. A second layer of Delta Lite strips was applied subsequently to give more rigidity. The same steps of wetting with water and strengthening with polyester and woven fibreglass were followed. The two moulds were drilled at intervals around the edges so that they could be held together by nuts and bolts. This allowed the body to be turned onto either side at will.

The internal examination, sampling and removal of internal organs, necessitated a great deal of manipulation and movement of the body. This in turn required the supporting of weak areas and loose parts. Some gaps were filled with original loose peat and elsewhere a more permanent yet easily removable support was made of wet peat enclosed in cling film (Fig. 5). This was easily moulded to the correct shape.

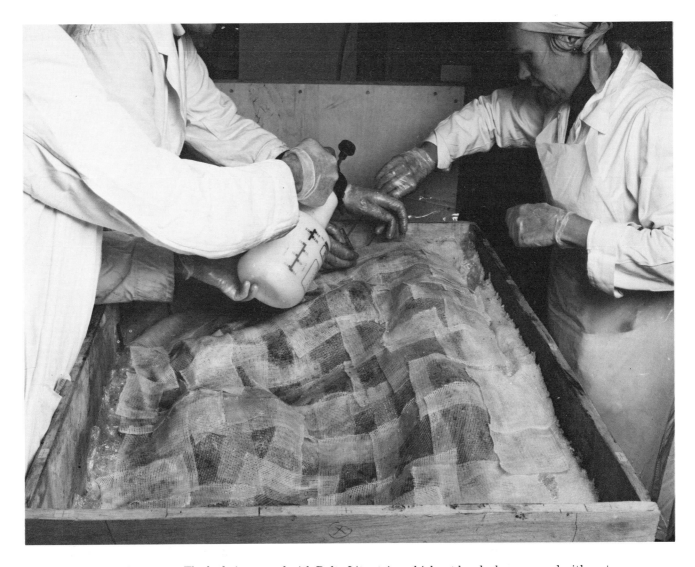

Fig. 4 Preparing the mount. The body is covered with Delta Lite strips which set hard when sprayed with water.

To allow an endoscope to enter the back of the head, and also the front through the mouth, the head had to be manipulated gently by hand. After the examination was completed, it was returned to its original position.

Travelling

The body was sent to a number of institutions for a variety of tests, such as: Radiography, CT (computerised tomography) body scan and MRI (magnetic resonance imaging) scan. A system for keeping it secure and cold was evolved, using the original wooden box made at Macclesfield Hospital. The box was lined with a polythene bag filled with polystyrene pellets which served as a cushion to the mounted body. A block of dry ice was broken into small pieces and these were distributed around the four sides in open polythene envelopes. Then the lid was screwed to the top allowing a thermocouple wire to pass through so that the temperature could be monitored throughout the trip.

The system proved to be adequate and protective, and achieved all the set requirements, e.g. control of temperature and the avoidance of damage by vibration.

Conservation

A search through the literature revealed that the only published material on the conservation of bog bodies originated from Denmark (Lange-Kornbak

Fig. 5 Lindow Man's head supported by wet peat enclosed in cling film.

1956; Glob 1977; Fischer 1980). As a result, the conservation was discussed with conservators and curators at the Danish National Museum, Copenhagen, the Prehistoric Museum, Århus (where the Grauballe Man was conserved) and Silkeborg Museum (where the Tollund Man is on display).

After viewing these bodies and discussing the conservation techniques which had been used it became clear that an alternative approach would be necessary for the Lindow Man. All those consulted agreed that freeze drying offered the best hope for a good result.

Freeze drying techniques have been successfully applied in the treatment of waterlogged wood and leather as well as in the preservation of natural history material, but there is no experience in the application of this technique to bog bodies. Hence experiments had to be undertaken before the body was treated.

Pigskin was chosen for experimentation due to its

similarity to human skin. Strips of pigskin were cut and packed in peat for several months to simulate burial conditions as far as possible. The skin was then removed and cut into small squares whose outlines were drawn on sheets of cardboard to record their dimensions before treatment began. The pig skin squares were then immersed in several different pretreatment solutions of polyethylene glycols with various molecular weights and in glycerol. The skin samples were left for a number of weeks then removed, and sandwiched between cardboard and frozen to $-26°C$. The cardboard containing the experimental pieces was then freeze-dried. Freeze-drying is a technique used to remove moisture from organic materials by sublimation, i.e. by turning the water into ice and converting that directly to vapour that can be removed. This technique helps preserve the internal and external structure of the material and avoids undue shrinkage, which is often associated with normal air drying. After the pig skin squares had been freeze-dried their dimensions were compared with the original outline drawings and the amount of shrinkage was calculated. Two solutions performed well in comparison with the others: polyethylene glycol (PEG) 400 and 2000. Of these two, PEG 400 was chosen as it did not leave a residue on the surface and did not affect the original colour or flexibility when freeze drying was complete. The residue from the PEG 2000 would also have created problems when cleaning the hair and could result in depilation.

The presence of waterlogged bone was a further complicating factor. Experiments on freeze-drying water-logged bone (Ellam 1985) have shown that PEG 400 gives good results, although at a much higher concentration than that envisaged for the treatment of Lindow Man.

The body was supported on a perspex sheet and bandaged with Tyvek strips (polyester bonded fabric) to stop it from floating to the surface and then immersed in a solution of 15% PEG 400 in distilled water for ten weeks. Pads and Tyvek strips were also used to support weak areas and loose bones (Fig. 6).

The body, with its support, was then removed, wrapped in cling film and frozen to −26°C for three days. It was then freeze-dried for four weeks in a machine at the Ancient Monument Laboratory. The body was removed from the freeze-drying machine and allowed slowly to acclimatise to a relative humidity of 55% at room temperature.

A permanent mount has been made so that the body can be handled and moved safely from one place to another and a special display case capable of maintaining a relative humidity of 55% has been constructed.

Measurements of reference-points on the body have shown that there was a shrinkage of less than 5% during the conservation treatment. The skin colour has become lighter and its texture much clearer. As a result of the drying process, the body as a whole has become more rigid, but it still retains some flexibility and can now be handled with relative ease. There is no offensive smell, and the freeze-drying process can be considered a success.

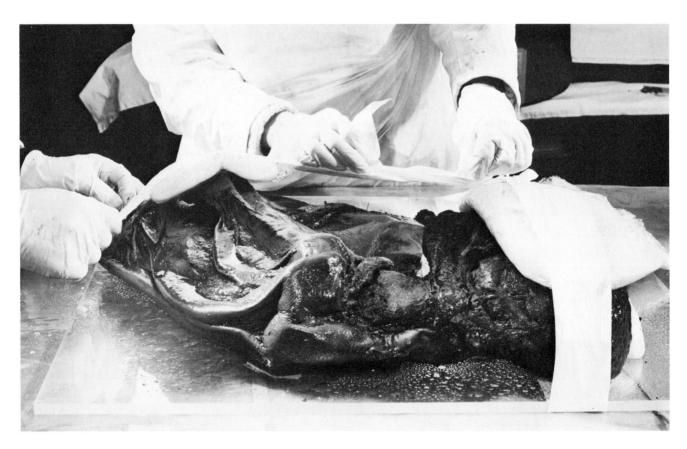

Fig. 6   Lindow Man strapped onto a perspex mount in readiness for immersion in PEG before freeze-drying.

4 The Microbiological Monitoring of Lindow Man

G. L. Ridgway   M. Powell   N. Mirza

Microbiological monitoring of Lindow Man was carried out on eleven occasions during the period September 1984 to March 1985. Cultures were performed on swabs taken from various sites on the body, from samples of the peat associated with the body, and from the distilled water used to spray the body. The body sites sampled were: scalp, skin from neck and under the garrotte, right shoulder surface (an area of possible decomposition), both wrists, ears, eye sockets, left loin, thoracic and abdominal cavities, and an anterior chest wound.

Swabs were immediately plated on two sets of media as in Table 1, and one set incubated at 37°C, and the other at room temperature. Cultures were examined after 24, 48 and 72 hours incubation.

Table 1   Media used for swab culture

Blood agar (aerobic)
Blood agar (anaerobic)
McConkey Bile Salt agar
Sabourauds (fungal) agar

Samples of peat were also processed on the media in Table 1. Samples of the spray water were cultured on blood agar, using the quantitative technique of Miles and Misra. In addition, 5 ml of water was filtered through a 0.22 μ millipore filter. The filter was divided into two equal halves, and plated on two plates of cysteine/lysine/electrolyte deficient agar (CLED), and incubated at 37°C and room temperature respectively.

Results

Initial growth was light, and slow. Cultures generally took 72 hours to become established, and organisms grew at room temperature only. This is consistent with the finding that the organisms isolated were soil and water commensals of no pathogenic consequence.

These included a number of *Pseudomonas* spp. Fungi and yeasts were isolated on a few occasions. Cultures were sent to Prof D. MacKenzie at the Public Health Laboratory Service Mycology Reference Laboratory for identification. Various species of *Penicillium, Mucor, Verticillium* and *Candida* were reported, consistent with the environment of the body. We were unable to detect any deterioration in the state of preservation of the body associated with fungal or bacterial contamination. We were however concerned by the persistent isolation of *Pseudomonas* species from the body. Quantitative cultures of the distilled water yielded heavy growths of *Pseudomonas* ($> 10^3$ organisms/ml) indistinguishable from the isolates obtained from the swabs.

Comment

The bacterial and fungal flora reflected the known origin of the body. We did not detect any deterioration associated with removal and examination of the body over the 6 month period of monitoring. However, we recommended that definitive preservation processes be expedited for two reasons. Firstly, *Candida* spp. was being consistently isolated, and the body was being colonised with a heavy growth of *Pseudomonas* spp. from the spray water, in spite of regular changing of the reservoir contents. Secondly towards the end of the period the body became colonised with white fly (? *Thysanura* spp) which are difficult to eradicate, and could lead to the establishment of secondary bacterial or fungal colonisation, with adverse effects on the body.

5 Accelerator Radiocarbon Dating of Ancient Human Remains from Lindow Moss

J. A. J. Gowlett   R. Gillespie   E. T. Hall   R. E. M. Hedges

The human calvaria with soft organic parts preserved, found in Lindow Moss in May 1983 and now known as Lindow Woman, was soon afterwards dated by radiocarbon accelerator to the Roman or early Dark Age period. It was the first bog-burial to be found in Britain this century, and incidentally the first in this country to be directly radiocarbon dated, preceding the discovery of Lindow Man by more than a year. Although some features of the skull were held to point to an association with a murder victim of 1962, Mrs Reyn-Bardt, the police arranged the radiocarbon date, which immediately demonstrated that the specimen was archaeological.

Mr P. Reyn-Bardt was in fact convicted in November 1983 of the murder of his wife, on other evidence. No remains of Mrs Reyn-Bardt have ever been found. If they were recovered, they would be clearly recognisable as recent by radiocarbon dating, since all modern organisms contain radioactive carbon derived from hydrogen bomb tests, and far exceed in activity any samples from AD 1950 or earlier.

The Radiocarbon Dating by AMS

The recently-developed Accelerator Mass Spectrometry (AMS) technique of radiocarbon dating allows Carbon 14 atoms to be isolated and counted directly (Hedges and Gowlett 1986). It contrasts with conventional radiocarbon dating, which detects and measures Carbon 14 through counting the number of radioactive disintegrations in a fixed period. The greater efficiency of the direct counting in AMS allows the use of a sample size about 1,000 times smaller than in ordinary conventional dating, and a factor of ten less than is possible in conventional 'small counters'. In the last three years several hundred dates have been produced, many of them concerned with later periods of British prehistory.

The accelerator technique allowed the calvaria to be dated from about one gram of bone taken from the base of the skull, and separately from a similar quantity of the dura mater, the cranial membrane. Following normal procedure, collagen was extracted from both specimens, and subsequently its constituent amino acids were isolated and purified (Gillespie et al 1984). The two measurements agreed very closely, and have been amalgamated to give the following final date:

OxA-114   Amino acids from skull 1740 ± 80 (BP)

Since this date is somewhat younger than those obtained for similar burials on the continent (Tauber 1979), it is worth considering its implications, and any possible sources of error. The possibility of a general systematic difference of results between the Oxford and Copenhagen laboratories can be ruled out in view of a dating intercomparison which has been carried out on Mesolithic remains from Denmark (Andersen et al 1986). The general accuracy of the Oxford accelerator to ± 1% (± 80 years) has been determined by large numbers of measurements on tree-rings, standards, and known age samples (Gillespie et al 1985; Gowlett et al 1986). In the particular instance, two further possible influences must be considered:

1 The use of formalin by the police as a preservative. Formalin is a 40% solution of formaldehyde (CH_2O) containing some methanol (CH_3OH).

2 The influence of humic acids in the peat on the body.

The extraction of structural collagen, followed by its hydrolysation and the purification of amino acids, is designed to eliminate the hazards of both these 'treatments'. Formaldehyde contains no amino acids, and should be separable from them. It is normally prepared from methanol, which itself is prepared from hydrogen and carbon monoxide. Methanol tested in the laboratory has been found to be radiocarbon 'dead': consistent with its preparation from coal products. If any formalin remained, it would therefore tend to make the radiocarbon date too old. This was observed in the case of the haft from a Bronze Age flat axe from Brittany, which had a 'date' of c. 10,000 years. Wood however contrasts with bone in having no constituent amino acids which through their precise characterization would be separable from formalin. In the case of bone or cartilage the amino acids can be isolated, and both the agreement between samples, and the relatively young age, indicate that the purification was successfully achieved.

Sample contamination by younger materials, such as humic acids, is encountered routinely, and does not normally present a problem for a sample of this age. The laboratory has achieved satisfactory results on Bronze Age material from peat, and indeed also for Palaeolithic finds, where the danger of contamination should be far greater (see for example Gillespie *et al* 1985, for dates at Monte Verde, Chile, and Jacobi *et al* 1986 for the accelerator dating of the Poulton elk). To make this point plainer, for a sample of 2,000 years old, a contamination by entirely modern material of 5% would be required to make an age difference of even 100 years. To be able to date at over 20,000 years, as the laboratory does regularly, it is necessary to remove such contamination to a level of below 1%.

Material preserved in peat could in some circumstances present other difficulties. In general bone is best dated from the structural protein, collagen, and purified amino acids derived from the collagen offer the ideal means of doing this. Pretreatment of the sample is intended to isolate the insoluble component of the collagen, so that free amino acids circulating in the environment do not affect the dating. In the case of peat, however, the chemical environment can produce a natural tanning reaction and it is possible that organic components derived from the peat will become bound to the collagen of interest. Such contamination would be limited by the radiocarbon ages of the components involved. There is now considerable evidence that at the relevant levels of Lindow Moss the peat is rather older than the human remains, at least of Lindow Man (Oldfield *et al*, pp. 84–5). On that assumption, the influence of components in the older peat appears to have been slight, since there is a clear difference of radiocarbon age between the peat and the human remains.

The only way to resolve any remaining doubt is for a bone sample from a peat context to be dated from the single amino acid hydroxyproline. This occurs at about 10% in bone collagen, but is ex-

tremely rare in other environments. It is envisaged that such dating for Lindow Man will take place soon.

The date of 1740 ± 80 years on the head of Lindow Woman can best be interpreted in historical terms through calibration on the high precision curve of Stuiver (1982) or Pearson and Baillie (1983). On either of these curves the mean value for the date coincides with a 'plateau' which occupies much of the third century, demonstrating the difficulty which radiocarbon has in offering dating precision for the Roman period. At two sigma, or 95% confidence, the span embraced is c. AD 80 to AD 550. Nevertheless, as the first standard deviation and one tail of the distribution occupy the Roman period, it can be said that there is approximately 85% chance of the find being of Roman date, and only 15% chance of it belonging to the early Dark Ages.

Dating of Lindow Man

In 1984 a further find was made at Lindow Moss, of the nearly complete body of Lindow Man. The chronological relationship between the two individuals now represented from the bog is clearly of importance for their interpretation. A Harwell radiocarbon determination obtained soon after the new discovery was reported as indicating an age of c. 550 bc (Stead and Turner 1985), but it is now accepted that this date was anomalous. All subsequent radiocarbon dates are later.

Accelerator dates available as of November 1985 are as follows:

OxA-531	Hair of head	1920 ± 75
OxA-604	Vertebra	1850 ± 80
OxA-605	Muscle attached to vertebra	2125 ± 80

All the dates were obtained on purified amino acids. Although collagen from human bone contains C14 accumulated over a period of several years, to all intents and purposes the three specimens should have the same radiocarbon age. The combined value of the three dates is c. 1960 ± 60 BP. OxA-605 for the muscle appears considerably older than the other two dates, but the significance of this difference is on the borderline at the 95% level. This difference may be purely statistical, but it could reflect the greater difficulty of removing peat amino acids totally from soft muscle tissue as opposed to bone or hair. As this issue is being investigated further the results discussed below cannot be regarded as a final radiocarbon age for the body. If weight is given only to the other two dates (OxA-531 and OxA-604), these have a combined value of 1890 ± 60 BP.

Calibration of these dates cannot be achieved very satisfactorily from data yet available in print. The Seattle curve runs back to AD 0, and the Belfast curve to AD 50. These high precision curves cannot therefore accommodate the older tail of possibilities for the dates. They do provide the best source for calibrating the means and later possibilities. The whole period is also covered by the curve of Klein *et al* 1982. Historical ranges derived from these curves are given in Table 2.

Owing to the nature of past C14 fluctuations, it makes surprisingly little difference whether the muscle date (OxA-605) is included or not. In either case, a first century BC date is possible, but unlikely. At the later end, a peak at *c.* AD 310–320 offers itself as a very marginal possibility, if only OxA-603 and -604 are taken into account, but AD 240 is the latest likely date, even at two standard deviations. On balance the accelerator dates suggest a first century AD date, with a reasonable possibility that the true date could be a century earlier or later. The dates may be reasonably compatible with those for the underlying peat, taking into account that peat formation probably slowed down during the earliest stages in the development of the open pool in which the body must have been deposited (Oldfield *et al*, p. 84).

The closest known age dating comparison which we can offer for this period is that of Pompeii. Six dates which we have run from material preserved by the AD 79 eruption cluster at 1960 ± 25 BP (Gowlett *et al* 1986), corresponding with an expected value of *c.* 1940–60 BP on the Belfast curve (Pearson and Baillie 1983). The accurate dating of material from a peat bog may however present greater difficulties as discussed above.

Comparison of Dates for the Body and Head

The possibility that the Lindow head and the body subsequently discovered are contemporary should at least be considered, though there are no compelling archaeological reasons to suppose this. The chief result of this comparison is to see that at present not enough radiocarbon dates have been run to resolve the issue: the total group of Oxford dates on both specimens does not allow them to be regarded as of effectively the same age; on the other hand, discarding the oldest date (OxA-605) would allow the two burials to be regarded as contemporaneous, with a combined result having a mean in the second century AD, but allowing virtually the whole Roman period as a possibility.

The arguments for a Roman date for both specimens are strong on all dating grounds, but certain discrimination within the late Iron Age/Roman period cannot be expected to be easy. Larger numbers of dates are necessary to bring down statistical uncertainty. It must be remembered too that the Roman period is compressed in terms of a radiocarbon calendar: for example the period AD 180 to 380 is represented by only 100 radiocarbon years. Consequently the Oxford and Harwell laboratories have agreed to further dating in collaboration so as to reduce the uncertainties mentioned above.

Summary

On the basis of the radiocarbon accelerator dating Lindow Man, like the isolated head of Lindow Woman, appears to be of broadly Roman age, though a final Iron Age date for the body is equally possible. The majority of bog burials from Denmark have been dated to the late pre-Roman Iron Age (Tauber 1979), but this does not necessarily mean that an identical scenario is to be expected in Britain, and there is no archaeological evidence to contradict the radiocarbon dates which place the head of Lindow Woman in the late Roman/early Dark Age period.

Table 2

na = not accommodated in the specific curve, but necessarily in the BC range

Historical ranges of the accelerator dates for Lindow Man, with and without the outlying oldest date, OxA-605.

Raw C14 age	Curve	Calibrated Mean	Calibrated 68% range	Calibrated 95% range
1960±60 (3 dates)	Seattle	30–50 AD	0–125 AD	na–210 AD
	Belfast	50–70 AD	na–120 AD	na–210 AD
	Klein			155 BC–215 AD
1890±60 (2 dates)	Seattle	75–125 AD	30–230 AD	na–240 AD, and 310–320 AD
	Belfast	110–120 AD	50–210 AD	na–240 AD
	Klein			15 BC–235 AD

6 Radiocarbon Dates for Two Peat Samples

J. C. Ambers   K. J. Matthews   S. G. E. Bowman

The Samples

Four samples of peat were originally selected by Professor Oldfield of Liverpool University for radiocarbon dating. The basic stratigraphic data supplied with the samples were:

33C — One of 5 samples of *upper* body contact peat from the *upper* left hand part of the torso near and on the left shoulder (Algal mud and weakly humified *Sphagnum* peat)

14 — Column of peat from *underside* of upper arm surface downwards. Taken close to skull. (Weakly humified *Sphagnum* peat).

125, 0–3 — Peat column 125 (lower) 0–3 cm. Algal/detrital mud clearly above the recurrence surface (RY). The upper contact of the humified *Eriophonum* peat is irregular and lies between 10 and 13 cm. Between this and the mud sampled lie some 7–10 cm of fresh *Sphagnum* peat.

125, 16–19 — Peat column 125 (lower) 16–19 cm. Humified *Eriophonum* peat entirely below the recurrence surface. (See notes on 0–3 sample for stratigraphic context).

Of these four samples, the first and third were dated by the Harwell radiocarbon laboratory and the other two, reported here, by the British Museum laboratory.

Pretreatment

For the purposes of radiocarbon dating, peat can be considered to have two main components: humins that are insoluble in alkali and an alkali-soluble fraction. If there has been no penetration by younger rootlets, the humins should represent the remains of the original vegetation from which the peat formed. The soluble fraction can be further subdivided into humic and fulvic materials, which are acid insoluble and acid soluble respectively. Depending on the acidity of the bog, these materials are potentially mobile within the peat and hence may differ in age from the insoluble humin component. The two samples dated by the British Museum were therefore subjected to a rigorous pretreatment procedure to separate the humins, humics and fulvics. The actual procedure followed is that of the Natural Environmental Research Council's radiocarbon laboratory at East Kilbride: we wish to thank Dr D. D. Harkness for providing this information. Similar procedures are employed by other laboratories such as that of the Australian National University (Gupta and Polach 1985). The weights of the samples as supplied, when dried and of the separated humin and humic fractions are given in Table 3 together

Table 3   Weights of the samples and their major components

*The weight of benzene synthesised from each fraction is given in brackets.

Sample	Supplied weight	Dry weight	Humins weight	Humins C14 ref	Humics weight	Humics C14 ref
14	25.1g	5.0g	3.2g (0.90g)*	BM-2398	1.0g (0.64g)	BM-2399
125, 16–19	72.0g	9.0g	4.5g (1.95g)	BM-2400	3.8g (1.68g)	BM-2401

with their British Museum radiocarbon reference numbers. The fulvic component of each sample was less than about 0.1 g.

Radiocarbon Dates

The humin and humic fraction of the individual samples were each converted to benzene and the radiocarbon content evaluated by liquid scintillation counting (Barker *et al* 1969). It should be noted that the samples were relatively small for conventional radiocarbon techniques and hence the weights of benzene obtained (see Table 3) were significantly smaller than the ideal full-size sample yield of 5 g. To maintain standard counting geometry each benzene sample was made up to 5 g using dead benzene. All the samples were measured over the same time period and under the same experimental conditions together with two modern and two background samples.

The dates are given in Table 4. For a given sample, the error quoted is the counting error for the sample, combined with an estimate of the errors contributed by the modern and background samples. This estimate includes both counting and non-counting errors, and is computed from differences in the overall count-rates observed among the individual backgrounds and moderns. The errors quoted are therefore appropriate for comparisons with similar material measured under different experimental conditions. They also reflect the sample sizes.

Discussion

The chemistry of peat is complex with the humic and fulvic fractions potentially mobile. By isolating the different components and dating each individually two goals can be achieved. Firstly assuming no erosion of solid material, the humin fraction will provide a reliable date for the peat deposition, and secondly an indication of the mobility of the humic and fulvic fractions can be obtained. The results reported here are for humin and humic fractions separated by rigorous well-tested procedures. The fulvic component was a very small proportion of the total and too small for conventional dating. For each sample the dates for the two fractions agree well within the counting error. This indicates there has been little mobility of humic acids in the peat. The dates for the two samples also agree well which is as expected on the basis of the stratigraphy given above. The stratigraphy would also indicate that the weighted mean of the dates reported here should either be approximately the same as the combined date for the samples measured by Harwell (Otlet *et al*, p. 31), or be earlier. The appropriate single-sided test does show the British Museum dates to be significantly earlier at the 5% level.

Clearly radiocarbon measurements on the peat do not directly date the Lindow body. Indeed both sets of peat dates (British Museum and Harwell, *ibid*) would suggest that the peat formation pre-dates the deposition of the body (Gowlett *et al*, p. 24 and Otlet *et al*, p. 31).

Table 4   Uncalibrated radiocarbon dates

Sample	C14 Reference	Fraction	Age (BP)
14	BM-2398	Humin	2590 ± 170
	BM-2399	Humic	2470 ± 250
125, 16–19	BM-2400	Humin	2450 ± 80
	BM-2401	Humic	2400 ± 100

7 Report on Radiocarbon Dating of the Lindow Man by AERE, Harwell

R. L. Otlet   A. J. Walker   S. M. Dadson

This report describes the measurement and results of six separate samples taken from the Lindow Man body and its surrounding peat and analysed during the period September 1984 to February 1986. This extended study was carried out to obtain as accurate a date for the body as was feasible with the latest 'state of the art' C14 dating of small samples, using the conventional decay-counting method of measurement. Because of the recent developments in small sample dating by this method and because of the special difficulties of pre-treatment (decontamination) of the body due to ingressed components of the peat environment in which it had been had preserved, the report is prefaced with a brief resumé of the present status of C14 dating which illustrates the procedures adopted and the interpretation given to the results obtained.

Present Status of the C14 Technique

C14 dating, first developed by W. F. Libby in the late 1940s, is now a well established technique for determining the age of organic remains, woods, charcoal, peat, bones, etc. Research on the basic techniques and upon understanding the strengths and limitations of the results they produce has been a continuing process since its original conception. This has included research into obtaining higher laboratory measurement precision, the measurement of very small samples and in establishing calibration curves with which to convert the measurement result to an absolute date. Running in parallel with this has been research into sample integrity, in particular, into the techniques of sample pretreatment which is necessary to eliminate post depositional (burial) contamination and is crucial to the obtaining of a valid date result in cases where the contaminant can be expected to have a significantly different age from the material being dated. Originally bones had a poor reputation as a dateable material due to contamination in the burial environment primarily from non-contemporary carbon, dissolved carbonates, in the ground water seeping through, but the introduction of the collagen extraction pre-treatment process for bones essentially reversed these previous misgivings. In this process precipitated mineral carbonates are completely removed by prolonged dilute acid treatment and any residual humic acid contamination is removed afterwards by washing in strong alkali. A further refinement which can be exploited with systems that can cope with extremely small samples (10 mg or less) is the extraction from the collagen of specific amino acids. Even with the now standard collagen extraction procedure, however, it is generally accepted that beyond the final calibration it is the measurement precision which becomes the main limiting factor of the accuracy in the result obtained. For most systems this precision, estimated in terms of a one sigma standard deviation, is around $\pm 1.00\%$ (equivalent to approximately ± 80 years) depending upon the process used and the size of sample being measured. Three systems of measurement are currently employed:

Gas counting
Liquid scintillation counting
Ion counting (accelerator mass spectrometry)

A full description and comparison of these procedures would be out of place in this report. At Harwell gas counting and liquid scintillation have been developed and utilised over many years. In general the liquid scintillation method is used for the larger high carbon yield samples (those from which around 5 gm of carbon can be extracted) and the gas counting method with miniature gas proportional counters for the smaller range (down to 10 mg of carbon).

Whatever counting system is chosen all samples are taken through the following stages:

(a) pretreatment, physical and chemical – to remove contaminants from the supplied sample and ensure that the carbon ultimately measured belongs only to the organism being dated.
(b) chemical processing – conversion of the sample to a form in which counting can take place; this may be a gas e.g. pure CO_2 for gas counting, an organic liquid e.g. C_6H_6 for liquid scintillation counting or solid graphite for the AMS method.
(c) measurement of the C14 – either by counting the emitted beta particles in gas proportional or liquid scintillation counters or direct counting of the C14 ions in an accelerator mass spectrometer.

These stages are listed as they will be referred to in the description of the specific procedures used in the dating of Lindow Man in the next section.

The Lindow Man

In August 1984 the British Museum approached the Isotope Measurements Laboratory, Harwell (IML) and asked if a quick result could be obtained on a sample of bone from a body recovered from the Lindow Moss bog in Cheshire. It was imperative that a result should be obtained within a week or ten days so that if it transpired that the body was of archaeological age it could be released immediately from the hospital morgue where it was being held. The IML agreed and the sample, consisting of some wrist bones, was thus put into process and a result obtained which showed the body certainly to be of sufficient antiquity to remove it from any present day police enquiries.

After the full counting period the date of this sample appeared to be approximately 2450 BP. However, some fragments of bone from a leg which had been found separately from the main torso but submitted for dating at the same time gave a result which was much more recent than that of the wrist bones (approximately 1600 BP). Accordingly it was decided that in order to establish as accurate a result as possible for this exciting find several more samples of both the body and the surrounding peat should be dated.

In all six different samples from the body and three from the surrounding peat have now been dated by Harwell. Those from the body include bone (wrist, leg, rib and vertebra) skin and hair. All were given the type of rigorous pre-treatment, mentioned above, but modified as indicated in some cases, to suit the obvious physical condition of the samples from this burial environment. Peat samples were given a fairly

severe alkali treatment even to the point of dissolving away some of the valid contemporary substance in an attempt to ensure that none of the later humic acid borne carbon remained in the actual portion dated. Weight losses in the pretreatment were thus about 30–50% of the original dry peat sample weight. In the case of the bone samples it was realised that dissolved carbonates contamination could not be applicable in the acid environment of the peat, although there was clear impregnation of humic substances from the peat, the bone being dark brown in colour and giving the appearance of tanned leather. Rather less acid demineralisation action than usual was thus required to extract the collagen and it was noted that the acid of the peat had already taken this step most of the way towards completion. Fully demineralised the residual collagen is a completely soft fibrous mass closely resembling wet bath-sponge. Only a very gentle alkali treatment was given to the residual collagen as it is extremely soft and light and rapidly dissolved away in even a cold alkali wash. The hair and skin samples received acid treatment only as they proved to be more fragile than the bone and disintegrated considerably in the treatment.

After pretreatment the samples were combusted in O_2 to form CO_2 in a high-yield tube-combustion line. Samples prepared for the gas counting system, i.e. all the samples from the body, were then further purified ready for counting by passage through a separate line, a series of copper, silver and platinum furnaces. In counting these samples three different 70 mg size counters and one 10 mg counter were used: all had been in constant use for over three years in the routine operation of the laboratory and have received regular calibration standards and background samples counted in them during the period (Otlet *et al.* 1983 and Otlet *et al.* in press). As a further check on the results obtained for the Lindow Man two '2,000 years' laboratory 'equivalent known age' standards were specially counted in the actual counters used. These were the well-calibrated benzene standards prepared by the laboratory as part of an intercomparison exercise organised jointly by Harwell and the British Museum and carried out in 1978 (Otlet *et al.* 1980). The peat samples were counted by the liquid scintillation method which is the main-line method used by the Harwell laboratory and is constantly subjected to reproducibility scrutiny as described elsewhere (Otlet and Warchal 1978 and Otlet 1979).

Results and Conclusions

The results of all the samples from the body, the surrounding peat and the 'known age' samples are listed in Tables 5, 6 and 7 respectively. Results are given in terms of conventional radiocarbon years BP, with the appropriate one sigma error terms. The errors express the one sigma standard deviation of the laboratory's estimate of the full replicate sample reproducibility, not simply counting statistics alone. Excluding the very first result (HAR-6224) the subsequent determinations on the body group into a completely statistically consistent set of values when proper regard is given to the individual measurement error estimates. The first result is clearly different and, although no positive explanation can be deduced at this time for the value obtained, in retrospect it is surmised that in the hurry to achieve some kind of result as quickly as possible on this first sample in order to secure its release from the morgue the pretreatment given was inadequate to remove the contamination of the associated peat.

No significance should be given to apparent differences between the individual results of the rest, however, and the weighted mean 1575 ± 30 BP (one sigma) becomes the recommended overall date result. This is clearly different from the peat dating results where an overall mean of 2290 ± 45 BP is the recommended result which should be taken.

The measurements made by the British Museum on the group of peat samples from the identified locations agree well with the Table 6 results. The discrepancy between the Harwell and AMS results for the body are as yet unexplained, although a series of intercomparative measurements are currently in hand (further sampes from the body, separately pretreated by each department as well as laboratory standards). However, the self-testing 'equivalent known age' laboratory standards given in Table 7 agree well enough with the earlier eight laboratory consensus result (2086 ± 8 BP) to give confidence that there is no significant scale shift (offset) in the miniature gas counter results.

The different pre-treatment procedure used by the AMS and Harwell may eventually provide a possible explanation but although the amino acid extraction recognisably dates a more specific fraction, that this fraction should provide an earlier date is not obvious

Harwell reference	Sample material	Age BP (years)	Notes
6224	wrist bone	2420 ± 100	
6235a	leg bone	1540 ± 100	Independent determinations
6235b	leg bone	1650 ± 80	from same initial sample
6491	skin	1550 ± 70	
6492	rib bone	1625 ± 80	
6493	skin and hair	1530 ± 110	
6856a	vertebra	1480 ± 90	Independent measurements
6856b	vertebra	1610 ± 80	from the same pretreated sample
Weighted mean (excluding HAR-6224)		1575 ± 30	

Table 5   C14 results from the Lindow Man

Harwell reference	Sample reference*	Age BP (years)
6521	LP/BF	2300 ± 70
6562	125, 0–3	2290 ± 90
6565	33C	2280 ± 70
Weighted mean result		2290 ± 45

Table 6   C14 results from the peat surrounding the Lindow Man

*LP/BF was between the right arm and the head; 33C is upper body contact and 125, 0–3 is from the peat monolith (p. 25).

Counter Number	Age BP (Years)
12	2000 ± 90
13	2070 ± 50
Weighted mean	2055 ± 45

Table 7   C14 results from 'known age' samples

for samples from this environment. The peat is itself clearly earlier than the body so that the process which removes it the more efficiently might be expected to give a later, not an earlier result.

Some small concern was felt that in the Harwell measurements of the body the contaminants from the peat might not have been absolutely removed, since the alkali treatment was less severe than would normally have been given to a more robust material. Thus on balance it is suggested that any residual error might be in the direction of an even later date than that given, but, in the authors' opinion this is very unlikely to be much beyond the range defined by the error estimates given.

For the conversion of the conventional radiocarbon results of the body and the peat to historical dates the calibration curves of Stuiver (1982) and Pearson *et al.* (in press) have been used. According to their recommendations the results have been expressed after calibration as ranges at the 68% and 95% confidence levels not as central dates with their associated errors. Table 8 lists these final calibrated dates.

Table 8   Calibrated dates of the Lindow Man body and the surrounding peat

	Conventional radiocarbon age (years BP)	Actual (historical) age ranges after calibration		Reference
		68% confidence	95% confidence	
Body	1575 ± 30	AD 425 to AD 540	AD 410 to AD 560	Stuiver (1982)
Peat	2290 ± 45	400 BC to 260 BC	400 BC to 200 BC	Pearson *et al.* (in press)

In the case of both the body and the peat the calibrated age ranges obtained are quite large. This is because the calibration curve shows very little variation in the relevant periods.

8 Photogrammetric Recording of Lindow Man

N. E. Lindsey

Introduction

Line drawings and paintings have long been used for recording in archaeology, to complement progress in investigation, cataloguing and conservation. In addition photography is employed to record the appearance of objects which are corroding, fading or are too fragile or toxic to handle. The results have generally been highly commendable and excellent archive material. In both cases however, the two-dimensional record does not provide a fully informative picture.

When discoveries are made, it is often necessary to record *in situ* before disturbing the relative and absolute positions prior to removal for detailed examination and subsequent conservation. Frequently the excavation and recording has to be completed with great speed as in most rescue archaeology occasioned by discoveries during construction work or natural disasters.

Thus a recording system which can register the bulk of physical detail quickly and reliably *and* regenerate that detail without loss is most attractive. Photogrammetry provides this facility, not always cheap, but when carried out with care, comprehensively effective and quick.

Photogrammetry

Photogrammetry is the art or science of taking measurements from photographs to determine the size, shape and orientation of the subject recorded.

A single photograph is an excellent perspective record in two dimensions of three-dimensional space, which on its own is a highly-prized data store. However, when two photographs are taken of an object in space, each from a slightly different vantage point, in the same way that human eyes register information, these two photographs can then be viewed to provide a three-dimensional model. The two photographs form a 'stereo-pair' which may be viewed naturally or with a stereo-scope. The stereo-model, which may be achieved with archive pictures, often, long after the subject has been lost, is available for inspection and interpretation at any time. In addition, the stereo-pair may be used in more complex photogrammetric instruments (Fig. 7) from which measurements and scaled drawings; plans; elevations; contours and profiles may be derived.

The use of three-dimensional, stereoscopic photography has been exploited mainly in aerial survey and mapping but it also has useful applications in architecture, civil engineering, mechanical design, medicine and for monitoring physical change or movement. In fact the growing interest and need to exploit photogrammetry in these subject areas is the main driving force behind the development of improved control systems, computer-aided drawing and data storage that may be used to handle the large quantities of information gathered in archaeology.

At present the use of photogrammetry is not standard on sites, largely due to the high cost of plotting equipment and the need for skilled operating staff. However, it would be worthwhile to allow for at least the acquisition of suitable stereo-pairs on most sites. These could be used as are single photographs at present, and in conjunction with a stereo-scope for improved interpretation, then stored in archives to await funds and new instructions, perhaps years later.

The Method

The acquisition of stereo-pairs of photographs for visual inspection and interpretation can be achieved using a variety of cameras. The basic rule is to use two camera positions separated by a known distance called the *base*. The two photographs are taken with the cameras facing the subject, their pointing directions parallel. The cameras should be between three and ten times the length of the base from the subject.

The camera can be hand- or tripod-mounted, and the only other requirement is that the lighting conditions remain constant for the two exposures.

When the stereo-pairs are required for measurement and plotting then more care must be exercised.

1. The camera should be a metric camera, i.e. one in which the geometry relating lens and negative is known and can be maintained.
   Cameras available include:
   (a) the Wild P32 which has a focal length of 64.32 mm and picture format of 60 mm × 80 mm and can use standard 120 roll film or glass plate.
   (b) the VEB Carl Zeiss Jena UMK which has a focal length of 100.00 mm and picture format of 180 mm × 130 mm and can use 190 mm wide roll film or glass plates.
   The two cameras mentioned are normally tripod mounted.
2. The base to taking distance ratio should lie between 1:2 and 1:8 for best results, for improved dimensional accuracy the ratio 1:2 is superior.
3. Roll film is available with a variety of exotic emul-

sions to suit most situations although the range is more limited for the wider film required for the UMK. Glass plates are only available with black and white emulsion and have a normal rating of 100 ASA.
4. Scale and orientation control. It is necessary to have 4 or 5 co-ordinated points in the object space to ensure dimensional integrity and each must appear in the stereo model i.e. each must appear in the common overlap of the two photographs.

The co-ordinates of the control points may be determined by conventional survey methods using tape, level, theodolite or electronic self-recording tacheometers.

After examination of the photographs to confirm that all the detail required has been recorded and the overlaps and control points are satisfactory, the optional stage of plotting can be initiated.

Photogrammetry and Lindow Man

Lindow Man probably qualified as a photogrammetric subject on each of the arguments usually

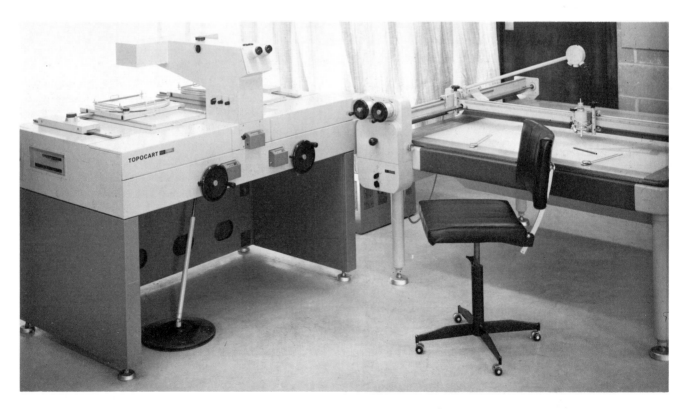

Fig. 7   VEB Carl Zeiss Jena Topocart, an analogue plotting instrument on which the body contours were plotted. Photo: The City University.

advanced to justify this form of recording. Here was a fragile subject, part-buried in refrigerated peat, likely to deteriorate if exposed to temperature and moisture variation and expected to be disturbed, moved, possibly taken apart and finally with a chance of disintegration. Photogrammetry offered a permanent non-contact, total recall record of the remains during excavation and exposure, useful for scientific analysis and for modelling a likeness for exhibition purposes. An added attraction in the modelling context is the ability to link the upper and lower surfaces of the body as they were exposed and thus to produce a total solid shape dimensionally correct. A number of other options have emerged since the photography was taken, the first to measure from the skin the circumference of limbs for stature determination, the second to provide a measured frame of the facial features to facilitate an artists impression of the face.

As a normal photographic subject the remains posed difficulties: they were dark brown, against dark wet peat, the texture was somewhat featureless and after each application of a waterspray surprisingly reflective.

In order to prevent deterioration of the body it had been kept in an ice box covered with foil and was only exposed for a few minutes at a time. The heating effects of television lighting and the presence of numerous scientists, technicians and other observers although kept at a distance, generated a somewhat hostile environment, for the body, whose well being was of paramount importance, and for the photogrammetrists who were of necessity afforded only brief intervals in which to examine, plan, control and obtain the stereo-pairs required.

Purpose of Photogrammetric Recording of Lindow Man

The main aim of the photogrammetric recording was to produce a contoured plan of the upper and lower surfaces of the body, as they were exposed, and to link them through a common datum to give a total body shape. Excavation of the body had, when the photogrammetrists arrived, reached the stage where it was half uncovered and standing about 80 mm proud of the supporting peat bed. After this first or upper surface had been photographed, the body was to be covered with a Delta Lite mount and the whole container turned over so that the second or lower surface could be excavated and revealed for photography. It was therefore necessary to establish suitable

measured control so that the two sets of contours when plotted could be firmly related to each other.

The box containing the body, approximately 1 m square and 0.3 m deep was supported on a work table under a low ceiling, and the camera, a Zeiss Jena UMK, was mounted on a sliding cradle supported on a Dexion frame just below the ceiling with a 1.5 m taking distance (Fig. 8).

It was decided to take five photographs of each surface as it was exposed at 250 mm intervals across the body to ensure full cover and to safeguard against processing difficulties or breakages (Fig. 9).

Photogrammetric Control

The photogrammetric control before the first session of photography was achieved in two stages. First a series of targets was established around the top edge of the wooden box. These were levelled using an instrument sighting a finely divided steel rule, and distances between the targets measured with a steel tape. All the observations were then used in a least squares survey adjustment to provide coordinate values in a local system for each target in x, y and z. Second a number of small mapping pins with 2 mm diameter spherical heads were placed round the body, pinned into the peat. These, it was calculated, would appear in the first photograph, remain in position as the foam was cast over the upper surface and reappear in the same relative positions when the peat was removed after the box had been turned over on the table. As an added safeguard, a number of extra targets were fixed on the floor on either side of the table.

When the negatives had been processed, a suitable stereo-pair of plates was selected with a separation of 500 mm and placed in a Zeiss Jena Stereo-comparator on which the image positions of the earlier coordinated targets were measured. This information was used in an appropriate computer programme to determine the two camera positions and then the mapping pin heads and floor target positions in terms of the coordinate system in which the targets had been established. Thus when the second set of photographs was taken, of the underside of the body, the mapping pin heads and floor targets were available as control, since the targets originally measured and coordinated were now out of sight under the box. The 2 mm diameter spherical heads to the mapping pins appeared not to have moved and their coordinates were simply adjusted to allow for the known diameter of 2 mm.

Fig. 8   Mounting system to support the camera in the five necessary positions over the body.

Contour Plotting

The stereo-pair of negatives recording the first or upper surface of the body was used in a Zeiss Topocart analogue plotting instrument (Fig. 7) and the contour plot (Fig. 10) produced. The control for this pair of negatives was provided by the calculated coordinates of the measured control targets.

Similarly a stereo-pair of negatives recording the second or lower surface of the body was used to produce the contour plot (Fig. 11). In this case the mapping pin head coordinates were used to control the plotting.

Since the same control network had been used for both surface contour plots, the contours were auto-matically linked and a solid shape was now available for profiling, modelling and analysis.

The contour interval on both plots was arranged to be 10 mm but the advantage of photogrammetry is that if the first interval is too coarse, subsequent plots may be made even years later from the glass negatives treated for archive storage. It would be possible to achieve a contour interval of 1 mm with the present photography and control if this is later required.

Comments

The whole project of contouring Lindow Man was

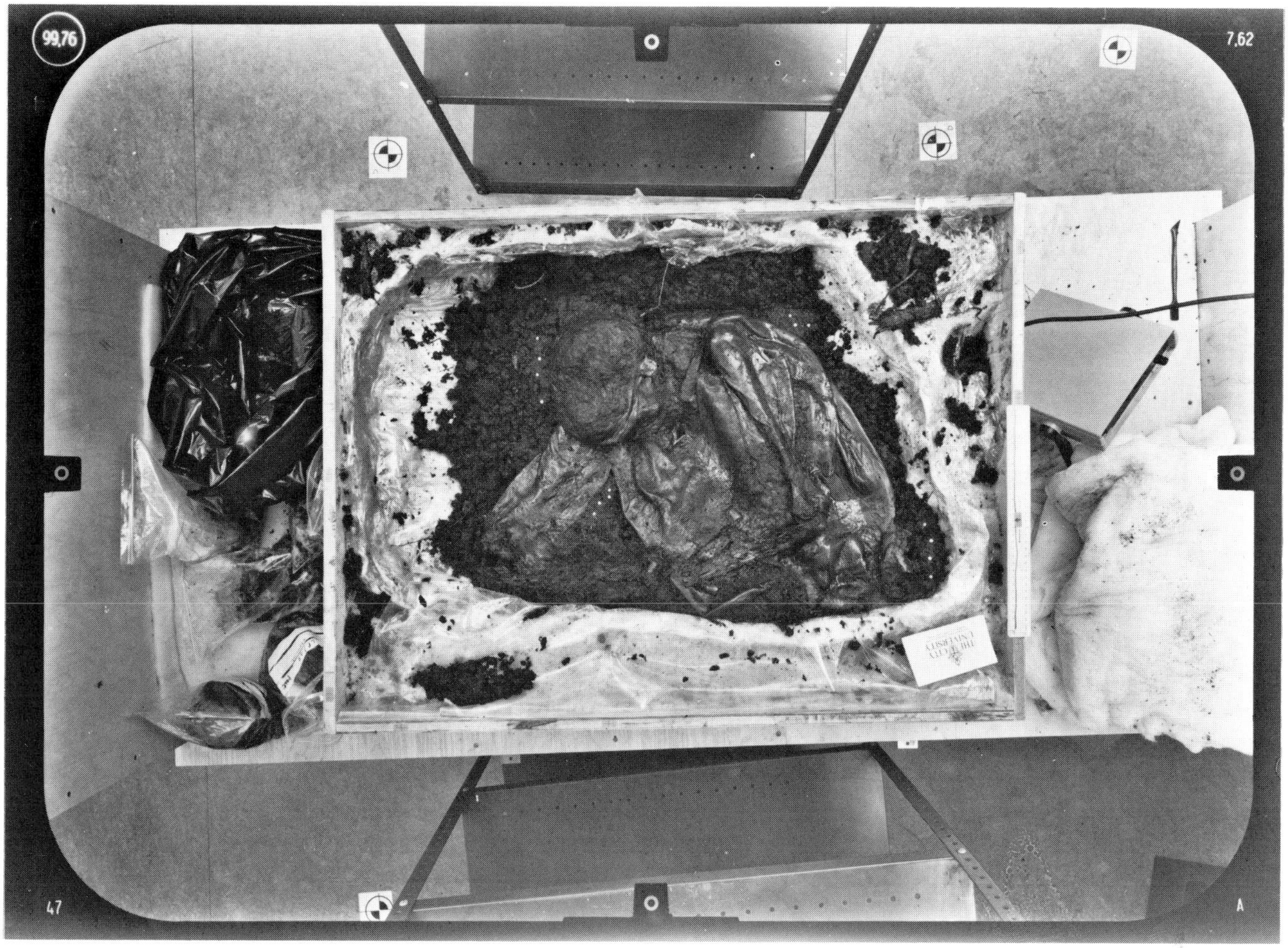

Fig. 9   Upper surface of body around which can be seen: a) marked targets on wooden container; b) mapping pin targets, around the body in the peat; and c) floor targets. Photo: The City University.

justified for all the correct reasons. The use of one set of conventionally measured control points which was subsequently used to extend the control to other points of detail too difficult or impossible to measure conventionally provided an almost limitless network of control. The question that is raised with this type of subject is whether the body sags or distorts during excavation. Possibly it does but the short time between photographs forming the stereo-pair is perhaps too short for excessive deformation. In the event of rapid movement or change, two synchronously linked cameras would serve most effectively to 'freeze' the changing subject.

A further potential use for the photography, would be to prepare a digital terrain model to be stored in a computer and displayed on a graphics terminal. The model would join the two surfaces and be displayed as a rotating solid shape for inspection by investigators and students under instruction.

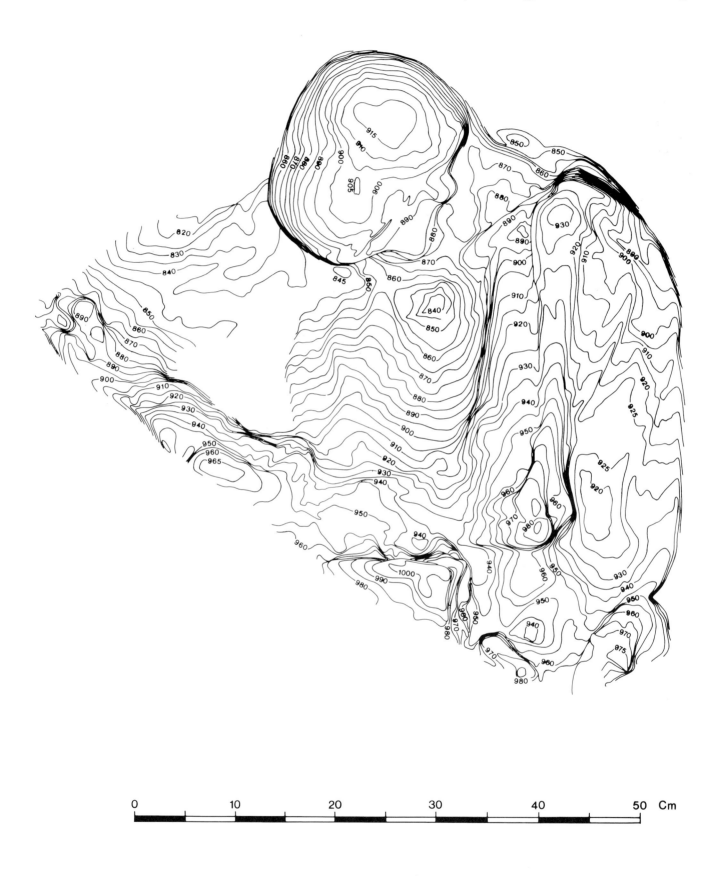

Fig. 10   Contour plot of the front of Lindow Man, produced by photogrammetry.

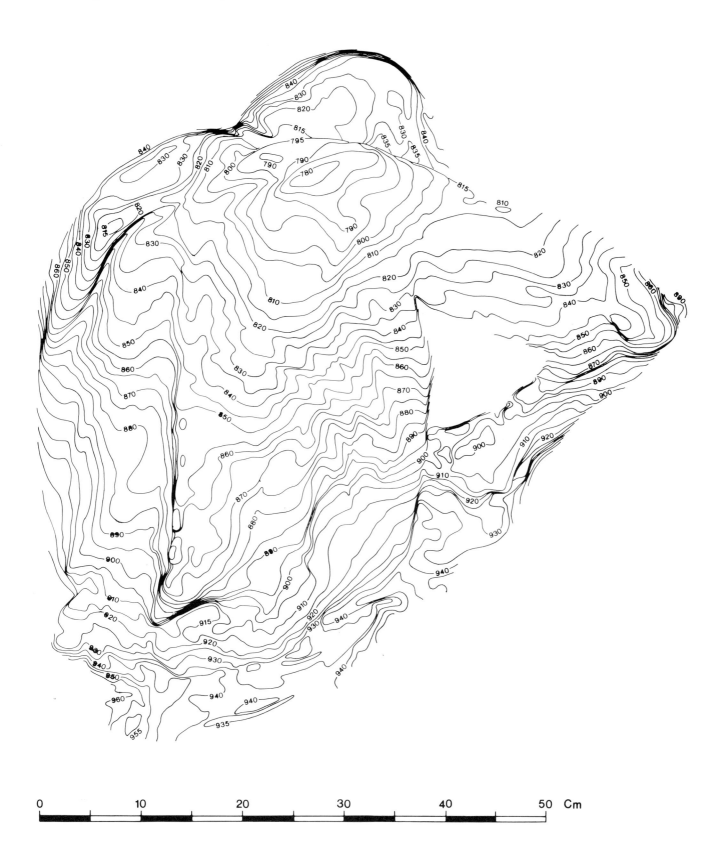

Fig. 11   Contour plot of the back of Lindow Man, produced by photogrammetry.

9 The Artefacts

Geoffrey Budworth   Margaret McCord
Ann V. Priston   I. M. Stead

(a) The 'Garrotte'

(i) The Cord

The cord remains firmly knotted around the neck of the body. By lifting the head carefully it was possible to measure the circumference of the neck and of the cord. A long flexible plastic tape was inserted between the head and shoulder and drawn to the required tightness. This was marked in ink, the tape withdrawn and the measurement recorded. For examination purposes the cord has been moved around the neck from its original position by about 30 mm so that the knot system is now visible at the upper back quarter (Fig. 12). The circumference of the neck is now 255 mm, and the length of the ligature 315 mm (allowing for the crepes it would have been perhaps 325 mm).

The neck cord is S spun on two fibrous strands of what appears to be sinew. The spin is medium hard at about 50° giving the cord a diameter of 1.5 mm. It has been overtwisted which has produced four backspin or crepe twist slubs, two small ones at the front of the throat and two slightly larger at the back of the neck on either side of the ligature knots.

A comparison between Continental and English collar sizes shows that 370 mm is the equivalent of

Fig. 12   The garrotte, moved slightly so that the knot can be seen under the shoulder.

size 14½, the smallest size given. Taking one English size as approximately 30 mm this makes the ligature a size 12 to 12½, considerably smaller than the average collar size of an adult male.

M.E.A. McC.

A very small piece of material from the garrotte, i.e. about 2 mm length, was extracted overnight in 4% ammonia. The extract was then tested by crossed over electrophoresis against anti-sera from cow, horse, human, deer, pig and sheep. No results were obtained against any of the anti-sera tested, but from its appearance under the microscope the cord was not of vegetable origin.

A.V.P.

(ii) The Knot

The attempt to identify the knots used to secure the cord around the victim's neck is based solely upon superficial observation within the time available. Loosening or untying the knots might reveal some other unsuspected twist or tuck which would change totally the character of the knots as deducted from external appearance alone. No firm conclusions are therefore possible; conjectures, however, can be made.

The knot joining both ends of the ligature is actually three simple overhand or thumb knots (see Fig. 13.1) which, closed up tight together, form a compound knot. All three knots are 'right-handed' (i.e. the two twisted parts helix clockwise). This is not linked to the handedness of the person tying the knots, but as knot-tying is a habitual process (hard to change, even deliberately), the indication is that they may have been tied by the same individual.

Each separate end of the cord is knotted. These two stopper knots serve to secure the third central knot, preventing the ends from pulling free. The third knot actually makes the ligature, if that is what it is, by forming a sliding noose with another overhand or thumb knot.

The three knots are snugly embedded alongside one another and the two ends are very short indeed, scarcely emerging beyond the knot. One is somewhat frayed. The extremely short ends are puzzling and are not typical in a ligature used to strangle someone.

Two possible explanations occur:

(i) Knots weaken the line in which they are tied. An overhand or thumb knot cuts down the breaking strength to 40% or 50% that of the unknotted cord. When a break occurs, it does so just outside the knot. if this was a garrotte, perhaps the

frayed end is evidence that the cord broke... a botched job!

(ii) It would not be possible to tie the knots with ends so short. Some adjustment would have been needed and this would slacken the ligature further. With no ends for an executioner to pull on, the task could have been done by inserting a stick and twisting the garrotte tight like a tourniquet. (This method was still being used in Shanghai in the 1930s.)

Cutting short the ends seems a needless preoccupation with neatness, given the grisly intent.

Conclusions

1. The compound knot consists of three simple overhand or thumb knots
2. A sliding noose results which will pull tighter but cannot slacken past the restriction of the stopper knots
3. No knot-tying skill is apparent
4. The short ends are not typical of a garrotte, and use of the cord as a sliding noose is thought unlikely
5. Tightening it like a tourniquet is feasible

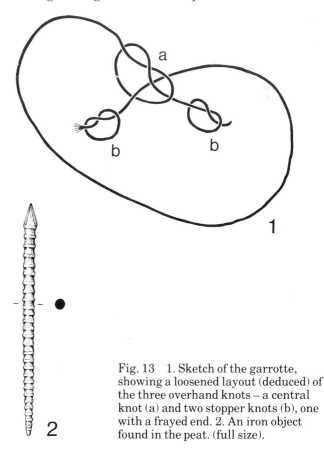

Fig. 13 1. Sketch of the garrotte, showing a loosened layout (deduced) of the three overhand knots – a central knot (a) and two stopper knots (b), one with a frayed end. 2. An iron object found in the peat. (full size).

It is worth noting that most cordage clues found at contemporary scenes of crime consist of a haphazard assortment of overhand knots, not best suited to the job in hand. Matters – it seems – may not have changed much through the centuries.

G.B.

(b) The Arm Band

Three sections of fur bearing skin were excavated, two from the upper surface of the left arm and one from between the arm and thorax. Fur was present in samples of peat taken from around the arm but as there was no evidence of skin remaining these have not been included in analysis of the arm band.

The largest piece is a curved strip of furskin which originally lay on the upper surface of the arm. It is fairly well preserved with a quantity of short hair on one side. There are no knots in the pieces but there is a twist or fold through 45° near the wider end. This strip is 135 mm long and varies in width from 5 mm at the back to 12 mm at the front of the arm.

The other easily identifiable piece of furskin is short and also of a rounded section. Its original site was to the front of the arm. There are no signs of knotting or twisting and the ends of this piece also appear torn or broken. The length is 55 mm and the width 10 mm.

The piece excavated from between arm and thorax is untwisted and flattened. it is more degraded than the other sections though some hair does remain. There are no signs of knotting and the ends appear torn or rotted. The approximate measurements are 25 mm × 15 mm.

The total length of the excavated section is 215 mm. This probably does not represent the original length of the band as an upper arm circumference for a mature person of average build ranges from 290 mm to 350 mm. There is no obvious evidence either that the band was knotted around the arm or that it continued untied across the chest or back of the body.

M.E.A. McC.

Samples were taken in an attempt to identify the source of the hair in the arm-band. They came away from the skin with no resistance and showed no obvious signs of any remaining attachment. They were transferred to glass containers and thereafter remained at 4°C. All the hairs were brittle and difficult to handle.

The hairs were washed in distilled water and their lengths measured. A proportion from each sample was mounted in XAM neutral mounting medium, first examined under low power using incident light and subsequently at a magnification of 400 using transmitted white light and a mixture of uv and blue.

A proportion of the hair was cross-sectioned by fusing hairs between cellulose acetate slides and cutting 10μ thick sections.

The scale pattern from a sample of the guard hairs was examined by preparing a cellulose acetate cast.

Observations

This was a mixture of fine body and coarse guard animal hair. All the hairs were short, 5 mm–10 mm in length. Many had roots and some were complete with root and tip. They were ginger and evenly coloured along their length. They exhibited a bright green fluorescence in uv light.

The scales were pronounced, particularly on the fine hairs, and diamond patterned for most of the length becoming flatter towards the root. In the fine hairs the medullae were of the uniseriate ladder type, the coarse hairs having a fine lattice medulla. In cross section the hairs were round.

Conclusion

The fur is from the fox, *Vulpes vulpes*.

A.V.P

(c) The Iron Object (Fig. 13.2)

A slightly tapering ribbed iron rod, now 61 mm long. It is broken at both ends, though probably only the tip is missing at the narrower end. It has been examined by specialists in Prehistoric, Roman and Medieval antiquities but no parallel has been suggested. Its function is obscure and it is of unknown date.

The ribbed iron rod is significant in that it was found and recorded at the same time as the severed head of Lindow Woman. But the two items were not closely associated – far from it, because they were found some 150 miles apart! The police investigating the discovery of the head made a detailed search of the surrounding peat. They were so thorough that they sieved peat recently removed from the site and it was in one such consignment delivered to Somerset that the iron object was found. Even if it had been possible to identify it and suggest a date it would have little relevance to the human remains.

I.M.S

10 Tests for Dyes

G. W. Taylor

(a) The Body

Four samples of peat taken from the fingernails of Lindow Man were received with a request for tests for woad and any other dyes. The hope was that the dye originally on the skin might have migrated to the surrounding peat.

For dye analysis, the samples were treated as textiles, making allowance for the water in which two of the samples were dispersed. All tests for indigotin (the colorant in woad) were negative; the test itself is very sensitive.

It was possible to recover two of the four samples and subject them to tests for mordant dyes – any such dye that had migrated to the peat should have shown up in the indigotin test, but it was worth checking. Again, however, the results were negative.

Infra-red photographs were taken of the body, but there was no hint of tattoos.

(b) The Hair

See Chapter 17, p.71.

11 Reconstruction of the Skull and the Soft Tissues of the Head and Face of Lindow Man

R. A. H. Neave   R. Quinn

The reconstruction of the soft tissues of the face utilising information provided by the remains of long-dead people is a subject which has intrigued and fascinated many people for many years. One of the earliest examples of this idea being put into practice must be the Neolithic plastered skulls excavated at Jericho in 1953 (Kenyon 1979). The features of the faces being delicately modelled in plaster on the skull, give the impression of artistic skills in portraiture far in advance of anything that was possible at that period.

In more recent times Kollman and Büchly (1898) reconstructed the head of a prehistoric female found in France, utilising measurements of the average thickness of soft tissue on the face obtained from fresh cadavers. Their methods and results can be regarded as the first scientific attempt in this area of study. Much work has been done since in the USSR (Gerasimov 1977) and the USA (Krogman 1962) to improve the accuracy of the techniques used. One of the most important requirements for these techniques to be successful is a complete or near complete skull, for it is the skull that provides the basic architecture of the head and face. Galen, in his book *De Anatomicis Administrationibus* written in about AD 130, sums it up perfectly when he writes 'As poles to tents and walls to houses so are bones to living creatures, for other features naturally take form from them and change with them.'

The realistic size and distribution of the features of the face are determined largely by the underlying bony structure to which the soft tissues are attached. By understanding the basic anatomical structure of the face and using specific measurements it is possible to reconstruct the soft tissues over the skull with a high degree of accuracy (Snow, Gatliff and Williams 1982). It must be made clear, however, that any reconstruction can do no more than give a reasonably good idea of the type of face that once existed. There are many variables that can occur, and the surface markings on the skin, folds, wrinkles, scars and hair lines, etc, cannot be detected from the skull alone. The production of a totally accurate portrait is not therefore possible.

When considering the remains of Lindow Man and the appearance of the preserved soft tissue it soon becomes clear why an attempt to reconstruct the head and face was undertaken, and why it was so difficult. Centuries of interment in the peat bog have distorted and squashed the whole body. This distortion, together with the natural preserving that has taken place, have combined to change the body and head into something that is almost unrecognisable as a human cadaver. All that can be easily determined against the surrounding peat is a dark brown, rather flattened figure with a face so squashed and folded that it is impossible to visualise with any degree of certainty how it may have appeared in life.

Anatomical and radiological studies indicated that this was the body of a 25-year-old male Caucasian. He would have been about 5 ft 7 in tall, well built and very strong. The head was quite large, with prominent brow ridges. The nose was straight with rather flared nostrils, and the ears were rather small. There was nothing to suggest that his face was scarred, pock marked or blemished in any way. The hair on the head was quite short and that of the moustache and beard seems to have been well trimmed.

Combining all these facts in a reconstruction presents them in a manner that is immediately understandable to both the professional and the casual observer, for it is at the face that one looks to gain some impression of another individual.

Due to the inaccessibility of the skull and the delicate nature of the body it was necessary to use indirect means and work from radiographs and photographs. The method finally adopted was to use a system previously devised for clinical use whereby a model of the skull is produced using information provided by radiographs (Neave, in press). Once the skull was ready the soft tissue reconstruction could be carried out in the routine manner. Fortunately, radiological studies had been made and copies of these images were kindly made available by Mr Reg Davis of the Royal Marsden Hospital. Although not of the type usually used for this kind of model they provided all the basic information from which the skull was made. On studying the antro-posterior and lateral views of the head it was clear that a considerable amount of bone distortion had taken place; the upper part of the skull appeared to have been pushed forward and the lower half backwards, at the same time as some flattening of the sides of the skull. A careful tracing was made of the lateral view of the skull's outline to eliminate the distortion. This outline was then modified as little as possible until it appeared acceptable by present day standards. The antro-posterior view showed considerable distortion also, being somewhat flattened, and with the right-hand side of the skull totally obscured. A tracing was made of the left half of the skull and then reversed to make up to the right half. The two halves were then modified into a more normal shape, compatible with the lateral view. Fixed points of reference could be seen in the radiographs at the temporomandibular joint and at the nasion, and were marked on the tracings. The adjusted antro-posterior and lateral views of the skull were transferred onto fibreboard from which templates were cut; these formed the basis of an armature upon which a model of the skull was constructed in clay. Under ideal circumstances a very high degree of accuracy can normally be achieved using this technique. The radiographs of Lindow Man however, provided a limited amount of information, and therefore the model could be no more than a reasonable approximation of the original skull.

Diagnostically, the information that could be gleaned from the radiographs was considerable, but details of some individual parts of the skull were very indistinct. The maxilla was poorly displayed, with the details of the orbits and zygomatic bone obscured by unidentifiable shadows. Unusually, the nasal bone appeared clearly and was undamaged and the outline of the nasal opening could just be seen. The mandible was not as robust as might have been expected in a skull this size and this fact played a big part in establishing the individuality of the face. Much of the mid portion of the skull had to be modelled in such a way that its form was determined as far as possible by those points that could be positively established. The final reconstructed skull, although lacking detail in some areas, was as accur-

ate as seemed possible under the circumstances. A plaster cast was prepared of the clay skull, providing the foundation upon which the soft tissues were developed.

Reconstruction of the soft tissue was started by first inserting small wooden pegs into the plaster skull at twenty-four specific points (Neave 1979a; 1979b). These project from the surface of the skull by an amount corresponding to tables of average soft tissue thicknesses as compiled by Rhine and Moore (1982) of New Mexico. These figures are of course only averages, and based on twentieth-century man, but they are the most up to date data available and are a good guide, eliminating the temptation to 'sculpt' instead of working to predetermined guidelines. Specially prepared blank glass eyes were then fitted into the eye sockets, which upon the advice of Dr John Storey of the Manchester Royal Eye Hospital were given a slightly larger anterior diameter than is usual. This simulates one of the characteristics noted in those of Celtic descent in Southern Ireland.

The face and neck were then developed, first in an anatomical manner, building the main muscles and muscle groups onto the skull. Next the glands of the neck and face and subcutaneous tissue were added. This stage is very much a means to an end as it ensures that the face develops from the surface of the skull outwards. The pegs limit the thickness of soft tissue that is built up, and ensure that the whole process is guided and controlled first by the skull, next by the anatomy, and finally by the measurements.

Surface details of the skin such as wrinkles and folds cannot be ascertained from the skull alone. The same goes for small scars, although deep wounds may well mark the bone (Prag et al. 1984). Hair and the eyes are features by which we often recognise each other and again cannot be ascertained from the skull. For this reason, an accurate soft tissue reconstruction may look very different from the actual person when alive because these details may be missing. In the case of Lindow Man however, fine details on the emerging face were less of a problem as reference could be made to the preserved body.

Although overall the details were grossly distorted it was possible, by looking closely at individual parts of the head, to determine to a large extent what was there and how it may have appeared in life.

The ears were small and lobeless. The forehead was highly creased, the nose straight with what seemed to be a slight tilt at the end and somewhat flared nostrils. The eyes and the mouth were not easily seen and here features that were compatible with the rest of the face had to be adopted. Every attempt was made to incorporate all these features into the final model as accurately as possible.

The results of this type of reconstruction are seldom predictable and any preconceived ideas as to the probable outcome are invariably wrong. Lindow Man was no exception in this respect. The face was broad and strong with a flattish nose, but a rather smaller lower jaw than might have been expected. The eyes were set under quite heavy brows. The head is set on a strong neck as one would expect in a powerfully built man.

Although the head and face were completed, at this stage it did not look like a living person. It is not until eyes, skin tones and hairs are added that a reconstruction of this type comes 'alive', for it is frequently the more superficial details of the face that give the strongest impressions.

We are deeply indebted to Mr R. Brammar, ocularist, for producing the eyes. They were made to a very carefully worked out specification and showed every detail that might be seen in a living subject with blue-grey irises, a colour frequently thought of as being suitable for a Celt of this period. The eyes were set into a wax cast of the clay head. Hair was then added, carefully observing the 'hair line', the length on the scalp and on the face, and the colour. The texture of the hair was very fine and soft and basically straight, unlike its appearance on the body. Subtle variations in its colour could still be determined but the overall basic colour was very dark brown. All these facts were taken into account when the hair was being prepared (and we are again much indebted to Carol Waugh for giving help with this part of the project and providing the hair that was incorporated in the finished model). Finally, the skin tones were added to the face and neck, and were those of a Caucasian living an outdoor life in Northern Europe.

This reconstruction was made using all the facts that were available at the time, and depicts Lindow Man looking very much as he would have done shortly before his death.

II
Medical and
Human Biology

Fig. 14   Lindow Man, the front fully excavated.

12 The Medical Investigation of Lindow Man

J. B. Bourke

The initial investigation was by non-invasive technique. The plain radiographs of the body were disappointing, which was perhaps not surprising as the body had become waterlogged while in the moss and the mineral elements, particularly calcium, would have been leached out. Its position is not anatomical (see Fig. 14) and makes the taking of radiographs technically difficult: the correct anatomical position is vertical with the legs together, the arms by the sides and the head looking to the front and in line with the spine.

Lindow Man made several journeys for special radiological examinations. He was taken to Picker International Ltd at Wembley for magnetic resonance imaging (MRI), a technique which allows hydrogen ions to be mapped, and which produced some useful images showing intracranial contents and arthritic degenerative changes in the spine: Schmorl's nodes which involved the five lumbar vertebrae and the lower four thoracic vertebral bodies. Schmorl's nodes are small, well marked depressions on apposing vertebral joint surfaces and are due to vertical prolapse of the nucleus pulporus (disc) into the adjoining vertebral body. This occurs through a small developmental or traumatic defect in the cartilogeneous end plate of a vertebral body and is typically asymptomatic.

A second journey was made for xeroradiography, a technique which uses selenium impregnated radiographs, and which has produced excellent images of mummies. The initial xeroradiographs of Lindow Man showed some interesting detail including a depressed coronal skull fracture fragment, but were disappointing because of the interference of a substantial amount of peat and the Delta Lite mount. However, a subsequent series of xeroradiographs was obtained after all the peat had been cleared and when Lindow Man had been removed from the mount. These excellent radiographs were obtained at the Royal Marsden Hospital and are reported in detail below (see p. 54) but the radiological technique which yielded maximum information was computed tomography (CT scanning) performed at St Bartholomew's Hospital (p. 63). Lindow Man, while lying in his Delta Lite mount, will easily pass through a whole body scanner. This permits transverse sections to be imaged which can then be converted into vertical and oblique images, a facility for reconstruction ideal for the study of a body which does not lie in the conventional anatomical position.

When the peat had been cleared away the remains were quite clearly those of a well nourished, young, bearded man whose skin and hair had been coloured brown by the indigenous water of the moss. The body had been transected at the level of the fifth (lowermost) lumbar vertebra. His pelvis, except for the left anterior superior iliac crest, was missing: presumably it had been taken by the peat cutter. The right leg below the knee had been previously recovered from the moss and was a separate item. Externally the skin had the feel and texture of soft leather. The head was flexed and turned so that the chin was resting towards the right shoulder. There was a transverse depressed fracture of the skull along the line of the coronal suture, and at its right hand end a skin wound (see Fig. 15). On inspection the base of the skin wound contained a bony flap of skull which had been driven down inside the cranial cavity. An endoscope was passed through the depressed fracture site to allow inspection of the inside of the cranial cavity. The convolutions of the normal brain were absent but there was a pulctatious material with the consistency of putty. There was some flattening of the occiput (back of the head) area and the CT scans and the xeroradiographs showed an occipital fracture.

When the neck was examined the reason for the awkward position of the head became apparent: a high cervical spine fracture dislocation had caused the head to be flexed on the neck and turned to the

Fig. 15   The top of the head, showing
the compound wound possibly caused
by two blows from an axe-like
weapon.

Fig. 16   The head soon after
excavation, with the top of the ear
still bent forwards.

right (see Fig. 16). Below the level of the fracture dislocation a sinew loop runs around the neck and makes a furrow in the skin, and above the loop on the right side is an incised wound about 6 cm in length. This is discussed in detail below (p. 79).

The trachea was identified in the cervical portion but the larynx could not be identified.

The ears, nose and throat were examined by Mr G. E. Mann of Cambridge. The pinna of the left ear was shrunken and soft, due to the deterioration of the cartilage. He removed some peat from the entrance to the meatus and debris from further in. This felt like wax but could equally well have been more peaty material. It was saved for further examination. The meatus was intact but collapsed and

the tympanic membrane was not identified.

The right ear could not be fully examined because of the position of the head. The pinna is present and has the same soft feel as the left one.

The soft tissue of the nasal tip has become separated from the nasal skeleton, leaving the bones exposed and giving direct access to the nasal cavity. This separation is continuous with a split in the skin which extends up to the left orbit and is probably *post mortem* in origin. The nasal cavity is large with no sign of any septal cartilage. Some soft tissue on the left lateral wall in the region of the inferior turbinate was removed for later examination. No normal anatomy was discernible in the nose.

Normal eyebrows and eyelashes were present but

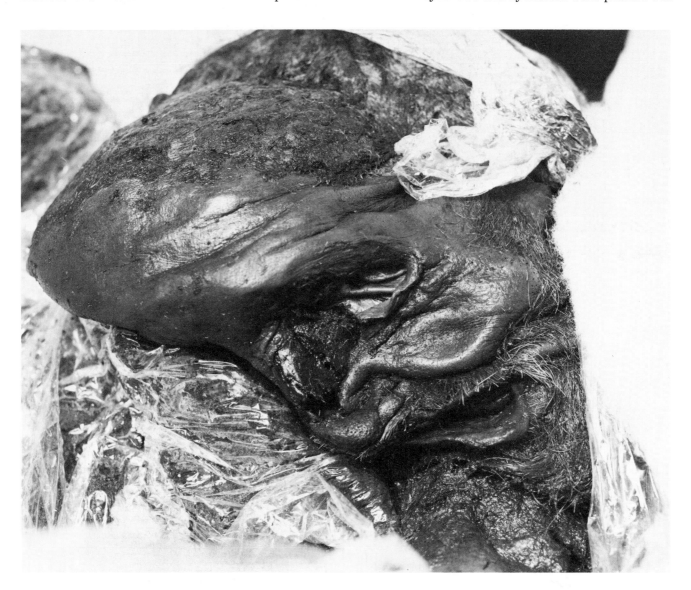

Fig. 17   The face showing the empty left orbit. The lips have been separated and the mouth opened by the excavators.

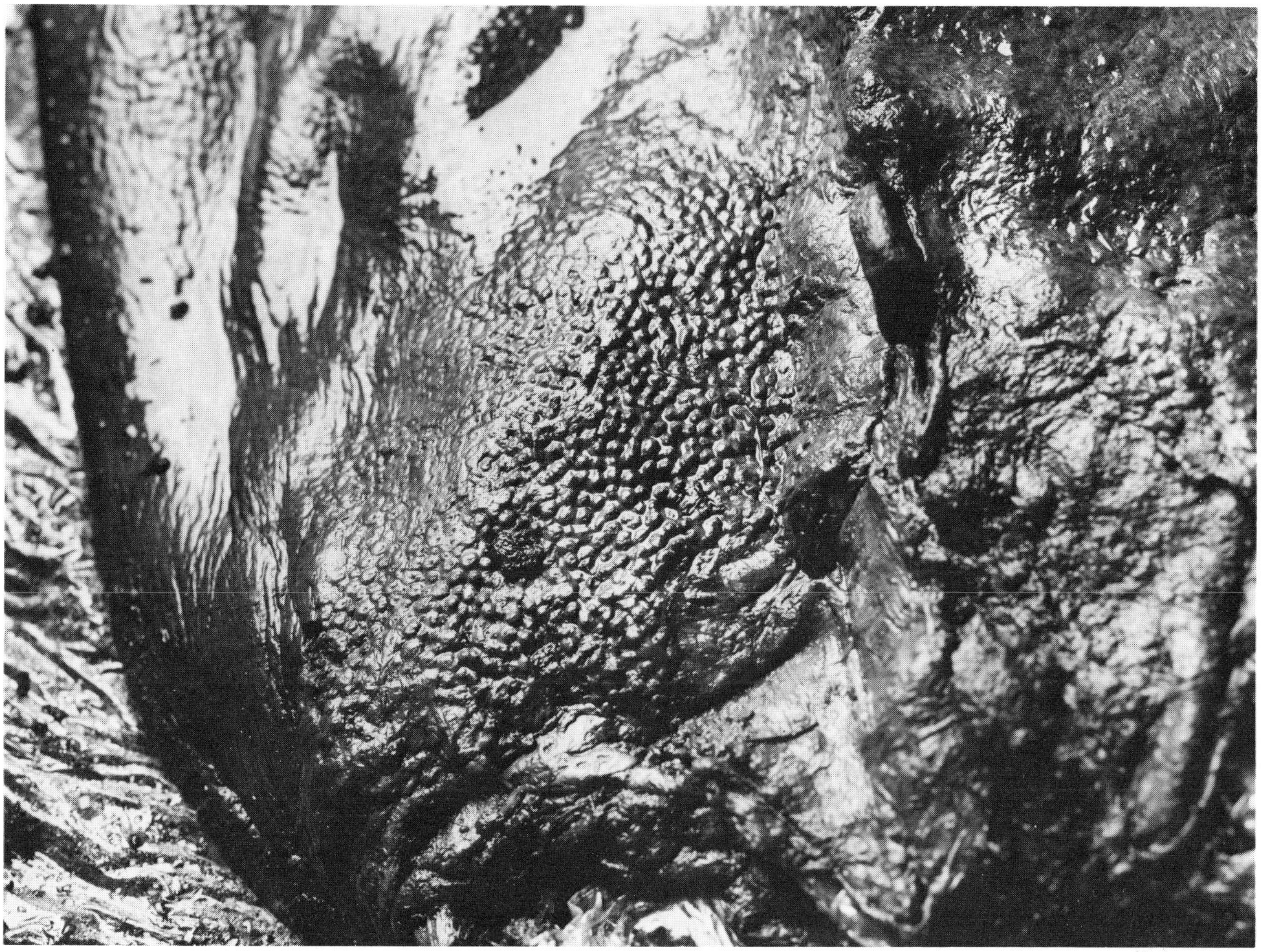

Fig. 18 Skin of the posterior abdominal wall showing the mammilated area.

both orbits were empty leathery pouches. The upper and lower eyelids were foreshortened and had become a little retracted. The frontal and facial bones were intact (Fig. 17).

The lips were closed together but could be easily separated. This allowed the mouth to be opened and several teeth were lying free in the oral cavity. The tongue had foreshortened into the floor of the mouth and could not be pulled forward. An endoscope passed into the mouth allowed the teeth to be inspected and located others in the back of the oral cavity. Presumably the dental ligaments which hold the teeth in the mandibular (lower) and maxillary (upper) sockets had been softened and loosened by the acid of the moss and the teeth had fallen out. After clearing the oral cavity of teeth the endoscope was passed onwards into the oropharynx. At this point the anterior and posterior walls of the oropharynx were com-

pressed together and the endoscope could not be passed any further. This obstruction corresponds with the site of the upper cervical fracture dislocation.

This oropharynx compression was very firm and the onwards passage of air from the endoscope did not occur. It is improbable that any fluid or peat material could have passed onwards after death, so any material within the gastrointestinal tract would have reached there before death and before placement in the moss. Admixture after death via the mouth was impossible. Ultimately thirty teeth were removed for further study (p. 60).

The anterior chest wall was flattened onto the posterior wall with externally no apparent space between them. In the right anterior apical area there was a small ulcerated area which may be the result of injury (e.g. a stab wound) or may be *post mortem* loss. The remainder of the anterior and posterior chest walls were normal to inspection and without injury. The umbilicus is a hole in the anterior abdominal wall where *post mortem* breakdown has occurred.

Inspection of the skin of the left posterior loin area showed a mammilated area (Fig. 18). A piece from here and from the skin of the left leg was obtained by punch and examined by Dr R. J. Hay of the St John's Hospital for Diseases of the Skin, London, who reports that the skin is grossly disorganised on both specimens. The epidermis is absent but there is residual supporting matrix consisting entirely of collagen fibres. There are no elastic fibres to be seen and no residue of other elements within the dermis. Both sides of the section are infiltrated with darkly pigmented fungal hyphae which do not appear to be infiltrating the collagen fibres themselves. There are no differences to be seen between the skin biopsy material from the leg or from the small lesions on the back. The collagen fibres seem to be slightly more closely knoted in the lesion from the back and the appearances on the surface are artefactual and due to some *post mortem* change in the fibres which go to make the skin.

The scanning electron microscopy confirmed that the vast majority of the integument is composed of collagen fibres. Intact hair shafts can be seen

Fig. 19 The stomach lying across the lumbar spine with the duodenum and upper jejunum attached to it.

attached within the substance of the fibres at intervals (Fig. 17). The outer cuticle of the hair is remarkably well preserved with an orderly arrangement of cuticular scales. It is not possible to see other structures in the scanning electron microscopy. The collagen fibrils are very well preserved and show regular cross-striations of the order of periodicity seen in fresh collagen. It is also possible to see a number of organic (non-human structures) associated with the outer sides of the integument. These include pollen grains, fungi and some bacteria.

Both shoulders and forearms were intact with normal skin cover. The right hand is present and four well manicured nails were found. It required careful dissection and removal of the peat because the bones were in a disordered state and most of the skin and soft tissue had decayed. The left hand was absent. No evidence of any rings, bangles or cords was found in association with the right wrist or hand.

Around the left upper arm just above the elbow was a fur band (p. 40) which was removed for further study. There was no wound in association with it.

At the level of the transection of the body by the peat cutter the anterior and posterior abdominal walls could be separated. The acid of the moss had given the skin the feel of soft leather, and the internal aspect of the abdominal cavity had the feel and consistency of suede leather. The anterior and posterior walls were separated and held apart manually and by chocks to allow inspection of the abdominal and thoracic cavities. No liver, diaphragm or lung was encountered on the right side and no spleen, diaphragm or lung on the left side. No heart or great vessels or intra-thoracic trachea was encountered.

However, on careful examination of the anterior aspect of the thoracolumbar vertebrae, a tubular structure was noticed which was higher on the left side of the body and lower on the right. This was then traced out and the upper end was found to extend up towards the thoracic cavity. The lower end extended downwards in the shape of a C. From the end of the lower limb of the C further tissue extended for about 12 cm. This tubular structure was part of the foregut comprising stomach, duodenum and upper jejunum (Fig. 18). No evidence of pancreas, liver, gall bladder or bile duct was found. Within the gut was intestinal content which could easily be palpated through the paper thin intestinal wall. The stomach, duodenum and upper jejunum were then removed as one specimen *en bloc*. Subsequently the stomach was opened along its greater curvature (inferior lower aspect) and the intestinal content removed for further analysis. The duodenum was also opened along its inner medial border and its contents removed for analysis. The stomach and duodenum were also submitted for histological examination.

The fifth lumbar vertebra was removed for further study. Dr Juliet Rogers of the Department of Rheumatology at the Bristol Royal Infirmary reported that it was that of a young adult and usual in every way except for a Schmorl's node on the superior surface of the body of the vertebra. This appearance was confirmed by X-rays and from the MRI and CT scans. In the CT scan the Schmorl's node appeared somewhat deeper than on visual inspection but this was probably due to the way that the body was lying when scanned.

Thus the body was that of a well nourished young man with a compound depressed coronal fracture of the skull, a posterior fossa (back of skull) fracture, a fracture dislocation high in the cervical spine and a sinew loop around his neck with an incised wound on the right side of his neck above the loop. Xero-radiographs showed that he had a left posterior 8th or 9th rib fracture (Fig. 22). His stomach, duodenum and upper jejunum have been recovered and they and their contents are available for further study.

13 The Remains of Lindow Woman

Don Brothwell

When found, the head of the first Lindow body (Fig. 20) consisted of parts of the skull together with some soft tissue (especially some scalp and hair, also part of an eyeball and optic nerve). When these remains were received by the British Museum, the soft tissue had mainly been removed and the skull consisted of most of the calvarium, that is, parts of the skull minus upper face and mandible. Owing to considerable decalcification, the calvarium is now very light in weight.

As the dentition and post-cranial skeleton are missing, a narrow estimate of age is not possible. However, in view of the size of the calvarium, the extent of the frontal sinuses, the development of the mastoid processes and the nature of the sutures (closed internally), there seems little doubt that it was fully adult. Bearing in mind the degree of sexual dimorphism displayed by roughly contemporary cranial samples from other parts of England, the very slight supraorbital development, medium development of the mastoid processes and no marked nuchal ridging suggest that the skull is likely to be female.

In terms of affinities, there is nothing in the cranial measurements which suggests that it falls outside the range of variation for contemporary samples from other areas. It should be noted, however, that these evaluations were made by reference to roughly scaled photographs because the bones themselves had shrunk considerably in the months since their discovery. The specimen measurements were reduced by 5 mm to 10 mm.

Details on non-metrical traits and abnormality may be briefly given. Possibly two lambdoid wormians were present, but no auditory tori and no metopism occurred. Similarly, there is no remarkable pathology or trauma, and no evidence of the cause of death. However, it should be noted that endocranially the pacchionian impressions are marked and the pattern made by the meningeal vessels is deeply 'etched' into the inner table (a feature which could indicate that the individual was an older adult). While there is no orbital osteoporosis, there would appear to be slight osteoporotic changes to the external surfaces of the parietals. The presence or absence of these traits is in no way unusual, and no special comment need be made.

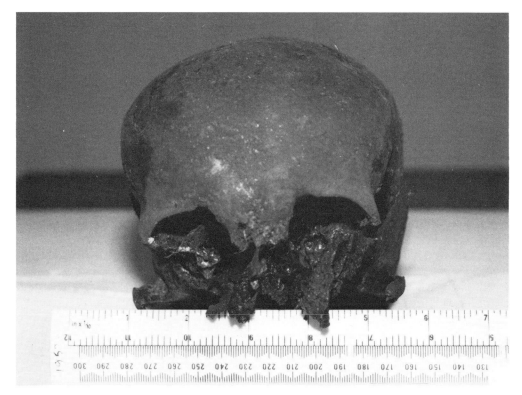

a

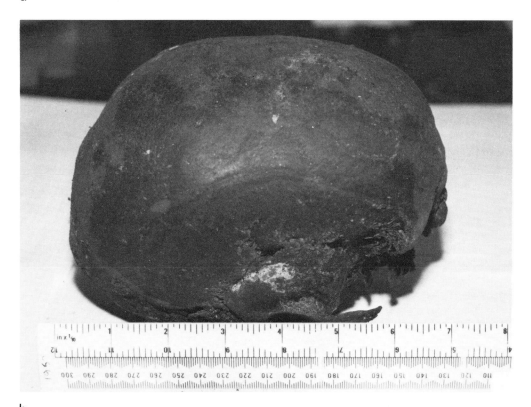

b
Fig. 20   a. Front view; b. Lateral view of Lindow Woman's head, taken soon after discovery.
Photo: Cheshire County Constabulary.

14 The Anatomical Description of Lindow Man

R. C. Connolly

There are four parts to the collection of human remains excavated recently from Lindow Moss, of which three are assigned to the single specimen Lindow Man. The three parts are the foot and lower part of the right leg discovered on 1 August 1984, the main section subsequently excavated consisting of the upper part of the body, and a series of bone fragments collected from the site but dissociated from the main body as a result of the commercial workings at the peat bog. There is no doubt from the anatomical studies that these three are all from the same body, that of Lindow Man. The fourth part, a female skull discovered in May 1983, is not directly associated with Lindow Man (see p. 52).

The right leg, severed at the knee by the peat-cutting operations had been subjected to extensive mechanical handling before being examined, as a result of which there was considerable *post mortem* damage and loss of material. Nonetheless it was in remarkably good condition principally on account of the relatively tough leathery condition of the skin which retained and protected much of the skeleton and internal soft tissue. As is apparent elsewhere in this body and in other bog bodies, the physical functions of the skeleton and soft-tissues had essentially exchanged their roles and the now fragile, demineralised skeleton is supported by the tough, inflexible, leathery skin. The well-defined external appearance of the leg is shown in Fig. 21, and the skeletal structure, although radiologically faint is clearly identifiable and anatomically ordered as seen in the radiographs, taken at Macclesfield District General Hospital on the day of discovery. The skin and some muscle from the back and sides of the leg extend well up to the popliteal fossa (level with the knee-cap in life) suggesting that severence occurred just above the knee. The patella, the femur and the upper (proximal) end of the tibia and fibula were destroyed and lost. The remaining tissue has allowed precise measurement of the apparent standing height of the lower leg of 44 cm and this value has contributed to the calculation of the final estimate of living stature. It has been assumed that no *post mortem* shrinkage has occurred – an assumption for which no contrary evidence exists or can reasonably be inferred. Little of the musculature of the leg remains: it was probably eaten by crows, foxes or insects during the long time that elapsed between excavation and discovery. The profile of the calf muscle is well-retained in the skin and clearly shows a well-developed powerful looking muscle of an equally well-formed leg. What remains of the musculature was mainly soleus and gastrocnemius. There were some well-preserved fragments of blood vessels and some tendon and fascia. The long bones of the lower leg (tibia and fibula) are present mainly as highly demineralised, paper-thin fragments of the outer (cortical) layer. There was some 30 cm of fibula, without either proximal or distal articular ends, and some 15 cm of tibia better preserved than the fibula and still articulating with the talus bone of the ankle. This section of tibia was destroyed for a radio-carbon date but was recorded in detail and is clearly visible in part on the radiograph (Fig. 22). Amongst the bone fragments retrieved from the peat-stacks around the main excavation was a 10 cm length of the distal end of a left tibia and a cuboid bone from a left foot. This tibial fragment, like the tibia in the preserved leg specimen, is large with a wide articular surface and a heavily built shaft. The dimensions of the articular head and the shaft of this specimen are identical to those of the tibia in the preserved leg, and there seems little doubt that they are from the same individual. The left cuboid bone is almost identical to that in the foot of the preserved specimen and this too must come from the same individual.

In spite of *post mortem* damage, the foot is remarkably well-preserved and almost complete but without toe nails. On some toes one, and on others two, of the small terminal bones (the phalanges) have also

Fig. 21   The detached right leg.

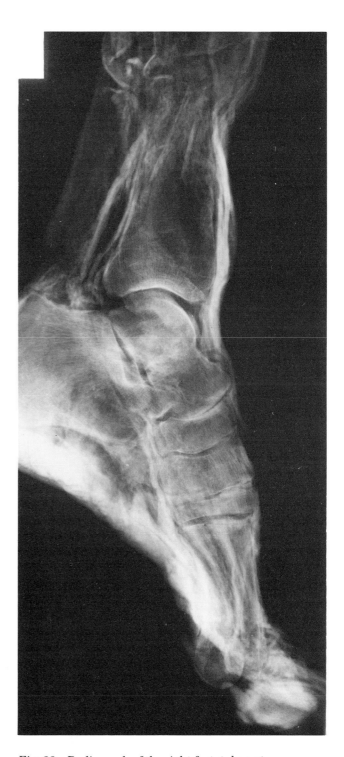

Fig. 22   Radiograph of the right foot, taken at
Macclesfield District General Hospital.

been lost *post mortem*. The small sesamoid bones associated with the first metatarsal (of the big toe) are present. Much of the skeleton of the foot and ankle is visible through the extensive lacerations but since nothing would be gained by dissection, no deep exploration was attempted. Like the dorsum of the foot, the sole is also damaged but the dermatoglyphic ridge patterns – equivalent to the finger prints of the hands – are visible.

The bones of the foot and ankle are characteristic of a fully mature adult and, like the leg, well-formed and heavily built. There is some osteoarthritic degeneration and some eburnation visible at the articulation of the talus and the tibia and also at the articulation of the talus and the navicular bone.

The skin-flap (Fig. 42) found projecting from the cut edge of the peat working, located the position of the body and was thought at first to be from the thigh. On closer examination, while still in the bog Dr Alan Williams and the writer concluded correctly that it was almost certainly from the lower anterior abdominal wall. After careful excavation, the top of the head and the position of the left shoulder were both sufficiently exposed to determine the dimensions of the peat block which needed to be cut to retain the entire body intact and in association with undisturbed peat. The success of this operation was confirmed by radiographs taken later in the day. The X-rays had to penetrate half a metre of heavily compacted wet peat so the resulting films were difficult to interpret. It was clear that the block contained a head, thorax, and arms but neither pelvis nor legs were visible. Reference was made in the original preliminary anatomical description published in 1985 to 'the damaged pelvic girdle'. This was the result of an incorrect interpretation of the X-rays taken through the peat-block, and it is now clear that the whole pelvis including the sacrum and coccyx is missing. After the removal of the block, examination of the cut edges of the bog showed no sign of severed or residual tissue.

The surface of the head and neck and most of the thorax are free of *post mortem* damage or degradation. Similarly the upper four fifths of the anterior abdominal wall and most of the associated musculature is well-preserved and intact but, although the preservation of the viscera is very disappointing, the identification of some internal organs was possible and is described elsewhere (p. 51).

The thorax is complete as far as the skeleton, superficial tissues and musculature is concerned and has been studied by computerised tomography (CT), xeroradiography and direct observation. The ster-

num is present, intact, fully formed but unremarkable, and the clavicles and scapulae and all the ribs are present. The fully adult state of the clavicles is important in the estimate of age. One of the lower ribs is broken, but it is not possible to determine if this occurred in life or is a *post mortem* artefact. The remaining ribs, although partly disassociated from their articulation with the vertebral column and the sternum (Fig. 23), are all identifiable, have retained their characteristic *in vivo* appearance and are considerably less demineralised than some other parts of the skeleton, still showing medullary and cortical bone.

The vertebral column is complete as far as, but not including, the sacrum, having been sectioned at the level of the fifth lumbar vertebra. The first two cervical (neck) vertebrae (atlas and axis) appear normal and undamaged but the next two (third and fourth) are very extensively damaged. The condition of this part of the neck is clearly defined radiologically (p. 64) and can also be observed directly by careful exploration with a probe or finger inserted in the extensive soft-tissue destruction on the back of the neck. If this damage is the result of a heavy blow from a blunt instrument sustained in life, the damage to the cervical spine and the displacement and disarticulation of these two vertebrae would almost certainly have severed or seriously damaged the spinal cord which, at this level, would result in instant death. In the rest of the vertebral column there is radiological evidence for some arthritis of the spine in the lower thoracic and lumbar regions with the presence of Schmorl's nodes (p. 64). The skeleton is clearly that of a well-built, young, mature individual and the presence of such arthritis is well within the range and distribution known from Roman, Anglo-Saxon and Medieval skeletons and even from some recent pre-industrial populations. The anterior aspect of the neck, thorax and what is present of the abdomen is generally well-preserved with respect to the body-wall, the thorax being of male appearance. There exist, however, several localised areas of destruction, one of which on the lateral aspect of the neck has the appearance of an incised wound (p. 79). The back, apart from the neck injury, is well-preserved and displays the well-muscled fully developed trunk of a typical male (Fig. 24).

The arms and hands are differentially preserved, the left being incomplete and in poor condition, with the hand absent. The different state of the two limbs is probably accounted for by two factors. First, the left arm was orientated so that it projected beyond the horizon of the cut peat edge and, along with the

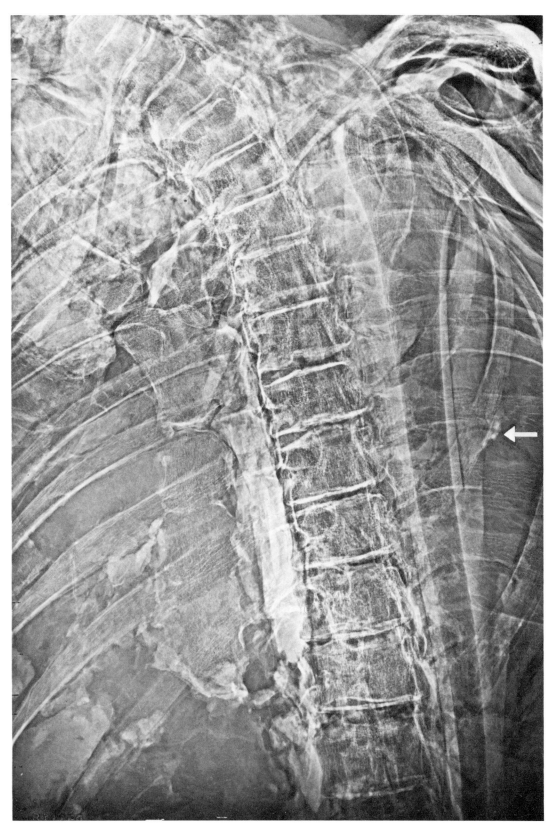

Fig. 23   Xeroradiograph of the back, showing a broken rib. By courtesy of Mr Reg Davis, Royal Marsden Hospital, London.

Fig. 24   Overall view of Lindow Man's back.

lower portion of the body, was severed above the wrist about one third of the distance down the forearm by the peat-cutting operation. Second, the actual chemical preservation of the tissues was less extensive on the left than the right forearm. It is possible that during the period immediately after death when most of the body was immersed, the left arm may have extended beyond the pool and thus been subject to decomposition. The present position of the arms, however, makes this hypothesis difficult to sustain unless there was considerable movement of the body some time after death. Unless such relocation occurred, much of the decomposed organic state of the left arm must be the result of recent exposure following severence. At the excavation site amongst the bone fragments collected was the distal 5 cm of a radius from a left forearm. The dimensions of this fragment equate exactly with those of the right radius of Lindow Man and there is no doubt that it is from the same individual. The remaining section of the left arm still attached to the body shows the upper (proximal) two thirds of the forearm with relatively well-preserved skin but poorly preserved musculature and only very fragmentary pieces of radius and ulna. The upper arm is complete, with the humerus, skin and musculature all well-preserved and the elbow joint and associated tissues with the proximal ends of both radius and ulna still present. Some 10 cm beyond the articulation fragmentation of the shafts begins and beyond this only the poorly preserved cut end of the arm survives. The right arm similarly shows a complete humerus with the skin and heavily-developed musculature of the biceps and triceps particularly well-preserved and the elbow joint and associated tissues also clearly defined. The right forearm, although undamaged *post mortem*, is in a relatively poor state of preservation with most of the mid-section of the shafts of both radius and ulna reduced to cortical shreds with much degeneration of musculature and skin. The hand, however, although much dissociated is complete as regards the skeleton and all the bones of the wrist, hand and fingers can be identified either directly or radiologically (Fig. 25). It is with this hand that the intact well-formed and rounded finger nails are associated. The nails, brown in colour from the peat water, show clear, straight, uniform striae and growth characteristics and none of the many possible signs which could be associated with malnutrition or with nutritionally derived growth disturbances. The palmar aspects of the hand and fingers are not sufficiently well-preserved to allow identification or description of any of the dermatoglyphic fingerprint patterns. Precise measurement of the humerus from both right and left arms was possible and values of 32.0 cm for the right and 32.2 cm for the left were obtained. Such lateral variation is well within the range of sidedness in modern populations but nothing regarding the individual's status as left- or right-handedness can be inferred either from this or from the muscular development of the right and left arms. These values, along with measurements of 22 cm for the right radius and 23 cm for the right ulna are valuable for the estimate of stature.

The last region is the compressed and much distorted head. This bears a healthy covering of hair with a characteristically male distribution on the similarly distorted face. The distortion, due to the pressure of the overlying peat, is enhanced by the increased weakness of the skull from a massive double impacted fracture of the frontal bone in the region just anterior to the coronal suture. This rendered measurement of the skull and calculation of even very basic anthropometric indexes too imprecise to be of value. It is, however, clear that the head is large with recognisable but not markedly prominent supra-orbital crests. The eyelids, without epicanthic eye-folds, are closed but the orbits contain no recognisable remnants of the eyes. The external pinnae of the ears are noticeably small, without free lobes. The flattened appearance is certainly a *post mortem* result of pressure and will not represent their appearance in life with the crus and the tragus showing so little detail. The nose is also greatly distorted and could not, without risk of damage, be manipulated sufficiently for precise measurements to be taken, but the flared nature of the nostrils is apparent even without manipulation. The soft tissue overlying the depressed fracture of the frontal bone bears a large wound through which three fragments of detached bone can be felt. They are clearly seen radiologically (Fig. 26) along with the widely spaced inner and outer tables of bone comprising the vault of the skull which is typical of a mature adult in 'the prime of life'. The occipital bone is also fractured, with a possible superficial soft-tissue wound and a radiologically detectable fragmentation of the inner table, presumably resulting, like the damage to the frontal

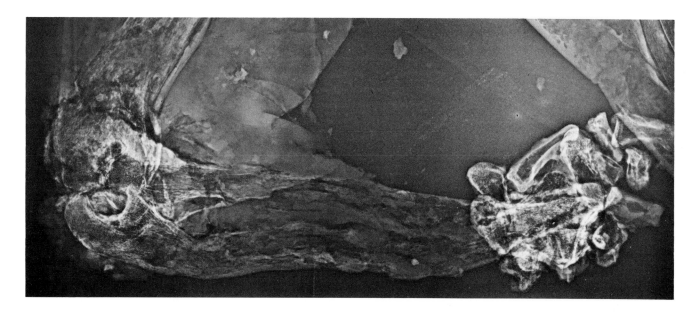

Fig. 25 Xeroradiograph of the right arm and hand. By courtesy of Mr Reg Davis, Royal Marsden Hospital, London.

bone, from traumatic assault with a heavy weapon similar to the injury to the neck. There appears to be no metopic suture nor persistent interparietal bone. The mouth and lips are not large, the tongue is normal and undamaged, and a short cartilagenous section of the trachea and some fragments of laryngeal cartilages persist. Compared with the face and the large size of the head, the lower jaw appears small and even and, allowing for *post mortem* disarticulation, it is remarkably non-prominent. The chin would have been small and rounded rather than the square profile which would customarily be associated with such a large mesomorphic head.

The teeth have been studied extensively by Mr Denys Goose and detailed data relating to attrition and dimensions will be published separately. Out of a possible full normal dentition of 32, there are 30 surviving teeth: the second upper right incisor and the second upper left pre-molar are absent. Because of the soft and decalcified state of the maxilla it is not possible either radiologically or by direct inspection to determine with certainty whether these teeth were lost during life or *post mortem* or even as a result of the assault which resulted in death. There is certainly no overgrowth of maxillary bone but the sockets are not distinct either. It is clear, however, from the attrition patterns on the opposing teeth of the lower jaw that the two missing teeth had existed in life and *post mortem* or time of death loss seems probable. All the teeth are well-formed and healthy in appearance, with no abcesses or evidence of caries,

no features which could be associated with periodontal disease and no apparent abnormalities. None shows any sign of damage or injury during life except the left lower second molar which has a vertical slice chipped from the meso-lingual angle (Fig. 27c). The edges of the chip are very clean and sharp with no sign of any abrasion or smoothing resulting from chewing or attrition so the damage occurred either *post mortem* or very close to or at the time of death. Since there is no *post mortem* process which would have produced such damage, it was probably caused by the blow which fractured the front of the skull. This blow would have jarred the teeth together and might have split the molar although the tooth fragment was not found in the mouth. The alignment of the teeth is good, but the wear patterns are markedly different throughout the dentition, some showing little or only moderate wear and others – notably the first molars – showing extremes of attrition. The acid nature of the peat has resulted in total dissolution of the enamel from all the teeth leaving them with the slightly pitted dentine exposed and, like the hair and fingernails, stained brown by the peat pigments. As a result of the total enamel loss they appear small, are loose in the sockets, and are now widely separated judging from the two pre-molars and first molar in a detached fragment of the right side of the mandible (Fig. 27a). Regressions have been calculated to determine the probable original sizes of all the teeth, but with the total absence of enamel the incidence or presence of dental caries can-

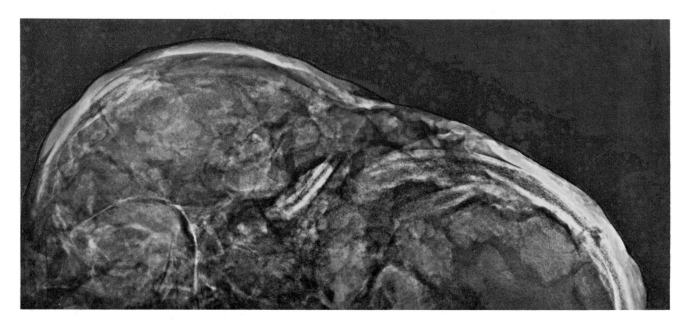

Fig. 26   Xeroradiograph of the skull. By courtesy of Mr Reg Davis, Royal Marsden Hospital, London.

a   b   c

Fig. 27 Teeth: a. fragment of right mandible with three teeth – note the spacing, showing loss of enamel; b. molar with deep erosion of roots, which is not pathological but due to immersion in the acids of the bog; c. a lower second molar which has lost a flake from the mesolingual cusp – presumably as a result of the blows to the top of the head. Photos: Liverpool University.

not be established. Many of the teeth have deep holes penetrating the roots but close examination indicates that they are due to *post mortem* chemical erosion although it is not impossible that they represent sites of cavitation which have acted as foci for this erosion (Fig. 27b).

Conclusions regarding mode of death are summarised elsewhere, but some reasonably certain conclusions about this individual may be drawn from this summary of the anatomical investigations. The sex is widely assumed to be male on account of the facial hair. There are no genitalia or pelvic viscera which would afford confirmation and the skeletal components offering the most reliable criteria are either missing (the pelvis and femora) or inaccessible (some parts of the skull and mandible). The data on sex which could be derived from dissection would not justify the resultant damage to the specimen. Despite the small mandible, the rest of the body is massive, highly muscular with well-built bones and a masculine chest wall, so it seems reasonable on anatomical grounds to assume the sex is male.

Using the lengths of the right and left humerus, the right radius and the right ulna, and the estimated lengths of the right tibia and right fibula, application

of Trotter and Glesers method and Breitenger's equations yields an estimate of stature centring upon 168 cm (approx. 5 ft 6 in). Of course, no calculation of upper and lower tolerance can be determined but, if it were estimated, it would probably approach ±4 cm. No estimate is possible for sitting height. Since the only limb-girths which could be determined by direct reconstruction are those of the upper arms, no direct estimate of body weight was possible. Working from the height to weight ratio, or Ponderal index $\left(3\sqrt{\dfrac{\text{Height}}{\text{Weight}}}\right)$, for an individual with an estimated height of 168 cm and a probable somatype of 352/262 an estimate of weight would be 60–65 kg, although the stature is smaller than might be expected from the massive head and thorax.

Determination of the age at death of an isolated single specimen from an unknown ancient population by reference either to modern data or to data from other ancient populations is beset with risk. However, recognising the limitations, some criteria can be considered. All the teeth have erupted, the lower third molars some time before death and the unworn upper third molars very close to the time

of death. In a modern population this would suggest
18–25 years +, and there is little or no evidence for
variation in ancient populations. Assessing the
degree of attrition of the teeth and applying Miles'
system, Goose estimates an age of 24–30 years. Little
can be determined even radiologically from the skull
except that there are no immature features. The wide
separation of the inner and outer bone tables of the
skull argues for an age younger than middle-life by
modern standards, and the vertebral column, the
bones of the hand and foot, the long bones and the
scapulae are all fully adult. It is unfortunate that
the pelvic girdle is absent for not only is it a good
diagnostic indicator of sex, it could also have provided some useful criteria for ageing. The epiphysis
of the iliac crest and ischium and the condition of
the pubic symphisis would have been useful in this
respect. Xeroradiographs of the thorax reveal both
clavicles and clearly the lateral or acromial head on
both sides is completely fused. The sternal ends of
the clavicles are rather indistinct and may be only
just distinguishable, suggesting recent or partial
fusion. Krogman's ages for fusion of this ossification
are 25–28 years.

The value of degenerative phenomena of the skeleton for assessing age are particularly vulnerable to
error in the cases of a single specimen. This specimen
is further complicated by the extensive dimineralisa-
tion of the skeleton which, if the conditions of preservation had been unknown would have advanced the
radiological estimate of age by several decades. Cau-
tious assessment of the arthritic degeneration is in
accord with a physically active individual in his mid-
twenties.

Lindow Man was probably a powerfully built,
mesomorphic man not much in excess of 25 years
of age, some 168 cm height and perhaps weighing
60 kg or more at death. He was probably physically
active but apart from minor skeletal lesions, there
is no reason to believe from his teeth, fingernails,
skeleton and soft tissues that he was other than a
healthy, well-muscled, well-developed, fit young
man, with little evidence of fat deposit, disease or
disability and certainly not approaching the end of
his natural life span.

15 Computed Tomography of Lindow Man

R. H. Reznek   M. G. Hallett
M. Charlesworth

Computed tomography (CT) (from the Greek: *tomos* a slice) is an X-ray technique which uses a computer to reconstruct an image of a thin slice of the body. The advantage of CT over conventional radiography is that very small differences in attenuation of the X-ray beam can be detected. This makes small differences in tissue density apparent and soft tissue structures within the bony skeleton are therefore well demonstrated. A CT examination usually entails obtaining a series of scans in the axial (cross-sectional) plane. The computer data so acquired can then be reformatted to reconstruct images in the longitudinal plane.

Recently there have been reports on the use of CT in the investigation of Egyptian mummies (Lewin and Harwood-Nash 1977; Yahey and Brown 1984). 'Bog people' have been discovered in Denmark with partially intact organs (Fischer 1983). This raised the possibility of imaging internal organs in Lindow Man, thereby permitting a more accurate approach to the dissection that was to follow. Furthermore, much of the calcium had been leached from the bones of Lindow Man and it was hoped that a CT scan would provide more detailed information about the skeletal remains than the limited data available on the plain radiographs.

The General Electric 9800 scanner used has a 70 cm aperture which allowed Lindow Man to be placed head-first into the scanner without disturbing his position on the Delta-Lite mount. Scans were performed at 5 mm intervals from the vertex of the skull down through the torso. This required approximately 100 images and the duration of the examination was 2 hours. Repeated spraying of the body throughout the study ensured that it remained cool and damp.

Findings

(1) The Skull (see Figs 28 & 29)
Lindow Man was scanned lying on his right side (Fig. 14) and so the left fronto-parietal bones are shown uppermost. An isolated, depressed fracture of the left fronto-parietal bone is seen. The bones of the right hemicranium are severely comminuted, distorted and disorganised, but a more clearly defined, depressed fracture of the right occipital bone can be identified (Fig. 29). It is impossible to determine from these images whether the fractures preceded or followed Lindow Man's death.

Amorphous soft tissue is seen within the skull, but its density is identical to that of the surrounding peat. It is therefore impossible to characterise the contents of the cranium further on the basis of its density alone. Furthermore, none of the characteristic macroscopic appearances of brain tissue – gyri, sulci, fissures, ventricles – can be identified. However, in the posterior fossa (Fig. 28), this material is symmetrically arranged around the midline and appears to be surrounded by air on its right and left lateral surfaces. These two features suggest that this may represent saponified, macerated brain tissue. Unfortunately, the eyes cannot be identified.

(2) Spine
(a) Cervical spine (Figs 29–31): Images of the spine yielded the most information. Excellent detail of the upper cervical vertebrae was obtained on the axial images. The atlanto-axial joint (between the first and second cervical vertebra) is well shown. The relationship between the arch of the atlas and the odontoid peg has not been disturbed (Fig. 29).

Lower down, a number of mid-cervical vertebrae are seen. Within the lateral masses of many of these vertebrae are small (about 3 mm) holes – the foramina transversaria, which transmit the vertebral artery. More remarkably, contained within the spinal canal of many of the vertebrae, there is a thin sheet of soft tissue with a triangular configuration. This appearance is consistent with the dura mater – the membranes protecting the spinal cord (Fig. 30).

No soft tissue structure can be identified within this dura to suggest the survival of the spinal cord.

The data acquired from the axial images was reformatted in the longitudinal projection (Fig. 31). Good vertebral alignment is seen from the fourth cervical vertebra inferiorly but there is a very sharp angular deformity at the junction of the third and fourth cervical vertebrae. The loss of spatial resolution inherent in the reformatting process does not allow the delineation of specific fractures, but it must almost certainly have occurred to allow this anterior dislocation. The site of this fracture/dislocation corresponds exactly to the superficial site of the garrotte.

(b) Thoracic Spine (Fig. 32): Multiple short segments of the thoracic spine are clearly outlined. The vertebral margins and joint surfaces are well preserved. Although intervertebral cartilaginous discs cannot be identified, there are multiple, small, well-demarcated depressions on apposing vertebral joint surfaces – Schmorl's nodes. These are due to vertical prolapse of the nucleus pulposus into the adjoining vertebral body. This occurs through a small traumatic or developmental defect in the cartilaginous end-plate of the vertebral body, is asymptomatic and of no clinical significance (Sutton 1980, 1134). Degenerative changes are not shown on the apophyseal joints between the articular facets on the posterior arches of the vertebral bodies.

(3) Other Skeletal Features
Both shoulder joints are well preserved. The left glenohumeral and subacromial joints are particularly well shown (Fig. 33). Initially the clear visualisation of the epiphyseal line of the left humeral head generated some interest in the possibility of assessing the age of the specimen. This line can however be identified up to any age in adults and with the surrounding loss of bone density in Lindow Man is likely to be more prominent.

An approximate measurement of tissue density can be inferred by measuring the extent to which the X-ray beam is attenuated by that tissue. An arbitrary scale of units (Hounsfield units) is used to quantify this attenuation. The usual attenuation value of bone is approximately 1,000 units, water 0 units, air −1,000 units. In Lindow Man this value varied between −267 to −650, reflecting skeletal decalcification that resulted in the failure of the plain radiograph to show bone detail.

Although ribs are clearly seen, disappointingly, no intrathoracic or intra-abdominal organs could be identified.

Conclusion

The enhanced tissue contrast resolution of CT provided superb images of the decalcified skeleton, showing fine detail of some minute structures. The ability to reformat images proved particularly useful in showing the dislocation of the spine between the third and fourth cervical vertebrae (C3/4).

One of the main hopes of the CT images was that preserved internal organs would be identified. Unfortunately, this expectation was not entirely fulfilled. It is not surprising that the gastrointestinal remnant discovered at the dissection cannot be identified. The normal empty oesophagus and stomach are difficult to image *in vivo* without the use of a contrast medium; in Lindow Man, surrounded by peat at the time of the scan, the task was impossible.

Nevertheless, it showed the persistence of the dura mater and suggested the preservation of intracranial contents. It proved a useful adjunct in the planning of the surgeon's strategy for dissection and confirms the impression of others (Lewin and Harwood-Nash 1977; Yahey and Brown 1984) that this technique is a powerful tool that provides previously unobtainable information in a non-invasive manner.

Fig. 28   Transverse scan through the skull at the level of the posterior fossa showing: a) left parietal bone surrounded by peat; b) fracture of the frontoparietal bone; c) posterior fossa (occipital bone); d) contents of posterior fossa – note symmetry and surrounding air; e) right petrous temporal bone; f) fractured, disorganised right frontoparietal bone; g) head of right humerus.

Fig. 29   Transverse scan done at a level slightly lower than Fig. 28 through the posterior fossa: a) left parietal bone surrounded by peat; b) contents of posterior fossa; c) fracture in posterior fossa; d) arch of atlas; e) lateral mass of first cervical vertebra; f) odontoid peg; g) fractured right frontoparietal bones; h) scapula.

Fig. 30   Scan through upper cervical vertebra and lower jaw showing: a) body of one of the upper cervical vertebrae; b) foramen transversarium; c) dura mater; d) lamina of cervical vertebra; e) teeth; f) scapula; g) clavicle.

Fig. 31   Longitudinal reconstruction of cervical spine showing: a) upper three cervical vertebrae; b) lower four cervical vertebrae; c) arch of atlas cut transversely; d) angular deformity between third and fourth cervical vertebrae.

Fig. 32   Scan through thoracic spine showing: a) Schmorl's node; b) pedicle of vertebra; c) articular facet; d) apophyseal joint between facets; e) intervertebral foramen.

Fig. 33   Scan through left shoulder joint showing: a) shaft of upper humerus; b) epiphyseal line; c) head of humerus; d) glenoid of scapula; e) acromion process of scapula; f) rib.

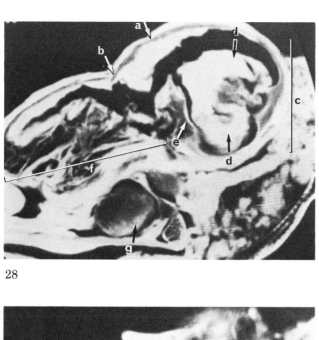

28

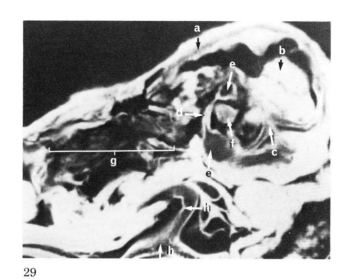

29

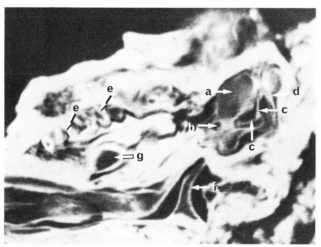

30

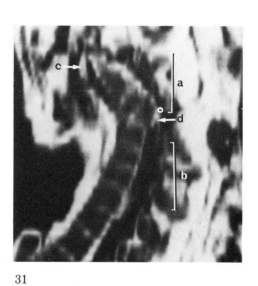

31

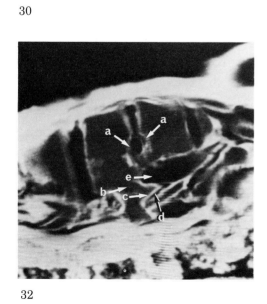

32

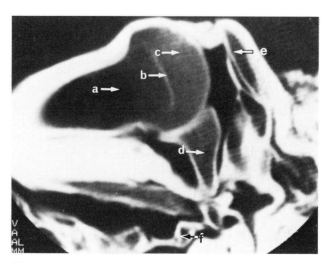

33

16 Studies on the Hair and Nails of Lindow Man and Comparative Specimens

Don Brothwell   Keith Dobney

Keratinous tissues, hair and nails, are known to preserve well in acid bog environments, and it was therefore no surprise to find that these remained intact for study on the Lindow body. The head and facial hair (see p. 2), appeared to be completely preserved, although flattened against the skin. There was, however, little evidence of body hair generally (although some axial hair remained) and in view of the good preservation on the head this suggests that the individual was relatively hairless. The pubic area and lower abdomen were of course cut away, and the forearms too rotted to display hair.

As for the nails, only those of the hands were recovered, and their position on excavation was affected by the surprisingly decomposed state of the hands and forearms. They were thus detached from the surrounding tissues, and a number had drifted some distance from the distal phalanges. Their state of preservation, on simple visual assessment, looked excellent, and we were struck by the smooth and 'well manicured' appearance of the distal edges (Fig. 34).

Hair

The head hair still covered all of the scalp, and was relatively short. Hair length was for the most part approximately 10 mm to 90 mm in length, with the hair of the occipital (neck) area generally the longest. There is no evidence of natural waviness or of any specially well trimmed appearance. Similarly, the beard hair has the appearance of being roughly cut, and in the case of the moustache, there is some 'notching' suggesting a fairly rough-and-ready attitude to hair cutting. Although not long, the moustache overlaps the upper lip by one or two millimetres.

Because of the apparently good state of preservation of the hair, and the 'notching' effect noted on the moustache hair, it seemed worth investigating a sample of cut hair ends to see whether the micromorphology would provide information about the

Fig. 34   A nail still attached to a phalange of the right hand.

cutting equipment used. For comparative purposes, modern European head and face hair samples were cut both by a razor and by scissors, and also submitted to scanning electron microscopy (SEM).

Methods used were as follows. A number of intact hairs were removed from the moustache of Lindow Man. Preservation was such that on some the follicle was almost completely intact. Each was carefully separated, making certain that the orientation to the face remained, then carefully placed in alcohol and cleaned for a few minutes by immersion in an ultraso-

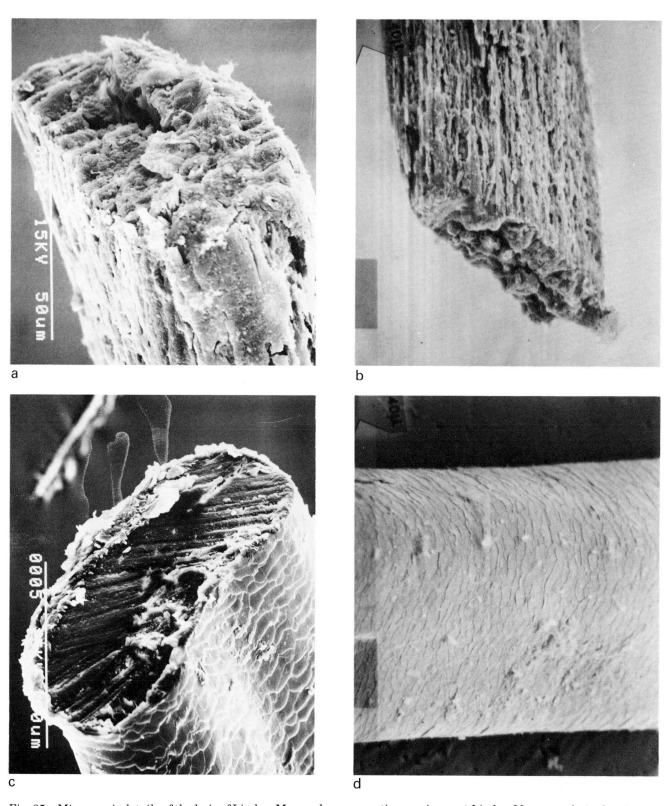

Fig. 35   Microscopic details of the hair of Lindow Man and a comparative specimen: a) Lindow Man, a cut hair showing stepped cut end. Hair shaft surface displays much *post mortem* erosion. b) Another hair from Lindow Man, with apparent cut end and noticeable erosion. c) Modern face hair with unstepped and relatively flat razor cut end. d) Lindow Man hair shaft with good preservation of cuticular scales.

nic cleaning tank. They were then removed, air dried and mounted on Cambridge stubs. Using a binocular microscope the presumed cut end of each hair was lifted slightly free of the surface of the stub in order to afford the best possible view of the hair section. Each stub was then coated with gold in an Edwards sputter coater and subsequently viewed with the Department of Human Environment's SEM located at the Institute of Archaeology. In the modern examples also, the orientation of the cut hairs was carefully maintained as each hair was washed in alcohol and carefully mounted and coated with gold. The freshly cut ends of each hair and the original ends were then viewed at magnifications of × 200 and × 300 in order to establish any differences between the two categories.

It should be remembered that at the time of this investigation, the date of the body (550 bc) would seem to preclude the use of shears as a means of hair cutting. We were advised that a cutting instrument of the razor type was the only one likely to be available for such tasks. However, in scanning the hair ends of the Lindow sample, we were impressed by the apparent 'stepped' ends of the hair. This step structure (Fig. 35a) was well defined even though at a microscopic level there was clear evidence of some post-mortem change and cuticular scale damage (Fig. 35b). When this step form was considered in relation to the high magnification appearances in the comparative specimens, it became clear that stepping was usually associated with cutting by shears or scissors and not by a single sharp blade being drawn across the hair (Fig. 35c). It thus seemed necessary to suggest from these comparisons that some form of cutting tweezers or shears had probably been used, even if such equipment is not known to be a common personal item in British Iron Age cultures. Scissors appear to have been introduced into Britain in post-Roman times.

The Nails

Finger nails were very well preserved on the hands of the Danish Grauballe Man, and were also present in other bog finds, although not studied in great detail. In this study, we undertook some comparative work with modern European nails, from four individuals with different work backgrounds, and were also fortunate in being able to include a consideration of the nails of a late medieval Irish bog body currently under investigation.

As in the case of the hair, the Lindow nails under the scanning electron microscope revealed some minor patches of microscopic erosion, but for most of the surface the detail does not appear to have been obscured. As seen in Fig. 36a the nail end is remarkably well rounded, and the upper nail surface is generally fairly smooth, with relatively few scratch marks visible. The nail was prepared and studied as follows. A part of the nail 'quick' area was cut away for biochemical analysis in the University of Liverpool (p. 74). The rest, and including the 'buffed' looking 'working edge' of the nail, was then mounted on an SEM stub and cleaned with alcohol until all visible loose peat matrix was removed. The nail was then fixed to the stub by carbon cement and coated with gold in a sputter coater. Comparative material was similarly prepared, and consisted of one specimen from an Irish bog body, together with modern samples from an agricultural labourer, an Institute staff member and the artificially buffed (filed) nails of a housewife. The results were interesting, and we suggest may be roughly suggestive of occupation. As was the case using normal microscopy, under the SEM at relatively low power (i.e. × 50) the nail appeared almost totally smooth, rounded and undamaged, especially along its working edge. At magnifications of around × 200 a discrete zone some 100 mm wide was visible at the distal edge. At × 1,000 this discrete zone was quite clearly an area of erosion with small areas of the cuticular layer being removed, giving a very ragged, flaky appearance (Fig. 36b).

The surface of the nail retains its smooth, undamaged appearance even at magnifications of × 1000. There are, however, a number of larger scratches or shallow grooves which appear to cross the surface of the nail approximately parallel to the working edge (Fig. 36c). There are also a number of much finer scratches, more obvious around the edge of the nail and mostly orientated parallel and at right angles to it (Fig. 36d). These are puzzling in view

Fig. 36 Surface detail of a nail from Lindow Man, and comparative specimens: a) Low magnification showing rounded nail edge and restricted *post mortem* damage. b) Close-up of *post mortem* damage (× 500). c) Near the edge of the nail, showing scratch marks, some quite deep. d) Zone just behind eroded working edge showing fine linear marks with some orientation. e) Detail of modern nail and edge. From adult female who manicures the trimmed ends. f) Nail edge without marked damage. Adult male teacher. g) Rough well-scratched nail surfaces of agricultural worker. h) Detail of nail edge in a medieval Irish bog body. i) Medieval Irish nail in close-up, showing a number of old deep scratches. Broken edge in top left corner.

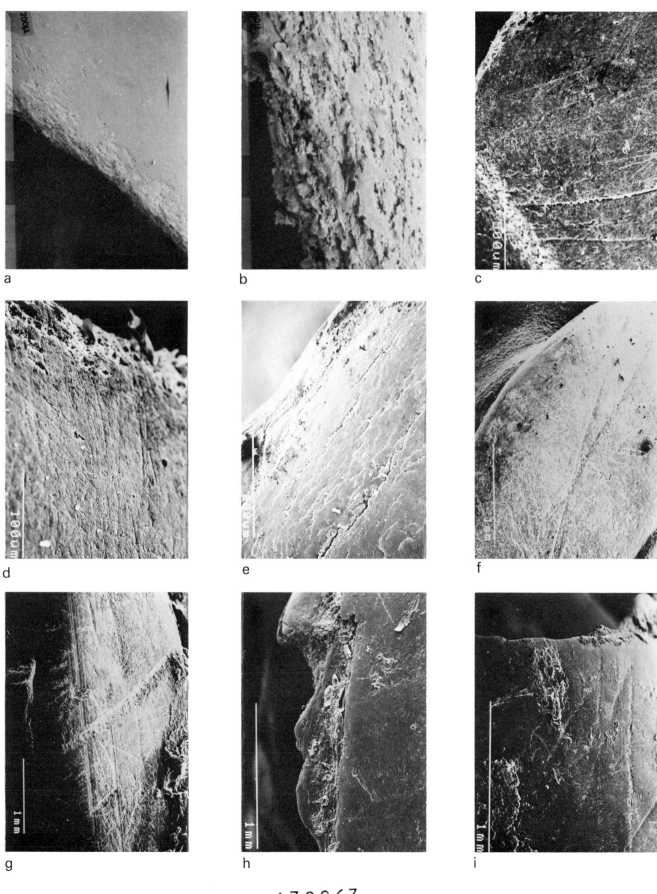

of their limited extent, and seem to be suggestive of some form of limited scratching action.

When compared with the modern nail clipping which *has* been artificially buffed no similarities can be noted. The latter, far from showing visible evidence of nail-filing, appeared rounded and very smooth at high magnification (Fig. 36e). However, a number of small cracks were apparent randomly scattered over the nail surface.

It is certain that the Lindow nail had not recently been trimmed, since characteristic compression of the cuticle, of a kind seen where the nail was trimmed with scissors for analysis, is not apparent.

The nail cutting taken from the agricultural labourer exhibited the most obvious surface damage of all the modern European samples. The whole outer surface was 'criss-crossed' with deep scratches, mostly running parallel to the working edge, but with several noticeably deeper running at right angles to it (Fig. 36g). The appearance of the Lindow nail is in complete contrast to this heavily worn modern specimen, as are all the other modern comparative samples, which does tend to suggest an occupation or vocation removed, if only recently, from physical labour of any kind.

Finally, compared with the nail from the Irish bog body, although at low magnification the outer surfaces both appear smooth, when magnification is increased the distal edge of the Irish nail is obviously chipped and broken (Fig. 36h). The rounded, smooth nature of these breaks do, however, suggest that these occurred during life rather than as a result of post-mortem erosion. At magnifications of ×300 deep surface scratching is apparent on parts of the nail (Fig. 36i) but the finer, more organised scratching which was visible around the nail edge of the Lindow Man is not present.

There is thus no evidence that the differences between the Lindow and modern European nails can simply be explained in terms of surface erosion in the archaeological specimen, especially as *post mortem* changes would accentuate the roughness of nail surfaces and not result in the smooth Lindow appearance. The Lindow nail is also very different in appearance to the Irish late medieval bog body, and here both bodies have undergone the same preservation in acid peats.

17 The Hair

Ann V. Priston

In order to determine the condition of the head hair and establish whether or not it had been dyed, samples taken from the cranium, nape of the neck, sideburn and beard were treated in the same way as the hair from the arm-band (p. 40). Like the arm-band, these hairs came away from the skin with no resistance and showed no obvious signs of remaining attachment.

A single ginger hair, 42 mm long, from the left cranium and a single brown hair, 36 mm long, from the nape of the neck, together with a sample of the original peat in which the body lay were extracted for 45 minutes in a mixture of piridine and water (57:43) at 90°C. The extracts were then spotted onto pre-prepared silica gel coated plates and run in a mixture of water; ammonia; chloroform; methanol (1:1:11:7) until the solvent front had moved 2 cm from the origin.

Observations

(a) Head Hair
The hairs were short and straight and evenly coloured along their length, either ginger or brown. The lengths ranged from 10 mm to 50 mm. Most were medullated, showing a range from continuous to fragmentary medullae. The scales were not pronounced. Some of the fine hairs had tapered tips, but most of the tips were either square or frayed. No dye was detected in either of the hairs examined or in the surrounding peat. After extraction of these hairs their microscopical appearance was unchanged.

(b) Beard Hair
These were short, 6 mm to 20 mm, and coarse and were darker than the head hairs but still showed an even colour along the length. The tips were straight across but frayed; some had bulbous roots.

All the hairs exhibited a strong green fluorescence when examined in uv light.

Conclusions

The head hair was in an extremely good state of preservation and there was no evidence of it having been dyed. The ginger colour is most likely due to the destruction of the less stable brown pigment (eumelanin).

18 The Chemical Composition of some Body Tissues

R. C. Connolly   R. P. Evershed   G. Embery
J. B. Stanbury   D. Green   P. Beahan   J. B. Shortall

Introduction

The study of the chemical composition of ancient tissues and other organic material has been made possible in recent years by the availability of a wide range of non-destructive techniques and techniques which although destructive use extremely small quantities of material which can be removed from important antiquities without prejudicing principles of conservation. A number of notable sources for ancient organic material of both human and non-human origin have been the subject of analytical studies. They include excavated skeletal material, specimens which have been mummified either intentionally or by chance, frozen carcases, material recovered after prolonged aquatic submersion and the generally more ancient sources of arthropods preserved in amber and residual organic isolates extracted from fossils. To this range can now be added peat-preserved human tissues to complement the wealth of information on other organic constituents and intrusions in peat. Of the sources of human material which yield significant quantities of skin, muscle, viscera and hair rather than just bony material, mummified and frozen specimens are particularly important and a comparison of mummification, freezing and peat-preservation may be made. Although the procedures for mummification adopted in Ancient Egypt involved the use of a wide variety of embalming substances and other additives, many of which persist either intact or as breakdown products in the mummified tissue and which severely complicate present-day analytical methods, the overall basis for mummification is one of controlled dehydration of tissues. Despite, or as a result of this controlled dehydration, a range of molecular types have been isolated and characterised including blood-group substances, and DNA which can be replicated in the laboratory using genetic cloning techniques. Many tissues have been re-hydrated and shown microscopically to have retained much of their original cellular structure. Similarly, there are frozen examples both human and non-human, including mammoths dated to 40,000 BP. Like the mummified material, it has been possible to isolate and characterise at least from mammoth a range of intact tissue constituents including clonable DNA, although this may be contaminated rather heavily with modern bacterial DNA. Mummification and freezing preserve DNA much better than the acid, aqueous environment of Lindow Moss. However, preliminary experiments by Dr M. A. Hughes and Dr D. S. Jones in the Department of Biochemistry at Liverpool University suggest the presence of intact DNA in muscle tissue of Lindow Man. Drying and freezing are methods of both natural and intentional preservation which result in the persistence for many thousands of years of several undegraded tissue components. The process of peat-preservation, although in some respects as effective as freezing or mummification, is totally different in its effector mechanisms, and the end product both chemically and in physical appearance is quite unlike the results of freezing or mummification. Peat-preservation of animal tissue depends upon the unique combination of three conditions: an almost complete absence of oxygen, complete absence of putrefactive micro-organisms and a very acid aquatic environment containing a complex and variable mixture of constituent organic acids. Each of these conditions either singly or in combination contributes to one or more of the processes preventing putrefaction and enhancing preservation.

Since Lindow Man was not buried deep in the wet peat like some Danish specimens, but deposited face-down and submerged in a pool of surface water, the normal processes of putrefaction were not immediately and completely inhibited by the acid, sterile, anaerobic conditions of the peat-bog. Almost certainly enzyme-induced degradation and microbial colonisation resulted in the rapid and almost complete putrefaction and total structural degradation of all internal organs except the stomach and part of the jejunum and duodenum.

The skin and muscle of mummified and frozen specimens appears to remain unaltered chemically and the cellular appearance can be readily restored. As is described elsewhere, the cellular structure of the tissues of Lindow Man is completely destroyed presumably by a combination of the osmotic and other physical effects of waterlogging along with microbial, enzymatic and other chemical degradative processes. Although it has not yet been unequivocably demonstrated in Lindow Man, it seems probable by analogy with some commercial tanning techniques that the collagen in his skin has been 'fixed' by acid tannins and phenolic derivatives in the peat water, with a similar preservation occurring elsewhere in the body wherever collagen is to be found.

R.C.C.

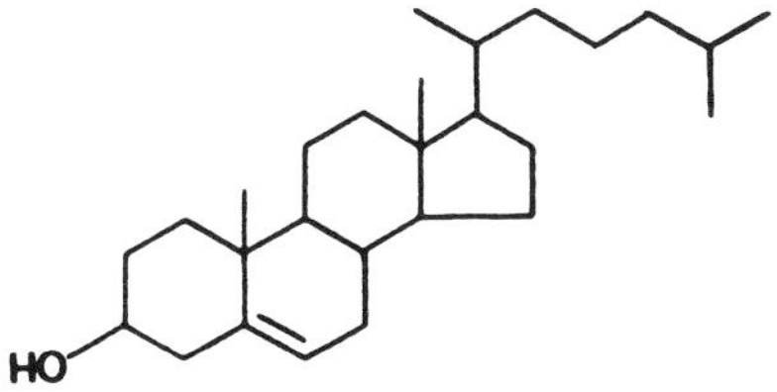

Chemical Investigation of Lipids and Tannins

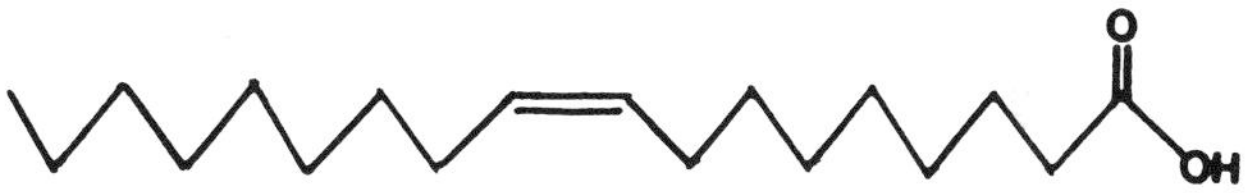

Chemical investigations have been initiated to examine the extractable lipid composition of various tissues of Lindow Man. Microanalytical chemical methodologies similar to those used on pitch samples from the Mary Rose (e.g. computerised-gas chromatography/mass spectrometry) are being used to compare the lipid composition of Lindow Man and normal modern human tissue. Through these investigations, it will be possible to determine changes which have occurred, at the molecular level, as a result of prolonged burial in the peat. So far cholesterol and fatty acid mixtures (including palmitic and oleic), which bear definite similarities to those from normal modern skeletal muscle, have been isolated.

A further area of interest involves the pursuance of chemical evidence for the presence of extractable tannins. Such evidence would corroborate the hypothesis that the preservation of bog people is essentially a collagen tanning process, a hypothesis widely quoted but as yet not fully confirmed.

R.P.E

The Non-Collagenous Components of Teeth

The principal non-collagenous components of the ground-substance of bones and teeth are proteoglycans which are composed of high molecular weight glycosaminoglycans linked to a specific core protein, and glycoproteins. They have both been extensively

Fig. 37   Molecules of cholesterol (1), and palmitic (2) and oleic (3) acids.

studied in modern specimens but have not been investigated in any ancient examples of teeth or bone.

One of the molars of Lindow Man had become partially fragmented and one small fragment, 35 mg, was sufficient for a limited study of the proteoglycans. Like the rest of the body, the teeth are demineralised and waterlogged with a moisture content determined by lyophilisation of about 60%. An alcohol insoluble fraction of proteolytic enzyme extract from the tooth fragment yielded on cellulose acetate electrophoresis several anionic components, one of which has been identified as chondroitin-4-sulphate, a major component of the teeth of modern man and several other mammals. In addition, a series of as yet unidentified glycoproteins and glycopeptides have also been shown. The demonstration of chondroitin-4-sulphate in teeth of this antiquity is of note and although its stability in prolonged acid medium exposure is predictable from its known structure it is of particular interest that it has survived apparently undenatured for so long. Samples of peat collected from around the body at the time of excavation were subjected to the same extraction procedure but were unaffected by proteolysis and no electrophoretic bands corresponding to either glycosaminoglycans or glycopeptides could be demonstrated so it seemed unlikely that the chondroitin-4-sulphate had been derived from peat contamination. This was further confirmed by the dissimilar spectra of sugars isolated from the tooth fragment and the peat, details of which are published elsewhere.

G.E., J.B. Stanbury, D.G.

The Blood Group Substances

For certain of the known groups the term 'blood-group' is something of a misnomer since the chemically defined substances on the red-blood cells which determine the group are not confined to those cells but are widely distributed in other tissues throughout the body. It is this distribution of the 'blood-group' substances that allows the determination of some of the probable blood groups of bone and other tissue samples of ancient populations. The specific blood group substances in ancient tissues may be identified either using the depletion-by-absorption method of a specific antiserum or by extracting the blood group substances from the tissue, attaching them to red blood cells not possessing those determinants then grouping the cells in the usual way. In view of the aqueous solubility characteristics of the determinant substances of the ABO system and thus the probability of their quantities being somewhat reduced, the red cell absorption technique was used, but no AB substances were detected. Similarly using the antiserum absorption technique neither group A nor group B substance was detected. Applying the absorption technique using the plant lectin Ulex, substantial quantities of the blood-group precursor substance – H substance – were identified. Persons of blood group A, B, AB and O all synthesise H substance which in all but the latter group is converted into either A or B substance or both by the addition of a single sugar molecule, N-acetyl galactasomine for A substance and galactose for B substance. Exhaustive study over many years in this laboratory has failed to demonstrate the *post mortem* conversion of A or B substance back to H substance and the conclusion is drawn that the native H substance was present in life and therefore Lindow Man was blood group O, the blood group which in the present day United Kingdom distribution is associated with persons of Celtic stock.

Testing for determinants of the MNS/s system by antiserum absorption revealed only M substance.

The possiblity that these reactions were due to cross-reacting oligosaccharides or glycoproteins derived from plant material in the peat was explored. Although large quantities of N-acetyl galactasamine was identified in peat-extracts no specific blood-group cross-reactivity could be demonstrated to derive from this source.

Other blood group systems are known, but either the determinant substances are not widely distributed in tissues or, like the Rhesus system, they are susceptible to rapid degradation following death and precise identification is therefore not possible in ancient tissues.

It is thus concluded that Lindow Man was blood group O and blood group M.

R.C.C.

Inorganic Constituents of Bone, Hair and Finger Nail

The radiological appearance of the skeleton of Lindow Man is characterised by a marked reduction in radio-opacity resembling in some degree both the normal demineralisation of old age and certain metabolic disorders resulting in mineral sequestration or failure of mineralisation. The 'demineralised' state of the skeleton of Lindow Man is referred to on several occasions elsewhere in this study and this brief report will demonstrate the nature and pattern of the process and confirm some details.

The mineral content of bone represents between 60% and 75% of the dry weight of which almost all occurs as hydroxyapatite $Ca_{10} (PO_4)_6 (OH)_2$. Most of this is crystalline, but a small and rather variable portion is amorphous, the relative amounts of amorphous and crystalline decreasing with bone-maturity. Other trace elements including magnesium, zinc and sometimes fluorine and strontium can be detected in the inorganic matrix but phosphorus and calcium are the principal elements of this matrix. The remaining 25–40% of the dry weight consists of an organic matrix most of which is the protein collagen with some 5–10% of amorphous ground-substance consisting mainly of mucopolysaccharides. Hair and nails consist mainly of the protein keratin but exhibit a variable sub-structure of partly mineralised matrix.

Clear proof of demineralisation of bone, hair and fingernail samples from Lindow Man has been obtained using X-ray energy dispersive microprobe analysis (EDAX). Fig. 38a shows the three distinctive X-ray energy peaks of phosphorus and the $K\alpha$ and $K\beta$ shells of calcium present in a modern sample

Fig. 38   X-ray energy dispersive microprobe analysis
of a) modern bone; b) Lindow Man's bone; c) peat; d)
Lindow Man's hair; e) modern hair; f) Lindow Man's nail;
g) modern nail.

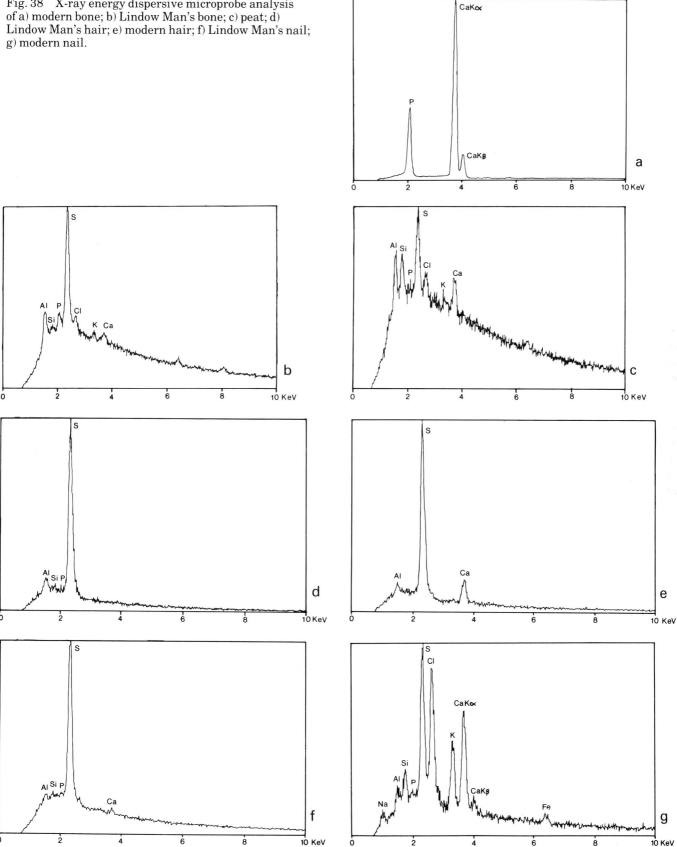

of bone whereas Fig. 38b shows the spectrum derived from a bone-sample from Lindow Man in which, with the vertical scale enhanced for clarity, sulphur appears as the principal constituent with only traces of phosphorus and calcium along with some aluminium, silicon, chlorine and potassium. Comparison of these two spectra with Fig. 38c which is from a sample of peat, shows very clearly that the spectrum of elements identified in the bone sample from Lindow Man reflects more or less passively the inorganic composition (with respect to these elements) of the surrounding peat. Although it is not possible from these spectra to determine with certainty whether all the native phosphorus and calcium of the inorganic matrix has been dissolved, and replaced at low level by a non-hydroxyapatite source absorbed secondarily from the peat, it is clear without doubt that true demineralisation has occurred. Further experiments are in hand to determine the form in which the residual phosphorus and calcium exists.

Fig. 38d shows the dissolution of calcium from the hair of Lindow Man compared with a spectrum derived from a modern hair sample (Fig. 38e), along with a possible but barely significant absorption of silicon and phosphorus. The keratin-derived sulphur which forms the principal peak in the hair samples is also very prominent in the samples of fingernail (Fig. 38f Lindow Man, Fig. 38g modern sample).

It is clear that all three tissues have become demineralised but bone most markedly so, depending now for almost all its structural characteristics on the barely supported organic matrix. The elemental exchange occurring in fingernail is complex and the dynamics have not been determined.

It is particularly unfortunate that these three tissues appear to have undergone such extensive elemental exchange of both dissolution by, and absorption from the peat since this prevents any conclusions being drawn from their composition which could have given valuable information concerning Lindow Man's diet.

These spectra do, however, suggest that of the three tissues, hair has undergone the least exchange and further trace-element studies which are in hand at the Joint Universities Reactor at Risley, Warrington, using neutron activation analysis, may ultimately reveal some details of diet and even by comparison with geochemical surveys perhaps give some indication of his local geographical origin.

P.B., J.B. Shortall, R.C.C.

19 Forensic Aspects of Lindow Man

I. E. West

The two important forensic aspects of the examination of Lindow Man centred around, first, the injuries and possible injuries on the deceased; and second, on the varying state of preservation which his body exhibited.

The head was in a good state of preservation, although there was severe discolouration of the skin and discolouration of the hair, beard, moustache and sideburn area and, to a lesser degree, to the head hair. Some of the scalp showed decomposition of the superficial layers, with sloughing of the epidermis, loss of some hair-bearing areas, and exposure of the tanned dermis and deeper scalp tissue. There was quite considerable flattening of the features, with loss of skin over the bridge of the nose, although the nose itself did not appear fractured. There was considerable angulation of the neck, which was flexed and pressed against the right shoulder. On the head and neck, the following injuries, or possible injuries, were seen:

(a) A laceration over the crown of the head (Figs 15 & 26).
(b) A possible laceration over the occipital region on the scalp.
(c) A sinew loop was present around the neck, with a visible ligature mark on the front and sides of the neck (Fig. 39).
(d) An apparent wound was present over the right side of the front of the neck (Fig. 40).

The presence of a fracture dislocation of the C3/C4 region of the cervical spine had been revealed by non-invasive techniques.

Further injuries were thought to be present over the trunk, including a possible stab wound on the right upper chest. A posterior rib fracture was subsequently demonstrated by xeroradiography.

The wounds will be dealt with in turn.

The scalp laceration was roughly v-shaped, *c.* 35 mm in length, and appeared to be formed by two lacerations, almost completely separated by a narrow triangular bridge of hair-bearing skin. Examination of the wound margins, using a stereoscopic dissecting microscope, revealed the typical features of a laceration with irregular split wound edges, displacement of hair follicles into the wound, small tissue bridges and splits on the margins. It also indicated some persistent swelling of the wound margins and this feature indicated the wound was entirely consistent with an *antemortem* injury and that survival after the wound had been inflicted was of sufficient duration to allow swelling and, presumably, bruising of the surrounding tissues – although this bruising could no longer be seen.

The presence of the bridge of skin passing across the majority of the long axis of the wound indicates that the injury could not have been received by one blow from a blunt weapon – assuming that the weapon had a single striking surface. The presence of bone fragments deeply embedded within the remains of the brain would indicate that the laceration was of a penetrating type, and that it would be consistent with use of a narrow-bladed, relatively blunt-edged weapon, such as a small axe. Again, the skin bridge indicates that if such a weapon was used, two blows must have been struck. The presence of two contiguous injuries of this nature is not uncommonly seen in current forensic pathological practice. If one blow had caused the injury, then the weapon would be required to have two projecting striking surfaces, both of which were capable of penetrating through the crown of the head.

The position of the wound on the crown of the head would suggest that it was caused whilst the deceased was in a standing or kneeling position. It is an uncommon site for injury caused when somebody is lying on the ground, but would be quite consistent with an injury produced by a person striking the deceased from behind with a weapon, with one blow rapidly being followed by a second.

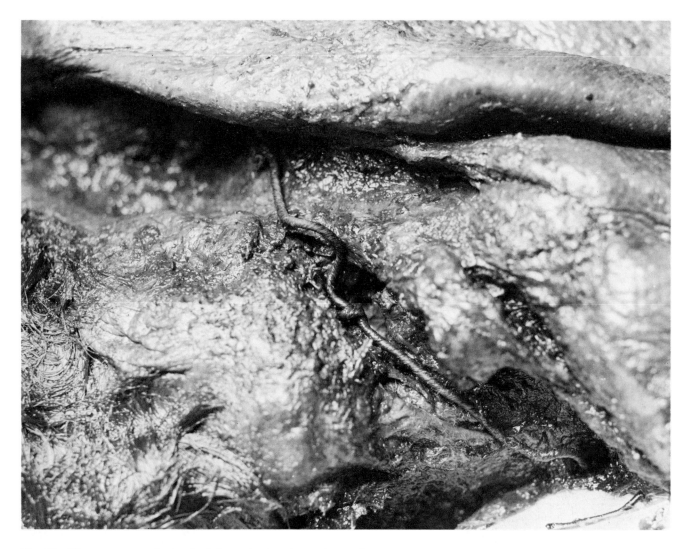

Fig. 39   The garrotte at the back of the neck, showing twists and a crêpe.

This injury would certainly have been fatal, but would not necessarily have been immediately fatal. The injury would have caused immediate loss of consciousness, but survival for a period of hours would be perfectly feasible.

The possible laceration over the occipital region could not be confirmed as a definite wound, owing to considerable scalp decomposition in the area. There are, however, fracture lines in the skull, in that area. If, however, a blow had been delivered to the back of the head with a heavy implement, such as an axe, then a full thickness laceration would have occurred. A more blunt weapon – such as a cudgel – of course would not necessarily cause a full thickness laceration, particularly if the striking area was relatively flat and broad.

There are a number of possible interpretations for the sinew loop present around the neck. Was this some ornament which the deceased had worn? Or was it deliberately placed there – perhaps after he had been struck on the head and rendered immobile? The use of a thin ligature of the diameter found here (1.5 mm) as a means of strangulation, in the traditional sense, would be highly improbable – unless of course the sinew had been longer and had been broken off, or cut off, at knot level. The presence of two twists in the ligature at the back of the neck would, in the writer's view, be highly significant if the sinew loop was used as a garrotte, rather than as a ligature which was tightened using the strength of an assailant's hands. The twists in the sinew at the back of the neck would be quite typical of changes which might be left if a stout stick, or a short piece of straight metal had been inserted into the loop and then twisted until the neck had broken, and/or closure of the airway occurred. It would be perfectly feasible to break the neck in this fashion, and would account for the injuries seen at the level of the third and fourth cervical vertebrae on the deceased. The presence of a well-defined ligature mark on the front and sides of the neck, but not at the back of the neck again, would be quite in keeping with the use of the sinew loop as a garrotte. The ligature mark was deeply indented and showed quite well-marked pressure abrasion of its surface, in keeping with a ligature compression of the neck occurring during life.

The circumference of the ligature indicates that it would have been extremely tight on the deceased's neck – even allowing for some shrinkage of the sinew, if it had been worn as an ornament.

The presence of the sinew loop is similar to the findings of a number of other bog bodies, and the knotting is not dissimilar to that seen in the rope on Borre Fen Man, and suggests, perhaps, that this was placed around Lindow Man's neck as part of a ritual sacrifice.

The wound on the right side of the neck initially looked as though it were an artefact produced by a combination of decomposition and the position in which the body was lying. At a subsequent examination, however, where the wound could be explored more fully, it was clearly apparent that the margins of this injury and the underlying soft tissues were cleanly incised. The superior border of the right lamina of the thyroid cartilage had been cut. The appearances of this wound indicated an incisional injury with a sharp-edged weapon, and the position of the wound would be entirely in keeping with a wound caused with the intention of severing the jugular vein. The haemorrhage from this wound would, of course, be accentuated if pressure on the neck was being applied by a garrotte as the venous bleeding which would occur when the jugular vein is cut would be caused by blood coming back from the head, not blood going to the head. Twisting of the garrotte below the incision would, provided the carotid arteries had not been closed, still allow blood to pass into the head via the arteries, and would accentuate the bleeding from a cut jugular vein. It would also obstruct the other jugular vein, causing all the blood to run via the cut vein.

The posterior rib fracture subsequently detected,

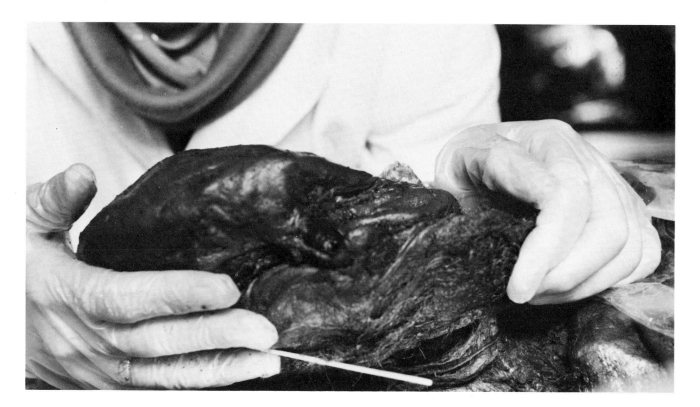

Fig. 40   Lindow Man's head lifted to show the cut throat with the garrotte below.

appeared to have been caused near to the time of death, and would be consistent with the effects of a heavy blow to the back of the chest.

The possible stab wound on the right upper chest could not be confirmed, as there was considerable decomposition to the skin in this area, and this defect could result purely from the effects of decay.

There was considerable variation in the state of preservation of the body of the deceased, but remarkable was the state of preservation of the skin of the face – where the hair-bearing areas were well preserved, with no evidence of previous skin slippage, which would undoubtedly have been present if putrefactive decomposition had occurred following burial. Loss of some head hair could well result from the effects of pressure of the peat overlying the body, but the fact that the deceased lay face-downwards would tend to protect the hair-bearing areas of the face. Similarly, the presence of the ligature mark caused by the sinew could not be explained in terms of putrefactive decomposition. The ligature mark did not have the appearance one commonly sees when

a necklet or necklace is pressed deeply into the skin of the neck by the swelling induced by putrefactive decomposition. If the neck had become distended by decomposition, then the beard area would show some signs of that process.

It is likely that the deceased was buried in the bog when the weather was cold, and that burial took place within a very few hours of death, before the processes of putrefaction had commenced. Subsequent to burial, the deceased's body would have had no exposure to warmth or air, and this would inhibit the processes of decomposition.

From a forensic point of view, the injuries on Lindow Man would be in keeping with the patterns commonly found in the bog bodies unearthed in northwest Europe. They suggest that Lindow Man was killed as part of some ritual sacrifice, with a possible sequence of wounding being two blows to the head, followed by the garrotting, and then the incision of the neck – although this was possibly performed before the garrotte was tightened sufficiently to break the neck.

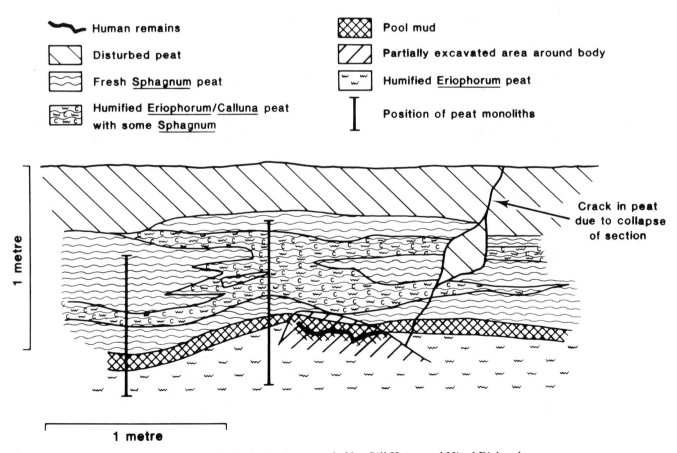

Fig. 41   Section of Lindow Moss with the body *in situ*, recorded by Gill Yates and Nigel Richardson.

III
Environment
and Food

Fig. 42   Section of Lindow Moss with the body *in situ*, (just above the trowel). Photo: R. C. Turner.

20 Pollen, Charcoal, Rhizopod and Radiometric Analyses

F. Oldfield   S. R. Higgitt   N. Richardson
G. Yates

Aims and Rationale

The present report summarises the interim findings from the various lines of study outlined below:

1 Visual peat stratigraphy. The section from which the body was removed was described and surveyed accurately by N. Richardson and G. Yates. Their section (Fig. 41) forms the stratigraphic context for all the studies which follow as well as for K. E. Barber's contribution (p. 86) and for two of the five peat samples used for C14 dating (pp. 25 and 29).

2 Pollen-analyses have been carried out on a limited number of samples from peat monolith 1.25 which was removed from the section at a within 0.5 m of the edge of the body whilst the body was still present in the peat.

3 During the course of pollen counting, charcoal fragments and rhizopod remains present in the pollen preparations were also counted, the former as a possible index of the use of fire in the neighbourhood of the site, the latter as an additional source of evidence for surface moisture conditions at each stage in bog growth.

4 At the suggestion of W. R. Schell, the gamma radioactivity of a peat sample taken from directly in contact with the body was measured to test the possibility that detection of radon diffusing from bones as a result of the radioactive decay of radium-226 might provide a novel method for detecting further bodies buried in peat.

Methods

Samples for pollen, rhizopod and charcoal analyses were prepared by digesting 0.4–1.0 g of dried peat in 10% NaOH and sieving through a 125 μ mesh. For samples from 50 cm upwards 5 tablets, each containing $11,267 \pm 370$ *Lycopodium* spores, were added before preparation in order to determine pollen concentrations per gram of dried peat (Stockmarr 1971). The preparation was stained in aqueous safranin and mounted in silicone oil (viscosity 1,000 cs). Counts were normally continued to give a pollen sum in excess of 150 non-mire pollen. Rhizopoda were identified using the diagrams given in Tolonen (1966). Charcoal frequency was estimated by measuring the length and width of each fragment and calculating surface area assuming a rectangular shape. The estimated area is then plotted in relation to the total pollen sum and shown on the pollen diagram as $\mu^2/100$ pollen grains. Comparison between the criteria used in the present study and those used by Dr R. Clark (*pers. comm.*) suggest that the present counts may be consistent overestimates.

Sample 33A, one of several taken on Sept. 27 1984 during the process of exhuming the body from its envelope of peat in the B. M. Laboratory, was used for gamma assay. The sample came from directly above and in contact with the upper left hand part of the torso close to the shoulder. Gamma assay was carried out using a low background hyper-pure germanium well-type detector with a 4 inch lead castle, NaI anti-compton device and copper shield, (Appleby *et al* in press). The sample was ashed at 550°C and placed in a specially constructed plastic holder designed to fit inside the well. The daughter isotopes of radon include ^{210}Pb and ^{214}Pb, the activities of which can be recognised at 46.5 keV and 352 keV respectively and used to estimate radon activity assuming secular equilibrium is attained in the sample.

Results

Figure 43 summarises the results obtained from pollen, charcoal and rhizopod analyses. Pollen samples taken from below the change in humification recorded at *c.* 60 cm both in the visual stratigraphy and in Barber's account are dominated by tree pollen types, with indicators of disturbed and open ground

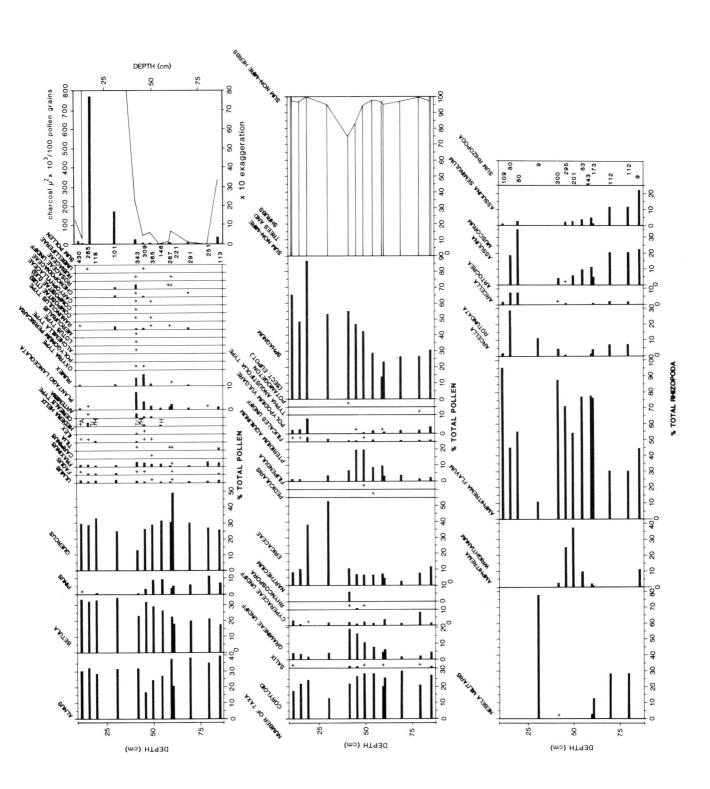

Fig. 43   Pollen, charcoal and rhizopod diagram from monolith 125, Lindow Moss. Cereal pollen types: A-*Avena* type, T/H-*Triticum/Hordeum* type.

only sparsely represented. Between 60 cm and 40 cm there are steep declines in tree pollen representation (notably *Quercus* and *Pinus*) and these are paralleled by significant increases in the relative frequencies of Gramineae, *Plantago lanceolata*, *Rumex* spp., and *Pteridium aquilinum*. Cereal pollen types (*Triticum*/*Hordeum*) and *Artemisia* are also represented. In the uppermost samples, grass and weed pollen representation is much reduced and *Quercus* values have largely recovered. However Cereal types are present in slightly increased frequency. Pollen concentrations range from *c*. 97,000 non-mire trees and herbs per gram at 49–50 cm to just over 10,000 at 19–20 cm.

Of the rhizopod types recognised and counted the most useful from the point of view of indicating surface moisture conditions is *Amphitrema wrightianum* (Tolonen 1966; 1979). It is restricted almost entirely to bog pools and in the present profile it is found only in samples between 60 cm and 41 cm. It reaches peak values between 55 cm and 45 cm.

Charcoal values are very low below 60 cm, peak modestly at that depth, decline immediately above, then rise between 49 cm and 30 cm to extremely high values which persist to 19 cm then rapidly decline to a minimum at 15 cm.

The results of the gamma assay show very low concentrations of ^{210}Pb and ^{226}Ra, of the same order as the standard errors associated with the measurements (Table 9). They give no encouragement to the speculation that anomalies in radon emanation can be used as a basis for locating bodies in peat.

Discussion

The radiocarbon dates which span the body and are based on peat samples directly above and below the torso and in contact with the skin, place the age of the 'envelope' of peat within which the body lies, between *c*. 2200 bp and 2500 bp. The radiocarbon dates spanning the part of the adjacent monolith considered contemporary and stratigraphically continuous with this peat 'envelope' indicate an age between *c*. 2240 bp and 2400 bp. These dates confirm the stratigraphic integrity of the section, and quite specifically, the synchroneity of the peat enclosing the body and that between approximately 55 cm and 60 cm in the monolith. They also reinforce the initial suggestion that the humification change recorded immediately below the body, and recognised not only as a distinctive horizon in the section shown in Fig. 41, but as a major feature across all the preserved areas of the bog, is in fact roughly contemporary with

the 'Grenzhorizont' or RYIII, a Recurrence Surface usually dated to around 600 BC (but see Barber, p. 88).

Evidence from visual stratigraphy, plant macrofossils, rhizopods, cladoceran and chironomid remains all concur in indicating that the body was emplaced in a substantial and persistent though not necessarily deep bog pool formed above the change in humification.

The pollen-analytical and associated evidence shows that formation of the peat within which the body lies coincides with the beginning of a major phase of forest disturbance, burning, and occupation for farming. Cereals were cultivated, probably wheat (*Triticum*) and/or barley (*Hordeum*), and possibly oats (*Avena*), but (pending further analyses) no rye (*Secale cereale*). Non-mire pollen concentrations decline during this period to values between 10 and 30 percent of those at the beginning of the episode. Although variations in peat growth may contribute to this decline, it probably reflects the dramatic impact of forest clearance on pollen supply. This phase spans up to 35 cm total depth in the peat and is thus likely to have lasted for centuries (perhaps two to four) rather than decades. This phase was preceded and followed by periods of lower activity each spanning 10 cm or more in the peat column. The pollen analytical evidence so far is consistent with a date before rather than after the birth of Christ for this major forest clearance and farming phase. If the humification change in the peat at 60 cm represented the 'Romano-British' Recurrence surface (RYII) of *c*. AD 400 (*q.v.* Barber p. 88) pollen analytical evidence for high levels of human activity would be expected below the humification change, with some decline above (*q.v.* Oldfield 1963; Oldfield and Statham 1963, 1965). The converse is the case. Moreover, rye pollen is so far not recorded. The archaeological record for rye macrofossils points to its first extensive cultivation during the Romano-British period, and it is considered improbable that rye was ever cultivated as a bread crop in prehistoric time in Britain (Godwin 1975). If rye crops had been cultivated locally in addition to the other cereals, then it would be expected that rye, an anemophilous high pollen producer, would be present at these levels.

In brief, the chronological, stratigraphic and palaeoecological evidence from the peat appears to present a coherent and internally consistent story. Yet comparison between the range of radiocarbon dates available so far from the body, and those presented here for the peat leave us, in our present incomplete state of knowledge, with an age discrepancy of between 300 and 1200 years. Of the possible causes for this apparent incompatibility, several lie outside the scope of this discussion. Questions inevitably arise however about stratigraphic factors which might have contributed to the contradictory chronological indications. By the time detailed stratigraphic investigations were possible, the body had been removed from the section and the envelope of peat both depleted and disturbed. This makes it quite impossible to state categorically, from the stratigraphic evidence alone, that the emplacement of the body was not accompanied by some displacement of overlying peat or some sinking within the loose infill of the pool. The radiocarbon dates and the stratigraphic evidence are inconsistent with the proposition that such factors alone could account for a discrepancy greater than two to three centuries at most. A further possibility is that the carbon accumulating within the pools which developed above the recurrence surface included some derived from erosion of older underlying pre-recurrence surface peat. This possibility cannot be precluded, nor can its likely effect be objectively quantified. It would however be a more credible suggestion if the stratigraphic changes and the humification contrast at the boundary were very much more dramatic than those actually recorded. For the moment, we conclude that the chronological discrepancies are very difficult to reconcile by invoking stratigraphic factors alone.

Table 9.   Radiometric (gamma activity) measurements on a peat sample adjacent to the body

Lindow Moss Body Peat sample 33A, 0.80 g
Count Time: 220000 Sec (Well Detector + AC Shield)

Isotope	Energy KeV	Counts Gross	+/−	Net	Conc. pCi/g
PB-210	47.0	432.7	39.5	26.3	0.19 ± 0.33
PB-214	353.2	119.0	24.8	26.3	0.09 ± 0.09

21 Peat Macrofossil Analyses as Indicators of the Bog Palaeoenvironment and Climatic Change

Keith Barber

Introduction

The waterlogged anaerobic bog environment which preserved the remains of Lindow Man for so many centuries also gives us the means of determining the conditions on the bog surface before, during and after the emplacement of the body, from the analysis of the plant remains making up the peat. The bog was also ombrotrophic during this period, receiving all its moisture from the atmosphere and not from groundwater inflows, due to the sodden mass of peat having built up like an inverted saucer into a true 'raised bog' (Godwin 1981). This enables us to infer the regional climate and its changes, since the stratigraphic changes in such bogs have been shown to be intimately connected with climatic variations (Aaby 1976; Barber 1981; 1982). The plants making up the peat are a really quite restricted group of species, able to tolerate the anaerobic, acid conditions, and comprise species of bog-moss, the genus *Sphagnum*, cotton sedges of the genus *Eriophorum*, heathers such as *Calluna vulgaris*, common ling, and cranberry, *Vaccinium oxycoccus*. Within the nutrient-poor (oligotrophic) habitat of the raised bog each species has a niche, the dominant factor in which is the water level (Ratcliffe and Walker 1958; Boatman 1983). Hence the bright green *Sphagnum cuspidatum* is characteristic of pools, hollows and wet 'lawn' situations whilst the tussocky cotton sedge *Eriophorum vaginatum* is most characteristic of drier hummocks on the bog surface, though along with its related species, *Eriophorum angustifolium*, it can invade infilling bog pools.

Peat is composed of the partially decayed remains of bog plants together with a complex of acids resulting from this decay (humic and fulvic acids) in the form of colloidal gels, as well as the remains of insects, algae, fungi etc. The accuracy with which the past vegetation of any peat mire may be reconstructed from the plant remains depends upon the degree of decomposition or humification of the peat – the less humified the better – as well as the inherent identifiable characteristics of the plants themselves (Grosse-Brauckman 1963, 1982; Barber 1981; Godwin 1981). The degree of humification has been shown to depend primarily on the rate at which dead plant material passes from the microbiologically-active zone near the surface where the water table fluctuates – the acrotelm – to the zone below which is permanently saturated, anaerobic and rich in sulphides – the catotelm (Ingram 1982; Clymo 1984).

While single shoots of *Sphagnum* may grow several centimetres in a year the rate at which peat accumulates (as determined by radiocarbon-dated profiles) averages between fifteen to twenty years per centimetre over the last 2500 years, with extremes of around 3 yrs/cm to 50 yrs/cm (Walker 1970; Barber 1985). Clearly, with a high water table at the time of Lindow Man's death, the rate of accumulation would probably have approached the former figure, say about 10 years/cm, but only a detailed series of radiocarbon dates can resolve this important question relating to how quickly the whole body was blanketed by the growing mire.

Methods

Macrofossil plant remains were analysed from two monoliths made available by Professor Frank Oldfield in December 1984. The position of these monoliths is shown in Fig. 41, the field stratigraphy diagram – the writer was not involved in this fieldwork or monolith sampling. The monoliths, designated 45 and 125 by reference to their distance in centimetres from the lefthand edge of the recorded section, were subsampled by slicing triangular-sectioned pieces from the length of each monolith. Due to secondary oxidation and the wet state of the peat very little stratigraphic detail could be seen in the monoliths but the relationships drawn in the field stratigraphic diagrams were broadly confirmed and further detail left to the interpretation of the macrofossil analysis. The sub-monoliths were frozen and cut by a hacksaw into contiguous 1 cm slices, placed in sterile vials and stored at 4°C. This gave 81 samples from monolith 45 and 92 samples from monolith 125.

The sampling strategy then adopted was to concentrate effort on monolith 125, this being much nearer to the body and passing through the other side of the hummock against which Lindow Man's head had rested, with fewer but contiguous analyses through the pool layer in monolith 45 to show up any variations in the contemporaneous pool environment. A basic interval of 2 cm was adopted, with contiguous counts across the humification boundary in monolith 125 and through the monolith 45 pool, and a 4 cm interval above and below the main region of interest in monolith 125. This entailed analysis of 20 samples from monolith 125 and 12 from monolith 45.

Sample treatment and identification followed the methods used on ombrotrophic peat from Bolton Fell Moss, Cumbria, on material covering the period

1400 bc to present (Barber 1981). The present results are therefore directly comparable with those from Bolton Fell Moss and have been presented in the same way in Fig. 44. After assessment of humification using the well-known von Post scale (Davies 1944; Clymo 1983) each sample was sieved through a 250 micron sieve using three litres of tap water. Previous experience has shown that material passing through a 250 micron sieve is usually unidentifiable plant fragments and humic material, and this was assessed by the degree of darkness of the water in the 3 litre beaker on top of which the sieve was placed. The material caught by the sieve was then transferred to a glass trough, examined with a stereozoom microscope, and its composition assessed on the same 5-point scale as used by Barber (1981) and many other macrofossil analysts, where: 1 = rare, 2 = occasional, 3 = frequent, 4 = common, 5 = abundant.

After assessment of total Sphagna, unidentified organic matter, (result averaged with that from 3 litre beaker) rootlets and the five categories of higher plants shown on the right of Fig. 44, a slide was made

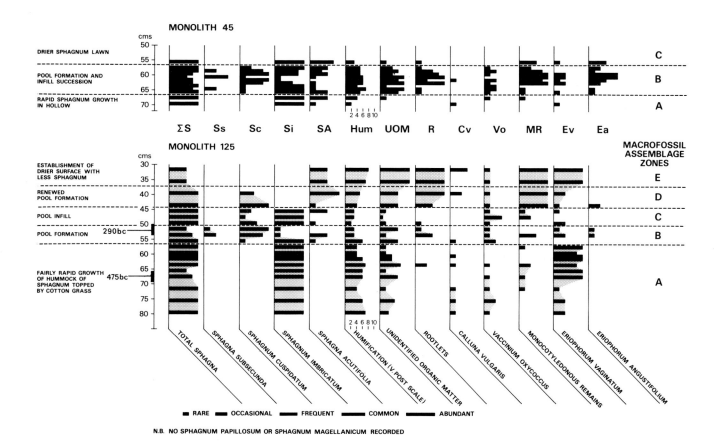

Fig. 44   Chart of plant macrofossils.

up from 3–4 subsamplings with a small spatula of the material in the trough. This material was mounted in Farrants Medium under a 18 × 50 mm cover slip and all fragments, leaves etc. examined at magnifications of 40–400 to identify *Sphagnum* species using the criteria explained in Barber (1981, 62–6). Notes were also taken of various odd occurrences of mites, beetle elytra etc and all record sheets, slides and sieved samples are archived at the Palaeoecology Laboratory, Southampton University. The resulting diagrams were split into macrofossil assemblage zones, representing distinct collections of macrofossils, for ease of discussion.

Results and Interpretation

In monolith 125, zone A, we see the typical build-up of peat dominated by the major postglacial peat former, *Sphagnum imbricatum* (Dickson 1973). Humification is moderate, mainly 4–6 out of 10 and some samples are almost entirely composed of *S. imbricatum* (e.g. 125: 71–72 cm). In the upper half of the zone *Eriophorum vaginatum* becomes abundant, but humification remains only moderate. This would be unusual for pre-*Grenzhorizont* peat, the black, cheesy, almost structureless peat which precedes the Recurrence Surface known as the *Grenzhorizont* or RY III (Godwin 1954, 1975), generally dated to around 600 bc (Barber 1982), but fits in well with the commonly seen peat types between RY III and RY II at about ad 400 or RY I at about ad 1200–1300. Correlation with the stratigraphy of the core studied by Birks (1965) is best done using pollen-analysis rather than simply depth criteria. The radiocarbon dates on the peat from this monolith 125, reported elsewhere in this volume (Otlet *et al*; Ambers *et al*), lend support to the idea that we are dealing with peat formed *after* the major event of the *Grenzhorizont* and that this *Grenzhorizont* lies below the level of peat monolith 125. However, the exact timing and nature of this major humification change in European bogs has long been a matter of controversy (Barber 1982; 1985) and is the subject of a new investigation by the writer and C. J. Haslam, utilising a transect of bogs across Europe from oceanic west to more continental east. Turner (1981), in her review of the Iron Age environment, cites a number of cases of major Recurrence Surfaces dated around 1200–700 bc including that at Chat Moss, only 20 km (12 miles) to the north-west of Lindow Moss, where the pool layer is dated at 695 bc and humified peat 11 cm lower in the profile at 1,120 bc

(Godwin and Switsur, 1966). The peat dated from monolith 125 (290 bc for 50–53 cm; 475 bc for 66–69 cm) gives a peat accumulation rate of 11.6 years/cm, which can be extrapolated roughly to date the base of monolith 125 at 92 cm to 760 bc. The dates on monolith 125 also enable us to give extrapolated dates to the samples analysed in Fig. 44 – 60 bc for the top sample at 31–32 cm; 615 bc for the lowermost sample at 79–80 cm, and 310 bc for the sample from 53–54 cm, the first occurrence of felted pool peat. It may well be therefore that a major Recurrence Surface, equivalent to the *Grenzhorizont* lies below the peat seen and sampled at Lindow Moss, and that the Recurrence Surface seen in the field stratigraphy is a lesser magnitude climatic change, as is also evidenced by the rapid accumulation rate and only moderate humification. The local environment in MAZ 125A is therefore thought to be a spongy, distinctly wet, hummocky bog surface with knots of cotton sedge establishing themselves and developing into small tussocks. *S. imbricatum* is now almost extinct in lowland Britain (Dickson 1973; Barber 1981, 199) but an analogous local environment can be seen today on actively growing bogs such as those at Tregaron and Borth in mid-Wales. In monolith 45 zone A is also dominated by almost pure *S. imbricatum* peat, of lower humification as expected in a wetter hollow situation and with very little cotton sedge. The water table would be within 10 cm, possibly 5 cm, of the surface.

It will be noticed from Fig. 44 that *Sphagnum papillosum* and *S. magellanicum* were not recorded from either monolith. These are now common species on many British bogs and it appears that they have taken the place of *S. imbricatum*, which is now rather rare. The situation at Lindow Moss some 2,000 or so years ago – of interactions mainly between *S. imbricatum*, *S. cuspidatum*, and *S. acutifolia* (probably mainly *S. capillifolium* (= *rubellum*)) – is paralleled by the situation at Engbertsdijksveen I, the Netherlands (Van Geel 1978, fig. 9) and at Bolton Fell Moss (Barber 1981).

Macrofossil assemblage zone B, in both monoliths, represents the formation of the widespread pool feature in which the body was resting. This may not be exactly contemporaneous in both monoliths, and is probably slightly earlier in monolith 45, perhaps at the same time as the change to lower humification in monolith 125 at 60–61 cm. The formation of the pool should not therefore be seen as a catastrophic flooding of a dried-out bog surface; it certainly represents a wet phase-shift (Barber 1981) from an undulating wet lawn situation to a definite open-water pool laying down felted mats of *Sphagnum cuspidatum* and *S. subsecunda* covered with algae. The yellowish-green algal pool mud consistently present in some fossil pools (e.g. Bolton Fell Moss, Barber 1981, plate XVIa and fig. 53) is not well-developed here as a separate stratum, rather the algae consist mainly of greenish coatings on the Sphagna. This would be consistent with shallow (say 10–20 cm) pools, almost filled with Sphagna, such as may be seen on Tregaron bog (Cors Caron NNR) rather than some of the deep pools of the Silver Flowe bogs (Boatman 1983) in which Sphagna are much less abundant. In this zone in monolith 125 we have a marked change in species composition with *S. imbricatum*'s dominance lost to a mixed *Sphagnum* carpet, including species of the section Acutifolia for the first time, and *Eriophorum angustifolium* which, as would be expected, reaches higher values, along with Sphagna from section Subsecunda, in the lower wetter microhabitat of monolith 45.

Zone C in monolith 125 is a good example of a pool infill succession (cf. Barber 1981, fig. 53). Sphagna subsecunda are extinguished, values of *S. cuspidatum* fall, *S. imbricatum* reasserts itself forming an almost pure *Sphagnum* peat of low humification. Such was the spongy, springy carpet of Sphagna, with frequent trailing stems of cranberry (*Vaccinium oxycoccus*) which rapidly covered the body of Lindow Man. Had he died later, in zone E, he would have decomposed much more rapidly. Boatman and Tomlinson (1977) and Boatman (1983) recorded increases in height of *Sphagnum* lawns of 0.7–1.5 cm per year, with maxima of 3 cm per year; peat formed within the last millenia has been rated as high as 3 years/cm, so that depending upon how far Lindow Man's body sank into the soft peat one can envisage him being covered by a wet blanket of Sphagna within a few years.

Zone D, monolith 125, is rather curious in recording a setback to the gradual drying out of the surface as the pool infilled. In a return to wetter conditions. *S. imbricatum* is extinguished, *S. cuspidatum* becomes abundant once more, accompanied by abundant monocotyledonous (sedge and grass) remains and rootlets. This wet phase-shift was, however, not as extreme as that of zone B, in that humification values are now higher, and Sphagna subsecunda are absent.

Zone E, monolith 125, records the establishment of a relatively rather drier surface dominated by cotton sedge and Sphagna Acutifolia – the sort of surface seen on many British bogs today (e.g. much of the south-east bog at Tregaron) which is firm enough

to walk on without difficulty and where the dominance of *Sphagnum* bog mosses has rather given way to a bog surface rich in cotton sedge and heathers. Under this cover Lindow Man's body would now be firmly in the catotelm zone of minimal microbial activity, and completely hidden from view.

Conclusions

(a) For several decades before Lindow Man was emplaced on the bog the surface wetness conditions could best be described as 'spongy', with a water table just a few centimetres (5–10 cm) below the surface. The bog could certainly have been walked upon without difficulty but not without getting wet feet. The best present-day analogy is probably the surface of Borth Bog NNR in mid-Wales. Climatic conditions would also probably approximate to those of the present day.

(b) For a short time before Lindow Man's death, and for some decades afterwards, the surface of the bog was distinctly wetter with widespread pools full of aquatic bog mosses – the abrupt change between zones A and B reported above – though there are indications of a shift to these wetter conditions a few centimetres below the level of the pool in which Lindow Man rested. Since the bog was ombrotrophic this phase-shift to much wetter bog surface conditions must be seen as a result of a change to a wetter and/or cooler climate. It is difficult to be precise about how cooler and wetter the climate became, but similar changes in peat profiles from Bolton Fell Moss dating from medieval times (Barber 1981) allow us to draw the analogy with estimates by Lamb (1982, figs 30 and 31) showing temperature values declining by $-1°C$ in July and August, and summer rainfall increasing 10% or so. Individual years could of course have been much wetter and cooler – indeed the summer of 1985 may be a good analogy – and undoubtedly would have had severe effects on the harvest.

(c) At the time of Lindow Man's death the bog would have been very difficult to walk upon, and impossible to do so without getting wet and probably frequently sinking in to knee-depth.

(d) The infill of the pool and the covering of the body by growing moss and cotton sedge (represented by 56–36 cm, monolith 125) would have proceeded relatively rapidly, perhaps about 3 cm per year in terms of unconsolidated *Sphagnum* mats.

22 The Insects Associated with Lindow Man

Maureen A. Girling

In order to investigate the insects associated with the body, samples of peat from around parts of the body, and the water used for cleaning the hair and skin, were reserved for analysis. Ten samples were investigated and in the following list, the letter assigned to each identifies the sample in Table 10.

The samples were processed and sorted by Mr A. Moss at the Department of Geography, Birmingham University, and the insects were sent to the writer at the Ancient Monuments Laboratory for identification and analysis. Dipterous remains were extracted and are the subject of a separate report (Skidmore, p. 92). The list of insects and arachnids is given in Table 10 and the numbers for each represent a minimum based on any common part. The nomenclature for Coleoptera follows Pope (1977).

As samples were small (washings 50 g of organic sediment, peat 150 g), the assemblages of insects were impoverished. Furthermore, the retrieved insects were rarely represented by the full complement of exoskeletal parts (i.e. heads, thoraces, beetle wingcases etc.) and those which were recovered were often fragmented. The incompleteness of the insect remains rendered identification difficult. Members of five insect families were recorded in addition to numbers of mites and two spiders. The larval Trichoptera (caddis) were identified and commented on by Miss Bridget Wilkinson, but the remains were generally too sparse to allow specific identifications. Larval Tipulidae (leather-jackets), which burrow below ground, were recorded in all but one sample.

Inferences about the immediate environment of the bog body are based largely on the twenty or so

Table 10

A	Hair areas: water	G	Abdomen area: water
B	Hair and beard area: water	H	Back, general: peat
C	Hair – back: water	I	Spinal cord cavity: water
D	Right ear-hole: water		
E	Impression of skull: peat	J	Final cleaning, top side: water
F	Abdomen area: peat		

Insect Name	A	B	C	D	E	F	G	H	I	J	Total
INSECTA											
HEMIPTERA											
HOMOPTERA											
Gen. et spp. indet.	—	—	—	—	—	—	2	—	—		2
HETEROPTERA											
Gen. et spp. indet.	1	1	—	—	1	1	—	6	—	—	10
TRICHOPTERA											
LIMNEPHELIDAE											
Limnephilus griseus/ignavus	—	—	—	—	—	—	—	1	—		1
Limnephilus sp.	—	—	—	—	1	—	5	—	—		6
Limnephilidae indet.	—	—	—	—	1	—	1	1	—		3
Trichoptera – 'species a'	1	1	—	—	1	—	—	2	—		5
COLEOPTERA											
CARABIDAE											
Pterostichus diligens (Sturm)	—	1	—	—	—	—	1	—			2
DYTISCIDAE											
Hydroporus obscurus Sturm	—	—	—	—	—	—	1	—	1		2
Hydroporus sp.	—	1	—	—	—	—	1	—	—		2
Graptodytes granularis (L.)	—	1	—	—	—	—	—	1	—	1	3
Agabus ?bipustulatus (L.)	—	—	—	—	1	—	—	—			1
HYDROPHILIDAE											
Helophorus brevipalpis Bed.	—	—	—	—	1	—	—	—			1
Enochrus spp.	2	1	—	—	—	—	4	—	—		7
HISTERIDAE											
Paralister sp.	—	—	—	—	—	—	1	—			1
STAPHYLINIDAE											
Lesteva heeri Fauv.	—	—	—	—	1	—	—	—			1
Philonthus sp.	—	—	—	—	1	—	—	—			1
Aleocharinae indet.	1	1	—	1	—	1	—	2	—	—	6
SCARABAEIDAE											
Phyllopertha horticola (L.)	—	—	—	—	—	—	—	1	1		1
SCIRTIDAE											
Gen. et spp. indet.	—	1	—	—	2	1	—	2	—	—	6
CHRYSOMELIDAE											
Plateumaris discolor (Panz.)	—	—	—	—	—	—	1	—	1		1
Plateumaris discolor/sericea (L.)	—	1	—	1	1	1	1	1	—	1	7
Altica britteni Sharp/ericeti (Allard)	—	—	—	2	—	—	1	—			3
Chaetocnema sahlbergi (Gyll.)	—	—	—	—	1	—	—	—			1
CURCULIONIDAE											
Rhyncolus lignarius (Marsh.)	—	—	—	1	—	—	—	—			1
Ceutorhynchus sp.	—	—	—	1	—	—	—	—			1
Limnobaris pilistriata (Steph.)	—	—	—	1	—	1	—				2
Rhynchaenus ?quercus (L.)	—	—	—	1	—	—	—	—			1
Curculionidae indet.	—	—	—	1	—	—	—	—			1
COLEOPTERA LARVAE	1	1	—	—	1	—	—	2	—	—	5
HYMENOPTERA											
PARASITICA	—	1	—	—	1	—	—	1	1	—	4
FORMICIDAE											
'Myrmica type'	—	—	—	—	1	—	—	1	—		2
'Lasius type'	1	1	—	—	1	—	—	3	—	—	3
DIPTERA											
TIPULIDAE											
Gen. et spp. indet.	2	2	1	—	5	4	1	30	1	2	48
ARACHNIDA											
ACARI	10	17	—	2	10	4	1	11	3	8	66
ARANAEA	1	—	—	—	2	—	—	—	—		2

taxa of Coleoptera (beetles) present in the samples. In particular, the more stenotopic species, which display particular habitat requirements, provide most data. The fauna largely reflects the conditions at the site into which the body was introduced; few, if any, beetles appear to be related to the presence of the corpse. The implication from the beetles and other insects are for a neutral to acid bog with peaty pools fringed with wetland plants and other bog vegetation growing in the vicinity. Whilst the paucity of insect species is consequent on the sample size, the nutrient-status of the bog is also a contributory factor as the insect numbers are inversely proportional to the nutrient supply. Neutral to oligotrophic bogs are characterised by faunas which are relatively low in diversity and numbers.

Two species of predaceous water beetles were recorded from the site. *Graptodytes granularis* is a small species with a variable colour pattern on the elytra. The identification was confirmed by features on the ventral coxal plate, examples of which were recovered. Balfour-Browne (1940) regards *G. granularis* as a stagnant water species frequenting detritus ponds and drains and it occurs locally in England and Wales. *Hydroporus obscurus*, a reddish-coloured species, is generally paler than others in the genus. Its identification was also confirmed on coxal plate features. Records of the species from the north of Britain are mainly from acid water bodies such as *Sphagnum* pools and peat mosses according to Balfour-Browne (*ibid*), although he notes that in Norfolk it occurs in freshwater drains. In north France, the species is found in stagnant peaty pools around Pas-de-Calais and the Somme, although it is rare elsewhere (Guignot 1931–3). A further species of *Hydroporus* present in the samples was too incomplete to be identifiable. A scrap of striated cuticle, also of a water beetle, may be referable to *Agabus bipustulatus*, a very widely occurring species, but this suggestion must remain tentative.

The Hydrophilids *Enochrus* and *Helophorus brevipalpis* inhabit the weedy margins of pools although the latter flies readily and is frequently found away from water. The evidence for pools is reinforced by numbers of Scirtidae, a family adapted for aquatic conditions although hibernation is on land (Crowson 1981). Caddis-fly larvae, which unlike the adults are aquatic, are represented by Limnephilidae, inhabitants of small pools often in peaty areas, and by parts of another type, termed 'species a', which occurs widely from the tundra to temperate areas but has yet to be recognised (B. Wilkinson *pers. comm.*). The staphylinid beetle *Lesteva heeri* is usually found in wet vegetation adjacent to water.

The phytophagous, or plant-feeding, beetles mainly indicate vegetation found around ponds or other damp situations. The most frequent records in this category were eight examples of *Plateumaris*, a reed beetle. Unfortunately, most of the remains were fragments of undersides, appendages and elytra, although the latter were referable to two of the four species in the genus – *P. discolor* or *sericea*. The single, complete elytron, in peat from the back of the body, belonged to *discolor*, a feeder on *Eriophorum* (cotton-grass) and species of *Carex* (sedge). The base of another elytron appeared closer to *P. sericea*, but this identification was not confirmed as the overlapping sutural margin near the apex was missing. It is possible both species were present; *P. sericea* also feeds on *Carex* as well as *Iris pseudacoris*. Sedges provide one of the food plants of *Chaetocnema sahlbergi*. In addition, Fowler (1890) notes occasional records of this beetle on *Vaccinium* (cranberry) and Joy (1932) gives as another host *Glaux maritima* (seawort), a plant of coasts and inland salt areas. According to Hoffmann (1950) *Limnobaris pilistriata* feeds on various Cyperaceae including *Scirpus sylvaticus*, the leaves of which are eaten by the adults, and *Juncus* (rushes). Reitter (1916) also includes *Cladium mariscus* as a host.

Two of the weevils suggest the presence of some trees; *Rhynchaenus* is a deciduous leaf-miner and *Rhyncolus lignarius* is found in decaying, mainly deciduous trees. Hence, there is a slight suggestion of carr woodland in the vicinity although the beetles could relate to trees on drier ground. One of the species in the fauna more likely to originate from such a location is *Phyllopertha horticola*. The larvae are root-miners on grasses, cereals and clover, often occurring in meadows where they can be destructive. The adults, which fly readily, often damage young trees, but they are also recorded on bracken (Fowler 1890; Britton 1956; Horion 1958).

One beetle whose occurrence at the site may be due to the corpse is *Paralister* sp. The peat from the back yielded a single elytron which most closely matched *P. obscurus* (Kug.) and *P. puparescens* (Herbst), but without the important pronotal character of the single or double striae near the lateral margins, a specific identification is not possible. Many Histeridae are associated with carrion, where they are predaceous on Dipterous larvae, although dung or rotten vegetation serve as alternative habitats. This single specimen is insufficient to imply any fauna of decomposition and the body must have been rapidly submerged.

23 The Dipterous Remains

P. Skidmore

The paraffin (kerosene) flotation technique used to recover the beetle remains (Girling, p. 90) is equally efficient in concentrating the fragments of other insects. Diptera (true flies) were poorly represented in the samples directly associated with the corpse, with only a few indeterminate Nematoceran larval head capsules and the puparium of a (?) Sphaeroceridae fly. Any corpse lying exposed to the atmosphere provides a very rich pabulum for numerous Diptera (cf. Megnin 1894) and, in any such situation, large accumulations of puparia of Calliphorids (i.e. *Calliphora* pp., *Phormia* spp., *Lucilia* spp.), Muscids (*Muscina* sp.), Fanniids, Heleomyzids (*Heleomyza* spp., *Neoleria* spp.), and Phorids, etc. occur. Whilst several of these groups would not be active in winter, the Heleomyzids, in particular, would infest a body on the surface at any time of the year. The total absence of a necrophilous fauna suggests that the corpse was *not* exposed to the atmosphere and total submergence in the bog would accord with the evidence.

24 Animal Remains – the Cladocera and Chironomidae

Judith A. Dayton

Introduction

The peat environment in which Lindow Man was found was potentially an ideal site for the preservation of certain water-living invertebrates, being expected to combine acidic and oxygen-low conditions. Under such conditions, the chitinous exoskeletons of such animals preserve very well, leaving a record of the animals living in the vicinity at the time of Lindow Man's death. By extracting these skeletal remains from the peat matrix, and identifying them, some idea of the environment at that time can be gained, provided that something is known about the ecological requirements or preferences of the species found.

In this report, the Cladoceran and Chironomid remains, and their contribution to the reconstruction of the environment, will be discussed. Both are essentially aquatic organisms, but chironomids are found in a greater range of water bodies, at least as far as salinity goes, cladocera being more or less restricted to freshwater.

Cladocera (or water fleas) are small (mostly microscopic) crustaceans (class Branchiopoda), which exist in many sizes of water body, often in large abundances. Chironomids are small flies or midges (Insecta, Diptera), which mostly spend the larval stage of their lives in water. It is therefore the larval stage which is found as sub-fossils in sediments.

A brief consideration of the animals' structure follows, with an outline of the development of their use in palaeoecology; detailed aspects of their interpretation is included in the discussion.

(a) Cladocera

It has been recognised since fairly early in the century that Cladoceran remains in lake sediments can be identified, often to species (e.g. Meyatsev 1924; Rossolimo 1927 – cited by Goulden 1964), but it was largely through the work of Deevey (1942; 1955) and

especially of Frey (1955; 1958) that they became recognised as indicators of palaeo-environments. They preserve well in sediments, especially the families Bosminidae and Chydoridae, and seem not to have altered morphologically for at least one hundred thousand years (Frey 1962). This allows confident identification of remains, and assumptions that their ecology has not altered greatly either. This latter point is clearly important if environmental reconstruction is going to be made on the basis of present-day ecology.

The most abundant remains tend to be of three parts of the exoskeleton. These are; the carapace, or body shell; the head shield; and the postabdomen, which covers the hind portion of the gut and is used for propulsion in many species. Other parts of the body also preserve, but are irrelevant to this particular report.

(b) Chironomids

The preservation of the tough head capsules of chironomid midges in sediments has also been recognised for some time, with important work being carried out by Stahl (1959; 1969) and others. Analysis of Chironomid remains has often been carried out in conjunction with that of Cladocera (e.g. Goulden 1964; Harmsworth 1968), the different groups of animals throwing light on different aspects of the water body in which they lived. (See the discussion for examples.)

Although a number of sub-families of Chironomids exist, the largest, and most commonly represented in sediments, are the Chironominae, Tanypodinae and Orthocladiinae. These are separated on the basis of the form and shape of the mentum – a chitinous plate which is very different in the different groups. Depending on the sub-family, other features may be useful in further identification of particular remains, such as plates to either side of the mentum (ventro-mental plates) in the Chironominae, or the size and morphology of the antennae.

Methods

A number of samples was provided for Cladoceran and Chironomid analysis. The material had already been processed and disaggregated in order to extract the Coleopteran remains, and so it was merely sieved through a mesh with an aperture size of 1 mm in order to remove large pieces of vegetation. It was then sorted in alcohol using a binocular microscope, and Cladoceran and Chironomid remains picked out and mounted on standard microscope slides in DMHF

(Di-methyl hydroxin formaldehyde). These were examined under a binocular microscope and the animal remains identified, principally with the aid of papers by Frey (1958; 1962; 1965) and Scourfield and Harding (1966) (Cladocera); and Wiederholm (1984) (Chironomidae).

Results

The material provided had already been treated, and so it was not considered valid to make any estimates of the relative or absolute abundance of the Cladoceran and Chironomid faunas present. The Cladoceran remains were relatively easy to identify to

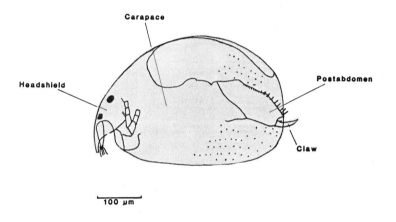

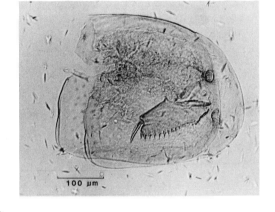

ALONA RUSTICA Sars showing exoskeletal components   (After Frey 1965)

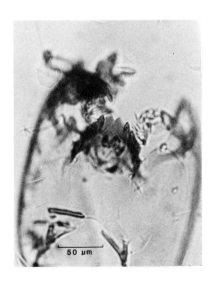

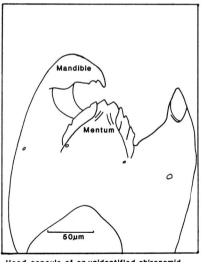

Head capsule of an unidentified chironomid, sub-family Orthocladiinae.

Fig. 45   Above: sketch of *Alona rustica* Sars with a photograph showing its carapace and postabdomen. Below: photograph and sketch of an unidentified chironomid, sub-family Orthocladiinae. Photos: G. Dowling, Department of Geography, University of Birmingham.

species level (although see below) since there are relatively few species which are mostly very different with regard to their gross morphology, and the skeletal characters are actually used in the identification of living animals. The Chironomids proved far less easy because the group is poorly known; there are many genera, often containing a considerable number of species, and the characteristics used for identification in the living animals do not preserve well, if at all, after death. Only the mentum was present in many cases examined, and so the remains were almost all identified to sub-family level only.

There was a very small number of taxa of both Cladocerans and Chironomids, representing a very depauperate fauna. All the Cladocera belonged to the family Chydoridae, and the Chironomids to the sub-family Orthocladiinae. The Chydorids are benthic members of the Cladocera, mainly living in the surface mud or rooted vegetation of water bodies, and in relatively shallow water. In deeper water planktonic forms such as *Daphnia* and *Bosmina* tend to predominate. Orthocladiinae are mostly found in the cold and temperate zones both sides of the equator. Most are herbivorous, and some groups have become secondarily terrestrial or marine (Fittkau and Reiss 1978).

(a) Cladocera

Only five species were identified with certainty (see Table 11), and the majority of the Cladoceran remains were of small species of the genus *Alona*. These are notoriously difficult to identify from disarticulated skeletal components, particularly from carapaces; but fortunately there were many postabdomens and head shields, and these are considerably more diagnostic.

All postabdomens examined appeared to belong to *Alona rustica* (Scott 1895), characterised by denticles well separated at the bases and a well-rounded post anal angle (Scourfield and Harding 1966). Frey (1965) considers the possession of setae along the anal groove as a more reliable feature; the postabdomens found agreed with his description and were therefore confidently identified as *A. rustica*.

Considerable confusion was caused by the presence of head shields closely similar to those of *A. costata* (Sars 1862) as illustrated by Frey (1959), in contradiction to the identification of the postabdomens as *A. rustica*. However, on comparison with the illustration and descriptions in Frey's paper of 1965, it became clear that these head shields were, in fact, also of *A. rustica*. Many carapaces also conformed

to the description in the same paper of the latter species.

It still remains possible that other species of *Alona* were present, especially *A. costata*, but were not recognised. However, the vast majority of the *Alona* remains were undoubtedly of *A. rustica*, since all the head shields and postabdomens looked at were of the latter species. A single large specimen of *Alona affinis* (Leydig 1860) was found.

Of the other genera present, the genus *Alonella* was represented by numerous remains, chiefly carapaces of *A. excisa* (Fischer 1854), and a few of *A. nana* (Baird 1850). The other species present, often in considerable numbers, was *Pseudochydorus globosus* (Baird 1850), represented by head shields and carapaces.

Many of the *Alona* remains were of tuberculated forms, the carapaces and head shields being covered with tubercles at more or less regular intervals. Harmsworth (1968) voiced a popular view that there may be a link between the presence of tuberculated forms and boggy conditions, finding similar forms in Blelham Bog, whilst non-tuberculated forms of the same species were living in the adjacent Tarn.

Also in the material examined were a number of ephippial females, apparently of *Alona* species. Ephippia contain sexual resting eggs, probably often produced under stressful environmental conditions.

(b) Chironomids

Many of these remains were extremely small, and difficult to examine, often consisting only of the mentum and the adjoining parts of the head capsules. Problems also occurred due to fragmentation to the mentum itself, or to distortion caused by mounting. It was therefore extremely difficult to identify the remains, beyond assigning them to the sub-family Orthocladiinae on the basis of the shape of the mentum and the lack of ventro-mental plates.

It was clear that at least two or three separate taxa were involved, each with a very differently shaped mentum, but only one was tentatively identified to genus level as *Smittia* (Holmgren 1869).

Discussion

(a) Cladocera

Cladocera have been used in a number of ways in palaeolimnological investigations in the past, because of their extremely good preservation in lake sediments (at least in the case of families Bosminidae and Chydoridae), and the ease of identification of remains, often to species level. Frey found that examining off-shore sediments for their Cladoceran remains gave a better picture of the species present in the lake than collecting live animals over considerable lengths of time did. This was true for both the shallow and deep water communities (Frey 1960). Therefore, when used in studies of aqueous environments of the past, the Cladoceran fossils should give a very faithful picture of the communities as they existed then, both in terms of species composition and abundance (Mueller 1964).

Large numbers of fragments are often preserved in lake sediments: Deevey (1942) found 67,400 remains per cubic centimetre of sediment in Linsley Pond, Connecticut, and Frey (1961) found up to 440,000 in the same volume. This sort of number allows the statistical treatment of results (e.g. Mueller 1964; De Costa 1964; Cotten in prep.). When abundances can be calculated, the quantities can give a rough indication of past primary production levels (Frey 1960; Deevey 1942), whilst the change in numbers through time can also give information on climatic conditions (Megard 1967; De Costa 1964), particularly temperature. The influence of man on a local and/or regional scale can also be detected, for instance the initiation of eutrophication (Goulden 1964; Harmsworth 1968). From a knowledge of the species' ecology, information about the lake itself can be deduced, such as the size, depth of water, amount of rooted vegetation, water transparency and acidity. One of the most recent applications of Cladoceran studies has been in the acidification debate, with attempts being made to monitor acidity levels of lakes through time by the analysis of Cladoceran (and other animal) remains (e.g. Batterbee and Renberg 1985; Paterson in prep.).

However, a number of problems do exist in the use and interpretation of cladoceran remains. As in all palaeoecological work, there are inherent problems with regard to the preservation of the animals after death, with not all animals, or even parts of animals, preserving equally well. Although studies such as that of Frey (1960) have supported the idea that the death assemblage of chydorids reflects the living community in terms of both species composition and abundance, it can never be certain that this is so. Unfortunately also, non-chydorid taxa, with the exception of the Bosminidae, do not preserve well, or are difficult to identify without an extensive reference collection, and so potential information is lost. Losses of the remains that do preserve also occur during treatment of the material, particularly if it is sieved to remove silt and clay particles. In the present study, some material had probably been lost,

since no postabdomens of the small *Alonella* species were found. When species abundances are required, this is clearly a source of error.

Perhaps more pertinent to the case in hand is the existing confusion over species identification. Species names being used in Europe were applied to similar species as they were discovered in America and other parts of the world, so that many species are now described as cosmopolitan. Not only might this be erroneous, as many workers, especially Frey (pers. comm.) now believe that subtle morphological differences may indicate that very similar species on either side of the Atlantic are *not* the same; but it also makes it hard to deduce anything about lake conditions on the basis of these species' presence, since, if cosmopolitan, they must be assumed to be tolerant to wide ranges of climate and environmental conditions. At present, whilst the 'cosmopolitan' label still adheres to many species, all that can be said is that ecological information deriving from outside Europe, or perhaps even North West Europe, must be treated with extreme caution when interpreting British sites.

Bearing this in mind, many species *do* seem to be very widespread, indicating broad ecological tolerance, since they exist in many different areas and habitats, but little is known about their precise requirements. This is true of Cladocera in general, even those with more restricted distributions. Despite this drawback, conclusions *can* be drawn about palaeoenvironments, but it is important to consider the overall assemblage, as far as possible, and not to regard an individual species as an indicator of particular conditions.

From the small number of species found and the presence of ephippia, it seems that the habitat was stressful and not particularly suited to Cladocera as a whole. Harmsworth (1968) found a similar array of species when investigating Blelham Tarn and its adjoining bog. As the bog developed, Cladocera became very scarce, with only one or two species present at times. Fryer (1985) found that the Chydorids were strongly associated with larger water bodies, and were less abundant and diverse in smaller ones, for no clear reason. This tendency, along with the water chemistry and other factors may help to explain the apparently low diversity of cladocerans in bogs.

All the species found (listed in Table 11) have a wide modern distribution over a variety of temperature zones and habitats. *Alona rustica* was described as cosmopolitan by Frey (1965), *Alonella nana* as 'ubiquitous' in the littoral (near to shore) zones of northern lakes (Goulden 1964), and *Pseudochydorus globosus* as present throughout the Holarctic (Harmsworth 1968). *Alona affinis* and *Alonella excisa* are also widespread species. Clearly, these are all species which exist across a wide range of ecological conditions and are able to cope with the rigours of existence in a bog.

Alona rustica, although found in a variety of habitats, is often associated with small acid pools (Fryer 1968), and it also tolerates peaty conditions. Harmsworth (1968) considers it to prefer a polyhumic situation. According to the same paper, *Alona affinis* will also tolerate such conditions. *Alonella excisa* is also linked with acid waters, such as suit *Sphagnum* (Fryer 1968) and is often found among and on vegetation. *Alonella nana* doesn't seem to prefer any one habitat above another, being tolerant to an exceptional sweep of ecological conditions.

This assemblage of species then, is entirely consistent with a peaty, rather acidic site, possibly with some rooted plants in the pool itself, and also with some bare substrate, since *Alona affinis* in particular seems to prefer such conditions if they are available (Fryer 1968). The total absence of non-chydorids, the presence of ephippia and the very low number of species does not support the idea that a large or deep body of water was present. The dominance of littoral species also suggests the idea of a fairly shallow pool.

The presence of *Pseudochydorus globosus* was very interesting, since this species is the only scavenger amongst the Chydorids. Its food is usually described as the carcasses of other small crustaceans (Fryer 1985), but its presence in relatively large numbers so near a corpse is highly suggestive, particularly as it is usually found in small numbers only (Goulden 1964).

(b) Chironomids

Stahl (1969) claimed that the commonest insect remains in lake sediments are those of midges (i.e. Chironomids), although they are generally much less abundant than cladoceran remains. They have, like Cladocera, been used to investigate a number of different aspects of lake ecology. They are particularly important and useful in the context of stratified lakes – that is, those which have several distinct layers of water at different temperatures at least part of the year – where the profundal (deep water) chironomid fauna depends on the oxygen concentration of the lower layer of water, and on the food resources within the sediments. The trophic status of the lake is also indicated to some extent, and this, along with the oxygen concentration is the information generally made use of in palaeolimnological investigations (e.g. Goulden 1964; Stahl 1959). Changing trophic state is often culturally induced; for instance when European man first arrives in an area (Warwick 1975).

The lake typology developed on the basis of chironomid associations (especially by Brundin 1949; 1956; 1958) has been tested statistically, and seems to be valid (e.g. Kansanen *et al* 1984). However, in shallow water stratification does not occur, and the relationships between particular taxa and lake type are not yet established, although Kansanen *et al* (*ibid*) consider that a typology for shallow water should be possible. In the present case of a non-lacustrine habitat, therefore, it is important not to draw conclusions from data intended for a deep-water situation. The fauna themselves can indicate if a lake was deep and/or stratified in the past, and so help decide whether to use such data.

Chironomid remains can also indicate other environmental conditions, since some midges are fairly specific in their ecological requirements; temperature and salinity may be implied for instance. Unfortunately, the difficulty of identifying remains below the level of genus can limit the amount of reconstruction possible, since a genus may include species from a great range of habitats. Confusion over taxonomy and lack of knowledge about many taxa also cause

Sample	Beard	Back	3	4	5	6
Species						
Alona affinis			x			
Alona rustica	x	x	x	x	x	x
Alona indet.	x	x	x	x	x	x
Alonella excisa	x	x	x	x	x	x
Alonella nana	x				x	
Pseudochydorus globosus	x	x		x	x	x
Orthocladiinae indet.	x	x			x	
Smittia (?) indet.		x			x	

Table 11   Presence of Cladocera and Chironomids

problems in interpretation, and as with cladoceran remains, it is important to look at the whole assemblage wherever possible, and not base too much upon a single identification.

Unfortunately, the small number of Chironomids recovered from the peat associated with Lindow Man, and the difficulty in their identification, makes such an approach difficult. Orthocladiinae are associated with polyoxybiontic conditions in stratified lakes, and may be indicating conditions that are not constantly anaerobic, but in this situation could also be indicating that nutrient levels were not particularly high, or at least that the bog was not eutrophic. The identification, albeit tentative of *Smittia*, is interesting, this group containing many species associated with terrestrial conditions, that is, the larvae do not develop in water bodies as such. Fittkau and Reiss (1978) describe the genus as 'inadequately known', but of the 9 species presently known to occur in Britain, 5 are associated with marsh or damp earth, 2 with bogs and one with lakes. Sendstad *et al* (1977) found several *Smittia* species; this was actually in the tundra, but the important points are that they were present in a situation with an impoverished chironomid fauna, both in quite dry and slightly wetter areas. The presence of this genus, therefore, is not inconsistent with the habitat suggested by the Cladocera: of a rather limited body of water, in size and depth, with plant matter freely available for the mainly herbivorous Orthocladiinae. The midges could have been living in the pool, or the body could have been close to the pool's edge, and the Chironomids were living in the area immediately by it.

Summary

The presence of cladoceran and midge remains in organic sediments can be used to gain environmental information through a knowledge of the species' ecology. Although hampered by problems of identification and lack of detailed ecological data, the five species of chydorid Cladocera and several taxa of Orthocladiinae found give a consistent picture of the environment as it existed at the time of Lindow Man. The low diversity of species suggests a constrained environment as far as these groups are concerned, in which only eurytopic species (e.g. *Alonella nana*, *Alona affinis*) or fairly specialised ones (*Smittia spp.*) can survive. Nutrient levels were probably fairly low in the bog, although high abundances of *Pseudochydorus globosus* may have been in response to the presence of the corpse. There is, in my opinion, evidence for only a shallow pool, perhaps with some rooted plants in it. The usefulness of pursuing several lines of evidence in palaeoecological investigations is shown; plant remains for instance throw further light on this question.

25 Plant Foods in Ancient Diet: The Archaeological Role of Palaeofaeces in General and Lindow Man's Gut Contents in Particular*

Gordon Hillman

Types of Palaeofaeces

Palaeofaeces come in many forms:

(i) They normally survive as intact 'hand specimens' only when preserved by desiccation as in the vast assemblages by coprolites at Salts Cave in Kentucky, Lovelock Cave in Nevada and Hinds Cave in Texas.

(ii) In the temperate zone it is more usual to be confronted by faecal remains in *disaggregated* form – preserved either by waterlogging or mineralisation. In this state, they may be encountered either in convenient concentrations in, for example, ancient cess pits, garderobes, latrines and sewers, or else in more widely scattered states as in many of the medieval deposits recently excavated in urban centres such as London.

(iii) We have lately been confronted with a third class of faecal remains, in the form of superficially amorphous fragments preserved by charring, as, for example, at the Late Palaeolithic site of Wadi Kubbaniye in Upper Egypt and in the Epi-Palaeolithic site of Tell Abu Hureyra in Syria. In both cases, the faeces appear to derive primarily from infants.

(iv) Gut contents such as those from Lindow Man are perhaps the rarest of all, as they generally survive only when freshly dead humans have been promptly desiccated (mummified), frozen in ice or pickled in peat. However, a puzzling exception now exists in the form of what may well be mineralised gut contents from an inhumation in the damp aerobic soils at Khok Phanom Di in Thailand (Higham and Thompson, pers. comm. 1985).

The following references provide examples of analyses of plant food remains from each of the classes of palaeofaeces mentioned above. (Analyses of pollen, phytolith and plant crystal remains are excluded here, though pollen studies are covered by Scaife elsewhere in this volume, pp.126–35). *Class* (i): Callen (1965, 1967 and 1968); Roust (1967); Heizer (1967 and 1969); Callen and Martin (1969); Yarnell (1969); Heizer and Napton (1970); Fry (1970); Paap (1976) (though possibly dog turds); H. Hall (1977) Williams-Dean (1978); Fry (1980); Stock (1983)[1]; Thomas (1984); *Class* (ii): Knörzer and Müller (1968); Knörzer (1975); Knörzer and Müller (1975); Wilson (1975); Greig (1976); Kawolski (1976); Girling (1979); Green (1979); Greig (1981); Knörzer (1979); Bakels (1980); Jørgensen (1980); Knörzer (1981); Greig (1982); Lynch and Paap (1982); Hall, Kenward *et al* (1983); Hall, Jones and Kenward (1983); Maier (1983); Knörzer (1984a) (summarised results from 15 sets of ancient latrines); Paap (1984); Shay (1984); Hillman (undated); Tyers (forthcoming). *Class* (iii): Hillman (in press); Hillman, Colledge, Harris and Vaughan (forthcoming); Vaughan (in prep.). *Class* (iv): Warren (1911); Wood-Jones (1912); Netolitsky (1906 and 1931); Helbaek (1950); Brandt (1950); Helbaek (1958); Yarnell (1970). *General*: Callen (1969); Bryant (1974a and b); Bryant and Williams-Dean (1975); Fry (1985).

I The Archaeological Potential of Plant Macro-Remains from Palaeofaeces

Many questions relating to past diet, past culinary practices, alimentary disease and the ancient uses of medicines and drugs remain unresolvable unless faecal remains are found on archaeological sites of the period under study. To archaeologists, then, palaeofaeces are pearls beyond price, and the uniqueness of their archaeological role deserves to be outlined in some detail.

---

*Note: (a) 'Palaeofaeces' are ancient remains of faeces, in this case *human* faeces, and throughout this paper they are taken to include ancient remains of gut contents; (b) the paper is essentially concerned only with plant *macro* remains. (Pollen remains are discussed in this volume by Dr Rob Saife).

Inadequate Information on past Diet from Plant Remains of the sort usually Recovered from Archaeological Sites: the Special Role of Palaeofaeces

(a) Remains of food plants are almost always recoverable from archaeological sites if appropriate methods of extraction are applied on a large scale. Such remains are preserved most commonly by charring in domestic fires, and, in the temperate zone, often by waterlogging as well. However, the recovery of remains of edible plants does not prove that they provided human food: crops such as barley or vetch may have been used only for fodder, as was the barley identified in remains of horse dung from Roman Lancaster (Wilson 1979); and the edible seeds of some wild species may have come from plants that had been growing as mere weeds of the crops or on middens in the settlement. We can be certain that particular species were actually *eaten* by the local population only when we find remains of them in human palaeofaeces.

There is also the related matter of how much they ate of each of these foods. Even though the charred remains of burned grain stores can sometimes provide useful hints on the relative importance of particular species in the food economy of the ancient settlement, it is only from palaeofaeces that we can finally deduce the precise proportions in which the various foods were eventually eaten by the local inhabitants.

Nevertheless, there are certain limitations on the potential of palaeofaeces in this regard, and some of these limitations are usefully evaluated by Knörzer (1984) in respect of his own studies of 15 sets of latrine contents from sites in the Rhineland.

(b) Normal archaeological remains of food plants also suffer from a more specific limitation when used in attempted reconstruction of ancient diet. Except on sites where extreme aridity allows total preservation of organic matter[2], normal botanical remains seldom provide information on anything other than grain foods, nuts and those fruits such as plums that contain hard, resistant stones[3]. Altogether lacking, then, from the normal (non-faecal) archaeobotanical assemblages from sites in the temperate zone is evidence of consumption of leafy foods, edible barks, stems or 'roots' (here taken to include stem tubers, corms, rhizomes etc), though it is probable that their apparent absence is, in part, a reflection of our inability to recognise their remains. (For some exceptions, see Greig, 1983.)

Absence of such evidence is particularly frustrating, because ethnohistorical records suggest that these leaves, shoots and roots may well have played a major role in past diet, not only in pre-agrarian societies but also, perhaps, in later agrarian economies such as those of Iron Age Britain (see, for example, the ethnohistorical records summarised by Maurizio, 1927, Sturtevant, 1919). Such a dearth of archaeological evidence of vegetative foods is not surprising, as they are unlikely either to be preserved in identifiable form by charring, or, indeed, regularly to end up nicely waterlogged in wells and ditches. And even when we *do* find identifiable, waterlogged remains of, say, some of the many edible species of wild leaf, the chances are that the preserved specimens had arrived fortuitously on autumn winds: cases of deliberate gathering are unlikely to be distinguishable in most cases[4].

As things stand, then, our only realistic hope of assessing the role of leaves, shoots and roots in past diet lies in recovery of many more examples of human faeces and gut contents from sites of every period. The recovery of Lindow Man complete with a small section of gut (and contents) therefore raised hopes that vegetable foods might be present, though we were destined to be disappointed in this regard. Of course, the contents of a single set of guts derive, in any case, from only a couple or so meals (in healthy individuals) and, at best, represent a diet typical of only one season of the year. Nevertheless, they offer some steps towards rectifying the present imbalance in evidence of diet in prehistory[5].

By contrast the vast conclaves of coprolites recovered from dry sites such as Salts Cave in Kentucky or Lovelock Cave in Nevada may appear to offer a much more representative picture of prehistoric diet. But even here, the coprolite contents are not as representative of year-round diet (within any one cultural phase) as might initially be supposed. At Lovelock Cave, for example, C14 dating revealed that the total of 300 coprolites had accumulated during a period of c 3000 years (Heiser and Napton 1970). On average, therefore, they provide a record of just one or two meals every ten years – assuming healthy alimentary habits. The equivalent figure for the assemblage from Salts Cave is one coprolite for every three years (from Watson 1969). Only at sites such as Hidden Cave in Nevada do we encounter large numbers of coprolites accumulated under seemingly exceptional conditions over a short period of time and offering a more representative picture of diet, albeit probably for only one season of the year (see Thomas 1984)[6].

It is hopefully clear, therefore, that the importance

of even the most meagre find of faecal remains for studies of past diet must not be underestimated, especially in Britain where prehistoric finds of palaeofaeces are still few.

Incomplete Recovery of Dietary Data from some Earlier Finds of Palaeofaeces

Deficiencies in the data from certain of the earlier studies of palaeofaeces further underline the potential role of new finds. In some of the most important of the previous generation of palaeofaecal studies, dietary reconstructions have been based on identifications of only the most readily recognised, hard particles of food (mainly seed coats) and epidermal fragments sieved out of the re-hydrated disaggregated faeces. Altogether ignored, it seems, was the identity (in terms of source food) of the soft, amorphous matrix in which the seeds were embedded and which appears to have accounted for much of the original volume of the faeces. As a result of this bias, the ensuing dietary reconstructions automatically omitted any evidence of those soft, parenchymatous foods which contributed to the amorphous matrix of the faeces and which may have been central to survival, this despite the fact that the role of such foods in ancient diet can seldom be assessed by any other means (see p. 100). This omission appears to have resulted from (a) the use (by the analysts) of sieves which allowed much of the soft, amorphous matrix of the disaggregated faeces to flush straight down the sink, and, perhaps, (b) a very natural reluctance to get involved in the identification of parenchymatous tissues and epidermal fragments for which the necessary anatomical, histological and biochemical background studies of the full range of wild foods have yet to be undertaken.

At Salt's Cave, for example, the finest of the analytical meshes used was 210 μm, and the analyst's estimates of, say, the consumption of acorn and hickory 'flesh' was based merely on the numbers of accidentally ingested fragments of acorn and hickory *shell* (Yarnell 1969, 4), rather than on the amounts of soft, digested remains of acorn of hickory flesh itself[7]. Remains of such soft, parenchymatous foods could theoretically have made up much of the relatively amorphous matrix of the faeces, and in the absence of any systematic analysis of this matrix, it is clearly impossible to know whether or not acorns or hickory nuts played the central role in diet that was hitherto expected in an area such as Salts Cave in the Early Woodland period.

At Lovelock Cave, a 147 μm sieve mesh was used

(Heiser and Napton 1970), but even this would have allowed a fine suspension of parenchyma cells to pass through. The authors also make no mention of identifying any crumbs of amorphous parenchymatous tissue which *were* retained by the sieve. As a result, it is difficult for the reader of the published report to assess the validity of their claim that, for example, Piñón seeds were absent from the Lovelock diet.

Today, with the benefit of hindsight, we are in a position to begin concentrating our attention on the identification of these elusive vegetative food remains and the assessment of their role in prehistoric diet, and it was inevitably hoped that the Lindow remains might make a contribution to this area of study. At the same time, however, detailed histological studies have to be undertaken of modern specimens of each of the edible tissues (and associated inedible tissues likely to turn up in food waste) of each of those food plants which may have been used by earlier populations, with a view to isolating criteria which can then be used reliably to identify any fragments of similar tissues from palaeofaeces[8].

However, when it comes to the identification of some finely ground (or well-chewed) parenchymatous foods from which the epidermis and any endodermis were removed prior to consumption, it is possible that no reliable histological markers will ever be found. This was, for example, suggested for remains of pounded pulp of *Agave* and sotol (*Dasylirion* spp) by Stock (1983, 148 and 151) and for edible barks and roots generally by Bryant (1979, 14). Admittedly, certain exceptions exist here in the form of plant groups that produce (in their soft tissues) resilient microstructures such as plant crystals of types characteristic of specific taxa. For example, the identification of plant crystals in coprolites from Hinds Cave in Texas allowed Bryant (1974c) to demonstrate that the inhabitants had consumed certain types of cactus stem.

In most cases, however, it will ultimately be necessary to resort to the use of species-specific *chemical* markers – identified by use of gas chromatography, high pressure liquid chromatography, infrared spectography, pyrolysis mass spectrometry or even electron spin resonance. Each of these techniques is already showing promise as a tool for identifying both charred grain fragments and minute traces of organic residues in ancient pottery and stone tools (see, for example, Robins 1983; Robins and Gutteridge, in press; J. Evans *et al* 1980; 1982 and in press; C. E. R. Jones, in press; Hillman, Robins, Jones and Gutteridge, forthcoming). With faecal remains, however, the problem of excising or separately targeting each of the different food components is far more severe, particularly in charred faeces. Equally problematic for chemical analyses is the cross contamination of each food particle by the chemical breakdown products of (a) each of the other foods consumed in the same meal, and (b) a range of digestive enzymes, bile salts, etc secreted into the food by the host body. Clearly, methodologies for extracting dietary information from palaeofaeces are still in their infancy.

Uncertain Status of Last Meals of Earlier European 'Bog People'

The meticulous analyses of Hans Helbaek revealed that the last meals of Tollund Man and Grauballe Man consisted of intriguing mixtures of wild seeds, cereal grain and certain components of cereal chaff (Helbaek 1950; 1958). Helbaek suggested that the seeds of wild plants represented deliberate gathering of these seeds as food, and in support of this hypothesis was able to cite hoards of pure weed seeds from three different sites in Denmark: 1.7 litres of Fat Hen seeds (*Chenopodium album*) from a charred wooden storage bin at Iron Age Norre Fjand; 1 litre of Pale Persicaria seeds (*Polygonum lapathifolium*) from a hearthside heap at first century AD Alrum, and a remarkable 5.7 litres of Corn Spurry seeds (*Spergula vulgaris*) identified by Jessen (1983) at an Iron Age house at Ginderup in Jutland (Brandt 1950; Helbaek 1954, 1960). Certainly, it is well established that, even in agrarian societies, seeds of many wild plants continued to be gathered as supplementary foods until recent times (see, for example, Schwantes 1939, 146–51, and the many ethno-historical records cited by Maurizio 1927), and the remains of charred seeds from Fjand, Alrum and Ginderup are doubtless prehistoric examples of just such a practice. However, for the last meals of Tollund and Grauballe Man there is a more prosaic explanation:

In poor families and in times of crop failure it was quite usual in recent times to 'stretch' the meagre supply of grain by adding the weed seeds, runt grain ('tail grain') and dense chaff sieved out of the previous year's prime grain before it was put into storage (Maurizio 1927). Such a mixture would most often be eaten as some sort of porridge, and the 'waste' fractions (generally called 'fine cleanings') would come either (a) from the 'waste' stored after the previous year's grain cleaning, or (b) be bought or begged from the farms of the more affluent. Alternatively, in years of crop failure, they simply used as food everything harvestable from the field and processed it only

as far as winnowing and 'coarse sieving'[9]. At this stage of processing, the grain still contained all the small weed seeds, 'tail grain' and dense chaff normally separated as 'fine cleanings', and in really bad years these 'waste' components were more abundant than the grain itself. In such years Maurizio (1927) also records that, when making bread of such a mixture, they even added handfuls of light chaff separated in winnowing, this to 'bulk out' the bread and somehow fill their stomachs.

Returning, then, to Tollund and Grauballe Man, it is surely beyond coincidence that the range and relative abundance of weed seeds, runt grain and dense chaff fragments dominating their last meals was *precisely* what we today find in 'fine cleanings' from the sieve cleaning of grain from archaic crops such as glume wheats and barley when these are harvested and processed using traditional methods of the sort still applied in the remote parts of the Near East and previously applied in prehistoric Europe (Hillman 1981, 156–8). For a tabular presentation of the components of 'fine cleanings', see Table 1 of Hillman 1984, (p. 10). As for the particular species of wild plants which Helbaek recorded as abundant, every one of them turns out to be an archetypical weed of crops, with the sole exception of *Deschampsia caespitosa* (Tufted Hair-grass). Seeds of the latter, together with all the rarer seeds of other 'non-weedy' species identified by Helbaek, were doubtless caught up in the harvest from stray plants invading the edge of the crop, just as we find today. Mixed with the grain in granaries of present-day farmers in East Anatolia, for example, I have consistently found seeds of 'non-weedy' plants such as even the Water Plantain (*Alisma lanceolata*). Precisely the same phenomenon has been been observed by Pat Hinton (pers. comm. 1984) in fields of Bristle Oat recently cultivated on the Shetland Islands of Yell and Unst: weed seeds present in the threshed crop products included not only the usual annuals, but also biennials such as Wild Angelica (*Angelica sylvestris*) and perennials such as Marsh Marigold (*Caltha palustris*). Correspondingly, the charred remains of crops and weeds from sites such as Cefn Graeanog in Gwynedd (Wales) reveal that, under ard (scratch plough) cultivation, the cereal fields had been efficiently invaded by all manner of 'non-weedy' species from neighbouring bogs, woods and hillsides (Hillman 1984, 19–21). All the seeds present in the Tollund and Grauballe samples are therefore most likely to have originated from weeds growing in the cereal crops themselves.

We were therefore persuaded that the last meals

of Tollund and Grauballe Man consisted either of (a) 'fine cleanings' from grain crops with the possible addition of prime grain to make it more of a meal, or (b) sparse grain harvested from badly failed crops in which the 'fine cleanings' (waste) component was never removed from the grain. With the recovery of Lindow Man, it was naturally hoped that his guts would contain half-digested food of similar composition so that we might test the opposing hypotheses more fully. In this particular, however, we were destined to be disappointed.

The Possibility of Iron Age Use of Psychotrophic Drugs Prior to 'Ritual Killings'

In the last meals of Tollund and Grauballe Man, Helbaek (1950; 1958) identified remains of 'large numbers' of sclerotia (asexual propagules) of the ergot fungus (*Claviceps purpurea*). These toxic sclerotia ('ergots') contain a range of alkaloids including ergotamine, ergotoxine and ergomethrine (Forsyth 1968). The tranquil expression on the face of Tollund Man is perhaps not surprising in the circumstances (see fig. 5 of Helbaek 1950): with that amount of ergot in his system, he was quite possibly comotose or dead by the time the spliced leather noose was applied, though he may earlier have experienced wild hallucinations, a burning sensation in the mouth and extremities ('St Anthony's Fire'), acute abdominal pain and convulsions (see, for example, Moreau 1979 and Moeschling 1980)[10].

None of this explains how the ergots got into their last meals. There are at least three explanations:

(a) Ergot sclerotia are common components of both 'fine cleanings' (which include any small sclerotia) and prime grain (containing any grain-sized sclerotia), especially when the crops have been grown under the damp conditions necessary for sclerotia shed from last year's crop to sprout sporangia and thereby infect the ensuing crop. The most plausible explanation for the presence of ergots in the last meals of Tollund and Grauballe Man is therefore that they were already present as a natural component of the 'fine cleanings' and grain which made up the meal (see p. 102).

(b) It is nevertheless not impossible altogether to exclude the possibility that ergot was added as a humane or ritual act prior to execution. If so, those responsible for state-organised ritual executions in modern society may have something to learn.

(c) The third explanation is the least plausible of all. Aberrant behaviour of the sort often induced by inadvertant ergot poisoning may itself have prompted the executions. In Medieval times, the psychotropic effects of ergotism were often attributed to supernatural influence. Perhaps, in earlier times, those diagnosing cases of 'demonic possession' also prescribed death as the cure.

The recovery of further bog bodies, such as this from Lindow, therefore offered a chance of recovering additional evidence for or against the hypothesis that (a) an hallucinogen was deliberately added to pre-execution meals, and thence (b) that the Lindow and Grauballe killings were just as premeditated as the hanging of Tollund Man seems to have been. Clearly, evidence in favour of such an hypothesis can come only from the identification of drug remains in foods in which they would never be present by mere chance. With the Lindow remains however, we were again destined to be disappointed.

The Role of Palaeofaeces in Deducing Details of Ancient Crop Husbandry and Grain Processing

When faecal remains contain residues of crop products (such as cereal grain) or by-products (such as 'fine cleanings') it is possible to use the relative proportions of each of the components to deduce details of the operations and tool types applied in the cultivation of the crop in the field and its processing back in the settlement. A simple example is the use of the presence of seeds of certain low-growing weeds to suggest that the crop had been cut low on the culm rather than right under the ear. Detailed accounts of these systems of interpretation and of the ethnographic and ecological models on which they are based are given in Hillman 1973; 1981; 1984a; 1984b; 1985; G. Jones 1981; 1984a, 1984b; Reynolds 1981. Also, phytoecological models specifically developed for (and/or applied to) the interpretation of plant remains include, amongst many others, Körber-Grohne 1967, 209–31 etc, van Zeist *et al* 1976 and 1981, Behre 1980, Wasylikowa 1981, Greig 1984, M. Jones 1984, and Knörzer 1984b.

However, charred crop remains of the sort most commonly recovered from archaeological sites generally offer far greater potential for detailed reconstructions of past agrarian activities than do the contents of palaeofaeces. The role of palaeofaeces in this area of archaeological interpretation is therefore relatively peripheral.

The Role of Palaeofaeces in Reconstructing Ancient Culinary Practices

In this role, palaeofaeces hold the centre of the stage. Unless preserved as coprolites, prepared foods seldom survive in recognisable form on archaeological sites. Inevitably, exceptions exist in the form of, for example, the fossilised loaf of bread from Pompeii and, more recently, a remarkable collection of charred loaves from Viking period graves at Birka (Hjelmqvist 1984). (A useful review of the earlier finds is given in Brothwell and Brothwell 1969). Food accretions also sometimes survive in ancient cooking vessels and eating bowls (see, for example, Brandt 1950 and Helbaek 1960) and novel systems of chemical analysis are now permitting the cooking methods to be identified from these accretions with greater precision. (See Hastorf 1985, and Robins, in prep.). Overall, however, such finds are very rare, and where palaeofaeces survive, they generally offer the only direct evidence of culinary practice that is available.

There are at least three different aspects of ancient food preparation which can be studied via palaeofaeces:

(a) The first class of information survives by virtue of the fact that human mastication is relatively inefficient. As a result, the finer grades of fragmentation of plant material in faeces are essentially a function of what had been done to the food *before ingestion*. The most convenient examples come from grain foods:

(i) If whole cereal grains are eaten boiled (as in primitive forms of porridge or the Turkish *aşure*, etc), the grain coats (bran capsules) survive as single units; mastication serves merely to split them open if they have not already been split by boiling.

(ii) If, alternatively, they are roasted and then eaten whole, the now more brittle grain coats tend to be broken into a few very coarse fragments. In this state, they can be confused with fragments derived from crushed or 'rolled' grain eaten as porridge or muesli, although any fragments derived from roasted grain can thereafter be distinguished by ESR spectroscopy (see below).

(iii) Next, grain eaten as the properly stripped forms of groats or *bulgur* (Ar. *burghul*) is recognisable from the fact that the grain coats are again reduced to coarse fragments which, in this case, entirely lack the outermost layers of 'long cells' (the true pericarp). An archaeological example of faeces derived from some poorly digested meals of rye groats bearing fragments of grain coat in exactly this state was recovered in 1976 from a Medieval latrine at Usk in South Wales (Hillman n.d.). In this case the remains were preserved by total mineralisation of the sort described by Girling (1979) and Green (1979).

(iv) Finally, if most of the bran is relatively finely fragmented, then this implies that the grain was well-ground before ingestion. Such a meal was most likely, then, to have involved bread, dumplings or some sort of gruel, though the presence of any charred fragments would clearly argue in favour of the bread option. (ESR analysis also offers a means of distinguishing one from the other, see below).

An example of the recovery of similar information on ancient methods of preparing foods comes from Callen's (1967) work on the Tehuacan coprolites. The crushed state of certain millet remains suggested that the grain had been prepared by pounding, while others exhibited splits most likely to have resulted, apparently, from having been rolled back and forth on a stone metate.

(b) To decide whether the ingested foods had previously been cooked by boiling, baking or roasting, we can use ESR (electron spin resonance) spectroscopy. Only small samples are needed, so ESR can, if necessary, be applied to fragments of each of the different foods present in any one palaeofaecal sample. From the ESR spectra, it is possible to estimate the highest temperature to which the particular tissue was exposed, and from this, of course, we can then distinguish between boiling (100°C, baking (generally between 200°C/300°C) and perhaps grain roasting (presumably even hotter on the grain surface). This and other archaeological applications of information on thermal histories from ESR spectra are outlined in Hillman, Robins *et al* (1984 and 1985). In addition, Robins (pers. comm., 1986) and Sales now consider that ESR curves for 'saturation levels' might also yield information on the *duration* of heating, *i.e.*, cooking time. Any such information might well allow us to distinguish between long-baked leavened bread on the one hand and rapidly baked flat bread or 'griddle cakes' on the other.[11,12]

Somewhat more subjective criteria for identification of past methods of preparing food have been applied to remains of the cactus *Opuntia* by Riskind (1970), Bryant (1974a), H. Hall (1977), Williams-Dean (1978), Fry (1980) and Stock (1983), all of them reviewed by the last author. For Hinds Cave in particular, Williams-Dean (1978, 190) and Stock (1983, 140–44) were able to identify not only methods of de-thorning but, from patterns of discolouration of remains of stem pad epidermis and fibres, were also able to suggest that the pads had been cooked by roasting and boiling-cum-steaming respectively.

(c) The composition of palaeofaeces can also provide valuable information on the *combinations* in which various foods were eaten. However, the mixtures found in palaeofaeces may also be somewhat misleading in this regard. The pyloric sphincter at the duodenal opening of the stomach quickly constricts when food is eaten, and everything eaten for a while thereafter is thoroughly mixed by contractions of the stomach wall (J. Bourke, pers. comm. 1984). For the different foods in closely-spaced snacks, therefore, it will often be impossible to decide whether or not they were eaten together.

Identification of Season of Death and Seasonality of Site Occupation

Foods such as strawberries are available during only one season of the year and, prior to the modern availability of cheap(ish) sugar for bottling or jam-making, such fruits were difficult to store in large quantities for later consumption[13]. As a result, when the seeds of strawberries, raspberries or blackberries are found in the guts of bog bodies, they provide useful clues to the time of year when the individual died. Similarly, when these same species are encountered in remains of *voided* faeces, they provide information on which seasons of the year the site was occupied. Such information is particularly valuable on non-agrarian sites where assessment of the inhabitants' mode of subsistence is dependent on knowing their annual pattern of mobility and sedentism (see also below).

Unfortunately, there are few foods (plant or animal) which cannot theoretically be stored for later consumption should necessity demand it. As a result, conclusions drawn on the basis of seasonal availability of particular foods are often equivocal. For very early periods, however, it is generally assumed that food storage was, at most, short-term only, and therefore that the presence in palaeofaeces of even *storable* foods can be taken as implying that site occupation included those seasons when the plants were in fruit. For example, at Late Palaeolithic Wadi Kubbaniye (Upper Egypt) the presence in charred palaeofaeces of seeds of *Scirpus tuberosus* Desf. and a member of the Anthemidae (the mayweed tribe) is assumed to suggest that the site was occupied during seasons that included part or all of May to September when

these particular plants are in fruit (Hillman *et al* in press).

The Recovery of Information on Ancient Food Storage Practices

On non-agrarian sites, there are rarely any clues to food storage practices. And even on agrarian sites with remains of grain storage pits, silos and pithoi (with or without their original contents), we rarely unearth evidence for the storage of foods other than cereals and pulses. Regardless of period, therefore, the recovery of palaeofaeces offers a rare opportunity to explore this key aspect of subsistence and domestic life in the past.

The rationale is straightforward enough. For each of the foods identified in palaeofaeces, the extent of their trans-seasonal storage can be assessed from their pattern of association (in the same faecal specimens) with remains of soft fruits likely to have been eaten fresh. If, for example, we identified remains of acorn mush in a coprolite or gut that also contained strawberry seeds, then we could suggest that the acorns (which ripen in autumn) had been kept in storage through the winter and well into the late spring when the strawberries start to ripen. And if remains of acorn mush were found co-habiting a coprolite with seed remains of bilberry (*Vaccinium myrtillus*), this would imply that the family had stored its acorns right through until late summer. And in both cases, such long-term storage might well imply that acorns played a central role as a dietary staple.

Coprolites as a Source of Data on Seasonal Exploitation of Specific Ecosystems

When large assemblages of coprolites are recovered from non-agrarian sites (hunter-gatherer or pastoralist), the identity of the plant and animal foods contained in them can yield information on (a) what types of ecosystem were being exploited, (b) the seasons at which each was exploited, and (c) the directions and distances of the concomitant movements of the local 'hunter-gatherers' or pastoralists[14].

In this role, however, food remains from faeces offer no great advantage over other forms of food remains recoverable from archaeological sites. At Tell Abu Hureyra (Euphrates Valley, northern Syria), for example, the rich assemblages of the usual charred remains of plants have, together with bone remains, allowed just such reconstructions of seasonal exploitation of plant and animal resources of what, at

9000 BC, was riverine forest, steppe and arid zone *Pistacia* woodland (see Hillman, Colledge and Harris, forthcoming; Legge and Rowly-Conwy, in press). But although the infant(?) faeces from Tell Abu Hureyra have so far yielded little additional information in this regard, palaeofaeces from other sites may well prove more productive.

Pollen is the subject of the paper by Dr Scaife (pp. 126ff.), but it is nevertheless worth stressing here that pollen from palaeofaeces is often a particularly useful source of information on seasonality in plant resource exploitation. Except for the pollen from prolific pollen-producers such as the reedmace (Am. 'Cat-tail'), *Typha* spp, it was seldom stored – cooked or fresh – for later consumption, and may therefore represent instant, seasonal consumption of the flowers concerned (see, for example, Bryant 1974a, 416–19; 1974b, 208–09; Williams-Dean and Bryant 1975). With Lindow Man, however, this particular role of pollen remains was destined to be limited (see Scaife, p. 133).

Gut Contents of Off-Site 'Burials' as an Aid to Identifying their Area of Origin

When bodies such as Lindow Man are found far from known contemporaneous settlements, the gut contents may sometimes throw some light on the sort of terrain – or even identify the specific district – that produced the food of his final meals. This possibility arises from the fact that certain wild food plants and weeds grow only on specific soil types, and these soil types may, in turn, have a restricted distribution in the area concerned.

Palaeofaeces as Indicators of Social Stratification

Because the contents of palaeofaeces reflect the diet of their donors, they can cometimes offer an approximate index of the relative wealth or social status of the individual donor, family or group. In so doing, they supplement (or in some cases even surpass) information on social status gleaned from remains of artifacts.

The work of Paap (1983 and 1984) in medieval Amsterdam provides an example that, at present, is seemingly unique in Old World archaeology[15]. Here, the survival of so many cesspits within any one period of occupation and in different parts of the medieval town has allowed Paap to examine the cess contents for differences in diet that might reflect differences in the relative wealth of the donors. Most useful in this exercise were, apparently, the large

numbers of stones from the fruits of various varieties of Bullace (*Prunus institia*): despite the abundance of fruit-stones, the cesspits from certain streets produced stones derived from only small fruited Bullace varieties (var intermedia and var italica) while other streets of the same period produced stone remains that included both a large fruited, presumably more expensive variety of Bullace (var syriaca) and the even larger, and presumably yet more expensive, domestic plum (*Prunus domestica*). (I assume that most of the stones had not passed through the gut but, rather, derived from fruits eaten by users of the cesspits during their short sojourns, in the course of which the stones were spat into the pits.)

In future work, components of the ingested food itself will doubtless also be used in this way to build up a picture of social disparities in other urban centres. However, in the absence of detailed information on local dietary norms of the period, the gut contents of isolated individuals such as Lindow Man clearly cannot be used as an index of social status.

It should also be stressed that the use of palaeofaeces in studies of social stratification seems, in any case, likely to be limited to agrarian, pastoral and urban societies: our present-day, material-based concepts of ownership, 'wealth' and inter-familial hierarchy appear, in most (but perhaps not all) cases to have first emerged only with the establishment of agriculture, and by extrapolation from ethnohistorical studies, would seem to have been alien to many pre-agrarian, 'hunter-gatherer' societies (see, for example, the studies reviewed by Sahlins 1968). Nevertheless it is not inconceivable that palaeofaecal studies might yet play a role in testing this selfsame view of pre-agrarian society against hard archaeological data. In so doing, they would address some of the most fundamental uncertainties presently besetting our understanding of the origins and emergence of modern (post-Palaeolithic) society and its potentially self-destructive system of values. However, it must be admitted that the interpretive problems that would arise from any such analyses could well prove insurmountable.

Summary of Section I: The Archaeological Role of Palaeofaeces

Realistic reconstructions of prehistoric diet are rarely possible in the absence of detailed analyses of palaeofaeces. This is especially true when attempting to assess the role of plant foods from vegetative organs (roots, stems and leaves), though in this area of study, the methodologies are still in their infancy.

Palaeofaeces similarly have a central role to play in investigating (a) prehistoric uses of medicines and hallucinogens, (b) ancient methods of food preparation, (c) prehistoric patterns of food storage and, (d) in some cases, social stratification. They can also yield invaluable additional data to supplement those from conventional bio-remains (i) in reconstructing past human environments, (ii) in assessing seasonality of site occupation by non-agrarian populations and (iii) in deducing their seasonal patterns of exploitation of – and mobility between – specified ecosystems. Finally, in addition to all these roles, the gut contents of preserved human bodies can in some cases provide clues to the likely area of the individual's home settlement, his or her season of death and, if hallucinogens or other poisons are present, could even be used in arguments for or against particular ancient killings having been ritual executions.

With the recovery of Lindow Man and with the discovery that a section of his gut still survived complete with its contents, it was hoped that an analysis of his last meal would yield information on at least *some* of the aspects outlined above.

II Lindow Man's Gut Contents: A Preliminary Assessment of Plant Macro-Remains from the First Sample

Within the first few minutes of microscopic examination of the first sample we took from his duodenum, it was already clear that Lindow Man's last meal was quite different from those of any 'bog people' investigated hitherto and quite different from what we had expected. It appeared that his final meal had consisted almost entirely of a farinaceous food, most probably bread. (The reasoning behind this preliminary identification is outlined below). While this result was clearly of archaeological interest, it was also a disappointment in that it precluded any possibility of investigating, for example, the role of vegetative plant foods in Iron Age diet (see p. 100). The apparent absence of ergot and remains of any other hallucinogens also pre-empted any re-examination of the possible role of hallucinogens in 'ritual killings' (see p. 103). However, what we *did* discover is outlined below.

The Principal Components of His Last Meal

(a) The Fine Textured Matrix
The matrix of the first sub-sample consisted of a fine sludge and the same is apparently true of the remain-

ing material (see Holden, p. 117). Suspended in water and examined under a normal light microscope at ×400, this sludge appeared at first glance to consist of remains of dissociated parenchyma cells with, remarkably, large numbers of free starch grains. In view of the fact that most of the coarser components derived from cereal grains (see below), it seemed probable that most of these cell remains and starch grains originated from the starchy endosperm tissue of the cereal grains themselves. However, because accurate identification of starch grains is better left in the hands of those experienced in this particular application of polarising light microscopy (see, for example, Metropolitan Police Forensic Science Laboratory's *Biology Methods Manual* 1978), identification of components of the fine matrix was deferred, and samples were set aside for starch grain specialists at the Forensic Laboratories of the Metropolitan Police.

After separating all the finer components (<*c.* 0.2 mm), the coarse fractions were next screened with a low-power stereo microscope (Wild M8) at ×15 to ×75 with various combinations of incident and transmitted light:

(b) Cereal Bran
It was immediately apparent that the coarse fraction was dominated by fragments of bran from at least two types of cereal, including wheat. However, little more needs to be said on the subject in this paper, as the formidable task of identifying and quantifying the thousands of fragments of bran is being undertaken by Tim Holden, pp. 116ff. (see also Holden in prep.). His work necessarily includes extending the background studies of botanists such as Körber-Grohne (1967; 1980; 1981) to include yet more histological studies of patterns of variation in different parts of every one of the cell layers (artificially dissociated) of modern grains of each of the cereals and weed grasses likely to have been growing in Iron Age northwestern Europe.

(c) Cereal Chaff
Mixed with the bran fragments were occasional pieces of cereal chaff which, unlike the bran, were instantly identifiable:

(i) Barley Chaff. Most conspicuous were thin slivers of tissue derived from the paleas and lemmas of barley and recognisable both from the pattern of wavy-margined 'long cells' on what had been their outer surfaces and from the twist visible at the end of some of the slivers. This twist represents the bevel or fold present at the base of barley grains (see e.g. Atterberg 1899) and from its shape suggested that the barley had been a lax-eared variety. Also present were numbers of intact barley rachillas: these are minute, flattened, awl-shaped structures which are generally hidden within the base of the groove of the grain. One of the bases for classifying barley varieties is the size, shape and hairyness of these tiny rachillas, and whether or not the hairs on their margins are unicellular or multicellular; (see, for example, Harlan 1918; Orlov and Aberg 1941; Schiemann 1948, 71–3). In the Lindow sample, therefore, the presence of at least two forms of rachilla (one ciliate, the other almost glabrous) indicates that the barley used in his last meal included at least two distinct varieties. As was usual in the traditional 'land race' mixtures of more recent times, these two varieties were probably growing in the same crop. Also present in the remains were a couple of fragments of barley glumes. (For illustrations of barley glumes, see Charles 1984).

(ii) Wheat Chaff. In contrast to the problems of reliably separating the different wheats on the basis of bran histology (see Holden, pp. 118–21 and in prep.; Colledge in prep.), the remains of wheat chaff can generally be referred to individual species with some confidence. Indeed, morphological studies of a broad spectrum of present-day populations of archaic wheats have revealed a number of criteria which can survive in chaff remains and which are diagnostic at the species level (see Hillman, in press and forthcoming a and b). From an examination of these criteria in chaff remains in the first Lindow sample it was apparent that the chaff derived not only from Spelt wheat (*Triticum spelta*) but also from the more archaic Emmer wheat (*T. dicoccum*). In both cases the chaff remains involved glume bases in a somewhat crushed state (5 of Spelt and 2 of Emmer in the first sub-sample), though there was also an intact, albeit well-chewed Spelt rachis node (complete with glume stubs) which appeared to have originated from an abortive spikelet near the base of the ear. (For illustrations of these structures, see Charles 1984 and Hillman, in press).

(d) Other Plant Remains in the Coarse Fraction
The first samples also contained a few fragments of seeds from a Dock (probably *Rumex conglomeratus*), Pale Persicaria (*Polygonum lapathifolium*), Fat Hen (*Chenopodium album*), one of the Meldes (*Atriplex* sp) and a tiny fruitlet fragment of one of the Cow Parsley family (Umbelliferae). Barring the indeterminate Umbelliferae, all of these plants are today typical weeds of crops and waste places. Intriguingly, there were also two charred leaves of heather (*Calluna vulgaris*) present, along with a number of leaves of *Sphagnum* moss. In examining all the remaining samples, Tim Holden has also now identified two additional seed species (see pp. 116–25).

(e) Charred Farinaceous Fragments
Lastly, two small (*c.* 0.5 mm diameter) fragments of charred material came to light. The matrix of these fragments had the blistered, vesicular appearance typical of charred endosperm tissue (endosperm is the starchy interior of cereal grains), so it could theoretically have derived either direct from a piece of charred grain or else from bread or some other food based on ground grain. The matter was resolved by the existence within the vesicular matrix of three minute slivers of cereal husk (not bran) which were embedded at different planes and had their surfaces partly obscured by the charred matrix. Such a random arrangement accords with material from ground-up grains rather than fragments from a grain in its intact state. The most likely donor of the husk fragments was barley, whose candidature was supported by the fact that the wavy-margined cell walls of the 'long cells' visible on the surface of the husk fragments closely resembled the walls of epidermal cells of barley lemmas and paleas. Whether the matrix was derived only from barley grain or from barley and wheat mixed is impossible to say.

While the matrix was thoroughly black and charred, the husk fragments were only browned. With dry, husked grains, this pattern of differential charring would accord with exposure to temperatures of around 220°C for a couple of hours. However, in the presence of ample moisture (as in baking dough, for example), much higher temperatures might produce precisely the same effect.

(f) Correlations with Results From the Pollen Study
It will be seen from Dr Rob Scaife's palynological study (pp. 126ff.) that there is close agreement between the identifications of the macroscopic remains and the identities and relative abundance of his pollen types. This could perhaps imply that, in screening the macroscopic remains, we have not, after all, overlooked any major food category present in relatively unrecognisable form, though this fact can ultimately be established only from a full analysis of the fine fractions (additional to pollen) that have yet to be examined.

What Food had he been Eating? The Bread Hypothesis

From the preliminary analysis of coarse components, all the evidence pointed to Lindow Man's last meal having consisted of plain but nutritious fare – namely, wholemeal bread or some related farinaceous food. It would therefore be surprising if analyses of the as yet unexamined fine fractions were to generate a radically different hypothesis. The present evidence is as follows:

(a) That a grain based food provided the core of his last meal is indisputable: (i) the coarse components are dominated by fragmented bran of wheat and barley (see Holden's report, p. 116); (ii) the pollen is dominated by Cerealia types (see Scaife, p. 129); (iii) there is a generous admixture of chaff from two species of wheat and at least two varieties of barley; (iv) the fine fractions (other than pollen) appear, provisionally, to be full of starch grains quite possibly derived from cereal endosperm; (v) the wild seeds all derive from plants that, today, are archetypical weeds of crops and, as in my hypothesis for the origin of weed seeds present in the last meals of Tollund Man and Grauballe Man, they probably became mixed with the grain through having been harvested together with the parent crop. (Compare the discussion on pp. 102–3). Certainly all of the weed species identified here are common contaminants of cereal grain in areas of traditional agriculture, this even after the grain has been through the basic sequence of traditional cleaning operations involving multiple winnowing and several sievings. (For details, see Hillman 1981; 1983; 1984; 1985; G. Jones 1981; 1984a; 1984b).

(b) The low frequency of weed seeds and cereal chaff relative to cereal grain remains (in the form of bran) precludes the possibility that Lindow Man's last meal was in any way comparable with the last meals of Tollund Man or Grauballe Man: such low weed seed frequencies are concomitant not with the weed-seed infested waste fractions separated from the grain during its cleaning but rather with grain that was already cleaned and ready for bulk storage or preparation as food (see pp. 102–3).

(c) The grain remains (of both the wheat and the barley, see Holden, below) are much more finely fragmented than can be accounted for by mere mastication of intact grain: clearly both the wheat and the barley grain had been ground up prior to consumption and, presumably, prior to their final preparation as food. On this basis, therefore, we can discount a wide range of grain foods based either on whole grains, coarse groats or porridge (see p. 104).

This leaves us with bread and other flour-based products as principle contenders. Of these, it is the *wholemeal* varieties that concern us here, as the bran had not been sifted out in the manner bequeathed to us by the town-based Roman fashionables whose obsession with snow-white, fibreless, constipation-inducing pap rightly attracted the reproval of Galen in the second century AD (see Galen n.d.; also Moritz 1958).[17,18]

(d) To distinguish between the various coarse, wholemeal, flour-based foods likely to have featured in Lindow Man's last meal requires that the cookery method(s) be identified as outlined on pp. 104–5. However, the problem is here exacerbated by the fact that the wheat and barley may have been eaten as part of entirely different foods: the *wheat*meal, for example, may have been eaten as griddle cakes while the barleymeal could have been eaten as dumplings! The range of possibilities is considerable. For a start, flour from either wheat or barley can be prepared from either ripe or unripe grains. Secondly, ripe grains can be roasted before grinding and the flour eaten after merely mixing it into a paste with water, without the need of further baking (see Musil 1928; Hütteroth 1959). Thirdly, flour from unroasted grains can be eaten, not only as one of the almost infinite range of leavened and unleavened breads, but also as griddle-cakes, dumplings, thick gruel or, in the case of the barley of the classical Greeks, as *mâza*, which Moritz (1958) deciphers as 'kneaded things'. Yet further possibilities exist. For example, as a means of preserving more perishable foods such as yoghurt, cheese or eggs, flour was often mixed with them and dried into hard balls for winter storage. These products would then be prepared for consumption simply by boiling them in water and eating them as anything from a soup to a thick glutinous sludge. (These and other traditional grain-based foods are outlined in the second halves of Hillman 1984b and 1985).

What evidence of cooking method(s) do we have from the Lindow Man's gut contents? The charred fragments of farinaceous matter (see p. 108) clearly provide some useful clues. While cooking by boiling or stewing may occasionally result in ground grain foods being charred, accidental charring is far more likely to occur with baking or griddling. The charred fragments in the Lindow sample are therefore most likely to have derived from the charred crust of some sort of bread. Particles of husk which appear to originate from barley are present in the charred fragments, so, if bread is involved, then it was made from barley or, more probably, from a mixture of both the barley and the wheat.

If correct, this conclusion still leaves us with the task of establishing whether or not the rest of the meal (other than the charred fragments) also derives from half-digested bread as opposed to some other, fine-ground, farinaceous food. Here ESR spectroscopy has an obvious role to play (see p. 104). Its ability to establish the highest past temperature of exposure of organic materials should allow us to decide whether bran from either the barleymeal, the wheatmeal or both of them had been exposed to temperatures characteristic of baking rather than stewing. The plan, therefore, is to submit for ESR analysis at Queen Mary College, University of london, not only specimens of barley and wheat chaff remains, but also specimens of a few thousand fragments of each class of cereal bran, to be identified and isolated by Tim Holden. In addition Dr Keith Sales of Queen Mary College, University of London (pers. comm. October 1984) has underlined the necessity of first obtaining spectra for modern equivalent samples from each type of grain (barley, Emmer and Spelt) and all possible mixtures, each of them cooked by stewing, baking and griddling – and perhaps passed through a human gut as well. Only when the ESR analyses are completed will the precise nature of Lindow Man's last meal by firmly established.

In the meantime, however, present evidence suggests that his last meal was some sort of bread made of both barley and wheat. Mixed breads of this sort were, in fact, quite usual until recent times in poor areas where cereals such as barley had to serve as staples (for ethnohistorical examples, see Maurizio 1927; Gunda 1981). In such circumstances the relatively meagre wheat supplies were stretched by adding 50% or more of barleymeal: even a small quantity of high gluten wheat flour greatly improves the baking quality of pure barley-dough.

Conclusions Regarding his Last Meal

It has often been claimed that the average prehistoric farmer rarely ate his grain in the form of bread. The preliminary results of the Lindow Man study may tentatively be interpreted as either offering one item of evidence against this view, or as implying that he had enjoyed relatively 'up-market' fare immediately prior to his death.

Contrary to our hopes, evidence for the inclusion of any vegetative plant foods in Lindow Man's last meal appears to be lacking so far.

Was the Barley De-Husked?

Unlike wheat grain, the grain of most barleys have husks (paleas and lemmas) firmly attached to the grain surface. In 'pearl' barley, these husks are stripped off. This pearling of barley grain is recorded as well-established practice by classical authors such as Pliny (*Historia Naturalis* xviii, 84) and also evidenced in ancient remains from, for example, the palace quarters of Phrygian levels dated to c. 760 BC at the ancient city of Gordion of King Midas fame in present-day Turkey (Hillman, unpublished report). However, even in recent times, many groups have eaten barley products complete with the husks, whether in barley porridge, barley bread or even the barley component of muesli, though it has been suggested by O'Neil (1985) and others that silicified hairs and other fragments from the silicon phytolith-laden husks of cereals might be carcinogenic[18].

The presence of barley rachillas and husk fragments in the Lindow sample therefore suggests that either (i) the barley grain was used complete with its husks, (ii) that dehusking had, as usual, left quite a few husk fragments still attached to the grain, or (iii) that not all the detached husks had been properly winnowed out of the dehusked grain prior to its being ground to flour.

The Baking of the Bread

(a) The Fuel

The charred leaves of heather (*Calluna vulgaris*) presumably came from the fire used to bake the putative bread, so it may perhaps be assumed that heather witthies provided part or all of the fuel. When the various flat breads and 'griddle cakes' are prepared over open fires, there is every chance of the dough collecting light fragments of fuel carried up by the flames. Even when a traditional, thick-walled oven is used to bake bread (which was probably not the case here), it is generally fired ten or more minutes beforehand in order to heat the thick walls and floor which then re-radiate the heat which effects the baking. The dough is put in the oven only when the fire is dying down and, even though the bulk of the embers are pushed to one side, it is quite usual for the tacky dough to collect a number of fragments of the fuel on its exposed edges. While most of these are afterwards brushed off, a few, like these burned heather leaves perhaps, remain attached to the bread.

(b) The Type of Bread

With techniques currently available, we have at least four lines of evidence for the broad class of bread which was eaten:

(*i*) To produce light (aerated), leavened bread it is necessary to include in the dough a good measure of flour from 'hard' grains of bread wheat (*T. aestivum*). These 'hard' grains are produced only by certain varieties of bread wheat when grown under sunny conditions and, for bakers, their key property is their high level of 'gluten' – the complex of proteins which produces the elasticity needed for dough to retain air bubbles and thence to 'rise'. (The bubbles originate from (*a*) water vapour, (*b*) carbon dioxide produced by the yeast of the leaven. For further details, see Robins 1980). The possibility that 'risen' aerated bread was involved can therefore be eliminated if we demonstrate that all forms of bread wheat were absent. This is almost certainly the case in Lindow Man's last meal: the bread appears to have been made from coarse, wholemeal flour of Emmer wheat, Spelt wheat and barley, and there is therefore little chance of the bread having 'risen' sufficiently to produce a really light, aerated loaf, even if it was well leavened with plenty of sour dough rich in wild yeasts.

(*ii*) Archaeological evidence for the availability of ovens can also offer useful, albeit indirect, evidence of baking methods. In general, production of risen bread requires some sort of oven, and the absence of any oven remains on a well-preserved archaeological site raises the possibility that, if bread was eaten at all, then it was probably flat and unleavened. Exceptions inevitably exist here. In eastern Turkey, for example, they bake a half-risen loaf (Tur. *Bazlama Ekmeği*) from 'hard' bread wheats over an *open hearth*, though they do cover the dough with a special lid holding a mass of hot embers.

In northwest England, prehistoric rural sites excavated to date apparently lack any obvious remains of bread ovens (Sue Hamilton, pers. comm. 1986), and it seems probable, therefore, that, if bread was eaten at these settlements, it was prepared in its unleavened form.

(*iii*) It has been discovered by Robins, *et al* (pers. comm. 1986 and in prep.) that certain features of electron spin resonance spectra appear to provide a measure of the *duration* of past heating of ancient food remains, *i.e.* they tell us for *how long* the food was cooked. Most useful here, according to Robins, is the ESR 'saturation level' and, to a lesser degree, electron 'spin concentration', though the latter is affected by other variables and is therefore more difficult to interpret in terms of cooking times. Now in general, unleavened bread-cum-griddle-cakes are cooked as flattened buns or thinnish sheets for relatively short periods (often three or four minutes on each side), while loaves of risen, leavened bread have to be exposed to much longer baking times – generally at higher mean temperatures. ESR saturation levels should therefore reveal clear differences between the two.

(*iv*) Analysis of body tissue for the ratios between elements such as zinc and selenium provides a means of, in this case, identifying long-term, consistent consumption of unleavened bread, as this apparently results in a deficiency of zinc relative to other minerals.[12] Such an analysis of Lindow Man's body tissues would not, however, identify the type of bread eaten in his last meal as such.

The first two lines of evidence thus indicate that the bread in Lindow Man's last meal was probably unleavened. We now await the results from ESR spectroscopy with intense interest (see p. 140).

Medicines, Hallucinogens and Herbs

In this area of study, the Lindow remains proved a disappointment. Unlike Tollund Man and Grauballe Man, and in contrast to our own expectations, we have found no remains of ergot or any other hallucinogen that might be construed as having played a role in ritual killings. Also absent was any identifiable trace of (a) medicines or (b) herbs that might have been used in flavouring the food.

Evidence of Ancient Agricultural Practice

(a) The Crops Cultivated in the Lindow District
Lindow Man's last meal included remains of just three crops: Emmer wheat, Spelt wheat and a lax-eared form of hulled barley, and it seems reasonable to suppose that they had been grown locally by the settlement that provided his last meal.

Whether the two glume wheats – Emmer and Spelt – were grown as separate crops or mixed-sown as a maslin remains uncertain. Separate sowing would superficially seem more logical, as the different rates of ripening of most present-day varieties of either species ideally require them to be harvested separately. However, on marginal land in central Turkey, equivalent mixtures of glume wheats (Emmer and Einkorn) have in recent times offered useful insurance against complete crop failure in bad years (Prof. Osman Tosun pers. comm. 1970; and the villagers of Alaca Höyük pers. comm. 1973). The Lindow area would certainly not have lacked land made marginal for agriculture through poor drainage, especially in years of heavy rainfall. Mixed sowing of a high yielding Spelt with, say, a relatively low-yielding but waterlogging-resistant form of Emmer (see Davies *et al* forthcoming) might therefore have made good sense.

(b) Harvesting and Grain Processing

It was stressed above that charred remains of the sort recoverable from most archaeological sites are, in general, likely to be superior to palaeofaeces as a source of information on ancient agrarian practice. Nevertheless, the few weed seeds and chaff fragments identified in the Lindow sample provide useful clues to the methods used to harvest the cereal crops and to clean the threshed grain.

(i) Harvesting methods. Weeds such as Persicaria, Fat Hen and Melde which were present in the Lindow sample generally grow much lower than the majority of primitive cereal varieties. Seeds from these weeds would not normally be present, therefore, in crops which had been (a) reaped close below the ear (as reported for one area of Roman Britain by Pythaeus and thereafter quoted by Diodorus Siculus [5.21] (see Strabo), (b) harvested by hand plucking of the ears as explained by Reynolds (1981) or (c) stripped by tools such as the Iberian *mesorias* as reported by Sigaut (1974). Correspondingly, if the cereal crops had been harvested by uprooting (as barley still is in parts of Turkey and Syria), these free-standing weeds would probably have been left behind in the field together with their seeds. Thus the only harvesting method likely to have resulted in these particular seeds contaminating the harvested grain is that of reaping fairly low on the culm – presumably with some sort of sickle[19].

From his studies of texts relating to early agrarian practice in Europe, Francois Sigaut (pers. comm. 1985) has concluded that the most common reason for harvesting cereal ears separately from the straw was to provide unbroken (i.e. unthreshed) straw for thatching. (The straw itself was cut later in the summer.) Evidence from Lindow Man that the crops had been reaped low on the straw such that both ears and straw were harvested together may therefore

imply that, for thatching in the Lindow area, reeds, bracken or heather sods were preferred to straw[20].

(ii) Grain cleaning procedures. The low frequencies of weed seeds and wheat chaff relative to the probable numbers of wheat grains indicate that the farming families who produced this batch of grain had submitted it to a series of operations including threshing, a round of primary winnowings, coarse sieving (probably), spikelet parching (probably), pounding or querning of the spikelets to free the grain, secondary winnowing(s) and then at least two stages of sieve-cleaning of the grain to remove the bulk of (a) the coarse contaminants, (b) the fine contaminants ('fine cleanings'). Most of these operations are unavoidable, and to be feasible at all, have to be performed in precisely the order indicated.

It should perhaps be stressed that our knowledge of (i) the operations and tools involved in grain processing and (ii) their effects on the composition of crop products is based on studies of grain processing applied to the same archaic crops in recent times by farming communities which have retained a full complement of traditional tools and techniques dating back to the Iron Age and, in some cases, much earlier. Ethnographic models based on these studies and designed to allow detailed, testable interpretation of the composition of archaeological remains of crops in terms of ancient agrarian practice have been published elsewhere. (The relevant references were cited in on p. 103).

(iii) Dehusking the barley grain (or, rather, its possible omission) was fully discussed on p. 110.

Who Cooked His Last Meal?

Here we are concerned, not with the identity of the cook, but the location of the settlement which produced the grain for his last meal and which presumably prepared the meal itself (see p. 106).

None of the weed species present in the Lindow sample are characteristic of specific soil types. However, the sample also contained charred leaves of heather and uncharred leaves and shoots of a sphagnum moss (*Sphagnum cuspidatum*), and both of these plants have marked habitat 'preferences'. The mode of inclusion of the heather leaves was discussed above, and their presence suggests that the last meal was prepared in a settlement on or near heathland or moorland from which heather could have been gathered for fuel.

As for the *Sphagnum*, Tim Holden has concluded that it can be dismissed as an intrusive from the boggy pool in which the body was dumped (see his paper, below). And as Lindow Man was almost certainly dead before he arrived in the pool, he is unlikely to have actively swallowed the *Sphagnum* with the pool water; even if he did, it surely would not have got through to his duodenum. We are therefore left with two possibilities: either the *Sphagnum* fragments arrived with water he drank on his way to his death across the bog, or they were ingested with his last meal. In the latter case, the *Sphagnum* fragments may have become attached to the putative bread at some point between its baking and ingestion, or they may have been swallowed with water drunk with the meal. If either of these last two scenarios is correct, then the settlement must have been on or near moorland broken by boggy pools (see E. V. Watson 1963), and this, in turn, accords with one of the general habitats indicated by the heather remains.

Thus, while the evidence in this section is far from conclusive, it nevertheless raises the possibility that his last meal was eaten in a settlement on or near the peat-bog where he died. Whether he himself originated from this settlement is clearly another matter.

What was the Season of his Death?

Sadly there are no seasonal foods represented in Lindow Man's last meal: all the grain foods are storable and could therefore have been eaten at any time of the year. Similar limitations presumably apply even to the gut-derived pollen, which, in this case, is most likely to represent merely the pollen caught on the stigmas of the flowering cereals and thereafter stored and consumed with the grain (see Scaife, p. 133).

The Dating of Lindow Man: Evidence from the Cereals in the Gut

Studies of crop remains from archaeological sites in Britain have now reached a stage where it is possible to suggest a generalised crop chronology for the country as a whole, from the first arrival of farming through to the present day. This pattern of emergence and disappearance of different crops is presented diagrammatically in fig. 1 of Hillman 1981. The characteristic feature of crop chronologies for the mid- to late-Iron Age in Britain is the widespread, simultaneous cultivation of three cereals: Emmer wheat, Spelt wheat and hulled barley, and it is these selfsame three cereals that I have now identified in Lindow Man's last meal.

Of the three crops, the least period-specific is the hulled barley: it appears to have arrived in Britain with the first Neolithic farmers and has continued to be cultivated through to the present day, though the last century has seen the introduction of many new varieties, especially of the two-rowed type.

Emmer, too, arrived with the first farmers but, during the Iron Age, was slowly ousted by Spelt (another glume wheat) which, by Roman times, had become the principal wheat throughout southern Britain from East Anglia to the westernmost shores of Dyfed and Gwynedd. It is therefore during the middle Iron Age that the combination of Emmer and Spelt (together with the omnipresent barley) became especially characteristic, and the presence of precisely this combination in Lindow Man's last meal suggests that he lived during this period.

There are certain caveats, however. Agronomic advantages offered by Emmer, together with agrarian and culinary conservatism, will doubtless have ensured that pockets of Emmer cultivation survived in many areas. Even today, we find occasional fields of Emmer under cultivation in parts of Czechoslovakia, Hungary and Turkey (see Kühn 1970, Gunda 1981 and Hillman 1984b respectively). A few fields of Spelt wheat, too, are still cultivated in Schwabia and were, until very recently, still cultivated in northwest Iran (as *T. spelta*, var. kuckuckiana) and in eastern Turkey (as *T. spelta*, var. vavilovii). It is not impossible, therefore, that the crops in Lindow Man's last meal were grown by an isolated settlement which had continued growing these cereals at a time when most of Britain's farmers had long since forsaken such archaic crops for the more modern bread wheats and rivit wheats.

Despite this caveat, the balance of probabilities based on British crop chronologies clearly favours Lindow Man having lived and died sometime in the middle to late Iron Age.

Summary and Conclusions

The first half of the paper reviews the role of studies of palaeofaeces (here taken to include both coprolites and gut contents) in providing information on (i) ancient diet, (ii) the ancient preparation of foodstuffs and culinary practice, (iii) uses of medicines and drugs, (iv) social stratification, (v) seasonality of site occupation and resource use, (vi) the season of death of preserved bodies, and (vii) the location of the source settlements of individuals who ended up as off-site inhumations. It also examines the shortcomings of our existing methodologies, and cites recent applications of techniques which are now opening new avenues in studies of ancient diet. From the first half of this paper then, it is hopefully clear that palaeofaecal studies have a central role to play in our understanding of everyday life in prehistoric times, and that this role can only increase as new systems of analysis become available.

In its second half, the paper outlines (a) some of the results of analysis of the most conspicuous components of just one sample from the guts of Lindow Man, and (b) interprets these results with reference to each of the archaeological roles of palaeofaeces outlined in the first half. The greatest disappointment has been the complete absence, so far, of foods from vegetative organs such as leaves, stems and roots. As a result of their absence, the Lindow remains throw no light on that most conspicuous area of our ignorance, namely the role of wild and cultivated vegetative foods in prehistoric diet. Sadly, the Lindow remains also offer no information on the Iron Age use of natural medicines or the possible role of hallucinogens in 'ritual' killings, though it was admittedly clear from the outset that our hopes of recovering any information on this aspect of Iron Age life were at best tenuous. On the other hand, the Lindow remains have allowed a detailed (albeit provisional) reconstruction of his last meal and this, in turn, provides clues not only to one aspect of Iron Age diet, but also to some of their methods of preparing food, the harvesting method they applied to the crops, their method of cleaning the grain and, finally, some rather imprecise clues to the type of terrain occupied by the settlement in which Lindow Man's last meal was prepared. The remains have also allowed us to address the question of *when* Lindow Man lived.

Detailed work is still in progress in the hands of Tim Holden (p. 116). Not only is he undertaking the formidable task of devising schemes for identifying poorly-preserved fragments of each layer of bran of each of the cereals and weed grasses likely to have grown in Iron Age Britain (see Holden, in prep.), but he is analysing the remainder of all other plant food components of both Lindow Man and, hopefully, other northwest European bog people whose last meals have survived the intervening millennia

Within a few years, we should know a great deal more about the dietary habits of our forbears.

Footnotes

1. I am grateful to Cheryl Haldane and Professor V. Bryant of Texas A & M University for bringing this and related studies to my notice.
2. Prime examples of sites with near complete preservation of organic materials include dry caves such as Lovelock Cave in Nevada (Heizer and Napton 1970) where extreme aridity allowed even basketry decoy ducks to survive almost intact, and arid zone open sites such as Qasr Ibrim in Upper Egypt where *c.* 20% of the site is composed of organic debris of one sort or another (Rowley-Conwy, forthcoming).
3. Even within this narrow range of food types (grains, nuts and fruits with hard seeds) we generally encounter remains of only those items which were either (i) regularly brought into contact with fire and thereby preserved by charring, or (ii) dropped into wells, ditches or ponds where they were preserved by waterlogging. Of these, the only items which finally get recorded are those resilient enough to remain in identifiable form regardless of charring or waterlogging. Worse still, because, in the case of grain-based foods, the materials surviving in fires or ditches most commonly represent only the *waste* fractions from ancient grain cleaning (see Hillman 1981), we are seldom able to use them to deduce how the grain itself was prepared as food: cereal grain, for example, may have been eaten as bread, groats, porridge, griddle-cakes, dumplings, gruel or one of the many other traditional grain foods once popular in rural western Eurasia. From grain processing waste alone, we can rarely know which was involved. (For an outline of some of the traditional cereal-based foods of Europe and southwest Asia, see the second half of Hillman, 1985).
4. Again, some exceptions exist; for example, remains of an accumulation of gathered leaves of dye-plants were identified in waterlogged, urban deposits at Viking York (Hall and Tomlinson 1983). So far however, such finds are rare.
5. There are inevitably many cases where a single set of gut contents represents many more than a couple of meals. Of these, perhaps the most extreme are found amongst opium addicts, some of whom are reported to void stools only once in six months (Ann Butler, pers. comm. 1983). In such circumstances, however, most of the identifiable plant remains will presumably be broken down by gut bacteria and released as methane and other gases.
6. The 'exceptional circumstances' which Robert Heizer (pers. comm. to Thomas) suggested might account for the accumulation of coprolites in the receptacle at Hidden Cave were based on the now widely publicised observations by the Jesuit priest Baegert (1864–5) of Indians in Baja California. These Pitahaya Indians, having feasted on the fruits of the Pitahaya cactus, thereafter claimed what Baegert termed a 'second harvest' by retrieving from their own faeces the large numbers of small, undigested seeds of the ingested cactus fruits. The seeds were then apparently roasted and ground before being eaten a second time. Equivalent practices have apparently also been observed in southern Texas by Newcom (1961) as cited by Stock (1983).

    The procedure seems eminently rational: the small, nutritious seeds (a) cannot be properly digested *without* prior roasting and grinding, but (b) cannot in any way be extracted from the fresh fruit for separate roasting and grinding without automatically wasting the flesh of the fruit – complete with its vitamin C reserves. The indisputably imaginative strategy adopted by the Pitahaya Indians therefore represents (for societies lacking the electric liquidisers of the modern kitchen) the only convenient means of ensuring full corporeal utilisation of both the flesh of the fruit and its seeds, and of thereby avoiding wastage of either resource.

    Prehistoric evidence for 'double harvests' of this type appears to exist at Hinds Cave in southern Texas (Williams-

Dean 1978; Stock 1983, 142) where seeds of one of the fleshy-fruited *Opuntia* species were fragmented and darkened in a manner consistent with their having been roasted and ground as described above.

7. It should perhaps be explained that, in the course of most of the traditional systems for processing and de-toxifying acorns, the acorn 'flesh' is converted into a flour or mush before it is ingested, and the same is true of many other starchy foods which are bitter in their unprocessed state. (See, for example, Smith 1923, 66 and 1932, 401–2; Maurizio 1927, 55–57). This pre-treatment is omitted (and then, not always) only with the non-bitter species of acorn such as *Quercus alba* in the USA (as used by the Ojibwe, but not the Menomeni Indians) and *Q. ilex* var. ballota in the Mediterranean area.

8. Study programmes with just this aim have recently been initiated in at least two centres in the UK, and perhaps elsewhere in Europe. One (sponsored by the SERC and supervised jointly by David Cutler of the Jodrell Laboratories of the Royal Botanic Gardens, Kew and by the present author) aims to isolate taxonomically stable anatomical and histological criteria in parenchymatous foods (and associated inedible tissues likely to be found as waste) from tubers, corms, rhizomes, aerial stems and petioles. The objective is to provide reliable means of identifying even the most fragmentary remains of these foods and their waste fractions recovered from archaeological sites in palaeofaeces and charred food-waste respectively.

9. For details of the sequence of husbandry and grain-cleaning operations traditionally applied to crops in Europe and the Near East, see the references cited on p. 103.

10. I am grateful to Paul Halstead and Glynis Jones (now Halstead) for bringing these works to my notice.

11. Yet further applications of ESR in archaeology are under investigation: see, for example, Robins (1984); Robins *et al* (in press); Sales *et al* (in press).

12. It is apparently possible to identify past dependence on unleavened bread (i.e. flat or 'pide' bread) as a dietary staple, from deficiencies of zinc relative to other minerals in skeletal or other tissues from preserved bodies. It would seem that this deficiency does not develop in people who regularly eat *leavened* (risen) bread. While identification of such a deficiency does not specifically allow identification of the bread type preserved in any one palaeofaecal sample, it clearly addresses a question of far broader archaeological relevance. (I am grateful to Dr Don Robins of Sciencewright and Dr Tony Leeds of Queen Elizabeth College's Department of Nutrition, for bringing these facts to my notice. See also Bingham 1978).

13. Most people would have access to only limited quantities of honey which was, in general, eaten in the comb rather than drained out for use in preserving fruit, for example (see Tannahill 1975).

14. Interpretation of any form of plant or animal remains at these three levels clearly requires a great deal of background information. Level (a) requires knowledge of the precise ecological associations of each of the plants and/or animals represented. Level (b) demands details of (i) dates of flowering and fruiting of each plant represented by pollen or seed; (ii) seasonal patterns of palatability/toxicity of vegetative foods identified in the remains (see, for example, Gott 1983, 9–10); and (iii) patterns of birth, tooth eruption, tooth wear, herd migration and the hibernation/aestivation habits of each of the animal species present. Level (c) requires detailed ecological models (generally based on pollen or wood-charcoal data) of the distribution of ancient vegetation, in particular the position of major ecosystem boundaries, at the time of occupation of the site.

15. For a New World (albeit European settler period) example of work with some similar objectives, see Shay (1984).

16. There was clearly a finite risk in extrapolating from the results of the preliminary analyses of a sample from the duodenum and applying them to the entire meal (as, for example, in the 1985 television programme on Lindow Man). This extrapolation was based on the fact that the foods ingested in any one meal are generally thoroughly mixed, *before* they begin to be passed into the duodenum (see p. 105).

17. I am grateful to Dr Stephen Mitchell, now of the Institute for Advanced Studies, Princeton University, New Jersey, USA, for kindly translating for me the relevant texts from Galen's original Greek.

18. The apparently beneficial effects of high-fibre diets involving cereal bran should not be confused with the claimed carcinogenic effects of consuming silicified hairs and other fragments from the phytolith-laden *husks* of cereals. I am grateful to Ann Butler for putting me in touch with the O'Neal reference.

19. The case is even more convincing when grain remains are contaminated by still lower-growing weeds such as Parsley Piert (*Aphanes* spp), Knotgrass (*Polygonum aviculare* agg), Chickweed (*Stellaria media*), Creeping Clover (*Trifolium repens*), Scarlet Pimpernell *Anagallis arvensis*), Annal Poa (*Poa annua*), Early Hair-grass (*Aira praecox*) or Silvery Hair-grass (*A. caryophyllea*). (Details of the use of weed and chaff remains to indicate ancient harvesting methods are given in Hillman 1981, 148–53; and 1984a, 26 and 30). Despite the Pythaeus report (see Strabo) almost all the assemblages of charred crop remains from sites in Britain which have been scrutinised specifically for evidence of ancient agrarian practice have so far indicated that the crops were harvested either by being uprooted or else reaped low on the straw.

20. For eminently readable accounts of the traditional use of bracken, heather and peat sods in thatching, see Grant (1961), Rymer (1976), O'Crohan (1978) and Fenton (1978a and b).

26 Preliminary Report on the Detailed Analyses of the Macroscopic Remains from the Gut of Lindow Man

Timothy G. Holden

Introduction

The body of the Iron Age man recovered from Lindow Moss was, on the whole, exceptionally well preserved, with most of the external features still discernible. Internally however, most of the soft visceral tissues have long since been reduced to an unrecognisable state. The main exceptions to this are the organs making up the upper part of the alimentary canal. These have survived by virtue of the fact that the acid of the stomach has acted as a fixative and preserving agent. The stomach and the upper small intestine have in this way been transformed into inert waxy structures (James Bourke pers. comm. 1985) so enabling them to resist the forces of decay. The preservation of this part of the gut was such that there was little opportunity for contamination of its contents. Unfortunately, the lower parts of the digestive tract were lost when the body was truncated by the peat cutting machine at the time of discovery. The material under study therefore, is the contents of the intact stomach and upper small intestine only.

Three other 'bog bodies' have been recovered in recent years from Northern Europe in a state of preservation such that their gut contents were suitable for detailed study (Brandt 1950; Helbaek 1950; 1958). These three were discovered in the peat bogs of Denmark in the late 1940s and early 1950s. Although the Danish bodies are not necessarily contemporary with Lindow Man, it is hoped that certain aspects will be comparable.

Most of the evidence so far relating to the Iron Age diet has been based on data produced from the study of animal bones and carbonised plant remains recovered from a variety of archaeological contexts. Such contexts however, can yield only indirect evidence for the human consumption of these items.

The importance of a find such as the Lindow Man is that, together with data obtained from coprolites and other faecal material, it can provide direct evidence for the composition of the Iron Age diet. The exceptionally good state of preservation of the Lindow material also makes it possible to pose questions relating to other aspects of Iron Age life. These research questions, the answers to which, it is hoped will enlighten us at both the level of Lindow Man as an individual and at the level of his culture and environment, will include the following:

(a) What was the composition of his last meal?

(b) Can the composition of this meal add anything to the corpus of knowledge on the Iron Age diet?

(c) Do any of the elements of the meal support the theory that they may have been linked to a ritual killing?

(d) Are there any indicators of the season in which Lindow Man died?

(e) Can the state and the composition of the material reveal anything about the crop husbandry, processing and cooking techniques used?

(f) Can the various elements in the gut give any indication of the different types of environment that were being exploited by the Iron Age population?

In order to attempt an answer to these questions it has been necessary to overcome fundamental problems in both identification and quantification. It has also been considered desirable to carry out a certain amount of experimental work using new techniques in the hope that if they prove productive they will provide information on both the Lindow body and any future such finds. These points will be discussed below.

Method and Materials

The gut contents consisted of a dark brown semi-solid material with no obvious colour changes throughout the length of the gut. Nevertheless the contents from discrete parts of the surviving gut were removed and treated as if they had been totally separate contexts.

The total contents of approximately 20 g (fresh weight) was distributed through the gut as follows:

Fundus and body of the stomach	4.3 g
Antrum of the stomach	2.2 g
Duodenum	5.8 g
Upper small intestine	6.8 g

Fresh weight was used as the most convenient measure. However, in order that comparisons with other material can be made the conversion factors below were calculated:

1 g of gut contents = 0.9 cc compact volume (fresh)

1 g of gut contents = 3.8 cc of sediment in distilled water after shaking

It was not considered necessary to analyse the total content of the gut, therefore 0.5 gram (fresh weight) sub-samples from each section were taken for study. This was done in the hope that any significant changes in composition through the length of the gut would be detected. By doing this it should be possible to discover, (a) whether the composition can be used to identify different meals, and (b) whether there has been any differential settling out of material in the stomach (i.e. to discover whether the more dense fragments of food debris will be over-represented in the lower part and the less dense fragments over-represented in the upper part, thus biasing results based on a single sample).

Each sample was put into a measuring cylinder with approximately 200 cc of water and shaken. After being allowed to settle for 2–3 minutes the supernatant fluid was decanted. This was repeated until the extremely fine particles that had tended to remain in suspension had been removed. The more dense fraction remaining as the residue was composed mostly of free plant material although some still remained aggregated. These aggregates could be teased apart with relative ease, thus releasing their constituent parts. The material in the residue was then separated into two size categories by gentle agitation in a 500 micron sieve while still suspended in water. This enabled separation to be carried out with minimal abrasive damage. It was hoped that all those particles retained in the sieve could be sorted and an attempt made at their identification. Those particles not held in the sieve on the other hand, were kept for possible future identification. Preliminary sorting was carried out using a ×50 binocular dissecting microscope; for the more detailed sorting however (e.g. in order to distinguish between the bran fragments of brome and wheat) it was necessary to use a ×250 − ×400 binocular microscope.

The identifications were made using the reference collections of modern seeds belonging to the Department of Human Environment and to Mr Gordon Hillman, both of which are held at the Institute of Archaeology, University of London. Since the semi-digested and waterlogged plant remains presented particular problems for identification, it proved necessary to prepare this modern material in such a way that it could be directly compared with the degraded ancient material. This was prepared using the technique devised by Camilla Dickson (forthcoming) and then mounted on standard microscope slides for permanent reference.

Preliminary Results and Identifications

Table 12 represents a subjective assessment of the relative quantities of the different components identified. The components recorded have been recovered mainly from the fundus and body of the stomach. Those indicated by an asterisk, however, were identified by Gordon Hillman from a preliminary assessment of the contents of the duodenum. Other items identified by Hillman are indicated by the $ character. It is hoped that as work progresses a more accurate representation of the composition of both the stomach and the other areas of the gut will be possible. A four category system has been used to give an idea of the relative quantities. In this, X represents less than 5 items, XX represents more than 5 but less than 20 items, XXX represents more than 20 items but less than 100 items and XXXX represents more than 100 items. The order of the species list and the naming conventions for the non-cereal component follow Clapham, Tutin and Warburg (1962).

As stated earlier, the identification of the plant remains posed particular problems by virtue of their small size and their state of preservation. None of the cereal fragments were large enough to enable any identification based on either their gross morphology or on the layers of cells commonly used for the identification of carbonised fragments. It is therefore considered necessary to outline here some of the more important identification criteria used and some of the limitations imposed by the nature of the material.

Cereals and Grasses – General

One of the major components of the gut contents is the inner layers of the bran coat of the grains of several species of cereal. These layers have been given various biological names by different authors, for example, spermoderm and perisperm (Winton and Winton 1932), seed coat or testa (Percival 1921) and inner integuments (Helbaek 1950, 1958). In order to avoid confusion, the terms spermoderm and perisperm have been used throughout this paper specifically to describe the inner layers of the bran. The outer layers of the bran, that is, the longitudinal and transverse cells (often called cross cells) of the pericarp, are not present on the majority of fragments. This appears to be a common occurrence since the absence of these layers has been recorded in material recovered from other archaeological sites (Camilla Dickson pers. comm.; Hall *et al* 1983). It is interesting to note however, that modern faecal material tends to retain the transverse cell layer structure (Camilla Dickson pers. comm.; Schel *et al* 1980). The structure of these transverse cells on carbonised grains has been used to distinguish between the cereal types by other authors (Korber-Grohne 1981; Korber-Grohne and Piening 1980), however, only occasionally can the degraded remains of these cells be observed in the Lindow material (see Fig. 46a). For this reason it has been necessary to use the number of cell layers in the surviving bran fragments and their relative orientation in order to identify the cereal species.

Many chaff fragments have also survived although often in a much degraded state. The identification of these can be used to complement the identifications made on the basis of the bran layers.

Triticum/Secale species (wheat/rye)

Both *Secale* (rye) and *Triticum* (wheat) species have a spermoderm which is composed of two layers of long narrow cells with thin walls lacking pits. These layers are arranged such that the longitudinal axis of the cells in one layer all lie in the same direction. A characteristic chequer board effect can be seen when observed in surface view since the two layers run at approximately right angles to each other (see Fig. 46b). Bran fragments showing this characteristic arrangement were therefore put into the *Triticum/Secale* category.

Where fragments of bran occurred with the transverse cells still intact, an attempt was made at their identification by using the criteria given by Korber-Grohne and Piening (1980) together with observations taken from modern reference material. A number of transverse cells appear to show end walls that have a certain amount of thickening and no pits. The majority of cells had a length that varied from

Species	Identified components	Quantity
Sphagnum spp.	leaves and stems	XX
Chenopodium album.*	seed fragments	X
Chenopodium/Atriplex type.	small seed fragments	X
Umbelliferae indet.*	seed fragment	X
Polygonum lapathifolium.$	seed fragment	X
Polygonum convolvulus.	seed fragment	X
Calluna vulgaris.*	leaf	X
Rumex spp.*	small seed fragments	X
Galeopsis type.	seed fragments	X
Bromus sp.	bran fragments	XXX
Triticum dicoccum.$	glume bases	X
Triticum spelta.$	glume bases	X
Triticum indet.$	glume bases, rachis fragments	XX
Triticum/Secale indet.	bran fragments	XXXX
Hordeum sp.$	glumes, paleas, rachillas, lemmas	XXX
Hordeum sp.	bran fragments	XX
Avena sp.	bran fragments	XX
Avena/Hordeum indet.	bran fragments	X
Cereal indet.	glume, paleas, lemma fragents	XXXX
Small Animal Hairs		XX
Fungi	Hyphae, spores	X
Fine sand		X
Carbonised Fragments		X

Table 12

Fig. 46   a) Bran of Triticum/Secale, showing degraded transverse cells with underlying spermoderm layer (× 100).
b) Bran of Triticum/Secale, showing the chequer-board arrangement produced by the layers of the spermoderm (× 250).
c) Bran of barley, showing cellular arrangement of the spermoderm and perisperm layers as seen by focusing through degraded outer layers (× 400). d) Epidermal cells of the light chaff fragment, cf. Hordeum (barley) (× 250). e) Spermoderm and perisperm layers of Bromus (Brome grass) as seen through degraded outer layers (× 400). f) Cellular arrangement of sphagnum leaf (× 250). g) and h) Spermoderm layers of Triticum/Secale showing fungal hyphae (indicated by arrows) that have grown around the no longer visible transverse cells (× 400). i) Seed coat of Galeopsis type (× 250).

25 to 100 microns which was, on average, 2–3 times the breadth. In some places dark patches of cytoplasm could be seen concentrated towards the ends of the cells. These three characteristics, that is, thickened end walls, short broad cells and dark cytoplasm towards the cell ends can all be observed on modern grains of *Secale cereale* (cultivated rye). For several reasons, at this stage, however, it is felt that these criteria for the identification of rye should be treated with caution.

(a) The use of size criteria in order to distinguish between the cells of different cereals can be misleading. If transverse cells are observed at varying distances from the apices of the grains, it can be seen that as the apex is approached, the cells of most cereals become shorter, fatter and patterns that can be seen over the rest of the surface of the grain tend to break up. Because the bran is represented only by small fragments, it is impossible to determine from which part of the grain they came, and therefore difficult to assess whether the pattern and shape of the cells represents the 'typical' arrangement for any one species of cereal. One could also argue that the smaller, more thickened cells towards the apical ends of grains would be less likely to be degraded by either cereal processing, or by decay and digestion, and thus be over-represented in the final assemblage. Without further work on a wide variety of modern material, the use of the cell size criteria, particularly on small fragments of cereal bran, would seem to be unreliable.

(b) If the thickened and unpitted end walls of the cells are to be used as criteria for the identification of rye, then it must be remembered that *Triticum spelta* (spelt wheat), can also exhibit end walls that appear to be unpitted and thckened although they are neither as obvious nor as numerous as those in rye. Spelt, together with other species of wheat also shows a tendency for adjacent rows of cells to come adrift from each other. When this occurs the end walls of cells become separated. As with the thickening of cell walls seen in spelt wheat this can, in poorly preserved material, give the impression of the thickened cell wall characteristic of rye.

(c) Modern specimens of rye show a marked tendency for dark coloured cytoplasm to congregate towards the ends of the cells. Although this is a common feature in rye it also occurs on other species of the *Gramineae* (grasses) and occasionally on wheat species. Since it is impossible to gain an impression of the variation of this phenomenon across the surface of the grain, because of the small size of the fragments, this too would seem to be an unreliable criterion to use.

For the above reasons, and because the cellular characteristics of the transverse cells are often seen to vary more across the surface of one grain than between grains of different species, it would be premature positively to identify rye as a component on the basis of such small bran fragments.

Numerous fragments of chaff were also recovered from the gut. Of these, some of the more dense items have been positively identified as wheat chaff. Several rachis internodes were recovered but were in a state that did not allow any more detailed identification than that of *Triticum* indet. (wheat). Of the glume bases of wheat recovered two were identified as *Triticum spelta* (spelt wheat) and several others were identified as *Triticum dicoccum* (emmer wheat). This was done on the basis of the venation patterns on the glumes as outlined by Gordon Hillman (p. 108).

In conclusion, there is a large quantity of the bran of rye and/or wheat. The evidence from the transverse cells only tentatively suggests the presence of rye but the chaff fragments show that both emmer and spelt wheats were present. Only with further work on a wide variety of modern material can the presence of rye be conclusively demonstrated.

Hordeum species (barley)

The longitudinal and transverse cells making up the *Hordeum* (barley) pericarp have not been preserved in any of the samples so far studied. Only the inner part of the bran coat has survived. This is composed of two layers, an outer layer – the spermoderm, and an inner layer – the perisperm (Winton and Winton 1932). Over most parts of the grain surface both layers consist of approximately rectangular cells which have very thin non-pitted cell walls. The cells in the spermoderm layer can, however, in places become shortened in length (see Fig. 46c). The longitudinal axes of the cells in any one layer all lie in a similar direction, except in the apical region. The cells in the two adjacent layers can be seen to run parallel to each other and therefore differ substantially from the spermoderm layers of wheat or rye where the cells in the two layers run perpendicular to each other. Fragments of bran that had obviously two layers of cells running parallel to each other and possessing the characteristics outlined above were classified as barley. Some fragments of bran were particularly pale in colour and highly degraded although still showing traces of two cellular layers. Their delicate structure and lack of pigmentation has been noted in some of the modern reference material so far examined. Further work is needed in order that firm identifications of such fragments can be made. Those fragments that were particularly degraded such that only one layer of cells was clearly visible but were not altogether typical of *Avena* (see below) were included in the *Hordeum/Avena* indet. (barley/oat) category. It is hoped that this category may be resolved further as work progresses.

There were a large number of fragments of light chaff recovered from the gut. Many of these were suspected of being fragments of barley lemma and palea mainly because of the way in which they had broken into thin slivers. The cell patterns on the epidermis of this light chaff were also studied (see Fig. 46d). These resembled the cell patterns on the paleas of modern hulled barley more closely than any seen on modern wheat chaff. However, a full range of modern material has not yet been studied in detail. Certain items identified by Gordon Hillman (pp. 107–8), do however, confirm that at least some proportion of this chaff is that of barley. These include, two barley glume bases, numerous rachillas (both hairy and non-hairy type), three lodicules and possible basal parts of paleas with their characteristic twist towards the base. The fact that the lighter elements of chaff (lemmas and paleas in particular) have been incorporated into the meal would imply that the barley was a hulled variety. The lemmas and paleas of naked barley are easily separated from the grain and therefore tend not to be represented in meals made from it. Hulled barley lemmas and paleas, on the other hand, adhere strongly to the grain with fragments still remaining in position even after the dehusking process. As a result, these are often carried forward into the meal itself. There are no chaff fragments that enabled the distinction between 2 row or 6 row barley to be made. The wide variety of chaff components complement the barley bran, which may well be under-represented by virtue of its lighter construction and suggests that a substantial proportion of the meal may have been made up of a hulled barley.

Avena species (oats)

The bran coat of oats is composed of an outer layer of longitudinal cells with a layer of parenchyma internal to this (Winton and Winton 1932). There are no transverse cells as such but the spermoderm and aleurone layers can both be discerned in modern material. It would appear that only the spermoderm layer has survived in the Lindow Man's gut. This layer is easily overlooked during sorting since it is colourless and almost translucent with a tendency to roll up or stick to other items. Where preservation allows it can be distinguished from barley since the spermoderm is only one layer thick and its regular rows of oblique cells make up a distinctive herring bone pattern. Care, however, must be taken since this pattern can disintegrate over small areas of the *Avena* (oat) grain, particularly towards the hilum and the apices. Where there was any doubt the fragments have been included in the *Hordeum/Avena* indet. (barley/oats) category.

No identifiable remains of oat chaff have been recovered as yet. It therefore remains impossible to say whether these fragments of bran represent one of the domesticated species (*Avena strigosa* or *Avena sativa*) or one of the wild species (*Avena fatua* or *Avena sterilis s.1.*).

Bromus species (brome grass)

Numerous fragments of the bran coat of brome grass were recovered. In these, the outer cellular layers have been lost leaving only the spermoderm and the perisperm layers available for study. Both layers are made up of thin and unpitted long narrow cells with acute interlocking ends. Over substantial areas of the grain, the longitudinal axes of the cells in the two layers run parallel to, or at a shallow angle to, each other (see Fig. 46e). This situation alters towards the distal apex where the spermoderm layer changes orientation such that rows of cells are seen to radiate outwards from the end of the hilum. Brome grass bran would seem to be more strongly pigmented than most of the other cereals (although other species of wild grasses also exhibit this property) and can therefore be picked out from rye/wheat bran on this basis with experience. Pieces of bran showing the characteristic pigmentation with the above orientation of the cells were therefore classified as *Bromus spp.* (brome grass). It is not possible on the structure of the bran alone to decide which species of *Bromus* these fragments represent.

Seed and other Plant Remains

The seed fragments recovered consisted of very small pieces of the seed coat of various species; identification based on the overall morphology was therefore impossible. Preliminary identifications were made on the basis of the thickness, texture and surface sculpturing of the seed coat. Further work in this area may help to resolve the broad identification groupings further.

The sphagnum leaves were identified on the basis of the cell patterns of the leaves (see Fig. 46f). It is hoped that this identification can be taken below the level of genus and they have been made available to Dr Scaife at the Institute of Archaeology to this end.

Small Animal Hairs

Numerous small animal hairs have been recovered from all of the samples so far observed. These have been studied by Dr Ann Priston at the Police Forensic laboratory and have been identified as fine mammalian body hair. Unfortunately a more specific identification cannot be made because of the absence of any of the more diagnostic guard hairs that are also to be found in the coats of mammals.

Fungi

Fungal hyphae were noted on several fragments of wheat/rye bran. In some cases (see Figs 46g & h) the hyphae seem to have traced the outlines of the transverse cells which have since disappeared. Other types of hyphae that can be seen on the surface of some of the bran fragments resemble the hyphae of *Dematiaceae* as photographed by Helbaek (1958).

Dark spots have also been noted on some of the wheat glumes that have been recovered. These resemble the spores of *Ustilago hordei* as recorded by Helbaek (1958). These are only preliminary identifications and it is hoped to make positive identifications at a later stage.

Carbonised fragments

These items were studied under the Scanning Electron Microscope and would appear to represent carbonised food debris into which small fragments of chaff have become incorporated. At this point it is not possible to say which species of cereal the chaff represents.

Discussion

In attempting to assess the composition of the last meal of Lindow Man there are two points at which a bias can be introduced into the final results thus distorting our interpretation of its original composition. Firstly, the composition of the samples that eventually arrive in the laboratory for analysis represent only those constituents that have survived

the processes of digestion and some 2,000 years of post depositional decay. Therefore it can be expected that components such as cereal chaff and bran, will be better represented than more easily digestible material. Indeed one only has to look at modern faecal material after a meal of wholemeal bread to be impressed by the resilience of cereal fibre to the action of the human gut. Few traces, however, would be expected to remain of meat or dairy produce if these had also been present in the original meal. The second bias is brought about by the limitations of the identification techniques that can be applied. Readily digestible plant material such as certain root crops or tree nuts (where the shell is not incorporated), would be expected to leave only slight traces after possible grinding, cooking, mastication and digestion. Only with the close study of more modern comparative material, focusing on the identification of such slight remains using, for example, starch grain or plant fibre analysis, will such plant foods start to appear in the published records of the Iron Age menu.

Bearing in mind the bias towards cereals in the gut contents it still seems probable that this component made up the most substantial part of this Iron Age meal. This cereal component is represented mainly by wheat and/or rye bran and barley chaff. The evidence for wheat is supported by chaff fragments of both emmer and spelt whereas the evidence for the presence of rye, based solely on the transverse cells, at this stage remains only tentative. The relative abundance of barley chaff to that of barley bran is probably a function of their different survival properties. It may at first seem strange that so much chaff has been incorporated in the meal, however, this can be readily explained. Even when rigorously processed, for example by 'pearling', substantial quantities of lemma and palea from hulled varieties of barley are still to be found adhering to the grain. These can readily be consumed without severely detracting from the quality of the meal. Smaller but not insignificant amounts of brome grass and oats were also recovered along with smaller amounts of mainly segetal type weed seeds (weeds of cultivation). The most likely explanation for these components is that they have passed through the crop processing sequence along with the cereals having been initially harvested from fields in which they were growing as weeds of the main crop. Such contaminants are tolerated by most agricultural societies using traditional techniques unless they are found to detract from the overall palatability. It would therefore not be surprising to find such contaminants in the primary product of the Iron Age crop processing sequence. The small size of these weed seed fragments appears to support the above supposition since they seem to have been ground into pieces similar in size to that of the cereal bran. This would suggest that they had been processed along with the cereals rather than being added to the meal as a separate item, as for example a condiment might be. The number of Avena (oat) bran fragments is so small that it seems unlikely that they represent part of a crop grown in its own right. They are most likely to represent members of one of the wild type oat species which, along with brome grass, was possibly a tolerated if not encouraged contaminant of the cereal crops. Brome grass in particular is often to be found associated with the primary product of crops such as spelt wheat recovered in a carbonised form from archaeological sites (e.g. from Romano-British Droitwich, Vaughan 1982). None of the constituents of the meal give any indication of the season in which Lindow Man died. Both the cereals and associated weed seeds can readily be stored for long periods of time and it is therefore conceivable that they could have been consumed at any time during the year.

The above components of the meal were all recovered in the form of very small fragments with none being greater than 3 square millimeters, thus suggesting that cereals had been thoroughly ground prior to consumption. This would rule out the possibility that the cereals had been consumed as whole grains in some type of stew or soup, and would imply that they had been made into a bread (see Hillman, pp. 109–10).

A number of small animal hairs were recovered. In the absence of other evidence such as bone or sinew fragments it is not possible to say whether or not these represent the remains of some type of meat that had been a part of the original meal. It would seem equally plausible that they could represent some type of contamination of either grain as it was being held in storage or during food preparation. Further investigation focusing on the identification of meat fibres (possibly using staining techniques) may throw more light on these aspects of the meal.

So far the discussion has concentrated on aspects of the last meal in isolation, but how far can this be taken as being typical of the Iron Age diet in Cheshire? A single individual can, at best, be expected to reveal evidence of perhaps one or two meals. Such a small sample can in no way be considered to be representative of the Iron Age diet as a whole. The circumstances surrounding the killing itself give a strong indication that it was either a ritual event or an execution. As such, the last meal may have had a special significance and could actually have been part of the ritual. If this was indeed the case the meal may well have had a composition to match its ritual status. Likewise, if it had been an execution, the meal may have represented only the poorest type of fare, fit only for a condemned prisoner's last meal. The status of the individual could also have a bearing on the composition of the meal, with an individual of high status being unlikely to receive the same type of diet as the lower status individual. Having said all this however, there is nothing regarding the composition of this meal that would suggest that it was of an extraordinary nature. It would appear to represent only a rough bread that would not be considered an unusual meal in any twentieth century agricultural society using traditional agricultural techniques, bearing in mind that the weed seed component would not necessarily be the same. The cereals, barley, spelt and emmer wheats are all known from the archaeological record in Iron Age Britain, so it is not surprising that they are represented in the meal of Lindow Man. Rye, on the other hand, is not common in the British Isles until the post Roman period although Bronze Age finds of charred grains have been reported from Oxfordshire (Jones 1978). If rye is confirmed as a component of the meal it will therefore be of considerable interest.

In terms of identifying past crop husbandary and processing practices this type of essentially waterlogged material should have vast potential. The Lindow material, however, with its low frequency of weed seeds makes ecological reconstructions of the field environment almost impossible. Those weed seeds that are represented are all, with the possible exception of the Umbellifer, ubiquitous weeds of cultivation. As the identification of these weed seeds progresses and more samples are analysed it may prove possible to say more about these aspects of Iron Age life in Cheshire.

A number of Sphagnum (sphagnum moss) leaves were also recovered from the gut. Contamination from the surrounding peat as the corpse was being dissected would appear to be the most obvious explanation. However, in some cases these leaves could be seen embedded in the actual compressed matrix of the gut contents. This would imply that they had not been modern contaminations. James Bourke (pers. comm. 1985) suggests that the transverse laceration on the right side of the neck is such that damage to the oesophagus is very unlikely. This is therefore an improbable origin of contamination. The fracture of his cervical spine has collapsed the anterior and posterior pharangeal walls, thus making *post mortem* contamination via the mouth to the stomach another highly improbable option. It is therefore considered that these leaves entered the gut through the mouth while the man was still alive. As a contaminant in the drinking water would be one strong possibility, or perhaps by being incorporated into the food in some manner. The latter of these two possibilities may not at first sight seem probable but there are numerous ethnographic examples of the use of sphagnum and other mosses in domestic contexts from Northern Europe (Hillman pers. comm. 1985). If a more specific identification can be made for this moss then it may prove possible to comment on the uses to which it may have been put and on the types of environment from which it could have originated. The single leaf of *Calluna vulgaris* (heather) could well have had a similar type of origin to that of the sphagnum moss. Heather has often been used for thatch and for other purposes around habitation sites in Northern Europe.

Comparisons with other Bog Bodies

Three other bog bodies recovered since the 1940s have undergone full examinations of their gut contents. These are, the corpse from Borremose (Brandt 1950), Tollund man (Helbaek 1950) and Grauballe man (Helbaek 1958), all of which were recovered from Denmark in circumstances not unlike those surrounding the Lindow Man. They had all been preserved by being buried in the peat of raised bogs and have all been dated by C14 to between 2000 BP to 2700 BP (Tauber 1979), that is, in general terms, to the pre-Roman Iron Age. All of the corpses show obvious signs of violence, resulting in death. Although the evidence is circumstantial it has been suggested that these similarities are more than just coincidence and that they may represent part of similar rituals and/or executions associated with the bogs. Bearing in mind these points and their possible implications for the composition of the last meal (see above) these corpses, as evidence of past subsistence, still represent windows through which we can observe aspects of the Iron Age diet. For this reason it is felt that a brief discussion and comparison of the gut contents from the various corpses will prove interesting.

It is unfortunate that the Lindow body had been truncated by the peat cutting machine thus losing the lower intestines to scientific study, since the Danish bodies show that the volume of material held in the lower intestine could be up to 20 fold greater than that recovered from the upper intestines and stomach. The samples from the upper small intestine and stomach of the Lindow corpse are, however, in a similar state of preservation to those of the Danish bodies.

The overall composition of the Danish gut contents varies considerably from that of Lindow Man, the latter having a much lower diversity of plant remains represented. The Grauballe man, for example, produced a species list containing over 60 species of plants from his gut, and the corpse from Borremose contained only wild weed species with no contribution at all being made by cereals. Apart from the wide diversity of plant remains, (weed seeds in particular) the Danish material appears to have contained particularly high numbers of seeds of certain plant species, namely *Chenopodium album* (Fat Hen), various *Polygonum* (Dock family) species and certain oil seeds. This has led to the assumption that certain elements of these meals had been collected from the wild. There is, however, no evidence that this was the case in the Lindow material. Other aspects of the Danish meals also differ widely from the Lindow material. The amount of dense chaff included in the meals of Grauballe and Tollund men was higher than that of Lindow Man, with one whole spikelet of spelt wheat being recovered from the Grauballe gut. Gordon Hillman (1981) has suggested on the basis of their composition, that these meals could well represent cleanings from sieving processes carried out in the latter stages of crop processing. Such cleanings would be expected to contain large numbers of weed seeds with some of the more dense chaff fragments and cereal tail grains. They would not normally be consumed by humans except perhaps by the very poor or by the general population in times of famine. With the Lindow Man however, there is nothing to suggest that his last meal was anything other than a meal made from the finely ground primary product of the crop processing sequence. The average size of the plant fragments from the Danish material is also much larger than those recovered from the Lindow material, with whole seeds regularly being recovered. This would suggest that they were less finely ground and probably consumed more as a thin soup (Helbaek 1958) than as the bread postulated for the Lindow meal.

It would seem unrealistic to assume on the basis of three meals that the average Danish fare in the Iron Age was on the whole more coarse and contained more plant species collected from the wild than did the usual Lindow meal. The technologies and the crops available to both societies would have been approximately the same, remembering that hulled barley, spelt wheat and emmer wheat are well represented in the archaeological record from Iron Age Northern Europe. These differences may well, therefore, represent different points in the spectrum of meals making up the Iron Age diet. Whether these differences could have been produced as a result of choice or by the dictates of season and famine would at this point be impossible to say. Alternatively, the differing composition of the meals could be tied up with ritual aspects of a last meal or the differing status of the individual. It should, however, be stressed that the composition of the Lindow meal at least, shows no signs of having been in any way extraordinary. There is therefore no evidence to suggest that it could have had any particular ritual significance.

Finally, it is interesting to note that certain of the minor components of the meals have been recovered from more than one of the corpses. Of the four corpses, sphagnum moss has been recovered from three of the meals, charcoal fragments from at least two, small animal hairs from three and fine sand particles have been noted from at least three of the four meals. These correlations are important when trying to reconstruct the events by which they came to be incorporated into the meals. It seems likely that these events were neither accidental nor isolated incidents but part of some activity that was regularly being carried out on Iron Age sites in Northern Europe. It may therefore prove possible to reconstruct, given adequate ethnographic examples, the types of activities that could have given rise to such assemblages.

Future Research

It is hoped that further work will be possible into identification criteria that can reliably be used to resolve certain groups represented in the species list above. In particular, work on the *Triticum/Secale* (wheat/rye) group, and on certain weed species may help to answer outstanding questions about Iron Age diet, crop husbandry, and the crop field environments.

With the aid of the Department of Nutrition at Queen Elizabeth College, University of London, it is hoped to conduct experiments on the digestion of bran through the human gut. This may help to explain why the transverse cell layers of the cereals are not represented in either the Lindow material or other archaeological material. At the moment it is not known whether this has occurred as a result of digestion, decay or some process to which the cereals were subjected prior to consumption.

Further experimental work into Iron Age food preparation and cooking techniques would also prove interesting since this, together with the ethnographic records of recent agricultural societies using traditional cooking methods, could help in the interpretation of the practices used in Iron Age Britain. It is hoped that it will be possible to take up the offer of facilities and expertise at Butser Iron Age Farm, Hampshire.

27 Pollen in Human Palaeofaeces; and a Preliminary Investigation of the Stomach and Gut Contents of Lindow Man

Robert G. Scaife

Introduction to Previous Work on Human Gut Contents and Coprolites

There are now numerous data available illustrating the value of plant macroscopic and microfossil analyses of palaeofaeces (coprolite studies). This short resumé seeks to provide a review of the literature relating to those pollen and microscopic studies which have largely been carried out during the last two decades and to present the initial findings of the palynological investigation of the stomach and intestinal contents of Lindow Man. Plant macrofossil studies have been similarly reviewed by Hillman (pp. 99ff.).

Such studies of gut contents and coprolites have largely come from the United States where researchers have in some cases studied very large numbers of well-preserved coprolites from the southern United States, Mexico and occasionally from sites in South America. By virtue of the excellent preservation conditions afforded by the arid climate of these regions, faeces of human and animal origin are frequently well-preserved in desiccated but complete and morphologically little-changed state. In contrast, such studies are rare in Europe, due to the more humid climatic regime and resultant increased rate of biological and physical decomposition. The value of studying the internal contents of animals has also recieved attention as shown for example by those of late-Pleistocene mammoths (Krausel 1922; Farrand 1961), Shasta ground sloth (Martin *et al* 1961) and even plant remains from dinosaurs (Ostrom 1964) and Tertiary mammals such as Rhinoceros (Voorhies and Thomasson 1979). Coprolites of animals are, however, relatively frequent on archaeological sites (e.g. Wilson 1979). These are usually of animal origin and particularly of carnivorous animals such as dogs (Dimbleby 1965; Scaife in press), where preservation of faeces in their original morphological form has been aided by their high mineral (largely fragmented bone and calcium phos-

phate cement) content. These animal gut and faecal remains have been found to contain pollen, phytolith and seed remains which provide clues to their feeding habits. Human faeces from Europe have rarely been preserved in their original form although there are a number of notable exceptions. These have occurred in the middle Pleistocene–early Palaeolithic deposits at the sites of Terra Amata, Nice, France (Trevor-Deutsch and Bryant 1978), Lazaret, France (Callan 1969). A more recent and complete human stool has also been found in the excavation of Anglo-Scandinavian York (Jones 1983). Human faecal material has, however, been recognised in numerous – especially urban – archaeological contexts usually in its amorphous degraded form in cesspits, latrines and in areas where material emptied from these have been dumped in stream channels, ditches and on waste ground (Scaife 1979, 1982; Greig 1981, 1982; Hall *et al* 1983; Krzwinski 1979; Krzwinski *et al* 1983; Knights *et al* 1983).

The pioneer work in the field of coprolite studies comes from the United States where a series of standardised methods have been used in the recognition and analysis of prehistoric coprolites (Callen 1969; Heizer 1969; Heizer and Napton 1969). Vaughan Bryant Jr is notable in this respect and he has reviewed the role of coprolite analysis in archaeology (Bryant 1974; Bryant and Williams-Dean 1975). Such studies have been able to elucidate the food preparation techniques and dietary preferences of the aboriginal populations. It has also been possible to study aspects of seasonality of occupation of encampments where coprolites have been found and in some cases the health of individuals concerned from the analysis of intestinal parasite ova.

The study of prehistoric human coprolites has a history back to the work of Harshenberger (1896) who was perhaps the first person to realise the value of human coprolites to the understanding of such points noted above. Subsequently, Young's (1910) study of Salts and Mammoth Caves in Kentucky examined dietary aspects. Lord and Harrington (1929 in Bryant 1974) worked on Lovelock Cave, Nevada. Jones (1936) established the discipline providing further data on Lovelock Cave, and Newt Kash Hollow Shelter in Kentucky. The numerous analyses of Callan (1963; 1967; Callan and Cameron 1960; Callan and Martin 1969) are of great importance since it was he who devised the analytical techniques for the study of palaeofaeces through reconstitution techniques using trisodium phosphate (Callan 1960; 1967) rather than simple crushing of the coprolites thus destroying the plant cellular material. In comparison to palynological studies of human coprolites, macrofossil analyses have more frequently been carried out. Hillman (pp. 99ff.) has produced a detailed review of plant macrofossil data and their value to understanding aspects of prehistoric diet. Reference is made here, therefore, only to aspects of palynological investigation.

Pre-Holocene Human Coprolites

The earliest known or suspected human coprolites are, however, of *Australopithiecus (A. africanus)* origin from Olduvai Gorge, East Africa and dated at *c.* 1 million years (Napton in Leakey 1971). Two southern French sites have also yielded a substantial number (444, of which 40 were selected for analysis) of early Pleistocene (*c.* 4000bp), possibly human, coprolites although poor preservation and mineral replacement has caused some doubt as to their authenticity. These come from Lazaret (Callan 1969; Lumley 1969) and Terra Amata, Nice (Lumley 1966; Trevor-Deutsch and Bryant 1978). At the latter site, however, quantities of shell, charcoal, seeds and a single fish jaw were recovered in the analysis, thus perhaps giving some of the earliest evidence of prehistoric diet.

Pollen Studies

As long ago as 1938, Laudermilk and Munz had recognised the existence of pollen in non-human coprolites and a number of plant macrofossils and microfossils have been recovered from the gut regions and fossil coprolites of prehistoric creatures (*op cit*). Such studies have continued with a number of pollen analytical studies on a variety of faunal excrements such as for example canine (Dimbleby 1968; Scaife in press). It is only since 1964 with the work of Martin and Sharrock that pollen and microfossil investigations of human palaeofaeces have

been undertaken. A sample of 54 coprolites obtained from rocky alcoves in the Glen Canyon region of Utah, USA was analysed. Here Martin and Sharrock (1964) obtained evidence of the diet of the Pueblo Indians as comprising *Cleome, Zea, Cucurbita* and *Opuntia* flowers and other less frequent cultural pollen types. This study illustrated the value of pollen analytical investigation of coprolites to ethnobotany and ecology. Subsequently, a substantial number of such studies have been made and include notably the works of Bryant on South West Texas (Bryant 1969, 1975a; Bryant and Lasen 1968) and Mammoth Cave, Kentucky (Bryant 1974b); Coahuila, Mexico (Bryant 1975a); Napton and Kelso (1969) at Lovelock Cave and Riskind (1970) from Parida Cave, Texas. At Antelope House Cave (Williams-Dean and Bryant 1975), 46 coprolites were found to contain some 12 specific economic or perhaps ceremonial plant taxa identified from their pollen and/or macro-fossils. These were notably: *Cleome, Populus, Opuntia, Zea, Cucurbita* and *Typha latifolia*. As in a number of such studies, an assessment of seasonality, in this case, spring and summer, was made possible by the relatively high frequencies of insect pollinated types. In a relatively large sample such as this, Williams-Dean and Bryant were able to show that a range of 'background' pollen types (largely arboreal taxa) may be present from natural incorporation into food (at source or during preparation) or drinking water. This point is returned to in the discussion of the data obtained from the gut contents of Lindow Man. Coprolites (17) from Mammoth Cave, Kentucky were analysed (Bryant 1974b), the results of which clearly showed the presence of flowers which were used in food or drink. This evidence again comes from the high pollen percentages of zoophilous (entomophilous) taxa which include *Acorus*, Liguliflorae, and Liliaceae. Additionally, their presence enabled the season of occupation to be ascertained. Schoenwetter (1974) has similarly analysed sub-fossil palaeofaeces from Salts Cave, Kentucky, and illustrated the prehistoric use of flowers in the diet from high pollen percentages of *Acorus*. These studies have been based on the often abundant coprolites recovered from caves and rock shelters in these arid regions. Only in exceptional cases of long continued occupation and in a good preservational environment has it been possible to discuss dietary changes through time. Bryant (1974) in his analysis of site 41 VV 162, a large rock shelter 2 miles north-west of the mouth of the Pecos River (a small canyon of the Rio Grande) was able to study an assemblage of 43 coprolites spanning 800BC–AD500 where there was evidence of consumption of *Yucca, Agave, Dasylirion tenaxanum* (Sotol), *Opuntia, Persimmon* and *Prosopis* (Mesquite) flowers (Bryant 1974, 412–416). Interestingly, in his work on Hinds Cave, Texas, on a selected sample of 100 human coprolites from a total of 2000 (dated at *c.* 5600–5700bp) Bryant (1975b), concluded that the foods were (i) low in fats, (ii) high in bulk, (iii) nutritious, (iv) high in calories, (v) ample vitamin content, (vi) with a basic diet low in sugars – a healthy diet? All of the above studies are, however, related to a middle Holocene or later date and illustrate that palynological analysis of human coprolites can yield information on a variety of aspects of diet, seasonality of site occupation and of general palaeo-environmental conditions.

From the above discussion, therefore, it can be seen that whilst seed and vegetative crops both wild and cultivated would undoubtedly have formed an important dietary element, if consideration is given to overall diet it is possible that the use of the floral elements of plants will also have played an important role in both liquid and solid foods. The ingested pollen is subsequently and readily passed through the human digestive system with little alteration. Any pollen contained within the stomach and intestines may derive from one or more of the following sources:

(i) Direct Ingestion of Floral Parts

Ingestion of the floral parts of plants for, or in preparation of, food drinks or medicinal herbal remedies (Bryant 1974a: 208, 1974b: 415; Williams-Dean and Bryant 1975; Schoenwetter 1974). Archaeological evidence for prehistoric drinks is understandably almost unknown, but the mead postulated from residues in a Beaker by Dickson (1978) indicates the possible use of the wild flora. Food or medicinal sources of pollen are demonstrated by the use of mallow (*Malva*) flowers as laxatives which has resulted in the finding of large quantities of its pollen in a number of urban cesspits and latrines. Such usage of the floral parts including anthers has been noted in studies of human coprolites by their much higher percentages of total pollen than are normally encountered in 'natural' pollen rain accumulations.

(ii) Secondary Ingestion of Pollen in Food

Pollen associated with, and derived from, those seed crops which have been harvested may also be represented. This has been illustrated by Bryant (1974a: 207). Due to their long flowering cycle, *Chenopodium* and *Amaranthus* pollen may be present at the same time as ripening seeds. Gathering of these plants for their seeds might in such cases also incorporate a

substantial quantity of anthers. Pollen may also adhere to or become trapped in the seed and vegetative structures of plants until the period of seed maturation and harvesting. Such pollen may become incorporated into foodstuffs especially in the case of cereal crops where Williams-Dean and Bryant (1975) have shown that pollen of *Zea* adheres to the 'feathers' and is liberated during crop processing to become incorporated into the final crop products. Robinson and Hubbard (1977) have similarly shown that this occurs in European cereal crops and a number of experiments (Hall *et al* 1983; Krzwinski *et al* 1983) have proven this. This is now generally recognised as the primary cause of the high frequencies of cereal pollen recovered from analyses of a number of urban archaeological contexts (cess-pits, latrines and sewers) where amorphous faecal material occurs (Greig 1981, 1982; Scaife 1982; Hall *et al* 1983; Knights *et al* 1983; Krzwinski *et al* 1983). This factor is also fundamental to the interpretation of the large quantities of cereal pollen recovered from the stomach contents of Lindow Man.

(iii) Indirect Ingestion: The Background Component

Pollen analysis of human and animal coprolite samples often shows a regional background component (Martin and Sharrock 1964; Bryant 1974a, 1974b, 1975; Williams-Dean 1975) and this is the case with Lindow Man (see below). This component is frequently largely comprised of pollen of anemophilous (especially arboreal) taxa which may become incorporated into either food or drinking water. It is perhaps also for this latter reason that small quantities of aquatic and mire plants have been noticed in the stomach contents of the Danish bog folk and of Lindow Man.

The Palynological Analysis of the Stomach and Intestinal Contents of Lindow Man

The preservation of the Lindow Bog body in anaeorobic and acid ombrogenous peats was seen as a potential source of prehistoric stomach and intestinal contents which could possibly elucidate some aspects of prehistoric diet. This would naturally be representative of only a small number of meals consumed prior to death.

Pollen Analytical Procedure

Pollen analysis has been carried out on five samples obtained from the fundus and antrum of the stomach and from the small intestine of Lindow Man. The data presented here are the preliminary results and it is expected that further samples will be prepared and higher pollen sums counted. An initial investigation of the internal organic matter from the small intestine revealed the presence of a number of microfossil components. These comprised intestinal parasite ova of *Trichuris* sp. (whip worm) and *Ascaris* (roundworm) and have been described by Jones (pp. 136ff.); pollen; fungal spores; plant cellulose debris and inorganic components of plant opaline phytoliths, charcoal specks and small particles of mineral (non-biogenic silica). All of this material was set in a fine groundmass of organic residue which was perhaps starch.

A fuller and statistical count of pollen contained in four samples from different parts of the stomach and small intestine which remained has also been made. The pollen contained in samples of 0.5–1 ml of matter was concentrated using standard techniques. These included deflocculation using 10% NaOH and a short (30 second) treatment using Erdtman's acetolysis technique. The latter was found necessary to remove the starchy groundmass noted above. Pollen counts of 100–150 grains were made. The results of the initial investigation are presented (Table 13) and data from the quantatitive counts are given in Table 14.

The Cereal Pollen

Inspection of Table 13 clearly shows that pollen of cereal type is the dominant taxon of the pollen spectra of all samples analysed. The remarkably high percentages can undoubtedly be correlated with the predominance of cereal chaff and bran debris also recovered from the gut and intestinal tracts (see Hillman and Holden, pp. 99ff., 116ff.). Since it is the ripe cereals which are gathered, some mechanism has to be responsible for those cereal pollen grains remaining after dehiscence. A plausible mechanism has been described by Robinson and Hubbard (1977) where liberated pollen becomes trapped into the cereal inflorescences (Fig. 47). This process is now

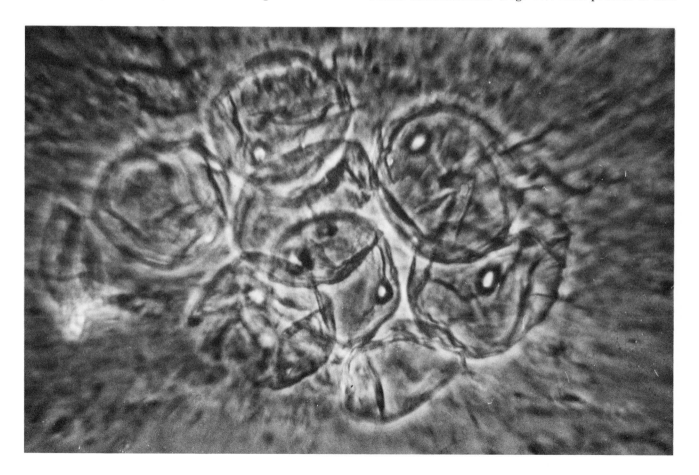

Fig. 47   Cereal pollen trapped in husk, from small intestine.

widely accepted and evidenced in the analyses of palaeo-coprolites and cess materials (Greig 1981, 1982; Scaife 1982). The cereal pollen grains (Fig. 48) were identified by their diagnostically coarse, columellate exine structure and by large pore and annulus. A sample of 214 grains was measured for maximum diameter. This showed that the overall size range of pollen grains of this character was from 32–85 µ but exhibiting a normal distribution with the modal class in the range 45–54 µ (51% of total). Small frequencies of 'wild' Gramineae pollen negated more detailed statistical comparison. However, of those grains recorded (13) the majority were of size smaller than 35 µ having also thinner exine, less distinct columellae and smaller pores and annuli. It is clear that the cereal pollen recorded is substantially greater in size and markedly distinct. At the present time, attempts are being made to identify these cereals to generic level in order to make comparisons with the cereal macrofossil remains identified (Hillman and Holden, pp. 99ff., 116ff.). It is also likely that the cereal spikelets would act as pollen traps or receptacles for pollen of arable weeds growing nearby and pollen of regional or even extra-regional sources (especially anemophilous types). Thus, for the former (i.e. local weeds) the pollen of Cruciferae (*Sinapis* type and *Hornungia* type), *Spergula* type, *Chenopodium* type, *Plantago lanceolata*, *P. major* type, and Compositae taxa (*Cirsium* type, *Taraxacum* type, *Anthemis* type and *Artemisia*), are likely to have come from weeds associated with the area of crop cultivation. The latter, that is regional input, is more enigmatic since it is such pollen rain that forms the natural spectra within the peat ombrogenous mire. Consequently, should contamination of the gut have taken place as a result of truncation of the lower half of the body, then such pollen types would be undifferentiable. From Table 13 it can be seen that a number of pollen taxa are exclusive to the lower part of the small intestine. These largely include the arboreal taxa which are also evident in the peat pollen stratigraphy (Oldfield *et al.* pp. 82ff.) and a number of taxa which may be specifically related to the ombrogenous mire including *Calluna*

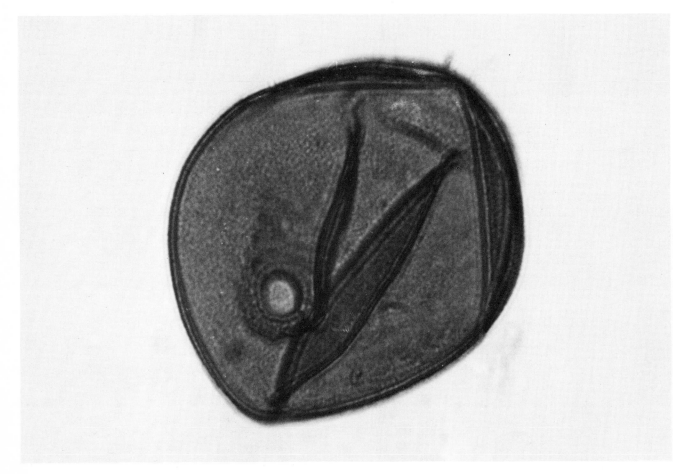

Fig. 48   Cereal pollen grain from the small intestine. Maximum diameter 55µ.

and *Sphagnum* (Oldfield *et al.* 1985). As these relate to the lower abdominal area close to where the body was severed during peat extraction, it is possible that minor contamination of the intestinal contents by *Sphagnum* pool water has occurred. Conversely, however, if such an ingress of contaminating peat had occurred, higher values of *Sphagnum* spores, Gramineae and Cyperaceae pollen might have been expected. Such points are important in that the presence of contaminant microfossils provides a good absolute measure of contamination at larger sizes. Very low percentages and absence of Cyperaceae (*Eriophorum*) and much *Sphagnum* (Oldfield *et al.* pp. 82ff.) suggest that if substantial contamination had taken place this would have manifested itself by higher values of these and other taxa. Furthermore, the presence of *Sphagnum* leaves have been noted in the gut contents of Danish bog men and in that of Lindow Man where Holden has noted that the *Sphagnum* leaves appeared to be well embedded in the fibrous intestinal contents. Consequently it seems reasonable to suggest that these taxa, including those recorded which are characteristic of mires, are in primary context having been of either some direct dietary relevence or were present in drinking water sources.

The Herbaceous Component

From the analysis of plant macrofossils, Helbaek (1958) has shown a marked diversity of herbaceous taxa in the stomach contents of Grauballe and Tollund bog men. In addition to the microscopical investigation of the gut contents of Lindow Man, a number of samples of gut material from Grauballe Man were also investigated (material courtesy of Forhistorisk Museum, Moesgård, Denmark). These are still being researched but initial results (Table 15) illustrate that the macrofossil diversity shown by Helbaek is matched by an equally diverse herb pollen content (see below). Pollen of *Polygonum persicaria* type, *Chenopodium* type, *Artemisia* and cereals has been noted (Scaife in preparation). These findings correspond closely with Helbaek's macrofossil data (Helbaek 1958). Helbaek regarded these taxa as being due to the specific gathering of weed seeds for use in a gruel or porridge mixture. Clearly, pollen of these taxa remained in the seed and other vegetative structures in the same way as discussed for cereals. It may be argued that these taxa are all ruderal and segetal taxa and were associated with arable cultivation. It is possible therefore, that these taxa may have been accidentally incorporated when cereals were

harvested and processed. In either case it is apparent that the gut contents of Lindow Man show a much poorer spectrum of such elements with cereal pollen comprising the sole statistically significant element (76%–91% of total pollen and spores). This would therefore suggest that the cereals represented here formed parts of a bread or porridge mixture which was apparently made from 'clean' well processed cereals. Both seem likely possibilities. What is clear, however, is that those samples analysed from Grauballe Man, which were rich in weed pollen, corresponding strongly with the macrofossil content, illustrate the large scale incorporation of these weed taxa into the final meal. It has been shown by Bryant (1974a, 1975) that *Chenopodium* pollen, especially, becomes incorporated into foodstuffs because of the longevity of flowering whilst seed maturation and harvesting may also have been taking place. Consequently, pollen becomes easily incorporated into the gathered food. It seems from the discussion of Hillman (1981, and pp. 102–3) that the diversity of seed taxa in Grauballe (Helbaek 1958) and Tollund (Helbaek 1950) Men resulted not from the economic gathering of these weed seeds for deliberate inclusion into, or making of a gruel or porridge, but that at the end of cereal crop gathering, poor cereal chaff debris may have also inadvertently incorporated the numerous arable weed taxa. This is certainly reflected in the intestinal pollen assemblage of Grauballe Man (Scaife in prep.) with its high pollen percentages of *Polygonaceae*, *Artemisia* and *Chenopodium* type pollen. In contrast, from the relatively small percentages of such taxa in the Lindow samples it is suggested here that (i) the cereal crop was much 'cleaner', a fact confirmed by Hillman (pers. comm.) and (ii) that those few taxa represented by low pollen percentages result from pollen trapped in the cereal heads along with the more frequent cereal pollen itself.

Mistletoe

A small quantity of *Viscum album* pollen grains (4 in total) has been noted in each of the samples. This interesting occurrence may cause much speculation since mistletoe has had a long history in folklore (a symbol of the Folklore Society) used medicinally as a nervine, antispasmodic, tonic and narcotic substance (Wren 1941). Culpepper's *Complete Herbal* notes numerous uses of mistletoe in herbal remedies, including its value as 'a cephalic and nervine medicine, useful for convulsive fits, palsy and vertigo'. If it was used for such ailments it is likely that far higher pollen frequencies would have been found. Pliny (*Nat. Hist. XVI* 95) tells of the religious significance of mistletoe to the druids provided that it grew on a *robur* (oak) (cf. Ross p. 167). This in itself is of interest because of the rarity of this phenomenon (Perring 1973). Usually *Viscum* is saprophytic on apple, lindens, poplars and hawthorn. Apart from its medicinal properties, it is therefore clear that its use can also be linked with religious custom. The fact that only small numbers of pollen grains and as yet no macro-fossil remains have been recorded, leaves us with the obvious enigma as to the reason for its presence in the stomach of this perhaps ceremonially killed Lindow Man! Dimbleby (1978, 140) has noted that mistletoe has been used as winter feed for sheep and as such it is possible that it was present in settlement contexts where it could have inadvertently become incorporated into human foodstuffs.

The fact that *Viscum* is dioecious, may explain why only a small but nevertheless significant number of pollen grains was found. If berries were used, only a small quantity of pollen grains might be expected (if at all) to remain in the old stigmas by the time of fruit maturation in the autumn or winter. This will be a subject of future research. The present ecological status is also of interest being present in England at the limits of its climatic tolerance. Thus, it occurs primarily in southern England northwards to the Midlands with its major areas of growth centred on Gloucestershire and Herefordshire. However, a survey in 1969/1970 illustrated a broader pattern of distribution than previously expected (Perring 1973). This distribution pattern reflects its general requirement of continental type climate. The palaeoecological record has, however, shown that it was more widespread during the Atlantic hypsithermal period (*c.* 7000–5000 bp). Climatic change to a more continental regime during the ensuing Sub-Boreal period may have resulted in its extension to more northerly latitudes and perhaps Cheshire. Climatic deterioration (into the Sub-Atlantic) from *c.* 1000–500bc would, however, have had a correspond-

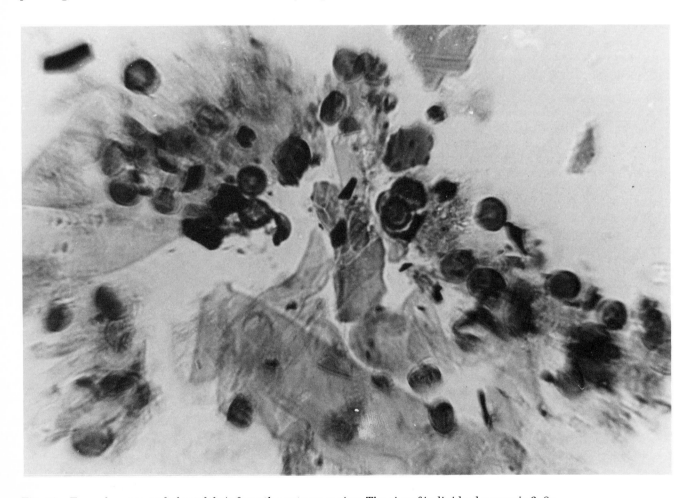

Fig. 49 Fungal spores and plant debris from the antrum region. The size of individual spores is 6–8μ.

ingly detrimental effect on its growth and avail-ability to Iron Age man.

Season of Death

There has been much debate on the feasibility of establishing the time of year in which death of the various bog men and women occurred. Such arguments seek to establish from the plant macro- and microfossils those floral elements which may be present in abundance but which fall outside of any means of storage or preservation for longer periods of time. Such studies in relation to pollen are far from easy because of the longevity and ease of preservation of pollen in certain environments unlike many soft fruiting taxa which decay rapidly. However, the potential of abundant pollen of taxa from inflorescences gathered at a particular time of year should be considered. There is also the possibility of the concurrence of pollen from soft fruited plants in which the pollen may have been associated in the manner described above. In the case of Lindow Man's gut contents it has not been possible to assess seasonality because of the likelihood that the pollen found may have been present in stored food raw materials (largely grain).

Fungal Spores

The use of hallucinogenic plant varieties must be considered in relation to the somewhat enigmatic deaths of those bog people so far encountered. Microscopic investigation by Helbaek (1958) has illustrated the presence of fungal sclerotia of *Claviceps purpurea*, fungal spores of *Ustilago hordei* a rust of barley and hyphae of Dematiaceae from the stomach of the Grauballe Man (Helbaek 1958, 113). Such fungal detritus may be derived from a number of primary direct causes or, as already illustrated, from the pollen from indirect sources. These sources may be summarised as:

(a) From the direct specific use of fungi as a food resource or even perhaps for their hallucinogenic properties (magic mushrooms!).
(b) Pathogens characteristic of cereal crops of which the best known is 'ergot' but of which there are many that could easily have been associated or contained within the cereals utilised in bread- or porridge-making.
(c) Post-mortem fungal development must also be considered as a source of fungal hyphae and of fruiting bodies.

In the present analysis of the Lindow Man, large quantities of individual fungal rust spores have been recovered from the fundus and antrum of the stomach and from the two samples from the upper and lower part of the smaller intestine (Fig. 49). These have not yet been fully investigated but appear to be similar to the *Ustilago hordei* illustrated by Helbaek (1958, plate VIIb). These are therefore likely to be associated with the marked quantities of cereal (presumably *Hordeum*) macroscopic and microscopic food remains present in all of the gut samples analysed (see (b) above and Hillman p. 107).

The Inorganic Component

The presence of a small inorganic fraction has been noted in the stomach contents of Egyptian mummies, the Danish bog men (Helbaek 1959, 114) and in sub-fossil prehistoric coprolites (Bryant 1974c, 22–23). Non-biogenic silica has also been found during the macrofossil investigation by Holden. It is likely that this resulted from the accidental incorporation of grit and dust into the food stuffs from using stone querns or grind stones, or during food preparation. Quantities of carbon found are also being subjected to analysis by electron spin resonance.

Comparison between the Gut's Macro- and Microfossil Contents

Preliminary pollen investigations of the gut contents of both the Grauballe and Lindow Men show a close correspondence. The majority of taxa in Grauballe Man (Table 15) are herbaceous taxa which relate to the macro-flora identified by Helbaek (1958). Helbaek (1958, 112) noted the presence of 'very many seeds of *Polygonum lapathifolium*' and this is confirmed in the pollen spectrum by the presence of substantial quantities of *Polygonum persicaria* type (49%) (Moore and Webb 1979). *Rumex*, *Spergula* type, *Chenopodium* type and Gramineae have also been noted in their seed counterparts in analyses of other Danish 'bog people'. It is interesting to note, however, that pollen of cereals are of little importance in the pollen record of Grauballe Man compared with the macrofossil remains and with both the pollen and macrofossil contents of Lindow Man. This is likely to be caused by the inclusion of weed floras in the 'unclean' grain comprising the last meal (see above and also Hillman, pp. 109–12).

Comparison with Hillman's and Holden's analysis

of the gut contents of Lindow Man shows similar close correspondence in (a) the relatively low values of weed taxa in comparison to (b) the large frequencies of cereal pollen and macrofossils. From the macrofossill analyses, *Triticum dicoccum, T. spelta, Hordeum sp., Avena sp.* have been identified by Hillman and Holden (pp. 107, 118). Identification to generic level has not yet been possible with the pollen recovered although this is being attempted. It is apparent that the overall diversity of taxa in the pollen record is greater for Lindow Man than the seed record. As noted above and when compared with the pollen data from human palaeofaeces this might be expected due to the potential use of flowers in the diet, the possibility of inclusion of the natural 'regional' pollen rain, and from pollen of nearby arable weed floras becoming trapped in cereal inflorescences. The possibility of contamination from adjacent peats has now been largely ruled out (see above discussion). However, pollen, spores and macro remains of *Chenopodium, Rumex, Calluna vulgaris, Galeopsis* (? *Mentha* type) and *Sphagnum* are present.

Holden has also noted the presence of fungal material (*cf. Ustilago hordei* and Dematiaceae) *in situ* on cereal plant debris. This would seem to confirm the microspore observations (above), but again in both cases further mycological examination will be necessary.

Summary

Five pollen samples have been analysed from the stomach and small intestine of Lindow Man. The pollen assemblage is notable for its very high frequencies of cereal pollen which undoubtedly represents that which had become trapped in the cereal head and which was harvested, turned into a bread or porridge and was ingested. The pollen had not been degraded in the gut and was found to be in a fine state of preservation. A range of other herbaceous taxa are present but are in relatively low frequencies especially compared with analogous material obtained from the Grauballe Man (Scaife in prep.). This would seem to suggest that the cereals gathered were of a much purer character than used by the Danish bog men – a fact supported by the plant macrofossil investigations of Holden and Hillman. In addition to the cereals and associated weed floras are a number of 'extra-regional' pollen types which may have been ingested accidentally from the same taphonomic processes or from drinking water. The analyses also showed the presence of inorganic fractions – plant phytoliths, grit and charcoal – and the intestinal parasites, *Trichuris* (whip worm) and *Ascaris* (round worm). Further study of the cereal pollen and total pollen assemblages is still being carried out.

Trees and Shrubs	Herb Pollen	Intestinal Parasites
Pinus	RANUNCULACEAE	Ascaris
Ulmus	Thalictrum	Trichuris
Betula	Sinapis type	
Alnus	Hornungia type	
Corylus type	Spergula type	
Quercus	Chenopodium type	
Salix	ROSACEAE	
	UMBELLIFERAE	
Calluna	Rumex type	
Erica	SCROPHULARIACEAE	
	Plantago major type	
	Bidens type	
	Aster type	
	Anthemis type	
	LIGULIFLORAE	
	*GRAMINEAE	
	*Cereal type	
	Pteridium aquilinum	
	Polypodium	
	Sphagnum	
	Unidentified pollen	
	Fungal spores	

Table 13:   Pollen, spore and parasite taxa recorded in a preliminary examination of a sample obtained from the small intestine. (*dominant groups)

	Fundus 1	Antrum 2	Small Intestine 3	4
Trees and Shrubs				
Ilex	0.5	—	—	—
Myrica	0.5	—	—	—
Betula	1.5	—	—	—
Corylus	1.5	—	—	—
Alnus	—	—	—	0.8
Quercus	2.5	—	—	—
Salix	1.5	—	0.8	0.8
Calluna	1.5	—	0.7	0.8
Herbs				
Hornungia type	—	0.5	—	—
Sinapis type	0.5	1.6	—	—
Spergula type	0.5	3.2	—	—
Chenopodium type	0.5	3.2	—	0.8
Medicago type	1.5	1.6	—	—
ROSACEAE	0.5	—	—	—
Viscum album	0.5	1.6	0.7	0.8
UMBELLIFERAE	0.9	—	0.7	1.6
Rumex	0.5	—	—	1.6
SCROPHULARIACEAE	0.5	—	—	—
LABIATAE	—	—	0.7	—
Plantago lanceolata	0.5	—	1.4	—
Campanula type	0.5	—	—	—
Anthemis type	0.9	1.6	0.7	—
Artemisia	—	—	0.7	0.8
Cirsium type	—	—	—	0.8
LIGULIFLORAE	0.9	—	—	0.8
cf. Tamus	0.5	—	—	—
GRAMINEAE	2.4	—	1.4	4.6
Cereal	75.6	85.5	91.4	85.0
CYPERACEAE	—	—	—	0.5
Pteridium aquilinum	0.5	—	—	—
Sphagnum	2.5	—	—	—

Table 14:   Lindow Man; pollen analysis of the fundus (1), antrum (2) and small intestine (3 and 4) calculated as a percentage of the total sum for each gut sample.

Viola arvensis type	3.5
Spergula type	14.0
Chenopodium type	3.5
Polygonum persicaria type	49.0
Rumex	12.3
Mentha type	3.5
LIGULIFLORAE	1.8
GRAMINEAE	8.8
Cereal	1.8
Unidentified	1.8

Table 15:   Grauballe Man; Preliminary pollen analysis of gut sample. Note – Percentages are based upon a small pollen sum of only 57 pollen grains.

28 Parasitological Investigations on Lindow Man

Andrew K. G. Jones

Summary

A sample taken from the small intestine of Lindow Man was examined for evidence of intestinal parasite ova. Ova of *Trichuris trichiura*, the human whipworm, and *Ascaris lumbricoides*, the maw worm, were present.

Introduction

Pollen analysis demonstrated that eggs of *Ascaris* and *Trichuris* were present in the gut of Lindow Man (p. 129). Recent work has established that the reagents used in the preparation of pollen samples can shrink ancient parasite ova (Hall *et al* 1983) and under some circumstances ova can be completely dissolved. In order to record accurately the numbers and size of the ova an unprocessed sample was examined.

Methods and Materials

Although the body was damaged by peat digging equipment, a short length of small intestine was recovered and its contents carefully removed. A small amount of this material, a dark reddish brown (Munsell soil chart code 5YR3/2) fine organic detritus, was submitted for parasitological investigation with a request to examine as little as possible of the sample. Consequently it was decided to adapt the procedure outlined by the Ministry of Agriculture, Fisheries and Food (1977, 3) for examining modern faecal samples. A 0.5 g subsample was placed in a 120 ml glass jar with 7 ml water. The flask was shaken gently for a few minutes until the sample was thoroughly disaggregated. The resulting suspension was poured through a freshly flamed 250 micron aperture sieve to remove coarse particles. Ten microscope slides were prepared by mounting 0.05 ml aliquots of the filtrate in glycerine jelly using 22 × 22 mm coverslips. One temporary mount was made by taking 0.15 ml of the suspension and covering it with a 22 × 50 mm coverslip. Slides were scanned at ×120 using a transmission microscope and all ova counted. A total of five counts was made. Where possible ova were measured using an eyepiece graticule; measurements were calibrated using a stage micrometer.

Results

Two kinds of ova were observed (Fig. 50). One, a barrel-shaped structure frequently possessing two polar plugs, was typical of the genus *Trichuris*. The other kind of egg typically possessed a mamillated outer shell characteristic of the genus *Ascaris*. Three kinds of *Ascaris* ova were recorded: fertilised ova; unfertilised ova; and decorticated ova. No other parasite ova were recognised.

The Condition of the Ova

The condition of the *Trichuris* ova was assessed by considering the numbers which fall into the following categories:

(a) complete, i.e. possessing two polar plugs;
(b) damaged, i.e. the shell is complete but the condition of either one or both plugs suggest that the ova are beginning to disintegrate;
(c) shell complete but polar plugs absent;
(d) shell broken or crumpled.

The majority of the *Trichuris* ova (54%) were complete possessing two prominent polar plugs. Only one ovum showed evidence of polar plug disintegration, while 44% possessed no polar plugs. No broken or crumpled ova were present. Comparing the condition of the ova with other archaeological samples from York and Oslo (Jones, 1984 and forthcoming) the material was classified as well preserved.

The *Ascaris* ova were also well preserved with only two broken fragments present in the samples. Fragments of *Ascaris* ova are frequently present in archaeological material.

The Numbers of Ova Present

Five counts were made on aliquots of the prepared sample. Four were 0.05 ml aliquots and one 0.15 ml. These have been multiplied by 300 and 100 respectively to obtain the numbers of ova per gram (opg). The counts are presented in Table 16.

The five counts show that *Trichuris* ova were slightly more abundant (3500–5700 opg) than *Ascaris* ova (2700–3900 opg) in the gut contents sample.

The Size of the Ova

Mean total length of *Trichuris* ova was 55.0 microns; mean length minus polar plugs was 51.4 microns and mean width was 26.1 microns (more details of egg measurements are presented in Table 17). These statistics show the ova from Lindow Man to be very similar in size to those quoted for modern eggs of the human whipworm, *Trichuris trichiura*. Beer (1976) reviewed the literature and tabulated the results of five papers which gave egg size data for the human and pig whipworms. Some of the measurements quoted in this paper show that the mean total length of modern human whipworm eggs is slightly larger (1.3–2.8 microns) than those from Lindow Man. By contrast, the *T. trichiura* ova Beer examined were slightly smaller (0.2 microns). Thus the size range of the Lindow Man *Trichuris* ova is consistent with published data for modern *T. trichiura*.

The Lindow Man *Trichuris* ova are considerably smaller than those produced by *T. suis*, the whipworm of pigs, the only other species of whipworm reported from man. *T. suis* produces ova that are between 6.0 and 9.3 microns larger than those found in Lindow Man. The eggs are also too small for *T. muris*, *T. vulpis*, and *T. ovis*, the whipworms of mice and rats, dogs, cattle and sheep.

The evidence from egg dimensions leaves no doubt that the eggs were passed by *T. trichiura*, the human whipworm.

Having identified the ova it is interesting to note that some of the measurements of the Lindow Man *Trichuris* ova were slightly larger than the measurements published by Beer (1976). For example, the maximum width of the Lindow Man ova was 30.5 microns, 0.5 microns larger than the largest egg quoted by any of the authors cited by Beer and 1.8 microns larger than the largest examined by Beer. Similarly the maximum total length for the Lindow Man *Trichuris* ova was 62.3 microns, which is up to 5.3 microns larger than those quoted by Beer (1976). It would appear that the modern studies have failed to examine the largest eggs produced by *T. trichiura*.

 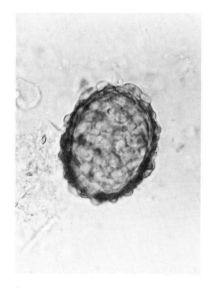 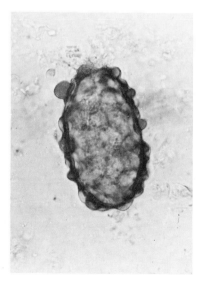

1   2   3

Fig. 50   1, A *Trichuris trichiura* ovum from Lindow Man. Standard length (minus polar plugs) 51µ; 2, A fertilised *Ascaris lumbricoides* ovum from Lindow Man. Length 62µ; 3, An unfertilised *Ascaris lumbricoides* ovum from Lindow Man. Length 70µ. Photos: York University.

The *Ascaris* ova have been identified as *A. lumbricoides* because of their characteristic appearance, their size, and their context – associated with ova of *T. trichiura* within a human intestine. (The eggs of *A. lumbricoides* and *A. suum* (the pig ascarid) are identical in morphology and size.)

Discussion

Both whipworms and *Ascaris* are parasitic nematodes which infest the lower intestine and caecum of man throughout the world. They are not common in Britain today but are widespread in warm climates and among poor people, and there is increasing evidence that intestinal nematode infestations were widespread in Europe before the development of mains drainage.

The two kinds of worm produce large numbers of eggs which are shed into the gut lumen and passed with faeces. The infestations are spread by ingesting embryonated eggs. Three main contexts for *Trichuris* and *Ascaris* transmission are in yards and houses that have been contaminated by faeces, especially those of children; to persons working in fields where human faeces is used as a fertiliser; and by consuming vegetables recently fertilised with human excreta (Feachem *et al* 1983).

Light infestations usually cause little harm to the host. Heavy worm burdens of *Trichuris* can cause prolapse of the rectum, diarrhoea and blood in the faeces. *Ascaris* larvae, which hatch from ingested embryonated eggs, migrate through the host tissues and can cause considerable damage. Heavy worm burdens may give many symptoms including digestive disorders, abdominal pain, vomiting and disturbed sleep. Nevertheless, many people harbouring small numbers of *Ascaris* do not suffer severe symptoms.

It is essential to remember that the material examined was a single 0.5 g sample and that it was collected from an unbroken section of small intestine found within the body; it was not a faecal sample.

Although one sample is described in detail it is thought to be representative of the gut contents for other samples examined for pollen grains also contained parasite ova. Furthermore, small amounts of the intestine contents were examined by making smears; these also contained many *Trichuris* ova and slightly smaller numbers of *Ascaris* eggs.

While it would be most interesting to estimate the

Table 16:   Numbers of parasite ova from Lindow Man

Count code	Number of Trichuris ova/g	Number of Ascaris ova/g	Total number ova/g
LM841	4800	3600	8400
LM842	5700	2700	8400
LM843	3600	3900	7500
LM844	3500	3800	7300
LM845	3900	3000	6900
Mean	4300	3400	7700

Table 17:   Dimensions of the *Trichuris* ova from Lindow Man

All measurements in microns
SEM = standard error of the mean
n = number of observations

	Total length	Width	Length minus polar plugs
Mean	55.0	26.1	51.4
Maximum	62.3	30.5	57.3
Minimum	51.1	24.3	47.3
SEM	0.5	0.1	0.2
n	30	74	74

Table 18:   The dimensions of *Ascaris* ova from Lindow Man

All measurements in microns
SEM = standard error of the mean
n = number of observations

	Fertilised Length	Width	Unfertilised Length	Width	Decorticated Length	Width
Mean	63.6	50.6	70.6	47.6	60.1	47.3
Minimum	42.3	39.8	62.3	42.3	51.1	42.3
Maximum	74.7	57.3	77.2	54.8	69.7	52.3
SEM	1.3	0.7	1.1	0.9	4.3	2.3
n	25	25	15	15	4	4

severity of the worm burden, because of the lack of modern comparative data this is impossible. As the sample was from the small intestine it is not appropriate to use modern egg concentration data obtained from the examination of fresh faeces in order to determine the severity of the infestations. Records of the concentrations of parasite ova in various parts of the human intestine have not been found during the course of this study. Even if they were available it is likely that egg concentrations would be distorted because the water content of the gut contents may have altered during the period of burial. So it is unwise to speculate on the severity of the infestation. However, most parasitological texts do not mention the small intestine as a common site for either *Ascaris* or *Trichuris*. This may indicate that the Lindow Man carried a relatively large worm burden.

Both *Ascaris* and *Trichuris* eggs have been previously reported from other human bodies recovered from peat bogs. In 1944 results of investigations on two well preserved bodies, the 'Drobnitz Girl' and the 'Karwinden Man' were published by Szidat (1944). Both contained eggs of *T. trichiura* and *A. lumbricoides*. The famous Danish bog burials 'Grauballe Man' and 'Tollund Man' contained only eggs of *T. trichiura* (Helbaek, 1958).

The Lindow Man find must be seen as increasing evidence that whipworm and *Ascaris* infections were widespread in the human population of Europe during the Iron Age.

29 Postscript: Last Minute Results from ESR Spectroscopy Concerning the Cooking of Lindow Man's Last Meal

Don Robins   Keith Sales   Duro Oduwole   Tim Holden
Gordon Hillman

It has been proposed by Hillman (p. 109 ff.) that Lindow Man's last meal involved some sort of coarse, wholemeal bread and that porridge and other farinaceous foods were unlikely candidates. He has further suggested (p. 111) that probably the bread had been baked on an open fire and eaten in a flat unleavened form or as 'griddle cakes'. These conclusions were based entirely on microscopic analyses and ethnographic parallels. In this short paper we see how further information has subsequently been obtained by looking at what we call the thermal history of the grains. Electron Spin Resonance (ESR) spectroscopy is a technique which we have, in the last few years, applied to the study of ancient foods and diet and which enables us to comment on Hillman's present hypotheses.

ESR is widely used in physics and chemistry to determine the structure and energetics of molecules which have unpaired electrons, an unusual state of affairs because electrons in molecules normally exist in pairs. Molecules with unpaired electrons, or, as they are normally termed, unpaired spins (because the electron spin is the important property here), are often very reactive and their study in, for example, biochemical reactions, can yield useful data about metabolism. In archaeology we are interested in materials with unpaired electrons which are stable over long periods of time and whose electrons will give us information about the past.

There are two main ways in which this can happen: dating and thermal histories.

ESR Dating

Dating by ESR can be applied to a variety of materials but most usefully to cave deposits and bone. This technique has been exploited over the last decade because it neatly fills the dating gap between about 50,000 and 1,000,000 years ago, i.e. between the end of the radiocarbon range and the beginning of the Potassium-Argon range. This gap is a period of great interest in studies of human evolution. We have carried out dating exercises on very ancient bone but our main interest has been in thermal history and this is how we became involved in the examination of the material from Lindow Man.

Thermal Histories of Food Remains

In ESR dating we detect unpaired electrons which have been produced by the effect of natural radioactivity upon the sample and which have been trapped within the sample. The number of unpaired electrons trapped corresponds to the length of time that the sample has been exposed to the radioactivity and so can be used to calculate the date of the object. With thermal history there is a different story. When you heat an organic material, such as bread, wood, starch, or meat, a certain amount of thermal decomposition occurs. Sometimes this leads to oxidation and at others to *pyrolysis*, which we define as decomposition by heating alone. You see this when toast is burnt but it is also useful in many areas of industry: for example, to increase the yield of petrol from oil and to prepare carbon black.

Pyrolysis of any organic material creates stable unpaired electron species of great chemical complexity which we simply classify as *radical carbon*. This species is related to graphite and has a chemical structure of great stability: once formed it appears to persist indefinitely. So, by identifying the presence of radical carbon with ESR we can tell whether something has been heated or not.

We have gone much further than this, however, in the last few years, because by studying the ESR signal in more detail we have been able to estimate the temperature to which the material has previously been heated and also how long it had been maintained at that temperature. This elaboration was prompted by the fact that archaeologists often presume that blackened objects found in ancient sites have been heated or charred. There are, however, many reasons why objects become black without heating having taken place, examples being absorption of iron and surface sintering due to decomposition and oxidation. The great advantage of ESR is that it can distinguish clearly if the blackness is due to heating, a matter of considerable importance when identification of heating is critical to archaeological interpretation, as in studies of ancient diet where the cooking regime has pronounced effects upon the nutritional value of the food of the sort reviewed by Stahl (1984).

In looking at grain materials we had first to calibrate the thermal decomposition of the grain itself using modern samples, and similarly for chaff which was the material actually used in this study because it had already been separated from the rest of the stomach contents. To do the calibration we had to pyrolyse samples at a range of temperatures from ambient to about 400°C and to study their ESR signals. We measured several parameters of the signal, the most important ones being the g value and the spin density, p (Fig. 51).

The g value is slightly smaller the greater the degree of pyrolysis of the sample. Since, however, the g value can be measured with great precision these small changes can be monitored. The spin density measures the number of unpaired electrons present and is directly related to the strength of the signal. It also gives an indication of the maximum temperature, for on heating the sample the signal

increases in intensity (unless the temperature rises above about 400°C when it starts to decline). The rate of signal growth at a given temperature depends both upon the maximum temperature of previous heating and upon the length of heating time in a complex manner. Study of this rate of change, and of other ESR parameters, allows us to give a measure of cooking or heating time.

Maximum Temperature of Previous Heating

Our early work on grain had led us to the establishment of a curve whereby g value varied with temperature, allowing us to determine the maximum temperature of previous heating of archaeological grain samples. For Lindow Man, as explained above, we had to carry out a study of chaff g value variation with temperature for modern material. Generally, this curve followed that for the grains except that it was slightly displaced upwards on the g value axis.

Our measurements of the g value of the wheat chaff obtained from Lindow Man's stomach have allowed us to give a maximum temperature of between 200 and 250°C, which is certainly consistent with the grain being eaten in the form of bread (for had it been porridge or gruel the g value would have indicated a temperature of about 100°C). This result agrees with the archaeo-botanical examination which suggested that the fragmentation of the grain is more consistent with bread than porridge, groats or other farinaceous foods (Hillman, pp. 99–115). The next question was whether we could say anything about the way the bread had been baked.

Length of Heating Time

The variation of spin concentration with temperature and heating time has already been mentioned and this provided the first pointer towards the type of bread. We have two possibilities: a leavened, baked loaf and a flat, unleavened griddle cake heated over a fire though intermediate forms do exist. Discrimination between the two might be possible on the maximum temperature attained, but it could also be made on the heating time, since the griddle cake would have had a much shorter exposure to its maximum temperature (p. 111). Our preliminary measurements show that the spin density in the chaff is low, which is more consistent with a short cooking time than a long one. This result accords, once again, with the expectations based upon the species of cereal present in the meal: Hillman has been able to identify

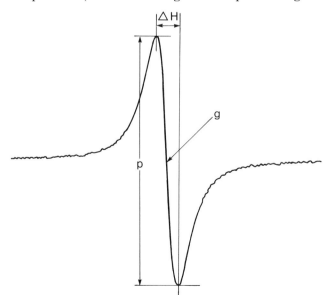

Fig. 51   A typical ESR spectrum; the spin concentration is proportional to p. $(\triangle H)^2$.

the cereal chaff as coming from Emmer wheat, Spelt wheat and barley, three cereals which are best suited for making *unleavened*, relatively flat bread (pp. 107–8). Holden's work on the bran remains (p. 116 ff.) also indicates the presence of cereals of broadly similar type.

The next piece of evidence comes from an examination of the undifferentiated stomach contents which visual inspection had revealed to contain minute fragments of charred material (see p. 108 above). Our examination of this residue produced a complex spectrum which consisted of a broad feature, which may be due to inorganic components, and a sharp, narrow radical carbon signal with a g value consistent with a temperature above 300°C. This is, of course, due to the presence of highly pyrolysed material, in other words charcoal, but present in very small amounts. It should be pointed out that ESR works on very small traces of material, so small as often to be below the level of detection of more conventional analytical techniques. Thus these minute traces of charcoal are sufficient for us to observe. So what does the charcoal tell us? Its presence indicates severe heating or burning of the bread, an event that is likely to occur much more often during the high-speed griddling of flat bread over an open fire than during the slower, oven-baking of a leavened loaf.

We have as yet, of course, only looked at the wheat chaff remains and a fine matrix of mixed materials from the stomach. Nevertheless, the ESR evidence supports the archaeo-botanical evidence on both counts: that Lindow Man's last meal was bread not porridge, and probably unleavened bread rather than leavened. It has been suggested above (see Hillman p. 108) that, because the charred fragments of ground farinaceous material (presumably crumbs of bread) contained slivers of barley husk, it is probable that the barley was also a component of the bread. The next round of ESR measurements will usefully test this point. To gain further evidence such as this we propose to undertake measurements on a series of loaves and cakes made from different cereals baked under different conditions and to study other ESR parameters to try to determine the cooking time more accurately. ESR studies such as those described above clearly open up a hitherto inaccessible area of the study of ancient diet and food preparation.

IV
Archaeology and Folklore

Fig. 52   The Haxey Hood Game (after Wright 1938).

30 The Bog Burials of Britain and Ireland

R. C. Turner   C. S. Briggs*

One thing had almost slipt me, how sometimes in mosses are found human bodies entire and uncorrupted, as in a moss near the Meales in Lancashire. These are the most remarkable phaenomena I have observ'd in morasses, I shall not therefore swell these sheets with unnecessary recapitulations, but according to our design proceed to the next chapter. (Leigh 1700)

Introduction

Lindow Man is a very remarkable discovery. It has prompted enormous public interest and great excitement in the archaeological world. It is, perhaps, the most deeply studied ancient human body ever. However, Lindow Man is not unique, but one of a very widespread set of discoveries coming from throughout Northern Europe and belonging to a wide span of time. It was Professor Glob's book *The Bog People* which first made the English speaking public and the archaeological world aware of bog burials and the tradition that some of them represent. But apart from the Countess of Moira's description (Moira 1785) and the figures, quoted by Glob, of 41 bog people from England and Wales, 15 from Scotland, and 19 from Ireland, the book gives no clue to the wealth of material from Britain and Ireland.

From earlier in this volume, it can be seen that Lindow Man was not the first bog burial, even from Lindow Moss. There has been no previous attempt to explain Glob's figures, or certainly in England and Wales, any recognition of bog burial as a widespread occurrence. Cotton, in a lecture to the Royal Archaeological Institute in 1959, introducing Glob's discoveries, (before the translation of *The Bog People*) said

'They (archaeologists in Great Britain) do not however, usually find burials in which the skin, hair and soft organs are preserved as in the case of the bog burials of north-western Europe. For these, a combination of suitable soil conditions and a specialised burial rite are required, a combination of circumstances which may not occur here.' (Cotton 1960).

Whimster, in 'Burial Practices in Iron Age Britain', a review identifying several classes of burial of this period, overlooked by earlier archaeologists, wrote, 'with the exception of a curious discovery of an undated but perhaps Iron Age, crouched skeleton buried beneath a construction of massive beams on the floor of a stream at Perranarworthal in Cornwall, we have no deposits of human remains from watery contexts to match those from Scandinavia or the numerious collections of votive metalwork or wooden objects recovered from peatbogs, streams and wells throughout Britain and Northern Europe.' (Whimster 1981).

The quotation which opens this section, written by Charles Leigh in 1700, is one of the earliest reference to bog bodies so far traced. It is interesting to see that these most remarkable phenomena almost slipped his memory as they have done with nearly everyone since then, but unlike Leigh, we intend to swell these sheets with recapitulations. The purpose of this chapter is to show that it is apparent that the finding of bog bodies was commonplace in Britain and Ireland, that they came to be there for a number of reasons and that they belong to a broad span of time. The contemporary reactions to the finds are almost as interesting as the finds themselves and these will be given in some detail (see Appendix, p. 181). Many more bog bodies await excavation from old newspaper articles, the antiquarian literature and obscure geological and natural history journals. Lindow Moss and elsewhere may produce more discoveries. This chapter should be seen only as a preliminary statement.

*R. C. Turner has written the Introduction, and Bog bodies in England, Wales, Scotland and Europe; C. S. Briggs contributes the History of Discovery, and Bog bodies in Ireland.

History of Discovery

> I know not if it will be worth the observing, that
> a *Turf-Bog* preserves things strangely, a Corps
> will ly entire in one, for several years; I have seen
> a piece of leather pretty fresh dug out of a *Turf-*
> *Bog*, that had never in the memory of man been
> dug before.
>
> (King 1685, 954).

This quotation is taken from a paper by William King, Archbishop of Dublin, entitled *'Of the* bogs, *and* Loughs *of* Ireland'. It was, however, concerned with economics, principally those of agricultural improvement through drainage, and the removal of those bogs which posed fatal hazards to communication, and not with bog bodies as such. His is one of a handful of accounts which were printed in the *Philosophical Transactions of the Royal Society* before 1695, when Bishop Gibson incorporated them into his first revised edition of William Camden's *Britannia*.

The location of the discoveries was predictable: notable human remains were found during peat cutting for the major drainage works and canalisations carried out by Dutch engineers in Restoration Humberside. Thorne Waste, Hatfield Chase and the Isle of Axholme provided the richest picking for local antiquarian correspondents and collectors, and here we find Richard Richardson of North Bierley and Nathaniel Johnston of Pontefract, as well as Abraham de la Pryme, listing buried trees, plough-marks and coins, as well as bodies. Sadly, the actual number of bodies either observed or preserved is not clear from their writings.

Elsewhere, Leigh, the Lancashire local historian, mentions discoveries at Meols near Southport (no. 21), prior to 1700 and in 1684 a coffin was exhumed just south of Cader Idris (no. 49) as noted by Edward Lhuyd. Despite King's remarks about Ireland there are no specific records of Irish bog bodies until later in the eighteenth century, but it is difficult to believe that bodies and coffins were not more common discoveries in seventeenth century Britain.

During the eighteenth century the Royal Society continued to serve as the main forum for the description of preserved cadavers and the peatbogs which had entombed them. In a letter communicated to the Royal Society in 1747 Mr G. Stovin described what was believed to have been the body of a woman shod in sandals preserved on the Isle of Axholme (no. 45). The same paper was read to the Society of Antiquaries, where her cold hand was exhibited alongside drawings which had been undertaken for both Societies (though only published by the more senior). A Mr Catesby observed that 'this shoe or sandal was exactly like what the *Indians* in *Virginia* wear at this Day, and call Mokasin,' (Stovin 1747, 575 *n.*) – an early example of an ethnographic parallel in British archaeology.

Contemporary fascination with bog bodies seems to have resulted from a general curiosity about the immortality of human flesh, which was part of the steady growth of medical awareness. Interest was therefore aroused by the discovery of a petrified human arm in an alum mine at Whitby, and that of several human ribs preserving the original flesh 'between and within them' which had been 'taken up by a gentleman bathing in the sea on the north side of the east pier [also at Whitby] and presented to Dr Dealtry, of York' (Gough 1789, III, 81).

Mummification was probably commonplace in some church crypts; those attributed to Crusaders and an early abbess at St Michan's, Dublin, are now well known, although they apparently remain unstudied. After the Great Fire of London, Braybrooke's body was found at St Paul's 'intire except an accidental hole in the breast through which his lungs might be seen and handled.' The skin was of a deep tawny colour, and the body very light and without any offensive smell. After being exposed some time in a coffin, it was re-interred (Gough 1789, II, 17). Stowe recorded a similar instance in the body of Alice, wife of Robert Hackney, Sheriff of London, 1321, found in St Mary Hill around 1497, the skin white, and the joints of the arms pliable; but after being exposed to the air for four days it began to decompose and was reburied (*ibid.*). During the later eighteenth century dried bodies were to be seen in the vaults of Whitechapel and St Martin's-in-the-Fields (*ibid.*), but in common with the other bodies already mentioned, these had a tangible history, and were not surrounded by the same mystery as bog bodies, the anonymity and geographical remoteness of which were to pose far-reaching questions about the earliest populations and their relationship to the land.

The advent of archaeological excavation saw rapid advances in answering some of these questions. During his tour of Scotland in 1772, Sir Joseph Banks was to witness the excavation of coffins on the Links of Skaill, Orkney, which held pagan, presumably prehistoric burials. One of them contained a quite remarkable 'highly preserved skeleton,' of which 'all the bones remained' and 'the flesh was like a whitish earth, lying about the bones of the thicker parts of the body; and on the arms, &c., was scattered a sort of blackish fibres, which Dr Lind supposed might have been the vascular system' (Lowe 1773, 273). This, the first known account of a preserved body from Scotland, was also the first to be published by the Society of Antiquaries of London.

Only ten years later, the Orkney account was surpassed in importance by the publication of a contribution to the *Archaeologia* from the Countess of Moira. This detailed the discovery in 1780 of a woman's grave beneath the peat bog in Drumkeragh townland, Co. Down, in North-east Ireland (no. 94), and, despite the author's obvious druidical proclivities, made a valuable contribution to contemporary scholarship.

The Drumkeragh lady described in this account had been deliberately interred between two headstones in a manner resembling that expected of graveyard burial. She was fully clothed in garments made of wool woven in a variety of ways, and (although not stated by the Countess) her costume would suggest that she was a woman of some consequence. Her situation in the bog indicates that she had been placed there with some care: possibly suicide, or unacceptable social behaviour had prevented proper Christian burial, or perhaps the woman was a murder victim. Although contemporary accounts claim that 11 feet of bog had grown over the body since interment, this can be disregarded. For such complete preservation to take place, conditions must have been anaerobic and the body must therefore have been placed within the bog's water table at the time of burial. Despite drawing upon Classical, Irish, English and French historical sources, and quoting from contemporary scientific literature on bog growth at Athelney, Lincolnshire, the Countess was still unable to date her find. There was a notable absence of linen in the dress, and it was eventually suggested that the lady might have been an Elizabethan, killed during civil disturbances or in wartime conditions. It is not improbable that the interment was relatively recent (perhaps as late as 1700 or 1720). Certainly, Elizabeth, Countess of Moira, went to a great deal of trouble to secure the surviving pieces of cloth (by buying them from peasants, some of whom had already re-cycled the cloth or the actual clothes, by putting them to fresh use after washing them) and thereby set a fine example for others to follow. It may still be possible to re-interpret the discovery since a handful of pieces of cloth survive alongside the lady's plaited hair.

Among the country clerics who were obliged to re-inter such bodies was the vicar of Grinton in Swaledale, in whose parish register for 1797 is recorded the burial of a body found in a neighbouring bog (no.

43). A similar interment took place at Ystrad Meurig church in 1811 (no. 48).

Earlier bog finds seem to have attracted more attention when it was thought they could be related to an accredited historical event. In Scotland, for example, reference is made to an individual thought to have been a Covenanter (Rennie 1810, no. 63). Gilpin, in an early tour (1772), heard the tale of a knight in armour accompanied by his horse, a find immediately and unquestioningly attributed to the Battle of Solway (1542). From Ireland come two accounts of 'Troopers'. One, from Charlemont (no. 69) in 1816, was thought to date from Queen Elizabeth's time and might reasonably be attributed to sixteenth-, or more likely, to seventeenth-century fighting in that area. If the testimony of J. Emerson Tennent, MP is to be believed, the second find, which carried chain armour and exotic livery in Gort-na-moyah bog, Co. Derry (no. 86), must have been deposited at a much later date. Nevertheless, it remains for historians to explain what a knight in armour would have been doing traversing a bog so far west beyond the Bann, outside the Pale of Anglo-Norman Ulster (Bradley 1985, 426, fig. 17.7). This one also seems likely to have been Elizabethan.

Similarly puzzling was the presence of a 'Highland soldier's hat' and a woman's body at Drumadreen (no. 79), thought to have been lost in the troubles of 1641. From Mulkeeragh came another, similar find, a man in full tartan dress, identified by his finders in 1753 as in full military uniform (no. 88). But it must here be remembered that the Medieval and post-Medieval formal dress of both Scots and Irish was of woven tartan, and that discoveries of tartan cloth needn't be ascribed exclusively to soldiers, Highland, Scottish, or otherwise.

It has already been suggested that the printed records of eighteenth- and nineteenth-century Britain and Ireland account for only a small fraction of contemporary bog finds, the majority having passed without notice. A source which demonstrates this far better than any other is the extensive manuscript collection relating to the activities of the topographical section of the Irish Ordnance Survey during the 1830s. Initiated to collect information on economic, social, demographic and scientific matters for political purposes, the Survey involved its officers in visiting and questioning virtually all the inhabitants of their chosen area. The resulting data sheets were submitted to a scholar in Dublin who synthesised them to create the Statistical Survey of each parish (Andrews 1975). Among the surviving original field notes for Co. Derry there are remarkable descriptions of bog bodies, skeletons, coffins and clothes extracted from local informants between 1835 and 1837. In the main they relate to events of the previous two decades, though exceptionally, extending into the previous century. In common with over 100 provenanced diagnostic prehistoric artefacts, these descriptions were never published (Briggs 1985), although Dr George Petrie, the archaeologist charged with the responsibility for collecting and collating this information, had himself produced a model account of the Castle Blakeney, Co. Galway, bog man in 1825 (no. 100). Petrie's neglect of the Ordnance Survey's remarkable store of information and the artefacts which derived from it was soon to be compounded by his inability to catalogue the Royal Irish Academy's collection (now that of the National Museum). It was thus left to Sir William Wilde to list all the early shoes, clothes and bodies, in his thorough catalogue (Wilde 1857, 280–93; 276–9 and 225–33). It is regrettable that the Drumkeragh body was not subjected to competent medical examination, but even without this Wilde was able to contribute a most distinguished analysis of the woollen fabrics which had survived, leaving an account which was unmatched in this field until the work of Henshall almost a century later (Wilde 1864).

Although Wilde's analysis of the Irish archaeological collections and his overall contribution to contemporary antiquarian observation should not be underrated or neglected, he provided no new cultural framework for Irish archaeology within which the bog finds could be accommodated. He seems to have presumed that they belonged to several different periods. Certainly, these particular human relics were not considered as important as those excavated from the stratigraphic contexts of bone caves or from cairns. Bog bodies make no appearance in the numerous editions of Sir John Lubbock's (later Lord Avebury's) *Prehistoric Times*, 1869–1900, nor in Sir Charles Lyell's *Antiquity of Man*, first published in 1863 (see the final edition for *The Everyman Library*, by R. H. Rastall in 1914, 7–25). But it is even more strange that Laurence Gomme did not index Lady Moira's paper, or any other similar account, in his *Index of Archaeological Papers 1660–1890*, of 1907, since virtually all other papers submitted to the *Archaeologia* were listed. It is obvious that nineteenth-century archaeological scholarship regarded this type of discovery as of ethnographic value, and of only peripheral interest to contemporary learning.

If, however, we turn to Lyell's *Principles of Geology* which was first published in 1838, we find in his dis-

cussion of Quaternary deposits, a discourse on peat, its growth and extent (1853, 718–19). Under the heading 'Animal Substances in Peat' (p. 722), Lyell rehearsed details given in 1810 by Rev Dr W. Rennie in his *Essays on Peat* on the best-known cases of animals and humans from peat graves. But in common with other geologists Lyell failed properly to understand the original published texts. For example, when quoting the Countess of Moira's account he takes literally the statement that the garments were made of animal hair, implying that they had not been spun from wool, and that the clothes must therefore have belonged to a period very early in the development of man. This was manifestly not the case, as the Countess herself had carefully demonstrated.

Rennie's and Lyell's remarks aimed to explain the nature of geological processes. That humans could be shown to have been preserved in peat was a fair illustration of the facility with which fossilisation could have taken place, and local experience of losing farm animals into bogs would clearly have brought home that message to many of his readers (p. 723) (see p. 152 for discussion).

Bog reclamation for agricultural purposes and for fuel continued throughout the British Isles until the Second World War. Mechanisation slowly replaced the activities of the manual workers, and the rise of the coal mining industry and cheap rail transport reduced the demand. Peat-cutting fell largely into abeyance in post-War years, although it still continues in Ireland on a drastically reduced scale.

Late nineteenth-century accounts of discoveries in England appear not to have reached national journals. Clothes were occasionally described from Scotland and skeletal material from beneath peat in the Cambridge region was of some interest to anthropological studies. Elsewhere, occasional parish and county historians noted such finds.

In 1906 Henry Morris, Secretary of the County Louth Archaeological Society, expressed a willingness to publish accounts of 'stone and bronze weapons, bog butter, and skeletons of primeval man and animal' ... 'found in bogs' (Morris 1906, 97), but sadly he appears to have had no takers. Any archaeological tradition of bog man which may have existed through the lineage of Moira and Wilde had died long before Cotton (1959) claimed that there were no bog bodies from these islands.

Yet, despite this lack of tradition, post-war Britain and Ireland saw a strong revival of interest in the subject. McClintock's *Old Irish and Highland Dress* which drew heavily upon the National Museum of Ireland's collection of preserved costume was published in 1950 and was to be followed shortly after by Miss Audrey Henshall's work on early Scottish clothes (1952). During this period Dr Lucas, Director of the National Museum of Ireland, was searching its collections and in 1956 published his seminal work on ancient shoes. Here again, a significant proportion of the footwear came from bogs and some had been closely associated with bodies.

Although this revival of interest paved the way for ever more specialist research upon early costume like that of Seaby and Henshall (1961–2) and of Shee and O'Kelly (1966) and Lucas (1972), no anatomical investigation of the bodies themselves appears to have been undertaken. Indeed, the whole subject might have remained in abeyance had it not been for the interest aroused by the discovery in Denmark of Grauballe and Tollund Man and the scholarly publications of Dieck.

Bog Bodies in England and Wales

The fifty sites from England and Wales have produced over eighty-five individuals recovered from peat deposits. Their state of completeness ranges from a single bone, to a complete body with tissue and bone surviving. The finds so far located do not come from the whole of England and Wales. The greatest number of sites is in the Norfolk and Cambridgeshire Fens, but in the main these remains are fragmentary and hard to analyse. More interesting discoveries come from the counties of the north Midlands and northern England. The examples from modern Lincolnshire belong to the Fenland group, but the Isle of Axholme now divided between South Yorkshire and Humberside is an important site. There are isolated discoveries in Cheshire, Nottinghamshire and Derbyshire and historic Lancashire has produced at least ten bog bodies. Of the northern counties only Northumberland and Durham have yet to yield finds. The five from Wales form no pattern.

This does not represent an even distribution of finds compared with the distribution of peat deposits in England and Wales. Of the large peat-filled river basins, the Somerset Levels have been subject to most detailed archaeological research, yet have produced no human remains. The small cauldron bogs or kettle-holes, where many of the Continental discoveries were made, are common in the West Midlands. There are no records of bog bodies from the upland blanket peat of South-West England.

The finds do not come from a single type of peat site. By far the largest number come from peat-filled lowland river basins, like the Fenland and the Isle of Axholme. In total these represent 27 of the sites.

Peat-filled glacial features are fewer and consist of (12) Lindow, (15) Scaleby and (19) Red Moss. There are several sites which are above 150 m: (14) Murchie's Cairn, (17) Hope, (23) Quernmore, (41) Austwick, (42) Grewelthorpe (47) Llyn Mawr Farm, (48) Strata Florida and (50) Gifron Farm (the numbers refer to the Appendix). The final group may be peculiar to England and came from sites exposed on seashores, or covered by shore sand. Here bodies are found in bands of peat formed during the periodic fluctuations of sea-level in post-glacial times (Tooley 1978b). This group is made up of (10) Meols, (11) Leasowe, (13) Hartlepool, (18) Birkdale and (20) Liverpool.

Bog burials can be dated in a number of ways. Four individuals have been dated using the radiocarbon method. The work on the two Lindow finds is described elsewhere in this volume. The site at Quernmore, Lancashire produced a burial in a wooden boat-shaped coffin and lid, one dated ad 610 ± 110, the other ad 650 ± 100. At Hartlepool Bay, the skeletal material provided a date of 2730 ± 60 bc, the earliest of the British finds. The baby's skeleton from Prestatyn will be C14 dated in the near future.

The largest group can be dated from their associated artefacts. This is most reliable when the human remains and the objects were found together and survive. In some cases, dates come from the description of artefacts found with the bodies, but are now lost. These show a strong bias to the prehistoric period, and the Bronze Age in particular. The two groups of burials from (32) Methwold, and (33) Methwold Severalls, were associated with artefacts, and would appear to be Bronze Age in date. The site at West Tofts, about 5 miles to the east, produced an oaken coffin and with the bones inside were 30 small beads of a blue colour, a cannel coal face and a gold funnel. The simple illustrations led Clarke to attribute the burial to the Early Bronze Age (Clarke 1960). Just to the west of Methwold, the same date was given by Grahame Clark to the Southery Fen Female, from the jet beads and bronze awl or pin found with her. In the northern Fens, near Spalding, a Late Bronze Age socketed axe was found with the skeleton of a man. From further north, the woman's head from Pilling, Lancashire, had two strings of cylindrical jet beads, with one string having a large amber bead at its centre. Edwards tentatively assigns the find to the Bronze Age from this description and in comparison with finds from a Bronze Age burial at Todmorden (Edwards 1969).

At Wymondham, Norfolk, part of a human skull was found in association with Roman pottery. Early authors ascribed a Roman date to the finds at Austwick and Grewelthorpe from the style of the shoes and the clothing, and a Saxon date was given for one of the finds from Hatfield Chase.

Some finds have been dated stratigraphically, for example Shippea Hill Man to the Bronze Age. The group of seashore finds, described above, must also have a prehistoric date. The great depth at which the finds were buried in peat, 9 ft at Scaleby, 10 ft at Austwick and about 4 yds for the 1665 find at Hatfield, convinced the first reporters of these finds of their great age. Some of the bodies have been given a date by physical anthropologists from the measurements of the skull, but the variability in any population, must make this approach very tentative. Three English bog bodies can be given very accurate dates of death. The man and woman at Hope, Derbyshire were known to have died in a storm on the night of 14 January 1674. The unauthenticated discovery of a man and horse in armour in Solway Moss must have belonged to the battle fought there in 1542.

Trying to quantify the evidence of those mentioned above, the following range of dates occurs. One individual belongs to the Neolithic, 16 to the Bronze Age, 2–4 to the Roman period, 1 to the seventh century AD and 2 to the post-medieval period. The period 650 BC–AD 30 into which the C14 dated Danish finds fall (Tauber 1979) seems poorly represented, but a number of the possible ritual sacrifices cannot be dated at all accurately.

This leads us to consider the causes of death and the reasons for burial in peat. We are hampered with the English and Welsh material because of the high proportion of skeletal remains. Out of 82 finds 61 are known only from skeletal evidence, though some of these may have had tissue originally, especially where the bones are described as light in weight and dark in colour. A lot, particularly the Fenland material, are single or small groups of bones, either found in disturbed deposits or unrecorded. Crania were collected for detailed measurement and comparison by physical anthropologists (see Duckworth and Shore 1911, in particular). In some cases, a cause of death can be deduced from the bone. At Runham, Norfolk, a male skull included by Dieck in his list, was found in mud dredgings. Wells showed that the head had been decapitated from front to back (Green and Wells 1961). This leaves 20 individuals where another cause of death could possibly have been determined. Very few can be given for certain. Lindow Man suffered a blow to the head and a slit throat, and he had a garrotte round his neck. No other is reported to have had a noose or anything similar round the

neck, as is quite common in the Danish finds. No other had a slit throat. The others which can be shown to have met violent ends, form a group of isolated heads. Of these the find from Pilling resembles the continental group from Stidsholt Fen and Roum in Denmark, and Osterby in Germany. The skull, with its long plait of auburn hair and with part of the first vertebra attached, was wrapped in a woollen cloth and buried on its own under a clod of hardened moss. There are three others where the circumstances are similar; Lindow Woman (where great efforts were made without success to locate other parts of the body), and (19) Red Moss and (24) Worsley. The description of the Red Moss find as female with a plait of red hair, is very similar to the find from Pilling. At (15) Scaleby, all that was mentioned as being found was part of the skull, some hair and brain, and a portion of garment, which may indicate another to add to the group above. These form a very close geographical group.

To those suffering violent death, must be added those buried naked, and/or in a crouched or unusual posture, with no evidence of deliberate inhumation. These also must be considered as belonging to the group identified as ritual sacrifices by Glob. Clearly Lindow Man fits these criteria. The most important group comes from (45) Hatfield Chase, Thorne Moss and the Isle of Axholme. Two of the finds are described in great detail. One was a man, apparently naked for no clothes are mentioned, 'lying at his length with his head upon his arm as in a common posture of sleep.' His skin, hair and nails preserved 'his shape intire' though most of the bones had gone. The second was a woman found in 1747, naked except for a pair of sandals, lying 'upon one side bended, with her head and feet almost together.' There are at least three other finds similarly preserved from this area. Parts of south Lancashire may have produced as many such finds as the area just described. The remark 'sometimes in mosses are found human bodies entire and uncorrupted' (Leigh 1700) has been quoted twice already. The man from (5) Shippea Hill, though only a skeleton, 'was found hunched up and crowded into a small space, less than two feet square, as if the body had settled vertically.' Even more unusual are the two bodies found upright in the peat, at (27) Spalding and (1) Burwell Fen. Glob records a similar occurrence at Bormswisch in Germany, noted briefly in parish records of 1450 (Glob 1969, 147). Not only was the Burwell Fen Man found upright but he was also dressed in a belted leather coat, his arm raised and standing in a dug-out canoe.

The mention of a dug-out canoe leads us to consider

another group of finds. These are buried in wooden tree-trunk coffins and include the Burwell Fen Man, the examples from West Tofts and Maes-y-Pandy, and from Quernmore. All must represent inhumation after death by natural causes. Inhumation is a large category. Both Methwold sites, with 12 burials in all, are considered as inhumations. At Murchie's Cairn, the body was laid on its back, covered by stone flags. The woman's skeleton at Austwick was found extended on her back with her head and feet resting on stone blocks. A pair of sandals was found at a little distance from the body.

Accidental death in bogs must not be discounted. Samuel Finney remarked of Lindow Moss that sometimes men and cattle had been lost in the treacherous bog (see p. 11). Grewelthorpe Man was considered to have lost his life this way. It is unfortunate that the description of this man is not more detailed. The clothing was very complete for an English bog burial and retained its colour, rather than having turned to a more uniform red-brown as is common with most bog finds. No indication of posture, hairstyle, age or depth in the peat is included. Fully dressed men are rare finds from an early period and it is hoped that an earlier account may be found to fill in some of these facts. The Shippea Hill Female was considered the victim of drowning, and the circumstances of the Hope and Solway Moss incidents are well known.

Totalling these figures, of the proportion where cause of death can be surmised, 13 would fit some of the circumstances of the ritual sacrifice victims outlined by Glob, 19 must be considered inhumation burials and 5 probably died by accident. The relative frequency of each category implies that the practice in late prehistoric and Roman times of sacrifice or execution followed by deliberate deposition of the victims in peat bogs, can be demonstrated for the northern half of England. More frequently found are inhumation burials, sometimes in wooden coffins, which are more widespread through England and Wales. Lhuyd's remark on the find at Maes-y-Pandy, 'and yet they who placed this coffin here might have regard to the perpetual preservation of it' (Gibson 1722, 775), may provide a motive for burial in peat. In the Fenland, the prehistoric landscape would have been dominated by peat moss and so bog burial would have been a necessity. Accidental death always remains a possibility for those trying to exploit the wide range of resources offered by peat bogs.

A brief mention of other human remains from watery places in England may indicate that bog burials are one aspect of a wider tradition. The crouched skeleton under a cage of wooden beams, recovered from a stream bed at Perranarworthal, Cornwall was mentioned in the introduction (Whimster 1981, 180). The Thames is a river producing a large amount of late Prehistoric metalwork of possible votive origin. An intriguing antiquarian note suggests human remains may also have been commonly found: 'Eleven skulls dredged from the Thames at Kew with bronze swords, spearheads, daggers, celts (stone and metal), British pottery, iron implements, bones etc. Quantities of human bones are met with by the dredgermen, who being superstitious heave them overboard.' (Tupper 1866).

Ross collected together a number of instances of human skulls from unusual watery places (Ross 1967). Oddest of these was the collection of 17 skulls made in 1946–9 in an underground pool of the River Axe in Wookey Hole Cave, Somerset (Mason 1951). The skulls were of adults, 25–30 years old, at least two of which were female. The pool also produced Roman pottery of the first to second century AD. A well at Heywood, Wiltshire also produced human skulls in association with Romano-British pottery (Pugh and Grittall 1909). The well known late Roman votive site of Coventina's Well on Hadrian's Wall, which produced many thousands of coins and metal objects, also contained a human skull. These incidents combined with the group of isolated heads from peat bogs support the conclusion: 'The cult of the human head then constitutes a persistent theme throughout all aspects of Celtic life, spiritual and temporal, and the symbol of the severed head may be regarded as the most typical and universal of their religious attitudes' (Ross 1967, 126).

Finally, not only well-preserved human remains come from peat bogs. English peat bogs have produced animals where the tissue survives. Lindow Moss produced a 'decomposed skeleton of a boar' (Norbury 1886). At Dulverton, Somerset 'many pigs were found in various postures, still entire. The shape was preserved. The hair remained on their skin, which had assumed a dry membranous appearance. Their whole substance was converted into a white, friable, laminated, inodorous and tasteless substance. When exposed to heat, however, it emitted an odour precisely similar to broiled bacon.' (Rennie 1810, 521). Other organic materials are found placed in peat bogs in Ireland, bog butter in particular. Because of the splendid preservation of these things, the same question arises over whether their presence results from deliberate burial, ritual sacrifice or accidental loss. Patterns must be looked for but a wide range of alternatives must always be kept under consideration.

Bog Bodies in Scotland

The Scottish discoveries present a very different picture from those found in England and Wales. The sample is smaller with only 16 sites producing 36+ individuals. Twelve of these come from a single site, (59) Bressay, where the burials are probably of quite recent date, but where very little of the bodies survived. The finds are concentrated in the Highlands and Orkney and Shetland. Lowland Scotland, rich in mosses, has so far yielded only two sites, (63) Ards Moss and (64) Greenhead Moss.

The most striking difference is the age of these discoveries where it is known. With the exception of the rather unsubstantiated finds from Stirlingshire, none of the Scottish finds is considered earlier than the sixteenth century, either by their discoverers or by those dating the associated artefacts. They cluster around the end of the seventeenth century, where two particular individuals are closely dated by the coins in their pockets. They come from (56) Quintfall Hill, and (61) Gunnister. This clustering has produced, on a number of occasions, the explanation that these people were Covenanters, caught in the religious persecutions of the seventeenth century. Many of the bodies have a wealth of associated clothing and artefacts, much of which survives for study (Henshall 1952). Up till now it is this aspect of Scottish bog bodies which has created most interest but before developing this theme further, another peculiarity of the Scottish material must be mentioned.

Preservation in Scottish bogs is much less complete than elsewhere. None of the finds had the appearance of Lindow and Tollund Man, and so they have not provoked the same interest or comment as remarkable human remains. Information about sex, age, cause of death, hairstyle etc, is seldom available. Indeed some Scottish bogs seem to dissolve away all human remains, both tissue and bone, with time. This is what Hunt found so remarkable about the Bressay find (Hunt 1866a). It was only after a number of coffins had been examined that they were shown to have had human occupants, when a fingernail was found in a pool of a fatty substance. Only the last of the twelve coffins found had a recognisable human body with tissue and bone, and this came from a greater depth and was fully waterlogged. The Bressay site, with its sawn Norway Pine coffins, could hardly be earlier than AD 1700. The other datable Scottish finds are almost all recorded as skeletons, sometimes with hair surviving. The baby at (58) Huntsgarth was only recognised by a few hairs and the shape of the space within the cloth, in which it had been wrapped. Chemical tests for human remains proved negative.

Typologically, the two earliest Scottish bog burials come from (52) Longside and (65) Oban. These sites produced three oak coffins made from single tree trunks, which compare closely with the finds from West Tofts, Maes-y-Pandy and Quernmore. This later group are thought to range in date from the Early Bronze Age to the seventh century AD. Oak tree trunk coffins can also be found outside bogs as in a tumulus at Gristhorpe, Yorkshire (Elgee 1930). Both the descriptions of these Scottish burials say that no human remains were found, and at Oban the fill was described as 'unctious and mixed with charcoal'. So the oldest Scottish sites, of medieval date or earlier, have lost all obvious traces of the bodies that they contained. It must be assumed, therefore, that the distribution of Scottish bog burials by age, is very misleading. Only the youngest may have survived and the practice of prehistoric bog burial may have occurred but nothing of it has been preserved, except at the as yet unlocated site in Stirlingshire.

What Scottish bogs do preserve, spectacularly well, is woollen clothing. This has received specialist study by Audrey Henshall in particular. Her conclusions on the style of the clothing and the techniques of production have led to the dating of most of the Scottish bog bodies. However, there must be some danger of a circular argument when looking at a closed group of material like this. Now other countries have produced woollen fabrics from the prehistoric period onwards, the greater age of some of the production techniques and styles of fabrics may be seen to apply to the Scottish finds. A new study of the clothing may broaden the unusually narrow range of dates given to Scottish bog bodies. The other point it raises is that apparently isolated finds of clothing within bogs may have represented a bog burial. This is especially true for Scotland where the preservation of bone and tissue can be shown to be shortlived. Objects of value like the hood from St Andrew's, Orkney, thought to be Viking in date, were unlikely to have been lost carelessly. In England and Wales, this may be true of leather objects, particularly pairs of shoes found together, which are recorded as finds from great depths in bogs (e.g. Scaleby, Stukeley 1776, 57; Chat Moss, Baines 1868, 596; Port Carlisle, Denny 1871, 166; Ince Moss, Owen 1982, xiii).

The explanation for bog burials in Scotland seems more straightforward than for England and Wales. Deliberate interment seems the most common reason. Sites nos 52, 53, 54, 58, 61, 65 and 66 would fit under this heading. Some sort of catastrophe, like shipwreck or battle, may explain the two larger groups of finds at (54) Culrain and (59) Bressay. The man found at (61) Gunnister seems to have died in a winter storm, been found later and buried on the spot; very similar to the circumstances surrounding the couple from Hope. Two victims may have died in suspicious circumstances, at (56) Quintfall Hill (killed with a blow to the head), and at (64) Greenhead Moss, (dumped in a shallow grave with evidence of sword cuts). At Quintfall Hill, robbery as a motive must be ruled out as the man's purse remained and no clothes were taken from the body at Greenhead Moss. The find from (55) Clayton Hill seems to have had a similar fate to these two.

None of the Scottish finds can be shown to have been ritually sacrificed. The examples from (51) Stirlingshire seem to have been associated with a quantity of Bronze Age metalwork and there may have been a votive origin to some or all of this material. The remainder may be far removed from the Iron Age, but the prevailing conditions of preservation in most Scottish peat may not preserve human remains for any length of time. The subtleties of preservation do favour woollen materials and have provided a unique collection of peasant clothing, which would have been lost under normal conditions. The sample from Scotland is another warning against oversimplifying the reasons for and the survival of bog burials.

Bog Bodies in Ireland

The Bogs of Ireland: their nature and recent history

The ubiquitous nature of bogs in Ireland, their instability, both seasonal and otherwise, made it quite certain that they should claim many victims. As early as 1633–6, Stafford's inquisition of land in Sligo stated that 'Carowtempeall, in the Parish of Emlaghfad, Barony of Corran,' ... was ... 'a great scrope of bogge and drowning places, which latter place is supposed to designate the holes and quagmires left when cutting away the peat for fuel' (Wood-Martin 1902, I, 113).

It seems that at a time when English bogs were being drained, and were therefore contracting in size, those of Ireland were growing, often at a prodigious and uncontrollable rate. In 1652, Gerard Boate clearly articulated definitions of four sorts of wet bog: dry heaths, grassy bogs, watery and miry bogs and hassocky bogs. After issuing warnings against entering boggy areas which were deceptively green, he went on to explain how some bogs did dry out in summer sufficiently to take the weight of animals for pasture, yet remained impassable to man and beast in winter. Permanent bog could only be crossed by narrow paths 'in which nimble trick, called commonly treading of the bogs, most Irish are very expert, as having been trained up in it from their infancy.'

'Watery bogs' he considered not to have been quite so dangerous: with water lying upon them they represented visible hazards. Although not strictly comparable to any modern bog classification, it is worth having Boate's account in mind when considering present-day explanations of the origins, morphology and growth of peat bog (e.g. Barry 1969).

The overall distribution and advance of bogs in the eighteenth century appears to have remained largely unchecked by fuel-cutting, superficial agricultural improvements or even by drainage. It is not easy to obtain statistics of the amount of land surface covered by bog at this time. The first twentieth century distribution map of peat, published by the Geological Survey in 1922, plotted some 3,028,000 acres of bog (Cole 1922), which is about one-seventh of the land surface – a fraction comparable to that suggested as recently as 1953 (Charlesworth 1953, Fig. 98, 254–5). Though apparently larger, allowing for differences in definition of the areas mapped, the 1922 figure was about the same as it had been a century earlier (Kane 1845, 35), at 2.83 million acres.

At present, peatland covers 16.2%, or 1.34 million hectares, of Ireland. Differences in the total recorded area covered, noted over the past half-century may probably be due more to varying investigational techniques than to real advances or regressions in the peat margins (Hammond 1981, 1–6). Without further detailed research it is not at present possible to assess bog diminution rates. The clearest impression of the area covered at present is to be had from Hammond's coloured map, pp. 26–7 in *The Atlas of Ireland* (Royal Irish Academy, 1979).

Whatever its conjectural area, by 1809 bog was considered so important as to have warranted the establishment of a Commission 'to inquire into the nature and extent of the several bogs of Ireland, and the practicability of draining and cultivating them' (Davies 1983, 20, 23). Over a million acres was surveyed within five years, and among those engineers undertaking it was Richard Lovell Edgeworth, who was to inform us of the empty woollen coat from Co. Longford in one of his written submissions to the Commissioners (no. 104).

Besides population pressure, there were other, more urgent reasons why government and learning should have required a clear idea of the nature of the bogs. By the time of the survey eight bog flows had been recorded from seven counties (Alexander *in press*). A bog flow is quite literally the movement of a water saturated peat mass carried away and re-deposited some distance from its origin. Precise details of these early flows are not always clear; nevertheless, the acreages involved were often staggering in size. For example at Castlegarde, Co. Limerick, in 1708, some three million cubic metres moved and was re-deposited. In 1745, at Dunmore, Co. Galway, material from a source area of 4 hectares was re-deposited over 33 hectares of ground.

A total of 38 major flows have now been recorded, from before 1697 (Molyneux 1697) to 1984 (Alexander *et al* 1985 and *pers comm.*) in some of which only a few acres of material moved or was re-deposited. In one case in 1885, at Castlereagh, Co. Roscommon, almost six square miles of ground was affected by peat re-deposition. Many smaller flows probably went unrecorded.

It will never be known how many lives have been lost through such natural disasters; according to Lewis's *Topographical Dictionary*, of 1837, 'near Doon [Doonmore], Co. Tipperary, at the close of the eighteenth century, more than 100 acres of bog moved from one townland into two others, destroying 13 cabins, the inmates of five of which perished.' Mortality through this sort of disaster may have been rare, but given ideal conditions of preservation, it would have required only a handful of similar occurrences to more than account for all the human bodies, clothing and shoes in the archaeological record.

Bog flows are therefore very strong potential progenitors of preserved material. The volatile peat having settled, drainage and farm improvement would probably have obviated the possibility of preserving a good deal of flesh; only in rare examples might this have taken place.

The Bodies

That bodies have been both lost and found in bogs since the seventeenth century has already been well-illustrated. In common with other antiquarian finds, records of their discovery relate closely to the availability of printing and the spread of an intellectual awareness of the past. Consequently, during the period of greatest dependence upon peat fuel, when both peasant agriculture and more sophisticated drainage projects were in hand, bodies were only recorded when they came to the notice of men (or women) of learning. That a great deal of useful archaeological information continued to be lost well into the nineteenth century may be inferred from the Ordnance Survey Memoirs for Co. Londonderry. Sadly, in Ireland, it has remained unfashionable to investigate anatomical details of the finds until relatively recent times. Having explained the complexity of the factors affecting recording and publication on the one hand, and discovery, on the other, the mean discovery date of *c.* 1870 for Irish bog bodies is not of any great significance. However, what must optimistically be conjectured from this discussion, and from the gazetteer, is that since Ireland retains great expanses of bog, and since both drainage and fuel extraction are continuous processes, greater public awareness should ensure that bog finds of all types will continue to be made, and be properly investigated and recorded.

Although gazetteer entries for Irish finds number 53 (excluding a number listed by Dieck in 1976 which cannot at present be accounted for), only 26, or roughly half, are of fairly complete well-preserved humans. There are otherwise three heads, (with hair), five skeletons, and eight skulls. For the rest, comprising nine or ten examples, we are dealing with empty suits of clothes, odd coffins and stray pairs of shoes.

The Irish sample contrasts strongly with the English in that a larger proportion of the English fen and bog material was exclusively skeletal. Upon present impressions fewer pieces of early costume have survived outside Ireland and Scotland. Some further idea of the wide geographical range of organic survival in Irish peat soils is to be had from the records of dozens, if not hundreds, of leather shoes, listed on a card index at the National Museum of Ireland.

Dating of the Bodies, and their Modes of Interment

Having explained something of the milieux likely to produce or to have preserved the bodies, it is now necessary to examine critically the evidence for the apparent interment of bodies in Irish bogs from Neolithic times. This will be undertaken chronologically, explaining certain problems of the study as the narrative progresses.

The difficulties of dating the Irish finds are very similar to those experienced elsewhere. So far, only three Irish burials have been investigated pollen analytically. The first, a skeleton now preserved in the Anatomical Museum, University College, Galway, was discovered in Stoneyisland Bog, Portumna, around 1929.

'It was found, according to Mr Dorphin [finder], lying on its back within a few inches of the marl at the base of the bog' at its centre, where the bog was 10 feet deep. 'The back of the head' was 'in contact with the marl at the base of the turf. The arms and legs were found in their natural relations to the body, the arms being extended and at right angles to the body.'

The retention of the natural relations of the limbs to the body and the different parts of the limbs to each other goes to show that the body had not sunk slowly down from an originally higher level in the bog; that it was lying in the position and at the level where it originally lay. The position of the arms does not suggest a burial, but rather that the body sank in the waters of what was then a lake, and settled on the bottom of the lake.'

Tree stumps and the ashes of fires had earlier been observed at a higher level than the skeleton. The only other artifacts from the same bog had been two dug-out canoes (Shea 1931, 73–4).

Comparative anatomical studies had shown the skeleton to have been of prehistoric origin. The diagnostic features had been wear on the joints of certain bones; heavily worn teeth, and a skull that fitted the contemporary notion of Neolithic man.

Pollen from the site was analysed by a Mr White from Queen's University, Belfast. Current terminology differs somewhat from that of half a century ago, so it is now difficult to assess his work. Prof Shea accepted Mr White's stratigraphic argument that the skeleton had been lying upon peat of about 4,500 to 2,000 BC. The published evidence includes no section or pollen diagram, and it remains possible that, as Shea originally explained, the body had entered a lake, or at least had fallen into a large bog pool; its peat base may have been Neolithic in origin, but only re-investigation will explain the full story of this mire.

Similar reservations must be expressed at the attempted pollen dating of the Mount Bellew, Co. Galway (99), skulls, found during drainage operations around 1935 (Martin 1935, 155–6), but only conjecturally dated later from peat samples taken at that time. The imprecise vegetation zones to which the finds were then attributed – the transition from Zone VII to Zone VIII (Mitchell 1945, 17), which suggested the possibility that the skulls could have been of considerable antiquity, was later to be changed, making more likely a date in the historic period (Mitchell 1951, 117ff).

Upon present evidence, neither the Portumna nor Mount Bellew finds appear to be datable within a close time bracket. However, in 1956 A. G. Smith examined peat samples from the Dungiven Costume (no. 85; Henshall and Seaby 1961–2, 136–7). His examination of a sample of 520 pollen grains produced a most tantalising result. On account of the high percentages of *Pinus* (pine) and low percentages of *Ulmus* (elm), it was felt that the peat had belonged to one of two widely separated periods; the Bronze Age before about 1000 BC on the one hand, or the Irish Plantation period on the other. Using other circumstantial evidence, it was convincingly argued that the latter seemed the more likely. So Smith's conclusion that this body had been deposited in a shallow water-filled ditch during the seventeenth or early eighteenth century coincided with the evidence for the dating of the costume. The obvious value of this investigation make it clear that further pollen analytical work is necessary.

Although many Bronze Age interments (mainly cremated), are known from sites subsequently covered by peat, there is no archaeological suggestion that at this time, or during the Iron Age, peat was habitually used as a medium for interment in preference to any other form of soil. It is now a commonplace among many prehistorians that prehistoric man was attracted to marshes and to water, and that the reasons why so may artifacts (particularly from the Middle Bronze Age to the Iron Age), have been found in such situations is attributable to this accredited attraction (Torbrügge 1972).

Sadly, it is likely that many of the types of artifact with which the theory is concerned would not, nay could not, have survived in any other types of ground condition. Metalwork is so vulnerable to decay that it usually rusts or corrodes unless buried deeply in the average type of North West European soil. Only anaerobic conditions preserved the more fragile metalwork (Briggs, *in press*). The same may be said of human and animal flesh, so that at present there is some circularity in the argument which appears to demonstrate bog or river finds to have been ritually deposited. Although it is true that La Tène Iron Age ritual deposits are known from the sites of springs in France, that is not to say that all water was held in veneration by all prehistoric men.

Both individuals, and their belongings could have been lost in bogs at almost any time in the past. In December 1954, drainage prior to peat cutting at Nahana td., Co. Offaly, brought to light a discrete collection of items thought to have belonged to a travelling man of Christian times (Raftery 1959). They have been omitted from the gazetteer since neither clothing nor body accompanied them. Nevertheless, they could have been the sole relics of a traveller, his body and clothes having perished. Detailed investigation of the pollen from near the site of the discovery, by Miss Parkes, and a radiocarbon date from material nearby led to the suggestion that the 'gear' was lost about a thousand years ago.

This traveller's equipment included two bone spoons and a horn drinking horn, a strike-a-light and various wooden fragments, probably from a container. The assemblage shares two or three pieces (the bone and horn items), in common with a late seventeenth-century clothed burial from Gunnister, Shetland (no. 61) (Henshall and Maxwell 1951–2).

It is difficult to accept that the evidence from Nahana td. provides a particularly secure date. One of the most telling problems of the discovery was that it had been made from beneath the mud floor of a former pool. So the loss might easily have been made when a traveller fell into the pool, or it could have been cast there by disappointed Tories (Irish robbers). Either way, as Raftery admitted at the time, 'these are items which correspond to those comprised in the well-known travelling sets of the eighteenth century; they represent the minimum that could be carried by a traveller in order to sustain some comfort on his journeys'. The horn objects could have been made at any time (Raftery 1959, 7–8).

In many of the accounts of discovery listed in the gazetteer, no idea is given by the original informant as to the sex or possible age of the body. Many were without clothes (see p. 149 above) probably due to the adverse conditions within the peat. In other cases, only the clothing has survived. It is worth emphasising the probability that bodies clothed in linen, or in the finer worsted would have become denuded through conditions of hyperacidity. To what age these naked bodies could have belonged may never, however, be ascertained.

It has already been noted that soldiers were believed to have been recognisable among the Irish bog bodies. However, without archaeological evidence of their armour, weapon or clothing, the dating of the Gort-na-moyah (no. 86), Charlemont (no. 69) and Drumadreen (no. 79) finds must remain conjectural. The claim that the male body from Mulkeeragh (no. 88) was in full military uniform, because his finders identified the clothing as of tartan, is one which raises questions fundamental both to the credibility of these antiquarian accounts, and to the date at which tartan (*sensu* the Scottish clans), was introduced into Ireland, if ever it was

(McClintock 1950 *passim*). Some caution over the credibility of the early informants should naturally be exercised, but in this case the matter seems to be less one of credibility, than of definition. By 'tartan', the finders were almost certainly concerned with what would nowadays be termed 'check' pattern (Dunbar 1949). Tartans as we know them were not developed in Scotland until later in the eighteenth century.

Over twenty-five of the remaining finds comprised either clothed bodies, or clothing suggestive of the former existence of a body which had disintegrated. Many of these were only fragments of cloth, or of ancient dress. Only a handful have been well-preserved and studied. Some were of wool, some of animal skin. Among the garments of animal skin is the cape from Derrykeighan (no. 67), and that upon the murdered body from Flanders (no. 84).

Clothed Bodies

A handful of complete costumes are well recorded and have been preserved. Two or three have been studied in some detail and upon stylistic considerations, appropriate dates of interment have been forthcoming. The best-known of these finds are: from the 'Hill Farm', Flanders td., Co. Derry (no. 85), dated *c.* 1590–1650; Carnanmoyle td., Co. Donegal (no. 91); Cloonbenes td. (no. 98) and Castleblakeney, (no. 100), both in Co. Galway; Emlagh td., Co. Kerry (no. 102) and Killery, Co. Sligo (no. 111), all ascribable to a roughly contemporary sixteenth–seventeenth century date. There is but one bodyless woman's costume, from Shinrone, Co. Tipperary (no. 115) at the National Museum of Ireland, and with that of the young girl from Emlagh, is all that survives of female attire of this same period.

Descriptions have come down to us of a small group of early clothes which are almost certainly now lost; the most important of these are the habit of the Drumadreen td. ? woman (no. 79), which may have been comparable to the 1954 Flanders td. find (no. 85); the earlier of the two finds from Flanders (no. 84), and the Mulkeeragh td. find of 1753 (no. 88), all from Co. Derry. These, together with the Drumkeragh burial (no. 94), already noted for its significance to the history of the study, might also be conjectured as having been post-medieval in origin.

A number of items of clothing mentioned in the gazetteer have yet to be re-located, if indeed they still exist. A more thorough examination of other pieces of early costume now at the National Museum of Ireland and elsewhere will no doubt shed more light on the period or periods at which bodies were being claimed by the Irish bogs. Artifacts other than clothing do not commonly accompany the known finds. There are, nevertheless, some noteworthy exceptions.

From Dunmore bog, Co. Derry (no. 83), came a wooden spoon and plate, probably carried by a traveller who died from exposure. The lady from Terrydremont, td., also Co. Derry (no. 89), had carried a well-turned wooden crutch; another from Carnanmoyle td. Co. Donegal (no. 91), had possessed a bag, woollen tassels and a kerchief. It is possible that the Drumkeragh lady had carried something metallic which stained her clothes. Two finds were accompanied by wooden staves; the Castleblakeney man (no. 100) and the Drumcroon skeleton (no. 82). The little girl from Emlagh (no. 102) carried a purse which contained some thread and raw flax, as well as a double-edged wooden comb.

Most tantalising of all, perhaps, was Edgeworth's account of the coat from Co. Longford (no. 104), in which he also described 'a razor with a wooden handle, some iron heads of arrows and large wooden bowls, some only half-made', with the remains of turning tools 'obviously the wreck of a workshop'. It is tempting to suggest that this assemblage had been overtaken by a bog flow, and to speculate as to what became of the owner of the jacket. Perhaps he perished in it, or was so fortunate as to have left it behind.

Modes of Burial

Although it is not possible to ascertain from the surviving records just how death took place in half the cases; conjecturally, a dozen or more (nos. 83, 86, 88–9, 91, 97–8, 100–2, 105, 111 and 112) appear to have fallen in by accident, or become trapped whilst crossing dangerous mires. Indeed, it has already been suggested that the Dunmore td. body (no. 83) died of exposure. Two individuals were believed by their finders to have been the burials of suicides, the identities of whom were known at the time of disinterment (nos. 68 and 76). A handful of descriptions relate to intentional burial where the reason for non-Christian burial is not clear (nos. 74, 90, 93, 94 and 118). The Drumard burial ground (no. 81) was obviously a secular killeenan or graveyard, which had been almost overtaken by bog-growth at the time it was surveyed.

More sensational are the four potential murder victims (nos. 75, 79, 84 and 119). The Ballygudden td. Co. Derry (no. 75) woman was accompanied by a child

with a strap around its neck fastened by a small buckle. Was this part of an old-fashioned papoose, or a case of strangulation, after which community justice did away with the infanticide? Or perhaps both had been struck down by disease. Alternatively this may have been the tragic case of a mother going out into the bog to rescue the child by lassooing it with the leather strap, only to find herself also victim of the mire.

It would be interesting to submit the clothes from Drumadreen (no. 79) to a forensic scientist, in order to ascertain if the diagnosis of the finder that the hole in the corpse's coat had been 'made by some sharp instrument, apparently for wounding the wearer to death, as for some inches around the cloth was clotted and stiffened with what had been formerly most probably blood.' Even more sinister was 'the sort of dagger, and several other deadly weapons, believed to have belonged to the murderous gang of robbers,' in Flanders td. (no. 84). The accompanying head may have become detached through natural causes *post mortem* rather than through murder. Finally there can be little argument against the verdict that a fractured skull indicated a violent end to the women from Thornhill Parish Church (no. 119).

Taken on balance, bodies seem to have been lost by accident, or more rarely, to have been despatched to the anonymous convenience of the bog by robbers, or even on account of domestic dispute. At present, the evidence seems to suggest that Irish bogs were at their most dangerous during the Medieval and post-Medieval period, during an expansion of peat growth. The recognition of considerable bodies and clothing finds attributable to the sixteenth and seventeenth centuries seems to bear out that this was the period when most victims were caught.

Bog Burials in Europe

Professor Glob's name will always be associated with bog burials, but it is really through the lifetime's research of Dr Alfred Dieck, now of Bremen, that the mass of information about these finds throughout Europe has been collected together. In a series of articles (e.g. Dieck 1958; 1963; 1972) and a monograph (Dieck 1965) he views the discoveries as a whole and publishes totals for each country. The totals rise from 465 in 1958, to 690 in 1963, and up to 1354 in 1972. The 1972 figure is presented in graphical form, country by country, to show the range and density of these discoveries (Fig. 53). Inevitably, the totals are biased towards Germany and Denmark, where the archaeological study of the discoveries has been carried out since the last century. Significant increases in totals for other countries could be made, as our researches set out to show. Dieck (pers. comm.) now gives a European total of over 1800.

The distribution map suffers from two shortcomings. Firstly, it only reflects where research has been carried out. Secondly, it can be argued that the map only reflects the distribution of peat deposits, which is limited by climatic and geological factors. This is an oversimplification. Fischer (Fischer 1979) analysed the known locations of the Danish finds and compared them with the distribution of peat bogs. He showed that West Jutland, with its many raised bogs, has significantly fewer bog corpses, compared with the remainder of Denmark. He compared more exactly the presence of sacrificed or lost pots of the pre-Roman Iron Age in bogs, with the finds of bog corpses. West Jutland seems to have been as densely settled in that period but there was apparently no tradition of depositing bodies or vessels into bogs. Such differential distributions have now been demonstrated in Great Britain.

Dieck's figures are presented uncritically. All human remains from peat deposits are included. The famous finds, such as Tollund Man, Grauballe Man and the Winderby Girl, had a high degree of preservation of tissue, but Dieck also includes sites where only skeletal remains are known. Which parts of the body survive does depend on the special qualities of the peat in which it was deposited. The state of preservation ranges from Damendorf Man, which is no more than a human skin bag, to those where the preservation is most dramatic and a range of soft tissues survive with skin, hair, and nails covering a framework of decalcified bone, and where the body cavity may preserve some internal organs, as with Tollund and Lindow Man. Skeletal material attracts less attention and is more likely to go unrecorded. Less information about the cause of death and few associated artefacts are recovered. Though there may be similar reasons for the presence of the body in the bog, it is hard to compare the finds or analyse them as deeply as those where tissue survives. Looking at the Scottish material in particular (Hunt 1866a; Henshall 1952; 1969), there may even be conditions where all human remains have disappeared and only associated artefacts, particularly clothing, survive. In such cases, distribution maps are hard to construct and the relative frequencies of occurrence have little meaning.

The different preservative qualities of the peat can be seen in Denmark. 'There is a concentration of finds in Central Jutland, where the soft parts of the corpses have not dissolved, while as on Funen and Zealand, the majority of corpses have been transformed into skeletons. This variation corresponds to the geographical distribution of different types of bog.' (Fischer 1979).

Such a difference occurs in England, where most of the Fenland finds are skeletal and those in Northern England have tissue surviving. This differential preservation also applies to associated organic artefacts, particularly clothing. Certain conditions will preserve only wool, others, linen. Often only the leather garments survive, shoes and belts in particular, which may give the impression of an otherwise naked body, which however may have been clothed on deposition. The specific qualities of peat from Lindow Moss have been discussed by others above, but it is a factor which should be considered in every case, before comparisons are made. It should also not be forgotten, that the ritual deposition of objects occurs in all types of watery places, lakes and rivers, as well as peat bogs, (Piggott 1953; 1965) and that the recovery of human remains from such places would be more difficult and would attract less comment. The example from Cornwall, quoted earlier (Whimster 1981), suggests that the practice was more widespread in watery places as a whole. Some rivers, like the Thames and the Witham, have produced volumes of prehistoric metalwork but any contemporary corpses would have decayed and their bones would have been dispersed. The distribution of bog corpses throughout Europe may be only a partial reflection of a more widespread practice.

The dating of bog bodies is a difficult problem. Most of the discoveries were made many years ago, usually by men digging peat for fuel by hand. The description of the circumstances and the associated stratigraphy is poor. Any artefacts from the bodies may be lost or too inaccurately described to allow a date to be confidently ascribed. The date of British and Irish bodies has been discussed above in detail, but an idea of those from the rest of Europe should be given. There were a great number of discoveries of bog bodies in the 1940s and early 1950s, in Denmark, Germany and Holland. Many of those preserved in museums were found during that period, and in Denmark none have been made since. During the war, coal was not available for domestic fuel and remained rationed or expensive in the years afterwards. Many small bogs were cut for peat for the first time and the amount of peat digging increased dramatically.

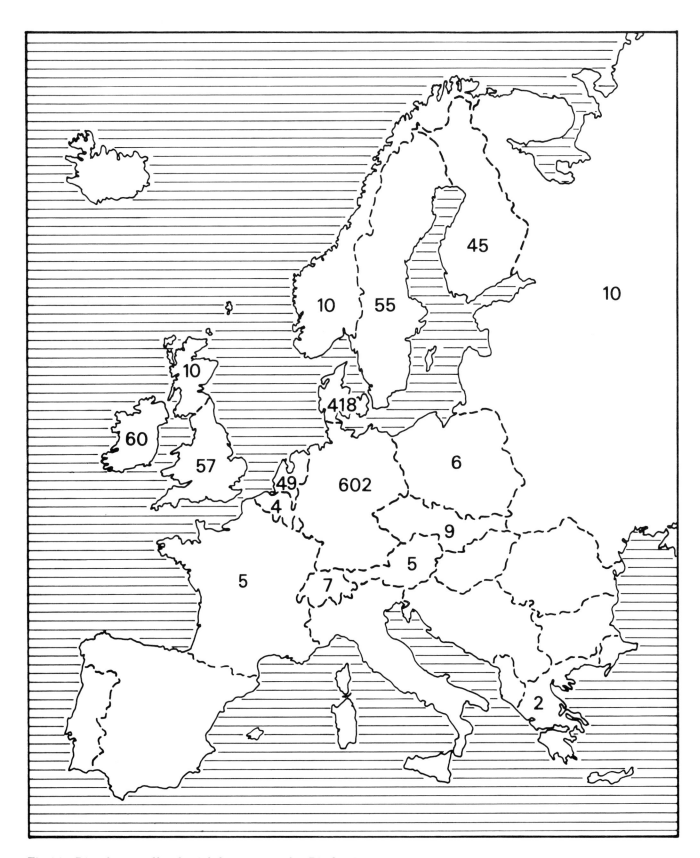

Fig. 53   Distribution of bog burials by country, after Dieck, 1965; 1972.

The latest discoveries were made just as radiocarbon dating became available as an archaeological tool. It was crucial in proving the antiquity of Grauballe Man (Glob 1969), as later it was important in dating Lindow Man. The original assay was AD 310 ± 100. However, it has been shown that bog bodies provide special problems to the dating laboratories. 'In contrast to cellulose and lignin of common plant materials, which are rather resistant to chemical reactions, proteins of animal and human tissues may react chemically with humic matter and other components in bog deposits.' (Tauber 1979).

Tauber redated Grauballe Man and dated for the first time eight other Danish finds (see Fig. 54). These formed a discrete group with their mean dates ranging from 650 BC to AD 30. The group consisted of the most studied of the Danish bog corpses, of which parts had been preserved, and where ritual sacrifice had been suspected. Again Dieck provided a less selective assessment. He gave a breakdown, (Dieck 1963) of the dates of those discovered throughout Europe, and included only the original date of Grauballe Man from the Danish group. His figures are shown in Table 19. About half, 153 out of 327, are given as prehistoric, and there is a significant Dark Age group, mostly from a single site, and a number from the seventeenth century, which are mainly Scottish and Irish in origin. There are discoveries from each prehistoric period and every century from the early Middle Ages onwards. Such a wide chronological spread gives a very different picture to the tightly dated Danish group, and suggests that there are many reasons for the finding of bodies in bogs.

Cause of death is the most tantalising fact to be learned from bog bodies. Most human remains from the archaeological record can tell us little, unless the fatal disease affects the bone. Many of the best preserved bog bodies have had violent ends and speculations on the events leading up to death really capture the imagination. In *The Bog People*, Glob is careful to select those individuals who contribute to his theory that Iron Age bog bodies are a ritual sacrifice to a goddess of fertility. It remains striking how this group of people, later confirmed as Iron Age in date by Tauber, do share a similar fate.

Nearly all have been executed or sacrificed by a method involving the neck. The following can be taken as examples. Tollund Man was found with a noose around his neck, and, like Elling Woman was probably hanged. Grauballe Man and the man from Raunholt had their throats cut. Several individuals had been beheaded, including the women from Stidsholt Fen and Roum, and the man from Osterby. One is thought to have been poleaxed and another knifed through the heart. These do not fit in and show there is some variation.

Both sexes are well represented and there is a wide range of age at death. The Winderby Girl was estimated at 14, the second Borre Fen Woman at 50, and Osterby Man at 50–60 years old. The first Borre

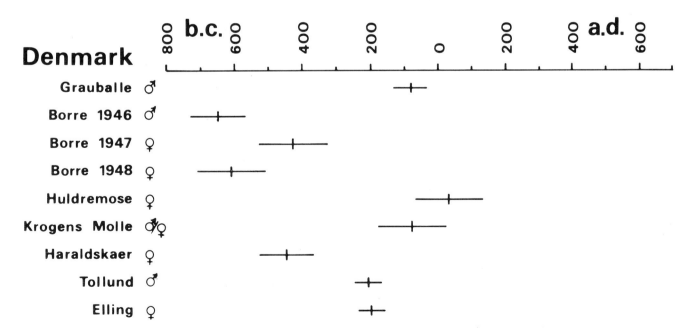

Fig. 54   Uncalibrated C14 dates of some Danish bog burials (after Fischer 1979).

Fen Woman may have been buried with her baby. The postures of the bodies were usually well described. Most are laid on their front or side with the knees bent into a crouching position. This position is said to be the one which a body naturally assumes after death. None of the bodies highlighted by Glob was laid out on its back, as in normal inhumations. Two were pinned down in the bog. The woman from Haraldskjaer Fen, 'Queen Gunhild', was held down in the bog on her back by wooden crooks driven into the bog at her elbows and knees, and by branches of wood crossing her chest; whose ends were similarly pinned. The discovery from Bunsok, Germany was very much the same. Other bodies were weighted down by stones or wood, either to stop the body floating to the surface of the pools in the bog, in which they had been deposited, or symbolically to stop their spirit escaping.

No general pattern emerges as to whether the bog bodies in this group were clothed or not. The majority of Danish bog bodies were deposited naked or with only items of leather, such as shoes, belts or caps. Commonly they were covered with leather capes or a blanket of woven cloth. Sometimes the clothing is placed alongside the naked body, the larger items rolled or folded up. Some women have been found fully dressed, the woman from Huldre Fen wearing the most complete surviving set of Iron Age costume. Dieck has published a fully clothed male body from Obenaltendorf (Dieck 1983). Much rarer are personal items of adornment or daily use. The first Borre Fen Woman had an amber bead and a bronze disc on a leather strap around her neck and part of a clay pot alongside her. A woman from Corselitze had a bronze pin and seven beads, and the Huldre Fen Woman had a bird-bone pin fastening her head scarf, and in her pocket was a horn comb. The bog man from Obenaltendorf wore two pendants. Sticks or rods were found with some bodies. Three hazel rods were found alongside the Undeler Fen Man and a willow post across Huldre Fen Woman.

The hairstyles show great variety and betray a greater interest in fashion than the clothing. The first Borre Fen Woman had apparently been scalped. The Winderby Girl had had her head partly shaved. Tollund Man's hair was neatly cropped. Many of the women wore their hair long and tied in plaits and knots, like the Elling Woman (Fischer 1979). Most famous of all is the Swabian Knot tightly tied on the right side of the head of the Osterby Man, just as described by Tacitus in his book on the Germani. The majority of men were clean shaven or with the stubble of a day or two's growth, but two were given as bearded, from Raunholt and Obenaltendorf.

The analyses of the contents of the last meals eaten by the men from Borre Fen, Tollund and Grauballe all suggest that the victims were killed in winter or early spring. But it can also be argued that only victims deposited in the cold weather of winter would survive to us. Those dying in summer or warm weather would begin to decay soon after death and the higher temperature of the bog-water could promote the continuation of this decomposition and thus leave no trace of the bodies, centuries later (Kjaerun, pers. comm). Comments on a number of the bodies include remarks on the delicate and undamaged nature of the hands and fingernails and suggest that these were not the bodies of working men or women.

Glob reviews all this evidence and also comments on the long tradition of depositing food vessels and objects of great value into Danish bogs. He sees bog bodies as part of this tradition and distinct from contemporary burial practices: 'Probably, then, the bog people were offered to the same powers as the other bog finds, and belong to the gods. Were this not so, there would be no reason for them to be in the bogs, which at this time in the Early Iron Age stood out as small woods in an otherwise almost treeless landscape. This matches Tacitus' account of the Germanic divinities: "Furthermore they do not consider it compatible with the greatness of the heavenly powers to confine their gods within four walls or to represent them in the likeness of a human face. They consecrate groves and coppices, and give the name God to that secret presence which they can see only in awe and adoration." Naturally we must except from this interpretation those who ended their days in the bog by accident, such as those who went astray in fog or rain and were drowned, one dark autumn day. We must also except those who were murdered and hidden in bogs, away from the beaten track. Several such are known amongst the bog people; but by far the greater number of the bog people, where proper observations are recorded, bear the stamp of sacrifical offerings.' (Glob 1969, 147).

Fischer is more guarded and stresses more the punishment aspect suggested by the accounts of Tacitus and Strabo, but concludes: 'The correspondence between finds of bog corpses and traces of activity in the bogs, that is, digging for peat or bog iron ore, indicates that it is logical to interpret the bog corpses as thank offerings to the god or gods who would have been disturbed by the activities of the people of the Pre-Roman Iron Age.' (Fischer 1979).

Lindow Man and Lindow Woman share many of the characteristics of the group of finds outlined above. Though they may not be comparable in date, both met with violent ends to do with the neck. Lindow Man was dumped almost naked in an open pool of water. His fingernails are neat and well-trimmed and his last meal was also lacking in any fruits or plant foods special to summer or autumn. However in the gazetteer appended each find must be viewed more critically and other reasons, perhaps just as interesting, must be sought for its presence in the bog. Deliberate burial, following death by natural causes, is the most common; accidental death and death in suspicious circumstances also occur. Glob mentions the burials from Hope in Derbyshire and two other incidents as exceptions to his theory. The proportion of bog burials of non-ritual origin in Britain and Ireland is very much higher and needs to be explained in other ways. Dieck's figures should not be taken as suggesting a common practice of ritual sacrifice across Northern and Central Europe, though this does appear widespread, but as a phenomenon occurring from many periods and with many origins.

Table 19: Dates of European bog bodies (after Dieck 1963).

| Period/Date | Dating Method | | | Other (Not always stated) | Total no. of bog burials |
	Pollen Analysis	C14	Associated Artefacts		
"prehistoric"	—	—	—	7	7
Mesolithic	4	—	1	2	7
Neolithic	5	+2	11	4	+22
Bronze Age	6	1	20	12	39
Iron Age	11	—	6	4	21
Pre/early historic	—	—	16	21	37
Century around AD 1	4	—	12	4	20
Roman	1	—	—	2	3
± AD 0–200	10	—	5	—	15
100–300	3	—	—	—	3
200–400	2	1	5	1	9
500–800	+37	—	1	—	+38
Dark Age	—	—	+3	1	+4
Early Medieval	—	—	4	—	4
Medieval	—	—	16	11	27
800–900	—	—	1	—	1
900–1000	—	—	—	2	2
1000–1100	—	—	—	2	2
1100–1200	—	—	2	—	2
1200–1300	—	—	1	—	1
1300–1400	1	—	5	1	7
1400–1500	—	—	4	—	4
Early post-medieval	—	—	6	2	8
Post-medieval	—	—	4	1	5
1500–1600	—	—	5	—	5
1600–1700	—	—	18	1	19
1700–1800	—	—	8	—	8
1800–1900	—	—	4	—	4
after 1900	—	—	3	—	3
Sum Totals	+84	+4	+161	78	+327

31 Lindow Man and the Celtic Tradition

Anne Ross

There are three important aspects of the Lindow Moss burial which, if considered in the light of Celtic religion and folk tradition, may lead to a better understanding of how and why Lindow Man met his death. The first factor to note is that he died the triple or threefold death, a well-known motif in insular Celtic and continental medieval literature. The second point to be considered is the role of bread in Celtic calendar festivals, especially the burnt or blackened bread given to sacrificial victims. The third and very important element is the discovery of mistletoe pollen in the gut of the bog man which would seem to cast light upon the season of the year when his sacrifice took place. Mistletoe (*viscum album*) was especially revered by the druidic priesthood. It is known in Irish as *druadh-lus*, 'the druid's plant', and in Welsh as *uchelwydd*, 'noble tree'. It was accredited with divine powers of both magical and medicinal nature, and was treated with great honour in druidic rites. The discovery of the severed head nearby is important, but will not be dealt with specifically here as publications on the all-important Celtic cult of the human head are listed in the bibliography (Ross 1957–84).

The Three Great Gods and the Motif of the Triple Death

The Roman poet, Lucan, (first century AD) refers to three mighty Gaulish gods to whom cruel human sacrifices were made (*De Bello Civili* I, 444–6). Each of these named deities is known throughout the wider Celtic world. Lucan records that victims were sacrificed to the tyrannous Teutates, 'God of the People', by being drowned in a vat or cauldron which was in all likelihood filled with some alcoholic beverage such as ale or mead, or perhaps water from a sacred well. A scene from one of the panels of the ritual cauldron recovered from the bog at Gundestrup, Jutland, Denmark, which casts much light on pagan

Celtic practice in the immediately pre-Roman period, shows the deity pushing his victim into a vat or well. Many vats and cauldrons have been recovered from boglands all over Europe and the victim may here have been offered to the presiding deity of the place and his body disposed of in the sacred bog. The second ruthless god named by Lucan is Esus, 'Lord, Master'. He would seem to have been equated with Mercury. His sacrificial victims died by hanging and stabbing. The third god whom the poet named is Taranis, 'Thunderer'. He was propitiated by fire.

The method of sacrifice apparently demanded by these major Celtic deities is, in true Celtic trinitarian fashion, reduced to a single sacrifice in the medieval literary tradition, the victims dying by stabbing, by burning and by drowning. These deaths are usually foretold by a druid or seer. In the story 'The Death of Diarmaid', a medieval Irish tale, the Irish king, Diarmaid mac Cerbhaill (sixth century AD), asks his wise men to foretell the nature of his death. They prophesy that he will die by a weapon, and he says he can easily avoid that. Then they tell him that he will drown in a vat of ale. Finally they tell him that his death will be by burning. Diarmaid scorns their prophesy and says that what they have foretold is highly unlikely. On the night of *Samain* (Hallowe'en), one of the four great festivals of the Celtic calendar year, a grim celebration which was attended by many sacrifices to the chancy gods, the king is in the feasting hall when his enemies attack him. One, Aedh the Black, runs his spear through the king, the hall is set on fire, he seeks safety from the flames in a vat of ale and is drowned. Only his head is preserved and this is carried off for burial at Clonmacnoise. Another king is killed in the same way and at the same season of the year, Muirchertach mac Erca, a cousin of Diarmaid's and a king of Ireland. Due to the treachery of his mistress he too is struck down by a weapon, the house is burnt down, and in trying to escape he drowns in a vat of wine.

Merlin the magician and the Irish Suibhne Geilt, both mad prophets, likewise meet with the threefold death. But the continental evidence is even more relevant. Two Latin poems by Hildebert, Archbishop of Tours in the early twelfth century, refer to the threefold death. A boy asks the gods how he will die. Venus tells him it will be in a noose; Mars states that it will be by a weapon, and Neptune tells him it will be by water. He climbs a tree above the water, falls so that his sword pierces him in the chest and, catching his foot in a branch of the tree, his head is submerged in the water and so he drowns (Jackson 1949, 535f.). The specific mention of the noose here is of great interest, and there are at least two other examples from the insular Celtic tradition, one, the earliest, being a prophecy made by Saint Columba of Iona in his seventh century *Vita*, where the burning episode is replaced by the falling from a tree – clearly referring to some form of hanging or garrotting. Lindow Man was killed by the noose, his throat was cut with a weapon, and he was deposited in a bog. This would seem to make the ritual and Celtic nature of his killing unarguable. There is no evidence that he had been brutally treated before death. If he was, as may well have been the case, of noble birth, perhaps even a chieftain or a royal priest, his death would have been regarded as a propitiation for the good of the whole community during some crisis such as inauspicious seasons, or threats from enemy tribes. Death held little fear for the Celts whose belief in the delights of the Otherworld made them indifferent to departure from their earthly state. Diodorus Siculus remarks: 'At dinner they are wont to be moved by chance remarks to wordy disputes, and after a challenge, to fight in single combat, *regarding their lives as naught* ... that the souls of men are immortal, and that after a definite number of years they live a second life when the soul passes into another body.' This theme of death and resuscitation is well-known in Celtic folklore and it is widely enacted in folk-plays throughout the British Isles. One of the most unusual and archaic of these plays was traditionally enacted until the late nineteenth century on the western sea-coasts and in the western Isles of Scotland, and was performed on St Michael's Eve (28 September). Michael was believed to be the guardian of the horses and the fishing grounds and his festival was one of the most popular in the islands and round the coasts of Britain. Moreover, as patron saint of heights, there is good reason to suppose that he has taken over the role of the pan-Celtic god, Lugos/Lugh/Lleu. There was a great deal of ritual associated with this benign feast, but the most impor-

tant feature was the death and resuscitation dance, *Cailleach an Dudain*, 'The Hag (Goddess) of the Mill-dust'. Like much that was associated with this festival it is extremely old and blatantly pagan. This account of the performance was witnessed at the end of the nineteenth century by the great Highland folk-lore collector, Alexander Carmichael:

> 'It is danced by a man and a woman. The man has a rod in his right hand, variously called *slachdan druidheachd*, "druidic wand", *slachdan geasacht*, "magic wand". The man and the woman gesticulate and attitudinise before one another, dancing round and round, in and out, crossing and recrossing, changing and exchanging places. The man flourishes the wand over his own head and over the head of the woman, whom he touches with the wand, and who falls down, as if dead at his feet. He bemoans his dead "carlin", dancing and gesticulating round her body. He then lifts up her left hand, and looking into the palm, breathes upon it and touches it with the wand. Immediately the limp hand becomes alive and moves from side to side and up and down. The man rejoices and dances round the figure. And having done the same with the right hand, and to the left and right foot in succession, they also become alive and move. But although the limbs are living, the body is still inert. The man kneels over the woman and breathes into her mouth and touches her heart with the wand. The woman comes to life and springs up, confronting the man. The tune varies vigorously and joyously ... the air is quaint and irregular, and the words are curious and archaic.' (Carmichael 1954, 207)

This strange death and resuscitation dance, a far cry from the simplicity of the Cheshire Soul-cakers' play, would seem to be a direct echo of Iron Age ritual and the man with his druidic wand, some distant, blurred memory of the pagan priest striking down his victim in the midst of ceremonial activity, for Caesar tells us that the whole community was present at the sacrifices. For the poor victims. however, their resuscitation, like that of Lindow Man, was to be in the next world. The druidic wand of the Hebridean dancer is reminiscent, for example, of the thirteen willow wands tied together with thirteen willow strips carried by King Boggan during the Lincolnshire Haxey Hood Game, enacted annually on 6 January, Old Christmas Day (Turner p. 171).

Another strange and archaic ceremony which took place in the Outer Hebrides until comparatively recently may have some links with the bog burials. Some of the 'victims' were found wrapped in animal skins or leather capes. The druids and seers of early Irish tradition wrapped themselves in bull-hides in order to communicate with the gods and see into the future. The Hebridean ceremony was performed by boys and young men who were known as the *Gillean Callaig*, 'Hogmanay Lads'. They paraded round the townships at night chanting a carol, of which there were several variations, called *Calluinn a' Bhuilg*, 'Hogmanay of the Sack'. Carmichael (1954, 149) gives a first-hand account of this performance. (The croft walls protruded beyond the thatched roofs.)

> 'One man is enveloped in the hard hide of a bull with the horns and the hoofs still attached. When the men come to a house they ascend the wall and run round sunwise, the man in the hide shaking the horns and hoofs, the other men striking the hard hide with their sticks. The appearance of the man with the hide is gruesome while the din is terrific. Having descended and recited their runes at the door, the Hogmanay men are admitted and treated to the best in the house. The performance seems to me to be symbolic, but of what it is not easy to say, unless the laying of an evil spirit. That the rite is heathen and ancient is evident.'

The most important man is the bull-man while the others run after him beating him as a scapegoat, who was, perhaps, originally sacrificed. The bull-man carried the Hogmanay skin and gave it to the man of the house, instructing him to put it in the fire, to go sunwise round his children and his wife. All who should inhale the fumes from the burning skin would be free from sickness and want for the coming year. The extreme archaism of rituals such as this which have survived into the twentieth century in a Celtic milieu is self-evident. The skins in which some of the bog bodies were wrapped may have had the same superstitious significance as the bull-hides of the druids and seers; the strip of fur around the arm of Lindow Man may possibly be compared with the strip of animal skin which was used in the Hogmanay ceremony, placed in the morass with the sacrificial victim to increase his powers of conveying health and prosperity to the community to which he belonged and, perhaps, over which he ruled.

Celtic Cake Ceremonies and the Blackened Bread

There were four major festivals in the Celtic calendar year. These were Imbolc, 1 February, sacred to the goddess Brigid (later turned into the Christian St Brigid) when the ewes began to lactate, the first day of spring. Next came Beltain, to be connected with the ancient pan-Celtic god, Belenos, 1 May, the beginning of summer. The third of these originally pagan feast days was the first-fruits festival held on 1 August, dedicated to the great god Lugos and known in Ireland as Lughnasa. The fourth, and most grim, sacred day was Samain, 1 November, when the world of the gods was laid open to mankind and he who dared could enter their perilous premises. These were all fire festivals, Beltain particularly so, for at that time the druids drove the stock through two great bonfires to purify and protect them against the hazards of the chancy summer. The summer and the winter solstices likewise received ritual acclamation. These ancient pagan feast days still survive in many parts of the British Isles and widely on the continent, under a Christian aegis and, naturally, in very aetiolated form. At each of these festivals, a flat round cake or bannock was the focal point of the feast, and its allocation to the man or woman, or couple, who would have the honour of breaking it and distributing it amongst the people was attended by much ritual and clear sexual undertones. In certain Celtic regions of Britain this ceremony is still observed, but it is rapidly disappearing. However, there are many records of it as it was performed, both in the past and, more recently, in the early twentieth century. Usually a large stake, often as much as ten feet in height, was driven into the ground in each individual township or community. On top of this, a large flat board was secured and the whole garlanded with fruits and flowers. In autumn, seasonal fruits were included in the display. A large flat bannock, usually made on a griddle, was then placed on the board. This structure clearly represented the sacred tree of pagan times for trees played an integral part in pagan worship in the Celtic countries. In some areas, all present danced round the 'tree', which in some places in Ireland was known as the 'bush'. Those who could dance the longest won the cake or bread which was then broken up and shared out amongst the company. Sometimes it was awarded to the prettiest girl and the most handsome lad, and he would lead her to the cake and present it to her for her to distribute it. Sometimes the dance was held at cross-roads, always a hazardous point. Sometimes the handle of the churn, on which the summer's supply of butter depended, replaced the stake. It was usually a communal performance, but individual households might put out a griddle cake on the churn-handle as an offering to the saint and a placation to other, more formidable beings. The following description of the sacred bread, baked for St Bride's (Brigit) Eve (Imbolc) (Danaher 1972) was recorded by an Ordnance Survey Investigator in Co. Derry in the 1830's. Rush crosses were made throughout Ireland, each region having its own design, many very intricate, and there are still people living who can make these traditional cruciform decorations. Before the ceremony the rushes for the crosses were blessed.

'A strone or large cake of oatbread is made in the shape of a cross. The rushes are thrown on the floor, and the strone placed on the rushes. All kneel round the rushes and the bread, and at the end of each short prayer a piece is taken off the strone by each person and eaten. When all is eaten the crosses are made, and when blessed by the priest or sprinkled with holy water, are placed over the door ... in the hope that the family may have a plentiful supply of bread until that time twelve months, and in honour of St Bridget.'

Strange heathen customs underlie many of these rituals. In Co. Kilkenny, for example, on the eve of Twelfth Night (Oiche Chinn), a large loaf known as the Christmas Loaf, was laid with much ritual upon the table. The doors and the windows were then closed and bolted. A member of the family, usually the mother, then took up the loaf and pounded it against the closed doors and windows, all the while chanting a *rann* (quatrain) in Gaelic. There were many variants of this custom, all of which were invocations for prosperity, fertility, health and protection from evil spirits. The Irish traditions which survive are rich and contain much of pre-Christian practice and belief. But it is in the Hebridean Isles that the most truly archaic rituals connected with the bread or cake festivals lie. One of the most fascinating records of the ritual attached to the making of the *struan* (anglicised *strone*) was recorded by Carmichael (1928, 201) in the west of Scotland, on the Eve of St Michael when 'pagan cult and Christian doctrine mingle like the lights and shadows on their own Highland hills'.

'A cake called "struan Micheil" is made *of all the cereals grown on the farm during the year*. It represents the fruits of the fields, as the lamb represents the fruits of the flocks. Oats, bere and rye are the only cereals grown in the Isles. These are fanned on the floor, ground in the quern, and their meal in equal parts used in the *struan*. The struan should contain a peck of meal and be *baked*

on a lamb-skin (uinicinn). The meal is moistened with a little milk, the sheep being deemed the most sacred animal. A *leac struain*, struan flag brought by the young men of the family from the moorland during the day, is set securely on edge before the fire, and the struan is set on edge against it. The fire should be of *crionach caon*, sacred faggots, such as faggots of the oak, the rowan, the bramble and others. The blackthorn, wild fig, trembling aspen and other "crossed" (evil, unlucky) wood are to be avoided.... If a member of the family be absent or dead, a struan is made in his or her name. The struan is shared among the family.... Various ingredients are introduced into the small struans such as cranberries, bilberries, brambleberries, carraway seed and wild honey ..., many cautions are given to her who is making the struan to take exceptional care of it. Ills and evils innumerable would befall herself and her house should any mishap occur to the struan. Should it break before being fired, it betokens ill to the girl baking it; if after being fired and before being used, to the household. Were the struan flag to fall and the struan with it, the omen is full of evil augury to the family. A broken struan is not used.... Next day, (the Day of Michael), the father puts the struan on a pure white board and divides it and a specially killed lamb amongst the whole family, and they take a piece of each in either hand and chant the triumphal song of Michael.'

That such elaborate ritual and deep superstition should persist until the late nineteenth century, not only verifies Carmichael's statement about pagan cults and Christian doctrine being closely intertwined, but provides us with a very real insight into the fears and superstitious beliefs of our Iron Age forbears and the lengths to which they must have gone, when human sacrifice was acceptable, and required by the gods, to ensure that no error was made when preparations for sacrifice, such as the bread for Lindow Man, in honour of the grim gods, were in progress. In the cautions given to the girl who baked the bannock, and the threatened evils which would befall her should she break it, one is reminded of the community of women (priestesses no doubt) who inhabited an island off the mouth of the Loire (Strabo, IV, IV, 6). Each year they took the roof off their temple and re-roofed it. This was a ritual act, in honour of their deity, and she who inadvertently dropped her load was torn to pieces by the other women and her remains carried round the temple as an offering to the god, or goddess. She had failed to perform the ritual correctly, and her punishment was death.

But, there are dark hints, still extant, that the scapegoat of the community was, at one time, sacrificed in Celtic countries. These may perhaps have occurred originally at all the festivals of the Celtic year, but the existing fragmentary stories known to the writer have all been associated with Beltain, when many sacrifices were made in the pagan past. These fragments are extremely important in our efforts to understand something of the nature of Lindow Man's end. Some very strange and pagan customs survived in Perthshire, Scotland, and were recorded in the eighteenth century by Martin Martin (1703). At the Beltain festival a specially prepared cake or bannock was broken up and distributed amongst those present. The person who received a certain *blackened* portion was called the Beltain carline (cailleach), and was referred to as 'devoted', i.e. devoted to the gods by sacrifice. The celebrants either seized him (or her) and made a pretence of throwing him into the great bonfire, or he had to leap through it three times, presumably when the flames had died down, and throughout the celebrations he was referred to as 'dead'. Martin says that wrongdoers were burnt in the fire, but gives no authority, although this certainly agrees with ancient practice. This record is very remarkable but even more astonishing is the fact that the custom survived in a remote part of Perthshire into this century. One of the best field informants in central Perthshire knew all about this Beltain custom although she had been too young herself actually to participate in it before it died out. In the wild mountainous country that surrounds Lock Tay, she pointed out a place which served as a kind of 'temenos', and which used to be regularly de-turfed and a great bonfire lit there, and where all the local people would assemble for the festivities. A large bannock was baked on a griddle but, no matter how carefully it was cooked, a blackened portion like a large thumb-mark always mysteriously appeared. When it was cooked, it was broken into pieces and distributed amongst those present. The person who had the misfortune to receive the blackened portion was regarded as the scapegoat and was chased out of the 'temenos'. 'But', the informant said earnestly, 'originally he would have been sacrificed'. Other people threw their portion of the Beltain bannock over their shoulder, invoking all the creatures who might harm them and their stock, natural and supernatural, saying, in Gaelic, 'I give you this, oh fox, preserve my horses',

'I give you this, oh eagle, preserve my lambs', and so on, including the local ghosts and bogles, the water-horse that haunts the river, and so on. She thought the scapegoat could only re-enter the community by leaping three times through the fire.

Another, less complete, but even more fascinating piece of information emerged in England. It is all the more surprising, because it comes from less than twenty miles from Lindow Moss, long before Lindow Man had been uncovered in his long resting place. It is in the High Peak District of Derbyshire where ancient Celtic beliefs still survive although, as is the case everywhere, these are rapidly disappearing. Stone heads were buried in the valley, wells garlanded with simple bunches of flowers at Beltain, the threefold mother goddess is known and acknowledged, and the Beltain bonfires lit on every farm. The writer watched them in 1977, and a splendid sight it was. The informant there, herself a native of the place, was brought up by her grandmother. Discussing the celebration of Beltain, she said that as a child she had been amazed that her grandmother, who was an excellent cook, always managed to burn part of the Beltain bannock. In Co. Cavan, Eire the writer has recently learnt that an old man of ninety-six there remembers the blackened bread when he was a boy. According to local information, five bog burials have been found in the county. Until comparatively recently in Ireland, peat-diggers have not cared to take away anything found in the bogs and have thrown objects of great interest and potential value 'back into the bog-hole', presumably because they had been 'offered'. More information about the blackened bread is likely to be forthcoming in the near future and this may cast further light on the contents of Lindow Man's gut.

Two further pieces of information about the burning of the grain, this time *before* the festive bread was made, would seem to be relevant here. Within living memory in Ireland, at the festival of Lughnasa, the first-fruits feast (Lammas), some of the grain must be harvested on the morning of the sacred day and prepared as bread or porridge before evening. When the harvest was late and the corn not yet ripened, or when time was short, a quicker method of procedure was employed known as 'burning in the straw'. The whole sheaf, or only the grain end, was set alight. This separated out the chaff and hardened the grain, which was then shaken reasonably clean of ash. In this way the cereal could be ground in the quern and the Lughnasa meal secured. Carmichael (1928, 250, f) recorded an interesting incantation in the Hebrides known as *Beannachadh*

Fuiriridh, 'The Blessing of the Parching' for, as in pagan times, all activity must receive the blessing of the Deity. He describes the process:

'When it is necessary to provide a small quantity of meal hastily, ears of corn are plucked and placed in a net made of the tough roots of yellow bedstraw, bent or quicken grass, and hung above a slow, smokeless fire. The bag is taken down now and again to turn the ears of corn. This net, however, can only be used for bere or barley; rye and oats, being more detachable, require the use of a pot or 'tarran' to dry them. This mode of drying corn is called '*fuirireadh*' parching ... Bread made of meal thus prepared has a strong peaty flavour much relished by the people.'

The Hairs in the Bread Content of Lindow Man's Gut

It is, of course, difficult to explain the presence of these hairs. It has been suggested that they stem from small rodents in the meal from which the bread was baked. This may well be the case. There are two possible alternatives. It has been seen that the bread baked ritually for St Michael's feast day was baked on a lamb-skin (uinicinn). That may perhaps have been used in the preparation of Lindow Man's last meal. Another possibility is the fact that in the Highlands of Scotland a substance known as 'bog butter' has been found, buried in peat bogs and contained either in a wooden trough or a tall keg (Close-Brooks 1984). A parallel to wooden troughs of this kind has been found at Glastonbury, dating to the pre-Roman Iron Age. Hairs are frequently found in this substance which would seem to indicate that it had been churned in a skin, a practice known in the Highlands as elsewhere. Bearing in mind the ritual nature of the baking of the St Michael bannock in a skin, these kegs of butter might have been deliberately made in a similar fashion. It is customarily said that the bog-butter was buried in the peat in order to preserve it. Crofters have always preserved butter made from the surfeit of summer cream by first salting it and then, after sealing the top of the stone or wooden crock with a thick layer of salt, pouring melted mutton fat over this to secure it further for use in the lean winter months. It is likely that these deposits of bog butter have a ritual origin, that they were offerings to the supernatural bog-dwellers in order that they should not entice the cattle into the morass, a hazard which is a constant theme in the incantations recorded by Carmichael and others. The hairs in Lindow Man's gut may thus indicate that the blackened bread itself had contained hairs from having been cooked in an animal skin, or that it was spread with butter which had been churned in a skin, or both.

Mistletoe and Druidic Rites

Mistletoe was accredited by the Celtic peoples with powerful magical and medicinal properties. But over and above its role in the popular beliefs of the people, it was greatly revered by the druidic priests. The oak was the tree which was most sacred to them, and when the strange parasitic plant with its moon-white berries, was found growing on an oak tree – the apple being its most common host – its sanctity was greatly enhanced. Pliny (XVI, 249) gives us the most succinct account of an impressive druidic rite in which the mistletoe plays a major part, and in view of the presence of mistletoe pollen in Lindow Man's gut, it would seem apposite to quote the passage in full here, in the context of this bog sacrifice:

'Here we must mention the awe felt for this plant by the Gauls. The Druids – for so their magicians are called – held nothing more sacred than the mistletoe and the tree that bears it, always supposing that tree to be the oak. But they choose groves of oaks for the sake of the tree alone, and they never perform any of their rites except in the presence of a branch of it; so that it seems probable that the priests themselves may derive their name from the Greek word for that tree. In fact, they think that everything that grows on it has been sent from heaven and is a proof that the tree was chosen by the god himself. The mistletoe, however, is found but rarely upon the oak; and when found, is gathered with due religious ceremony, if possible on the sixth day of the moon (for it is by the moon that they measure their months and years, and also their *ages* of thirty years). They choose this day because the moon, though not yet in the middle of her course, has already considerable influence. They call the mistletoe by a name meaning, in their language, the all-healing. Having made preparation for sacrifice and a banquet beneath the trees, they bring thither two white bulls, whose horns are bound for the first time. Clad in a white robe, the priest ascends the tree and cuts the mistletoe with a golden sickle, and it is received by others in a white cloak. Then they kill the victims, praying that the god will render this gift of his propitious to those to whom he has granted it. They believe that the mistletoe, taken in drink, imparts fecundity to barren animals, and that it is an antidote for all poisons.'

This remarkable account seems to point strongly to the ritual sacrifice of Lindow Man. When Pliny wrote his observations, human sacrifice had been banned by the Romans and it is not unlikely that the bulls were substitutes for what had originally been human victims. The purpose of sacrifice was not only to please and appease the gods. It was to ensure the fertility of the land, the stock and mankind. If Lindow Man took mistletoe pollen in drink, it would be a means of ensuring his potency which his sacrifice would then confer on the community. Kendrick (1927, 124) draws our attention to a tumulus at Gristhorpe, near Scarborough, which contained an oak coffin, covered with oak branches together with a large quantity of mistletoe, which had by then degenerated into a mass of vegetable material. The burial dates to the Bronze Age. The skeleton of an aged man, together with a bronze dagger and flint implements was found in the coffin. Kendrick also notes that something similar is recorded for Brittany where the funerary deposits were laid on a bedding of oak leaves, in the megalithic tombs. Whether mistletoe was also present is not mentioned. It is interesting to note, in the light of Pliny's remark that the Scottish Gaelic name for the mistletoe is an *t'uile-iochd*, 'the all-healing'.

Summary and Conclusions

The poet Lucan refers to three powerful Celtic gods, Teutates, to whom men were sacrificed by drowning, Esus, who was propitiated by the rope and the weapon, Taranis, whose sacrificial victims perished by the flame. The medieval motif of the threefold death occurs in Irish and in Welsh vernacular texts and was incorporated into later continental Arthurian literature. The victim was usually stabbed, burnt and drowned. In some versions he perished by the noose, by stabbing and by drowning. Lindow Man was subjected to the noose, his throat was cut with a weapon and he was committed to the sinister embraces of the bogland of Lindow Moor. *Bog*, adj. *bogach* are Gaelic words meaning soft. *Bograch* means 'a boggy place'. *Bogai* is Gaelic for bogey, *bobodha* means bogey-man. Boggane comes from Welsh *bwchi*. Turner has dealt with the very relevant Gawain material (Turner p. 178). The Green Knight is fully accepted as being identical with the Green Man who glares down balefully from the roofs and walls of our medieval churches and adorns many an

inn sign throughout the country. He may also be the Lord of the Crossroads of High Peak tradition, the 'Green Knight upon the Road', guarding the crossroads against all comers. Crossroads as we have seen were always places of danger, to be propitiated by dancing and by offerings and by images such as the benign 'Déesses Quadruviae', and the sinister, but evil-averting Sheela-na-Gigs, whose frank and hideous sexuality would frighten off the most daring of hostile bog-dwellers. Crossroads were especially frightening in boggy country where the wrong choice of route and the wiles of supernatural forces could well lead the lonely traveller into the horrors of the mossy morass.

The ritual of making and breaking bread, the communal eating of it, the fertility associations connected with gaining possession of it and distributing it, and the hints of its original sacrificial meaning, are well-attested in the Celtic world down to very recent times. The baking of the festive bannock was hemmed in by tabu. To break the bread before the correct time would be certain to bring ill luck and perhaps, at an earlier, pagan period, death.

Lindow Moss is a sinister, eerie place. It is situated in countryside which is rich in traditions which were probably Celtic in origin. The Cheshire 'horsings' are strange and many little known to the general public. That held annually at Antrobus, near Lindow, is perhaps the best-known, with its Soulers' play and its hobby horse ceremony which can be likened to the Welsh Mari Lwyd Christmas horse. These Cheshire horses would seem to have borne the generic name of Wild Horse; the name Antrobus has never been explained, but it could well be of Celtic origin. Sword-dancing, Morris dancing with stag antlers, stone heads fashioned and originally venerated and still regarded with superstitious respect, all these traditions based on ancient ritual are to be found concentrated in an area where the dark deities of the bog must always have presented a challenge and a threat to mankind.

The threefold death of Lindow Man, the blackened bread in his gut, the presence of mistletoe, sacred to the druids, are all pointers to the ritual nature of his death. The presence of the severed head found near him and at the same level in the bog, suggests that the place may have had a much greater sanctity than is at present demonstrable. The presence of the mistletoe pollen would perhaps suggest that the sacrifice took place at Beltain, which would accord well with the blackened bread, or at midsummer, again an important time for avoidance, observance and oblation in the early Celtic world. A journey into onomastics is always as hazardous as crossing a bog – full of pitfalls. However, it is possible that the name of the Cheshire Moss, *Lindow*, may mean 'Black Pool'. This is derived from Welsh *Llyn*, 'lake' and Welsh *Du*, 'black'. It should also be noted that Gaelic *dubh*, 'black' is anglicised to *dow*. Right or wrong, it is an attractive thought, if the entire site was indeed a votive pool or lake and the adjective would then have a *double entendre* – sinister pool or lake as well as dark in colour.

This brief paper is offered in an attempt to demonstrate the archaism of the Celtic tradition, and its relevance to the actual ritual which formed the nucleus of pagan Celtic religion. The oral tradition has an impressive ancestry, and it is known that the druids themselves taught their acolytes by word of mouth, scorning the use of writing for their sacred knowledge. Quotes of some length have deliberately been given from some impressive examples of rituals from the surviving Celtic world, the archaism of which is not in doubt. It is hoped that they may cast some light on Lindow Man's dark death, and provide some small clues which will stimulate other scholars in their future researches into bog burials and ritual deaths.

32 Boggarts, Bogles and Sir Gawain and the Green Knight: Lindow Man and the Oral Tradition

R. C. Turner

Introduction

The practice of ritual sacrifice must have left echoes in the oral tradition. The fears and forces which had to be assuaged must have been strong and felt long after they were superseded by a new religion. In parallel with the deposition of objects in peat bogs, this practice seems to have occurred across Northern Europe for much of late prehistory and into the early centuries AD. The tales of the Celtic and English oral tradition can be expected to have extended so far back and elements of the ancient ritual may be contained within them. This paper looks at the recurring themes suggested by those bog burials considered to be sacrifices, in the wealth of English and Celtic, dialect, poetry, folktales and custom.

Previous authors have looked in detail at the classical sources, Tacitus, Diodorus and Strabo in particular, and the light they throw on the contemporary or recently historic practices among the Germanic and Celtic tribes (see Kendrick 1927; Ross 1967; Piggott 1968; etc). Some tribes made human sacrifices for the good of the community and some punished severe crimes, like murder and adultery, with execution and burial in a peat bog. It is not the intention here to add to these assessments. Great sympathy with the underlying reasons for the fears represented by the finds from peat bogs is to be expected in the oral tradition, even though in its first written or recorded form, it may be further removed from the relevant period than the classical authors. However, archaeology can never reconstruct the intellectual framework to which the remains, identified as belonging to some ritual or religous ceremony, adhere. Therefore to understand why some bodies are discovered in peat bogs, some reliance must be put on the oral tradition.

Bogies and their Allies

Of the two main themes which have been detected, the first deals with tales and customs surrounding a class of fairies under the broad heading of bogies. Briggs in the *Dictionary of Fairies*, (Briggs 1977), gives the following list of variants: bogan, boggart, bocan, bodach, bogey-beasts, boggle boos, bogies, bogles, bogy, bugan, buggane, bugs, bug-a-boos, boggle-boos and bog bears. In their habits they can range from the mischievous to the outright dangerous. Their etymology clearly associates them with bogs and peat mosses. Some authors have gone even further and derived them from the Slav word 'bog' meaning god, brought by Danish invaders in the Dark Ages (Baring-Gould 1913, 85). The Oxford English Dictionary is contemptuous about this attractive hypothesis. 'That they are connected with the Slavonic bog, "god", is a mere fancy from the similarity of form without any evidence'.

Some of the different variants have a marked regional distribution. Boggart occurs in Westmorland, Lancashire, Cheshire and Yorkshire. Bogle is found throughout the north country from Cumbria to Lincolnshire. Bugan and buggane are Manx, Cheshire and Shropshire dialect words. These distributions match closely the possible distribution of English bog burials, identified by Turner and Briggs (see p. 144). This is a convenient correlation, but bogie and bogy are common throughout southern England, and they and the word, bocan, have been exported to America. Boggarts often haunt houses and move objects, causing minor irritations, like souring milk and turning butter. In modern recorded folktales, clever men and women can trick and overcome them. In other cases, of which two are given, their behaviour is more sinister.

The Bugganes of the Isle of Man are particularly common (Killip 1975). The most famous of Manx legends involves the Buggane of St Trinians. In Marown, on land granted in the 12th century by the Priory of Whithorn, stands a roofless church. It is rumoured never to have been finished because a terrible buggane destroyed it at every attempt. A tailor called Timothy is challenged to make a pair of breeches in the church overnight. As he sits and sews, the buggane with a head of coarse, black, hair, eyes like torches, long arms and strong claws, rises through the church floor and destroys the roof. The tailor escapes down the hill into the sanctuary of Marown Churchyard but 'the buggane couldn't follow him into this sacred place and was so furious that he tore his head off his shoulders and threw it over the wall at Timothy, where it burst into pieces among the gravestones'. Killip searches for an historical explanation for the destruction of the church without success and concludes:

'A pagan origin for the buggane is just as likely as any of these: an ancient god of some disestablished religion showing his disapproval when a Christian church was built in the place formerly sacred to him'. The image of an anti-Christ figure and the beheading will occur later in this chapter.

Of the calendar customs of Britain, the one that can be most closely associated, geographically, with bog burials is the Haxey Hood Game. This still takes place annually at Haxey, Humberside, a village on a small island in the great tract of marshes making up the Isle of Axholme. The bog burials from this region form a group which may represent ritual sacrifices (see p. 155). The Hood Game takes place on 6 January, Twelfth Day or Old Christmas Day as it is known, traditionally the heart of midwinter. The legend behind the game relates that sometime in the Middle Ages, Lady de Mowbray riding to church one Christmas Day, had the scarlet hood blown from her head by a fierce wind. Twelve men dashed forward to pick it up and return it to her. She was so impressed by this gallantry that she left a parcel of land, the Hoodland, the rent of which would provide a hood for an annual contest between 12 villagers dressed in scarlet jerkins and caps (Palmer and Lloyd 1972).

The modern ceremony is managed by twelve Boggans or Boggins, whose leader is the Lord or King Boggan, and a Fool. During the week before, these men go around and collect money for the ceremony. In earlier times, the day began with the Boggans and the Fool marching from Wroot to Haxey, where watch was kept from the churchtower and the bells rung when they were sighted.

At 3 pm, the Fool delivers an oration from the stump of the Old Cross at the centre of the village (Fig. 52). He carries a stick with a bran-filled sock tied to the end by a leather thong. Towards the end, a fire is lit at his feet and parts of his clothing are set alight, 'Smoking the Fool' as it is called. In earlier times, it is reported that the Fool sat within a loop of rope suspended from a tree during the 'Smoking'. The Fool ends his speech with the phrase: Hoose agen house, toone agen toone, if thou meets a man knock him down, but don't hurt him. The Lord carries a long wand of 13 sticks of 'celery' willow bound around 13 times. After the speech, the Fool leads the way to the field where the incident with Lady Mowbray is reputed to have taken place. The Lord throws up, one by one, the twelve sham hoods of sacking. If someone catches them and can get to one of the village inns without being touched or tackled by a Boggan then they win 50p or were entitled to free drinks in the past. At 4 pm, the main event begins. The Sway Hood, a leather bound piece of rope 25 in long and 9 in in circumference, is thrown up. Rival gangs from different parts of the parish then form the Sway, a huge rugby scrum. The aim is to get the Sway Hood to the home pub by any means. The Sway can last for several hours and there are often injuries. When it is forced into the winners' pub much carousing commences, and the pub then remains the proud holder of the Sway Hood for the rest of the year (Wright 1938; Palmer and Lloyd 1972). In 1985 the Sway Hood was stolen during the game but it is hoped that it will be recovered.

A number of comparisons can be made between the Haxey Hood Game and the ritual of bog burial. The custom is of great age and the incident with Lady Mowbray is considered to be just a legend. Wright comments that 'some, however, believe that the custom is a relic of rites performed in ancient Celtic times' (Wright 1938, 88). The game takes place on the fringe of the area which has produced the greatest number of bog burials of probable ritual origin. Similar practices survived elsewhere in Lincolnshire, in the 19th century, at Epworth and Belton (Gutch and Peacock 1908, 274) and so the Haxey Hood Game should not be considered an isolated occurrence, but remarkable in that it survives to this day. The game is run by the Boggans whose title give them a direct link to the group of fairies described above and to the evil spirits of the surrounding peat bog. They are dressed in red with floral hats, the Lord having an elaborate wand. A number of bog burials were found with sticks across their bodies or alongside (see p. 166). The other main character is the black-faced Fool. When at the cross, the Fool is smoked, is he being sacrificed? And by leading the procession to the Hoodland, is he a victim being taken out onto the peat bog? What are the hoods? Glob points out that 'several bog finds have produced caps or bonnets of skin', with the one on Tollund Man's head being the most famous (Glob 1969). The Sway Hood is a leather-bound, thick rope perhaps even suggesting the nooses found around some of the bogman's necks.

Finally, the ceremony takes place in mid-winter, on Old Christmas Day, and seems certain to be concerned with renewal and the replacement of one year with the next. Plough Monday follows the next week, when the village ploughs were blest all over England, before they began to turn the soil to prepare for the coming year's harvest. These customs are cyclical and not in response to some catastrophe and the Haxey Hood Game is enthusiastically re-enacted each year.

The Beheading Myths

The second major theme to be analysed is the group of Beheading Myths to be found in legend and in early English and Celtic hagiography.

These myths can be found in British, Irish and French oral tradition, and the earliest written source can be traced back to Beowulf and the 8th century Irish saga of Bricriu's Feast (Cawley 1962). From that date to the High Medieval period, the imagery of beheading becomes widespread and its symbolism is applied to a number of situations.

The most famous of the Beheading myths is Sir Gawain and the Green Knight which has the richest source of imagery and was written in the late 14th century (Tolkien 1975). Furthermore Gawain travels through North Wales into Cheshire and the Gawain-poet is thought from his style and dialect to have come from the North West Midlands (Cawley 1962), so there are geographical links with Lindow Man. Sir Gawain and the Green Knight combines the Beheading Myth with another common tale, the Temptation. Tolkien sees it as a romance, an adult fairy tale, which propounds the ideal of Christian Knighthood and courtly love. The difficulties it presents is in unravelling oral tales from later embellishments, for here similarities with the supposed ritual of bog burial may be found.

The story begins at Camelot where King Arthur and his court are celebrating New Year with a great feast. Gawain sits at Guinevere's side. In bursts the Green Knight, on horseback, carrying a great axe and a bundle of holly. Both the man and his garments were green. He issues a challenge to the court, 'a Christmas pastime'. If anyone is bold enough to

strike one blow with this axe, then he may keep it, on the condition that the Green Knight could return the blow a year and a day later. Gawain takes up the challenge and decapitates the Green Knight. The head falls to the floor and rolls around the feet of the onlookers, but the body of the Green Knight recovers it, remounts his horse, and calls out 'to the Green chapel go thou and get thee a nimble knock in return on New Year's morning.'

Gawain sets out on the following Feast of All Hallows (November 2), and travels though the mythical realm of Logres. He stays the night and continues his journey the next day: 'till anon he drew near unto Northern Wales, . . . and then over by the Holy Head to high land again, in the Wilderness of Wirral: there wandered but few'.

He then returns to countries unknown, travels 'through many marshes and mires' where he meets and overcomes many forces both natural and supernatural all alone except for his horse Gringolet. On Christmas Eve, Sir Gawain arrives at a castle where the Temptation episode takes place and wherein he fails. At the end of this episode, he is given a silken green riband which will be proof against death.

On New Year's Eve, he sets out to find the Green Chapel, in full armour, the riband tied around his waist. The Green Chapel turns out to be a mound, with an entrance at each end, 'a worn barrow on a brae by the brink of a water'. Sir Gawain hears the Green Knight sharpening his axe and challenges him. On demand, Gawain bears his neck and implores the Green Knight to take one blow only. But as the axe falls, Gawain glances up and flinches at the sight. The Green Knight stays the blow and reprimands him. On the second attempt, the axe falls but only nicks Gawain's neck, the scar to remain a symbol of his weakness and dishonesty in the face of Temptation.

There is much in this tale to suggest that the Beheading Myth it employs may be based on bog burial ritual. The tale is cyclical, with the main action taking place in the depths of winter on New Year's Day. It involves the Green Knight, a trickster, capable of changing shape and persona, closely associated with watery places, and whose chapel is a prehistoric barrow. His colour, clothing and associated objects all echo death, rebirth and fertility. The deprecatory use of the word 'old', his struggle with Christian forces and the ideals of courtly life, suggest he is pre-Christian (Burrow 1965): 'Originally he may have been the old sun-god surrendering to the might of the 'young sonne' or he may have been the Green Man, whose decapitation and revival represent the annual death and rebirth of vegetation'. (Cawley 1962, xx).

On the other hand, Gawain is a man of considerable status, for he sits beside the Queen at table. He goes to be sacrificed at a watery place, not in fear or disgrace, but full of courage and to fulfil a promise. When the axe falls it only makes a nick to let the blood. Lindow Man was killed and then his throat was partly cut for perhaps the same reason. Gawain wears a riband as a charm; Lindow Man's only clothing is a fur band around his left arm and Tollund Man wore only a belt and skin cap. It is very tempting to see Sir Gawain as the literary equivalent of Lindow Man.

The Beheading Myth has much earlier origins in a written form. These can be traced back to the 8th century and it must be re-emphasised that decapitation is seen in both British and Continental bog burials, (see p. 155). One of these is Lindow Woman, dated to the 3rd century AD, and the Celtic Cult of the Head identified by Ross, (Ross 1967) seems to exist throughout the Roman period. The gap to be spanned by the oral tradition is quite short.

Branwen, daughter of Llyr, is one of the great collection of medieval Welsh prose tales, the Mabinigion, and it contains a beheading incident. Bran, her brother, was raised to the throne of London. The King of Ireland and Branwen were married and there was great feasting, but the king received a deep insult. In compensation he was given a cauldron, whose discovery was described as follows:

> at the top of a mound which overlooks a lake called the Lake of the Cauldron, I saw a huge man with yellow-red hair emerging from the lake with a cauldron on his back; he was a great monstrous man with an evil thieving look about him (Gantz 1976).

The troubles were not over, and when Branwen had been taken to Ireland she was mistreated and held captive. Bran set sail with 13 ships to rescue her and the magic cauldron. In the battle which followed, the Irish used the powers of the cauldron to renew their troops. One of Bran's men, Evnissyen, managed to break the cauldron into four pieces and Bran's men finally triumphed but only seven men and Bran, mortally wounded, survived. Bran commanded them to cut off his head. 'Take my head and carry it to the White Hill in London, and bury it there with the face turned towards France'. The head became a talisman. It brings eighty years of good fortune at the Assembly of the Wondrous Head and later kept the plague from the whole island.

This legend brings together beheading and a magic cauldron found in a lake. Cauldrons, bowls and buckets have been commonly found deposited in peat bogs in Britain, Ireland and on the continent. In Wales, from the Early Iron Age, there are three finds of this type. There are two bronze cauldrons from the Llyn Fawr hoard, a bronze bucket from Arthog, and a gold inlaid shale bowl from Caergwle; all are from peat deposits (Savory 1976). These have also been considered as ritual sacrifices. In the Mabinigion, the cauldron is taken out of the lake by a huge man. His only description is that he had yellow-red hair, commonly reported as the colour of bogmen's hair from staining by the peat-water. The magic powers of the cauldron are renewal and rebirth and so provide a link with a central theme in Sir Gawain and the Green Knight.

The Irish have their own beheading myth recorded in the Champion's Covenant, the last chapter of the cycle of tales known as Bricriu's Feast (Henderson 1899). As the Royal Court of Ultonia were seated in their hall at eventide, 'they saw a big uncouth fellow of exceeding ugliness drawing nigh upon them'. The man claimed to have travelled Europe, Africa and Asia in a quest for someone to answer his challenge: 'Come whosoever of you that may venture, that I may cut off his head tonight, he mine tomorrow night'.

Fat-Neck, son of Short-Head, springs up saying: 'Bend down bachlach, that I may cut your head off tonight, you to cut off mine tomorrow night'. The bachlach replies that he could have got that bargain anywhere, but after some discussion he agrees. Fat-Neck dealt him a blow cutting off the head, but straightaway the bachlach rose, recovered himself, clasped his head, block and axe to his breast, and made his exit from the hall with blood streaming from his neck. For three nights he can find no-one to take the challenge. On the fourth, Cuchulainn, the most famous warrior of Ultonia, is present, and springs up and deals him a blow that hurls his head to the top rafter. Cuchulainn gives him another blow smashing his head, but again the bachlach rises and goes away.

When the bachlach returns, Cuchulainn, though frightened, resolves to keep his bargain. The bachlach takes a mighty swing but brings the blunt side of the axe onto Cuchulainn's neck. He is spared and the bachlach sings his praise then vanishes, for the monster is Curoi mac Dairi, the great magician, come in disguise to fulfil a promise he had given to Cuchulainn.

The similarities to the story of Sir Gawain and

the Green Knight are obvious and very strong, even though the Bricriu's Feast manuscript, considered 8th century, is very much older. However, it is missing the embellishments which suggest the strong link between Sir Gawain and bog burial ritual. The principals are a man of status and a monstrous trickster, capable of shape shifting. But the action is not cyclical and does not take place at a specific season. There is no connection with watery or boggy places and no strong symbolism of death, rebirth and the renewal of vegetation. No wounding or beheading of the hero takes place, no sacrifice of the hero is made. Perhaps the Irish bard had no direct knowledge of these practices or they had no place in his cycle of tales. Perhaps the Gawain poet grafted these onto the basic Beheading Myth. It is impossible to say.

The last of the great tales to be considered is perhaps the earliest. Beowulf is an anonymous English poem written between AD 680–800. Beowulf was a Geat from South Sweden, an heroic figure, a thane and a leader of men: 'That this poem should have a Scandanavian cast and background is a reminder of the shared historical and legendary inheritance that once bound the Germanic peoples together' (Crossley-Holland 1984, 70). Part of a shared archaeological inheritance has been brought to light by the finding of Lindow Man. The story can be briefly reviewed because the elements that may link with bog burial ritual only occur towards the end of the first part. Beowulf and his men come to the aid of Hrothgar, King of the Scyldings of Denmark, whose great hall, Heorot, has been ravaged by the monster Grendel for 12 years. Beowulf and his party sleep within the hall to await Grendel, who cannot be hurt by any weapon. When he arrives, Beowulf grasps Grendel by the arm and tears it off from his shoulder. Grendel's Mother, seeking revenge, comes to Heorot and carries off one of the thanes to the fens:

'These two live in a little-known country, wolf-slopes, windswept headlands, perilous paths across the boggy moors, where a mountain stream plunges under the mist-covered cliffs, rushes through a fissure. It is not far from here, if measured in miles, that the lake stands shadowed by trees stiff with hoar-frost' (Crossley-Holland 1984).

Beowulf and his warriors fearlessly offer to pursue her and they set off for the lake with the horn sounding before them. Beowulf dons his massive corselet and helmet and dives into the lake where Grendel's Mother grasps him in her claws. A great fight takes place in which Grendel's mother is finally beheaded. Beowulf sees Grendel on his death bed alongside and metes out similar treatment to him. To the great joy and delight of his followers Beowulf emerges out of the lake after a whole day. They return to Sweden, leaving the Danish kingdom to prosper.

It is possible to draw many threads out of this epic poem. Grendel and his mother are monstrous creatures who prowl the fens and misty moors. Their home is a terrible lake surrounded by trees caught in a hoar-frost of perpetual midwinter. Periodically they come at night to take human victims from the great hall of Heorot. These victims are thanes, men of status. Grendel and his mother are presented as anti-Christian, descended from Cain himself. They are found impervious to ordinary weapons and it is only the superhuman figure of Beowulf who can overcome them by strength alone. He is lead by ritual procession, the horn sounding to the fore, to this terrible lake. Here he dives in, like a body thrown into the pool of a bog, but he is protected by his armour. Beowulf overcomes the dreadful monsters by beheading them and frees the Scyldings from their predators. It is easy to see Beowulf's physical strength representing his moral strength and his armour, the protection of the Lord. So Christian virtue, in its infancy when the poem was written, has permanently overcome long-held pagan superstition.

The other main source of beheading myths is to be found in the Celtic and early English hagiographic tradition. Even Sir Gawain passes over by the Holy Head to the Wirral. Holy Head must be Holywell, Clwyd, where there is the shrine and holy well dedicated to St Winefride and there can be little doubt that the original readers of Sir Gawain and the Green Knight would have been aware of the reference to St Winefride, whose cult was at its height in the 14th century. This was further emphasised as Sir Gawain passes through there on 3 November, the saint's feast day.

The legend of St Winefride was first written in the middle of the 12th century by Robert, Prior of Shrewsbury, to where her relics had been brought in 1138. She was a 7th century virgin. One day Caradoc, a chieftain from Hawarden, attempted to seduce Winefride. She ran away from him towards the church at Holywell, built by her uncle, St Beuno. At the church door, Caradoc caught her and cut off her head. In the place where her head fell, a spring of water came up. St Beuno came out from the church, took up her head and placed it back on her body. He then prayed and raised her back to life. Robert wrote that 'a very thin white line like a thread encircled her neck, following the line of the cut; and this, for as long as the virgin lived, remained with her, always unchanged, as a mark of the cutting of the head and as a token of the miracle' (David 1971). Though this legend can have little basis in fact – Farmer calls it a 'tissue of improbabilities' (Farmer 1978, 408) – it is shared by a number of other saints. The power of the legend and the cult of St Winefride and the healing properties of her well, cannot be denied. During the Middle Ages, it became one of the three main centres of British pilgrimage, with Jesmond Dene in Northumberland, and Walsingham in Norfolk. It received royal patronage from Henry V, who invoked Winefride's aid at Agincourt, and later from Edward IV and Richard III. The most important patron of all was Lady Margaret Beaufort, mother to Henry VII, who had the very fine well chapel built and caused Caxton to produce a very early printed life. Even more remarkable was that pilgrimages and masses for the saint survived all attempts to suppress the cult during the Reformation of Henry VIII and Elizabeth, and during the Civil War and the Commonwealth. James II and Mary of Modena were the last monarchs to make a pilgrimage to the shrine. It remains the only Catholic shrine to survive undamaged and to have an unbroken history of pilgrimage in Britain. The well still gushes forth in the bath where pilgrims bathe, and the late Perpendicular well chapel is thronged on her feast days (David 1971).

The legend of healing and the springing forth of water is associated with other saints. But the mark of the thread around Winefride's neck is strongly evocative of the 'garrotte' around Lindow Man's neck. St Lludd was beheaded at Brecon, and where her head rested a gushing well formed. St Cynogs was also beheaded in Brecon, but here the well dried up and he picked up his head and took it off down the hill with him (Ross 1967). These legends are not restricted to Wales and the myth surrounding St Edmund needs to be looked at in some detail.

Edmund was a little known King of East Anglia in the 9th century. In 869, he refused to surrender to the Danes and was taken from his hall, bound to a tree, and had arrows shot at him. During this dreadful ordeal, Edmund constantly expressed his love of Christ. His head was ordered to be cut off and hidden, separately from the body, in a wood. Edmund's followers eventually found the head and, miraculously, it reunited with the body, when they were brought together (Whitelock 1970).

In a paper entitled 'The Body of St Edmund: an essay in Necrobiography', Scarfe traces the tales which surround the body of the saint (Scarfe 1970). Abbo, in his life of the saint written between AD 985 and 987, emphasised the remarkably incorrupt condition of the corpse. 'He said it might have been assumed that in the years since Edmund's death the body would have putrified; but on the contrary, there was no trace of his wounds or scars, only a tenuous red crease, like a scarlet thread round his neck'. (Scarfe 1970, 305). This incorruption was attributed to a life of chastity and the persecution that led to martyrdom, and was a reward for these trials. Theodred, Bishop of London between AD 942 and 951, checked the corpse and washed and reclothed it. A young magnate, on forcing a look at the body, went out of his mind. Leofstan, abbot at Bury St Edmunds (1044–1065) to where the remains had been moved, decided to check that the head had really rejoined the body. Whilst a monk held the feet, Leofstan pulled on the head, but nothing parted and his hands became paralysed and his speech and sight were affected. In 1198, Abbot Samson made an examination of the saint's body in the presence of 18 monks, and found it incorrupt and supple. The later history of St Edmund's body was just as eventful. It disappeared and was rumoured to have been taken to France. A skeleton was brought back from France but when doubts on its authenticity were cast it was rather hurriedly buried in Sussex on its journey up to Bury St Edmunds.

Where it can be checked, Abbo can be shown to have been historically very accurate. Scarfe believes his story of the incorrupt body must be taken as *prima facie* evidence and that the body had been embalmed. Alternatively, it could have been a bog man for it had 'no trace of his wounds or scars, only a tenuous red crease, like a scarlet thread round his neck'. The body remained incorrupt and supple. It could have been naturally dried like the find from Castle Blakeney, Galway in Ireland, made in 1821 (see p. 193). Perhaps the body considered to be that of St Edmund was in fact the earliest bog man of which a description survives and the earliest that was preserved. The incidents described took place on the fringe of the Fenlands and the Broads and the discovery of a well-preserved bog burial must have been considered miraculous: King Edmund's death and the mutilation of his body could have provided an explanation for such a discovery. If the story of the saint's death is true, it is hard to explain away the body as described by Abbo. This mixture of fact and legend, in part shared by the story of other saints, makes a tantalising puzzle.

Conclusions

Efforts have been made to show that evil forces, associated with peat bogs and watery places, underlie a whole body of English and Celtic folklore and dialect. The myths are so strong as to have survived over many centuries and some remain vigorous to this day. At Haxey, the Hood Game is still most enthusiastically enacted, and the cult of St Winefride, despite nearly two hundred years of attempted suppression by the Crown, still attracts a regular flow of pilgrims. It may only be coincidence that two of the great English poems of the medieval period, Beowulf and Sir Gawain and the Green Knight, share imagery with what has independently been surmised as forming part of the ritual of bog burial.

These myths from the oral tradition must have been written down long after the practices at which they hint, took place. Whilst the minstrels and oral poets must have shown great skill in memorising and passing on the myths which formed the basis of their people's history, by the time that they came to be transcribed, the intellectual and theological climate had changed.

Those tales, gathered together under the broad heading of the Beheading Myths, were all written down by Christians or people living in a Christian society. Some have overt references to Christianity. In them, the evil forces associated with wet and boggy places are subordinated or overcome by the heroes of the tales. Through the oral tradition, a belief which must be considered central to the yearly cycle of harvest and renewal must have slowly evolved during constant retelling but it may have been unable to cope with a complete change in religious belief. The versions which survive to us may have been defused and have lost some of their original power.

Similarly the class of fairies, the bogies and their allies, may have lost some of their terror. In some cases, they are no more than mischievous and would be hardly worthy of the types of sacrifice which have been suggested. Some, like the Buggane of St Trinians, are clearly anti-Christ figures, trying in vain to overcome the spread of Christianity. Christianity provides a loving, all powerful God, not a malevolent figure or a goddess of fertility, inhabiting wet and misty peat bogs and most active at night and in midwinter. To ensure the fertility of the land, valuable sacrifices had to be made to them. The Christian Hell is very different and its symbolism of burning fires is more appropriate to its origins in the Near East. The boggarts of Northern England must have retreated to occupy the role of ghosts and minor devils, vivid enough to fen dwellers and travellers across lonely moors, but of little power away from there.

Nevertheless, the wealth and consistent nature of the instances presented here, seem more than coincidence and they may provide reasons why some bog burials appear to be ritual sacrifices. The classical authors suggest that on the continent people were sacrificed both for the good of the community and for serious crimes. The oral tradition of the peoples involved, of which the English and Celtic have been briefly reviewed here, may suggest a more religious origin for these sacrifices. The strength of these forces can be suggested by the great value not only of the objects recovered from peatbogs but also by the apparent status of the human victims. For a community with few resources, the most valuable object which they had to sacrifice could have been a man or woman of status and they may have gone willingly to their death. The details of any ceremony must be left to the imagination.

The fascination and something of the horror inspired in the past by the bog burials remains today. The news of the Danish discoveries caused enormous public interest throughout the world. Professor Glob's book *The Bog People* must be the most widely read archaeological work published since the war. Many visitors 'tramp all the time up the suburban creak of the stairs' of Silkeborg Museum to marvel at the serene expression of Tollund Man. Lindow Man shared a similar worldwide exposure soon after his discovery and for a time an archaeological find became part of the public consciousness (see the cartoon on p. 16). The association of murder with a number of the bog men has the beginnings of a modern myth. Bog finds have already inspired a number of poems, those by Seamus Heaney and Geoffrey Grigson being the most notable. Lindow Man not only has a place in the oral tradition, but may father one of his own. As you warn your naughty children to beware of the bogyman, and toss coins into a wishing well, think of the more terrible fate of Lindow Man.

33 Summary and Conclusions

I. M. Stead

Lindow Man was well-built, in his mid-twenties, some 168 cm (5 ft 6 in) tall and perhaps 60 kg (almost 10 st) or more in weight. He seems to have been healthy, although he certainly suffered from worms. Very slight osteoarthritis has been detected, and some of the vertebrae have Schmorl's nodes – but he would have been unaware of that because they have no clinical significance. His head was quite large, with flared nostrils and surprisingly small ears; he had a full head of darkish hair, and a short beard, moustache and side-burns. Many vital pieces of information are unknown – his name, home, occupation – but there is a clue to his social status because his finger-nails are neatly rounded: he is unlikely to have been a manual labourer and may well have belonged to the upper levels of society.

On the day that he died (or the day before) he ate a meal, of which a major component was a mixture of wheat and barley, finely ground to make whole-meal bread – probably a flat unleavened griddle cake heated over a fire. The combination of two varieties of wheat, spelt and the more ancient emmer, is typical of an Iron Age context and provides the first clue to the date of Lindow Man. It seems very likely that he was already quite near the bog we now know as Lindow Moss, because the water he had drunk had traces of sphagnum moss in it and heather had been used as a fuel to bake the bread. Neither the food nor the pollen in the stomach gives any hint of the season in which he died, although the condition of the body may suggest that the weather was cold.

Little is known about the life of Lindow Man, but there are vivid details of his death. He seems to have been stripped naked, apart from a fox-fur band on his left arm – possibly a decoration, or perhaps a symbol of his status, or clan. While standing or kneeling he was struck from behind – twice on the very top of the head, with a narrow-bladed axe-like weapon. Perhaps at the same time he received a vicious blow in the back (? from a knee) which broke one of his ribs. Then a cord was tied tightly round his neck, and the loose ends were neatly cut at either side of the knot. A stick inserted into the cord at the back of the neck was used to twist it tighter and tighter. Unconscious, but not killed by the blows on the head (the edges of the wounds were swollen), Lindow Man was now strangled and his neck was broken by the garrotte. That was the moment of death – but the executioners had not yet finished with their victim. They slit his throat, with a short deep cut at the side of the neck. This would have severed the jugular vein and the flow of blood from the dead man's head would have been accentuated by the position of the garrotte just below the slit throat. At the end of this gruesome sequence the body was dropped face downwards into a pool in the bog.

Lindow Moss has changed over the years. In antiquity it was a natural bog in which peat accumulated as successive growths of moss and other vegetation partially decomposed and compacted. Eventually the depth of peat covering Lindow Man reached about 2.5 m. Then the process was reversed, when peat-cutters moved in and the bog was drained. At the time of his discovery in 1984 only 1 m of peat was left over the body, so the stratification that would have preserved a complete history of the bog from prehistoric to modern times had been interrupted and a large part of it destroyed. A detailed study of a 50 cm depth of peat near the body has shown that as the weather turned slightly damper and cooler a distinctly wet bog became still wetter, so that pools developed and sphagnum moss was dominant. Examination of the remains of water fleas, and of midges that spend their larval stages in water, has shown that they were in a constrained environment at the time that Lindow Man died. Certainly there was water, but it was only in shallow pools. Then conditions changed and it became rather drier, the pools disappeared, and a relatively firm surface was covered with cotton sedge and heather. The sequence available for study represents a span of about 500 years.

Pollen carried into the bog from the surrounding countryside has shown the changes in vegetation over a wider area. Lindow Man was dumped in the pool at a fairly early stage in a period of forest clearance, when agriculture was on the increase. Pine and oak pollen were starting to decline, while cereals and weeds were becoming more common. This represents a major farming phase, also reflected by a marked increase in charcoal, which probably lasted between two and four hundred years.

Carbon 14 has been used to provide an absolute chronology for these changes in the development of the bog and the surrounding countryside. Peat samples have been dated by two laboratories, and they tell a consistent story. The major forest clearance and farming phase occurred before the birth of Christ, and the pool in which Lindow Man was immersed flourished between the fifth and third centuries BC. But this neat story is disrupted by other C14 dates taken from the body itself. Various parts of the body – skin, tissue, hair and bone – have been dated by two laboratories, with different results. The one laboratory has had three samples: the results group reasonably and indicate a date in the first century AD. The second laboratory has worked on seven samples and produced closely grouped dates suggesting that Lindow Man died in the fifth or sixth century AD. The problem here is not only that the dates for the body differ from those for apparently contemporary peat, but that two laboratories have produced different dates for the body (Fig. 55). Part of the problem could be solved by arguing that the body cannot be contemporary with the peat: it must have been buried, or have sunk into the peat (but did it sink through 300 years accumulation of peat or 800 years?). However, this argument is not consistent with the recorded stratification: there is no hint of a grave, and the pool that was essential for the good preservation of the body is clearly defined in the peat sequence. Furthermore, the dated peat samples were carefully selected to include some contemporary with the body. It would be far better to date the body itself, rather than associated peat, but there is a difference of about 350 radiocarbon years between the two sets of body dates. Until the discrepancy can be explained perhaps the wisest course is to regard all the dates from the body as suspect. But the dates from the peat are not controversial, there are sound arguments for the body being more or less contemporary with the peat that surrounded it, and such a date makes good sense from an archaeological point of view.

Lindow Moss is not a normal burial-ground, and Lindow Man did not die a normal death. It has been alleged that he was mugged – beaten and robbed while crossing a lonely bog (Connolly 1985, see also the reply, Parker Pearson 1986). But this is unconvincing if the evidence for the complicated sequence of the killing is accepted, and it seems unlikely that a mugging victim would have been completely stripped and deliberately bled. It is more likely that Lindow Man was executed, and indeed execution is a reasonable explanation for the severed head of Lindow Woman found the previous year. Three other severed heads from bogs in the vicinity (nos 19, 22 and 24, pp. 183–4) may belong to the same category. Other British and Irish bog bodies could have met their deaths in a variety of ways; few have been examined in detail but there are no records of slit throats, smashed skulls or ropes round the necks.

Many bog burials have been found on the continent, especially in Denmark, and some of them have been executed in ways which recall the death of Lindow Man (Glob 1969; Fischer 1980). Grauballe Man had had his throat cut; Tollund Man had a rope round his neck and had probably been strangled rather than hanged; the women from Elling and Krogens Møllemose had been strangled or hanged; the woman found at Borremose in 1948 had a head wound. These Danish bodies are among nine that have been dated by C14, and all belong to the first millennium BC or the first couple of centuries AD (Tauber 1979). For most bodies there is but a single C14 date, and all were produced by the same laboratory. Opinion is divided as to whether the Danish bodies were executed criminals or sacrificial victims, or both (Munksgaard 1984), and the Roman historian Tacitus is frequently quoted in the argument. On the one hand: 'Traitors and deserters are hanged on trees; cowards, shirkers and sodomites are pressed down under a wicker hurdle into the slimy mud of a bog' (*Germania* 12, 1), and on the other a religious ceremony was 'performed by slaves who are immediately afterwards drowned in the lake' (*Ibid.* 40, 5).

However, there was little direct contact between Denmark and Britain in the Iron Age and Roman period (Parker Pearson 1986), and in terms of ancient ethnography the two countries were occupied by different peoples, with Germans in Denmark and Celts in Britain. But there is some evidence that Germans and Celts shared certain traditions: in particular, both placed votive deposits in bogs, lakes and rivers, and both engaged in human sacrifice. In Denmark and in Britain most of the fine metalwork from the first millennium BC has been found in watery places.

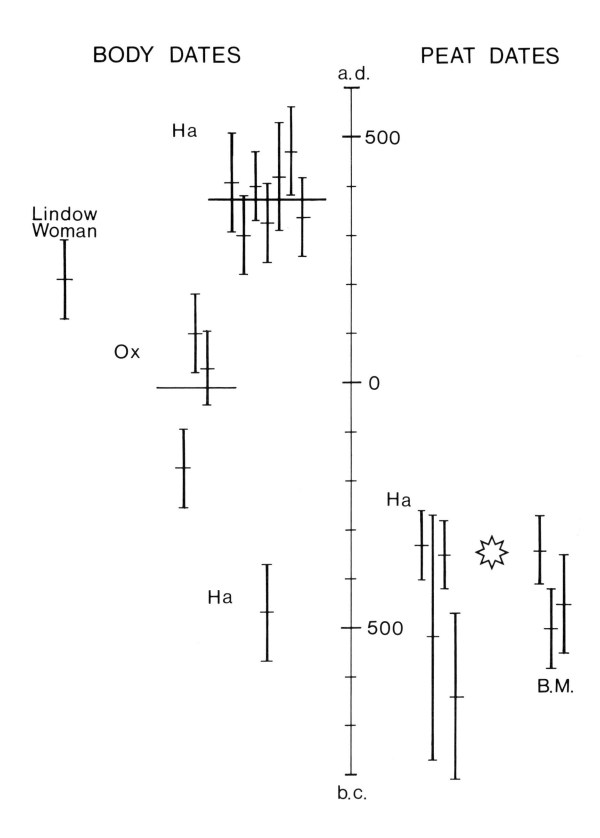

Fig. 55   Uncalibrated C14 dates for Lindow Man. Dates from the body are shown to the left of the scale (Ha = Harwell; Ox = Oxford), and dates from the peat are to the right of the scale. The star indicates the level of the body in the peat: dates to the left of it are taken from peat in contact with the body; those to the right are from the adjoining peat monolith.

Human sacrifice amongst the Celts is described by Diodorus Siculus (V, 31, 3; V, 32, 6) and Strabo (*Geographia* IV, iv, 5) following Posidonius, and by Caesar (*De Bello Gallico* VI, 16).

For Britain, Tacitus (*Annals* XIV, 30) records that the druids in Anglesey 'drench their altars in the blood of prisoners and consult their gods by means of human entrails'. On Anglesey, too, only eighty miles from Lindow Moss, a large votive deposit of La Tène metalwork had been placed in a lake at Llyn Cerrig Bach (Fox 1946). Mention of the druids recalls the discovery of mistletoe pollen in Lindow Man's gut, for the druids 'hold nothing more sacred than the mistletoe' (Pliny, *Nat. Hist.* xvi, 95). There was only a little mistletoe pollen in the stomach, but the coincidence is intriguing because it is not a common find. If Lindow Man had been sacrificed by the druids the ritual might well have taken place not in a temple but in a grove like the one in Gaul 'whose interlacing boughs enclosed a space of darkness and cold shade... gods were worshipped there with savage rites, the altars were heaped with hideous offerings, and every tree was sprinkled with human gore' (Lucan, *Pharsalia* III, 399–423). The site described here was destroyed by Caesar, just as sacred groves in Anglesey were demolished by Paulinus (Tacitus, *op. cit.*). Was Lindow Moss another sacred grove? It seems unlikely that human sacrifice would have survived into Roman times in Britain; the Romans, like the Greeks, regarded it as a barbarian practice (Hammond and Scullard 1970, 944), and the druids were specifically repressed (Piggott 1968, 127).

If human sacrifice was part of Celtic tradition, why is it that so few slaughtered bodies have been recognised? Lindow Man, even with some severed heads from bogs in the neighbourhood, hardly argues for a widespread ritual. The answer may be that it was more usual to deposit sacrificial victims in other watery places such as lakes and rivers that lack the preservative qualities of raised bogs. There bodies would have been quickly reduced to bones and commercial dredgers or drainers would then find unremarkable and perhaps disarticulated skeletons, and would never see the evidence for slit throats or hanging. At one of the most famous Iron Age ritual deposits, La Tène itself, de Navarro (1972, 17–18) accepted the evidence for human sacrifice, and certainly a skeleton is said to have had a rope round its neck. When the metalwork was removed from the Llyn Cerrig Bach votive deposit on Anglesey 'masses of (bones) were left, as I observed, and only a few collected' (Fox 1946, 3) – but all those examined were from animals (*Ibid.* 97). The finest collection of British Iron Age metalwork comes from the river Thames, much of it no doubt ritually deposited and most of it found by dredgers in the last century and the early years of this century. Bones were sometimes discovered at the same time, and in particular it is worth noting that in the vicinity of the Battersea shield there were 'numerous human crania, of two distinct types, mingled with weapons of bronze and iron... the skulls and weapons were scattered from the Middlesex shore to about the middle of the river, where the greater quantity were found' (Cuming 1857, 237–8). Countless sacrificial victims could have been lost in rivers and lakes.

On the evidence presented in this volume it seems reasonable to see the killing of Lindow Man in the context of the religious practices of the Celts in the centuries before the Roman conquest. Palaeobotanists have presented a convincing argument suggesting that he met his death around 300 BC, and there the matter must rest pending further work by the C14 laboratories.

APPENDIX
A Gazetteer of Bog Burials from Britain and Ireland

C. S. Briggs and R. C. Turner

This gazetteer is the result of six months intensive study, based on a long term interest held by one of us (CSB). Many of the finds and descriptions lie buried in obscure publications and manuscripts. The most important of the many individuals who have assisted in unearthing the many references, is Alfred Dieck, whose paper of 1958, was so fundamental to the writing of *The Bog People*. A list of all European human remains found in peat deposits was published in his 1965 monograph, and provided our starting point. This list gives the briefest of details; the date of discovery or first publication and a find spot. It did not consider the age or degree of preservation of the bodies, nor did it describe the peat from which they were taken. No bibliographical references were provided, so that it proved quite difficult to crack the code, reconstruct and check the original references and offer an appreciation if its worth. Most of this list has been identified and many others added.

Something of Dieck's methodology has been preserved. Again all human remains have been included, where they can be shown to have come from peat deposits. The discoveries are divided into three, England (compiled by RCT) and Wales (CSB & RCT), Scotland (RCT), and Ireland (CSB). The findspots are arranged alphabetically within each county or region. Bogs, turbaries and mosses producing several finds are treated under a single heading. A parish or township name and a grid reference are included wherever possible, and discoveries are listed in order of date of discovery or publication. Contemporary or early accounts are quoted *in extenso*, quite uncritically, in order to illuminate the reaction to these most remarkable events. Quotations are almost without exception taken from the earliest reference cited. This gazetteer must be considered only as a preliminary list. Apart from Dieck's work, there has been no attempt to draw this information together for the whole of the British Isles. Its main function is to show that Lindow Man is by no means a unique discovery in this country, or in Great Britain and Ireland as a whole, but part of a much wider phenomenon recorded over the past three centuries at least. We are sure that many more references are to be found, in Sites and Monuments Records, antiquarian histories, proceedings of local geological and natural history societies, old newspaper articles and manuscript sources. We would be delighted to hear of any such references which would expand the list here presented.

England and Wales
(50 sites, 85 + individuals)

CAMBRIDGESHIRE

1 Burwell Fen TL 58 66 (p. 149)
There have been at least six separate collections of human remains at this site, representing at least nine individuals. One of the references is to a Bronze Age jet necklace to which no body may have belonged and only appears on Dieck's list. Most of the rest are in the Sedgwick Museum Collections, Cambridge University, but nothing is recorded of the circumstances of their discovery, whether human tissue was preserved or if full skeletons were represented. Duckworth and Shore published four of the crania and two are so described as to give the impression that the bone was demineralised, suggesting that the conditions were favourable to tissue preservation. The final description is one of the most remarkable bog body accounts. However, this discovery is not mentioned in Clarke 1960 but only in the introduction to the second edition, and no other published account of it has been found.

before 1854 The plate of a third necklace of jet (from Burwell Fen), which was complete when found, is in the Cambridge Museum (*Camb. Ant. Soc. Rep.* (14) 1854, 13; Fox 1923, 55).

1884 Two male calvaria, a jaw fragment and a humerus (Sedgwick Museum Collections; Duckworth and Shore 1911).

1890 Lower jaw (Sedgwick Museum Collections).

1898 Female skull with mandible (Duckworth and Shore 1911 give date as 1890).

1901 Six skull fragments (Sedgwick Museum Collections).

before 1911   Three mandibles (Sedgwick Museum Collections; Duckworth and Shore 1911).

before 1971   'Most shudderingly entrancing of all was the Ancient Briton, who suddenly emerged from the peat in Burwell Fen, when the turf-diggers were at work. He stood upright in his dug-out canoe. His lank black hair dropped to his shoulders. The peat-dark skin was still stretched over the bones of his face. The eyes had gone but the eye-sockets were dark with mystery. He was clad in a long leather jacket, belted, with garters round his legs and the right arm was raised as though about to cast a spear. That body of the unknown hunter, the nameless warrior, had been preserved in the peat for uncounted aeons of time. It crumbled to dust in the sharp Fen air. The canoe is in the Downing Street Museum at Cambridge'. (J. Wentworth Day in Clarke 1971).

2   Isleham Fen   TL 64 74
1952   Two individuals, no account traced (Dieck 1965).

3   Isle of Ely
1874   'Mr William Marshall gave an account of the discovery of skulls in the peat of the Isle of Ely'. Skull, deformed by softening and pressure, male, moderate stature, just beyond middle age, bones light. Also a broken calvarium. (*J. Anth. Inst.* (3) 1874, 497).

4   Reach Fen   TL 56 66
1891   Lower jaw from peat (Sedgwick Museum Collections).

1901   Radius from peat (Sedgwick Museum Collections).

5   Shippea Hill   TL 66 84   (pp. 149, 150)
1911   'The Shippea Hill Man: The late McKenny Hughes, ..., seems to have been the first to appreciate the significance of finds made in the fen deposits. It was in 1911 that he hastened out to Shippea Hill Farm, a few miles to the north-east of Ely, in response to a letter announcing the discovery of human bones made by men draining. He found such of the bones as were still *in situ*, at about 4 in from the base of $4\frac{1}{2}$ ft of peat which rested on buttery clay. A sample cut through the lower peat and the upper clay is now preserved, together with the bones, in the Sedgwick Museum. Hughes records the "human skeleton was found hunched up and crowded into a small space, less than two feet square, as if the body settled vertically...." Unfortunately Hughes' observations were vitiated by his failure to recognise the true character of his find, which clearly represented a burial. Its true stratigraphic position is unknown.' (Clark 1933; Hughes 1916).

6   Barway Fen, nr. Soham   TL 54 75
1918   Skull and lower jaw from peat (Sedgwick Museum Collections).

7   Soham Fen
before 1923   'in the British Museum, where are also jet beads and plates of the second necklace from Soham Fen. The latter were associated with a skeleton – possibly a case of accidental death rather than of inhumation – and a socketed chisel-like axe of late type'. (Fox 1923, 55).

8   Upware   TL 53 70
before 1911   Male skull with mandible, undated mandible, mandibular frag, molar and metacarpal from peat deposits. (Sedgwick Museum Collections; Duckworth and Shore 1911).

9   Cambridgeshire
before 1911   Male skull from Cambridgeshire Fens. (Duckworth and Shore 1911).

before 1923   No account traced. (Dieck 1965). Perhaps from Fox (1923).

CHESHIRE

10   Meols (now in Merseyside)   SJ 22 90   (p. 148)
before 1863   'Man (Homo sapiens) – As these have been more carefully deposited than the remains of inferior animals, so they are of less frequent occurrence; but skeletons in whole or in part are occasionally found, not at the site of the ancient burying-ground, but protruding from the black earth.' (Hume 1863). Meols is a sea-creek site producing finds from late Prehistory to the Conquest.

11   Leasowe (now in Merseyside)   SJ 26 92   (p. 148)
1864   Perfect male skeleton found by workmen building Leasowe Embankment, 22/1/1864 under a sandhill *c.* 100 ft in height, 3–400 yds from the tide. '... a navvy preparing for his work as the tide receded, saw amid the black peat, a white substance ... proved to be human skull. He immediately carried it to his ganger who had the rest of the bones carefully removed.' The body lay E-W and the skeleton was placed below the peat and upon the blue clay. 'When first exhumed the bones were very white, but shortly after exposure to the air they became dark and inky.... Professor Busk lecturing the Ethnological Society reports that other skeletons have been found similarly situated in other parts of the country.' (Cust 1864). Busk measures the skeleton and concludes, male, powerful frame, 5 ft 10 in tall. (Busk 1866).

12   Lindow Moss, Mobberley   SJ 820 805   (pp. 148, 149)
1983   Female skull with hair, brain and other tissue, found by workmen at a peat depot. Dated 1740 ± 80 bp (OxA-114). For further details see this volume.

1984   Isolated foot and complete male torso excavated *in situ*. 'Lindow Man' is the subject of this volume.

CLEVELAND

13   Hartlepool Bay   NZ 50 32   (p. 148)
1972   'The skeleton was disarticulated in the "grave" and the cranium was upside down. Although most of the bones were concentrated in area and vertical range, three phalanges of the hand occurred at a higher altitude in the detritus gyttja. Most of the cranium and the right side of the skeleton were present ... The skeleton is of a male aged about 25 to 38 years of short, stocky stature ... There is evidence that during his lifetime, he received two blows on the head from which he recovered and one rib fragment displays a well-healed fracture ... A radiocarbon assay on a selection of cleaned but untreated bones yielded a date of 4680 ± 60 bp (HV-5220). The skeleton was uncovered by the sea on the beach. In the same layer, but at some distance, was a stuck flint flake.' (Tooley 1978a).

CUMBRIA

14 Murchie's Cairn, Bewcastle NY 596 765
(pp. 148, 150)

before 1873 Found about 25 years previous, half a mile to the north of Hessilgil Crags, near head of Bullcleugh Beck. 'The body had been laid north and south, a small dry wall built along one side, and then it had been covered with two thin flagstones, reaching from the wall to the peat brow on the other side.' The bones were in a good state of preservation and in a crouched position. 'The skin was still remaining on one of the arms, from the wrist to the elbow, having probably been tanned by the moss-water. One of the thigh bones dropped from the body when it was lifted, and had a large piece of skin under it. The hair was on the legs and generally over the body, and had been of a dark red colour.' Considered Pagan Saxon. (Maughan 1873).

15 Scaleby NY 46 SW   (pp. 148, 149)
1845 A portion of garment made of skin covered with reddish hair, and sewn with sinews; a fragment of one of the parietal bones, a lock of black hair and a small quantity of brain, the state of adipocere for the body of an ancient Briton, discovered nine feet deep in the bog, near Scaleby, Cumberland, 28 May 1845. Reported by the Rev J. Hill, Incumbent of Scaleby. (Bateman, 1855, 8). Stukeley reports, on visiting Scaleby Castle in 1725, being shown 'two Roman shoes found in the bog hereabouts'. (Stukeley 1776, 57).

16 Solway Moss NY 36 NW   (pp. 146, 149, 150)
before 1772 The moss is seven miles in circumference and lies between England and Scotland. 'At the Battle of Solway, in the time of Henry VIII (1542), when the Scotch arm, commanded by Oliver Sinclair was routed, an unfortunate troop of horse, driven by their fears, plunged into this morass, which instantly closed upon them. The tale was traditional, but it is now so far unauthenticated, that a man and a horse in complete armour, have been found by peat-diggers, in the place where it was always supposed the affair had happened. The skeleton of each was well preserved, and the different parts of the armour easily distinguished' (Gilpin 1786, quoted in Lyell 1838).

DERBYSHIRE

17 Hope SK 17 83   (pp. 148, 149, 150)
1703 A letter records the burial of a man and a woman lost in a snowstorm on 14/1/1674 but not discovered until 3/5/1674. They were buried on the spot in the moss. They were looked at again 28 years 9 months later, 'when some countrymen, having observed, I suppose, the extraordinary quality of this soil in preserving dead bodies from corrupting, were curious enough to open the ground to see if these persons had been so preserved and found them no way altered, the colour of their skin being fair and natural, their flesh soft as that of people newly dead. They were afterwards exposed for a sight 20 years, though they were much changed in this time, by being so often uncovered ... The woman, by some rude people had been taken out of the ground, to which one may well impute her greater decay ... He took out one of the fore-teeth, the upper part of which as far as was contained in the socket, was as elastic as a piece

of steel; and, being wrapp'd round his finger, sprung again to its first form; but this power was lost in a few minutes after it had been in his pocket. Mr Barber of Rotheram, the man's grandson, was at the expense of a decent funeral for them at last in Hope Church, where upon looking into the grave sometimes afterwards, it was found they were entirely consumed'. (Balguy 1734). This incident is the most celebrated of English bog bodies. Bakewell and Lyell use it to demonstrate the preservative powers of peat and Dieck uses the discovery as an early example in his history of the study of bog burials (Dieck 1958). However it seems that to the finders, the most striking aspect of the discovery and its constant exposure was that it could be explained, the history of the incident being well known and with it, a whiff of scandal. It also seems clearly implied that the finding of bog bodies was well known, including perhaps those from the nearby Hatfield Chase area.

GREATER MANCHESTER (see LANCASHIRE)

HUMBERSIDE (see SOUTH YORKSHIRE)

LANCASHIRE

18 Birkdale, nr. Southport (now in Merseyside) SD 32 15   (p. 148)
1872 During sewerage works, beneath a deep layer of blown sand in a peat layer, in Gloucester Road opposite the shop of Mr Kershaw, at 8 ft down, a human skull was found. The skull was severed by sheet piling and has been kept with fragments of red deer bone, and has been presented to the Museum of the Royal College of Surgeons. Reade compared the stratigraphy with the Leasowe discovery. (Busk 1874; Reade 1883).

19 Red Moss, Bolton (now in Greater Manchester) SD 63 10   (pp. 148, 149)
before 1960 The skull of a female with a plait of thick, reddish hair adhering to it. Nearby was a pick made of antler tine. This group of finds is lost. (Greater Manchester SMR).

20 Liverpool (now in Merseyside)   (p. 148)
1911 'On the 21 January 1911, two days prior to one of my visits, a human skeleton was found in No. 3 Bay of the cross-trench. The skeleton was incomplete, an arm and a leg being missing ... found in the surface layers of the upper peat band and were overlain by about five feet of shore sand.' (Travis 1913).

21 Meols, nr. Southport SD 31 NE (pp. 144, 145)
before 1700 'One thing had almost slipt me, how sometimes in mosses are found human bodies entire and uncorrupted, as in a moss near the Meales in Lancashire. In Eller Moss was found the skeleton of a stag standing upon its feet, these are the most remarkable phaenomena I have observed in morasses, I shall not therefore swell these sheets with unnecessary recapitulations, but according to our design proceed to the next chapter.' (Leigh 1700).

22 Kentucky, Pilling SD 441 462   (pp. 148, 149)
1824 'As some labourers were digging peat, on that part of Pilling Moss contiguous to the road leading to Garstang ... at a depth of six feet from the surface, a piece

of coarse woollen cloth, of a yellow colour, was discovered, in which were contained, the remains of a human skull, with a great abundance of hair, of a most beautiful auburn, and two strings of large black glass beads, together with a part of the first vertebra of the neck; the hair was plaited, and of great length; in many parts, about three inches from the extremities of the braids, it was cut off by some heavy cutting instrument, as the ends were exactly level, not a hair projecting, which could not have been the case had it been cut by scissors: a large piece of hardened moss, rendered so by exposure to the air, and bearing evident marks of having been dug with a spade, was found lying in immediate contact above the cloth, though the moss above was as solid as in any other part' letter dated 4/6/1824. A later letter, 5/2/1825, describes the beads in more detail, one link has only jet beads, half inch in length and cylindrical; the other similar jet beads of irregular length with a large round one of amber. (W. Birch, quoted in Edwards 1969). Baines gives the location as at a place called Kentucky (Baines 1868).

23 Quernmore   SD 5423 5735   (pp. 148, 151)
1973   Drains were being cut mechanically into stony blue clay after 25–40 cm of peat had been stripped from the surface on an intended car park at Quernmore, 290 m AOD. Two monoxylous oak boat shaped coffins were found, one intact, one broken by the machine into 16 pieces. 'No evidence exists as to the relationship either of the finds to one another, or of the finds to the stratigraphy. It is possible to say only that no mound or other surface indication had been recorded at the site and that a depression in the surface of the clay in which the canoe-/coffin had lain was clearly visible'. The intact coffin was 2.4 m by 0.4 m and lay approx E–W. Inside were two pieces of folded woollen cloth (later shown to be from an original piece, c. 1.5 m square) associated with which were quantities of human hair, 12 human nails and 3 whitish feathers. It is considered that the broken coffin was the lid to the intact one. (Edwards 1973). Two C14 assays, one from each coffin, ad 610 ± 110 (Birm-430) and ad 650 ± 100 (Birm-474) (*Radiocarbon*, 1974, 16 no. 3, 300).

24 Worsley (now in Greater Manchester)
SD 70 SW   (p. 149)
1958   A skull and lower jaw were found in Worsley Moss in 1958 and were thought to be between 100 and 500 years old. Some skin, hair and other matter were attached to the bones. (Greater Manchester SMR).

25 Lancashire
before 1911 'Crania from peat deposits, the anatomical and geological collections of Cambridge University. VII. A male skull (Mus. Anat. Cont. no. 658); from a "peat moss" Lancashire, described as "Ancient British". VIII. A male skull (Mus. Anat. Cont. no. 659); with locality and description as above' (Duckworth and Shore 1911).

LINCOLNSHIRE (also see SOUTH YORKSHIRE)

26 Bracebridge   SK 96 68
before 1911 'Crania from peat deposits, Cambridge University Collections. II. A male skull with mandible;

from Bracebridge, Lincolnshire.' (Duckworth and Shore 1911).

27 nr. Spalding   TF 22 SW   (pp. 148, 149)
? before 1724   In Gough's *Britannia* of 1789 (ii, 280), it is stated that 'at Crowle [=Goole] on the Don was found the body of a woman standing upright in the peat moss at Althorpe, and two ancient shoes.' Supporting references are made to the Spalding Gentlemen's Society Minutes, the *Phil. Trans. Roy. Soc. Lond.* no. 484 [1747=Stovin's account] and the *Gentleman's Magazine*, May 1749, 203. It seems likely that the Gentlemen's Society reference is to the MS Minutes of 1724 (folio 806), where it is noted that 'a socketted axe [was] found with the skeleton of a man found upright in the same moor by one John Lupton, a Quaker, and many oakes and firrs.' That the scrivener re-iterates that it was *in the same moor* seems to suggest the association of axe with skeleton was not a close one.
The *Gent.'s Mag.* account, which is accompanied by an illustration of a shoe (Fig. VIII), is that described in entry no. 45, from Amcotts.
There is obviously confusion here between the finds from Althorpe and Amcotts in the South Humberside area, and a putative discovery from closer to Spalding which may have related to a find from the general area of the Wash.

NORFOLK

This county has produced by far the largest number of instances of human remains buried in peat deposits. All except two were found this century, which contrasts strongly with the antiquarian bias seen elsewhere. As a result the majority come from disturbed deposits, mechanical dredgings or ploughed fields, and so the circumstances and the quality of the observations are less satisfactory. This twentieth century bias is also due to the enthusiastic fieldwork of firstly, Rainbird Clarke, and secondly, members of the Norfolk Archaeological Trust. Clarke probably provided Dieck with a large number of his English sites and several of these are not from peat deposits. These are included in the gazetteer but are not included in the totals for each country.

The Norfolk examples seem to stand apart from the rest of the English finds. All the remains are skeletal, no tissue seems to survive (though this must reflect the nature of the peat). A lot of the finds are fragmentary and possibly redeposited. Where more than fragments occur, deliberate inhumation burial seems likely, as at Methwold Severalls and West Tofts. The concentration of material in Feltwell Fen resembles that at the nearby Burwell Fen in Cambridgeshire.

28 Feltwell Fen   TL 68 NE
1901   A lower human jaw found 'laid on clay head beneath the turf' (Norfolk SMR, no 5302).
before 1911   A male skull (Mus. Anat. Cont. no 275); from Feltwell Fen, Norfolk, described as 'Early British'.
before 1923   Refers to the Feltwell Fen bone necklace which was 'in clay soil about 5 feet below the surface'. (Fox 1923, 55 and 65; Dieck 1965). Not from a peat deposit.
1948   No account traced (Dieck 1965).

29   Foulden   TL 745 992
1956   Human skull with jaw missing uncovered by dredger in peat. (Norfolk SMR no. 4735).

30   Harling   TL 9788 8574
1983   Frontal part of a human skull in dredgings, Thet Valley. Find encased in peat. (Norfolk SMR no. 19797).

Hockwold cum Wilton   TL 6963 8809
1952   Roman inhumation not from a peat deposit (Dieck 1965; Norfolk SMR no. 5338).

Worthing, Hoe   TG 0079 1954
1947   Dredgings from River Wensum produced human parietal bone, stained the colour of chocolate, with Roman material and animal bones. Not from a peat deposit (Dieck 1965; Norfolk SMR no. 2984).

Whitlinghorn, Kirby Bedon   TG 282 080
before 1945   Female skull in river dredgings. Not from a peat deposit (Dieck 1965; Norfolk SMR no. 9672).

31   West Tofts, Lynford   TL 837 929   (pp. 148, 151)
1720   '. . . was found an oaken coffin in a moist springy ground about two furlongs off West Tofts church in Norfolk, as some of Mr Partridge's labourers were digging a ditch to drain the grounds. It seemed to lie SE and NW, it was full of water, and besides bones was taken out about 30 small beads, a black face of Lancashire Coal, a golden funnell and a cipher as in the figures below. . . . The cypher and beads are of a blue colour. The beads are all square but irregular.' (Norfolk SMR no. 5137, from orig. ms.; Clarke 1960).

32   Methwold   (pp. 148, 149)
before 1945   TL 69 SE: In peat, a skull was found 2 miles west of Methwold village in Broad Fen (Norfolk SMR no. 2547).
1958   TL 631 941: Human bones ploughed up from near the bottom of the peat at a depth of 2 ft from the surface. Bones blackened and rather decayed. 1 flint flake and a flint pebble with a hole in it. Extended skeleton of an adult and 2 children (total of 4 bodies). Bone awl. Given as Bronze Age. (Norfolk SMR no. 2585).
1960   TL 6885 9712: Unfinished bronze rapier, with human lower jaw nearby, found after ploughing to 18 ins in the Fen to the north of Catsholm Island (Norfolk SMR no. 2540).

33   Methwold Severalls, Methwold
TL 6505 9685   (pp. 148, 150)
1968   Several bodies, partly articulated, surviving in peat; partly disturbed by ploughing but also some disturbance soon after death. The only other find; a bronze double-ended awl of quadrangular section. Peat sampled by Hibbert, Camb. Univ. (Norfolk SMR no. 2542).
1971   Three burials, 10 yds south and 50 yds east of 1968 Methwold Severalls. 2 white scrapers just under the bones. Found in peat 2 ft deep and disturbed by the plough. (Norfolk SMR no. 2542).

34   Southery Fen, Methwold   TL 6300 9425   (p. 150)
1932   'The Southery Fen Female: young female skeleton. In this case, we have to deal with a drowning, and the victim was fortunately associated with eight fusiform jet beads and a bronze awl or pin of Early Bronze Age date.' Found 3–4 in from base of 2 ft of peat above buttery clay (Clark 1933).

Postwick   TG 20 NE
1935   Human skull from river, not from a peat deposit. (Dieck 1965; Norfolk SMR no. 9654).

Runham, Mautby   TG 4631 1065   (p. 149)
1954   Male skull, found in blue mud dredgings. 'As the estimated depth of the skull and the condition of the upcast coincide so exactly with the transition from clay to peat, it is clear that the skull was resting in the basal estuarine clay on the uncompacted peat'. Head decapitated from front to back. (Green and Wells 1961; Dieck 1965).

35   Shouldham   TF 6948 1102
1954   Human skull from east end of Mere Plot, in peat. (Norfolk SMR no. 3464).

36   Wayford Bridge, Smallburgh   TG 34 24
before 1883   'In making a staithe-ditch on the Smallburgh side, several human skulls and bones were found, 6 ft deep in peat. A female skull was preserved in the Museum of the Royal College of Surgeons.' (Gunn 1883, 22).

37   Southery   TL 69 NW   (p. 148)
1968   'Found in peat at Black Bank Drive, an occipital bone from a human skull. It has a semi-circular gash on the exterior which has healed partly. Notable stress marks around the edges and across the bone; interior has very deep vein channels.' Child's skull or microcephalic idiot? (Norfolk SMR no. 16017).

Strumpshaw   TG 3338 0630
1954   Skull from bank of River Yare; not from a peat deposit (Dieck 1965; Norfolk SMR no. 10240).

Surlingham   TG 331 063
1956   3 adult male bones, in dredgings from River Yare; not from a peat deposit. (Dieck 1965; Norfolk SMR no. 10249).

38   Wroxham   TG 3029 1816
1959   Human skull with cut marks found *c.* 3 ft deep in peat in the bank of the River Bure. Possibly 13th–15th century, or 17th–19th century. Report by Wells. (Norfolk SMR no. 8424).

39   Wymondham   TG 0954 0296   (p. 148)
1961   Found in extending the sewage works, 6 ft deep in peat, part of a human skull, with Roman pot, leather and animal bones (Norfolk SMR no. 8901).

NORTHAMPTONSHIRE

40   Northamptonshire
1866   The frontal and parietal bones of a cranium, from a peat-bog in Northamptonshire 'From J. Prestwich, Esq., Dec. 1866' (Flower 1907, 63). Now in the Royal College of Surgeons, London.

NORTH YORKSHIRE

41   Austwick Common, Clapham   SD 76 69
(pp. 148, 149, 150)
1846   Labourers digging peat 'discovered the remains of a human skeleton beneath four feet of peat, from which

six feet had been previously removed, and also a pair of shoes; though not in close proximity, and therefore, probably not belonging to the same individual.' The shoes were of one piece, laced at the top and with open uppers. The outer soles were fastened by hobnails. 'The human skeleton found in the same locality and at the same period had two stones of calliard and gritstone, placed one at the head and the other at the foot, but there was no indication of a kist; so that it is evident the individual had not been accidentally lost in the bog, but carefully interred on this solitary spot.' The body was thought to be female, of small stature, long bone epiphyses fused, skull unfused. The bones were light and flexible. Speculates on the age and favours the Roman period but no firm conclusion reached. The skeleton was preserved by the Geological and Polytechnic Society, West Riding of Yorkshire. (Denny 1871).

42   Grewelthorpe Moor   SE 170 758
                                    (pp. 148, 149, 150)
1850 'The most remarkable discovery connected with this period (Roman) was made in the spring of 1850 by Edwin and John Grainge, while digging peat on Grewelthorpe Moor, when they came upon the body of a man, in an almost complete state of preservation, and from his dress evidently a Roman, which the peat had tanned and dried in a remarkable manner, somewhat like an Egyptian mummy. The robes were quite perfect when found, the toga of a green colour, while some portions of the dress were of a scarlet hue; the stockings were of yellow cloth and the sandals of a finely artistic shape, one of which was preserved and we believe is now in the Museum of the Yorkshire Philosophical Society. The flesh was tanned into a kind of white fatty substance, and had a very offensive smell. No coins or weapons were found about the body. He was probably some wanderer who had lost his way and perished in the bog in which he no doubt reposed for 1400 years. The remains were finally interred in the Churchyard of Kirby Malzeard'. (Grainge 1892). The grave is unmarked but a sandal and part of a stocking survive in the Yorkshire Museum (Tinsley 1974).

43   Grinton in Swaledale   (p. 146)
1797 '18 June 1797. A person found by Ralph Harker buried in the peat moss in Whitaside but from the changes in the body has undergone cannot be distinguished whether it is male or female having been examined by Messrs Barker, Thompson and Metcalfe surgoones.' (Grinton Parish Registers).

NOTTINGHAMSHIRE

44   Nottinghamshire
before 1868 Cranium of young person, from a peat-bog in Nottinghamshire, wanting the greater part of the base; presented G. Busk 1868 (Flower 1907, 63).

SOUTH YORKSHIRE

45   Hatfield Chase, Thorne Moss and the Isle of Axholme   centre SE 77 07   (pp. 145, 149)
This vast tract of peat moss is now divided by the boundary of two modern counties, South Yorkshire and Humberside. During the two centuries after Dutch engineers first began draining it in the mid-seventeenth century (Gaunt 1975), a number of important bog burials have been found. There seems to have been a minimum of five examples, and may have been more. It is difficult to locate them precisely from contemporary descriptions and some accounts confuse elements from earlier discoveries. Nevertheless, this area is the most important in England for bog bodies and can be compared with some of the Danish sites, like Borre Fen and Bjaeldskovdal, which have produced a number of finds explained as ritual sacrifices. Seventeenth century accounts make it clear that finds other than bodies were commonplace in the area; Roman coins, gates, hammers and shoes, as well as early plough furrows were known from this tract (de la Pryme 1694). More recently, palaeo-ecological work has demonstrated the existence of at least one Bronze Age track and evidence of prehistoric tree clearances (Buckland and Kenward 1973). Parts of the area are still worked commercially for peat, and there exists the possibility that further finds will be made here.

c. **1645** 'About 50 Years ago, at the Bottom of a Turf-Pit, was found a Man lying at his length, with his Head upon his Arm, as in a common Posture of Sleep, whose Skin being as it were tann'd by the Moor-Water, preserved his Shape intire, but within, his Flesh and most of his Bones were consumed and gone; an Arm of whom is now in the Possession of Dr. *Nat. Johnson.* Though these things may seem strange, yet many Authors have yet related the same.' (de la Pryme 1694). Details of the above were repeated by Gibson (1695, cols 725–6; 1722, col 850) and Gough (1789, III, 35).

before 1700 [at Goole SE 74 23] **and 1740** [near Thorne ?SE 73 15] 'As to this Water upon these Moors preserving human Bodies, it is most certain; *viz.* Part of a Body taken up at *Geel* by your Grandfather Mr. *Empson* 50 or 60 Years ago, and one in the great Moor near *Thorn,* about 7 Years ago, with the Skin like tann'd Leather, the Hair, Teeth, and Nails quite fresh.'.

1747 [at Amcotts, Lincolnshire SE 85 14] '. . a labouring Man, was digging Turf or Peat in the Moors of Amcotts; and, at about six Foot, from the Surface, his Spade cut the Toe of a Sandal, which dropped into the cut he was graveing Peat in; also Part of the Foot dropp'd in, which terrified the Man, and he left it. Hearing of this Discovery, I went and took some Servants with me, to make further Discovery; when we soon found the other Sandal (which I now send you whole and firm). It was very soft and pliable, and a tawny Colour, with all the Bones, of that Foot in it, and all the grisly Part of the Heel: And proceeding further, we found the Skin and Thigh-Bones, which I measured to be eighteen Inches long. We then found all the Skin of the lower Parts of the Body, which was of the same Colour of the Sandals, and very soft, with fresh Hair upon it &c. which distinguished it to be a woman. The Skin drew or stretch'd like a Piece of Doe-Leather, and was as strong. We then found the Skin of the Arms, which was like the Top of a Muff or Glove, when the Bones were shaken out. We then found his Hand I have sent, with the Nails as fresh as any Person's living; which are now, both Hand and Nails, shrunk very much, since it was exposed to the Air: This Hand is the Lady's natural Skin so tann'd, with the Nails. We left the Bones in the Fingers, where the Nails are, for fear the Nails should drop off, if that Joint was taken out.' Later, he added 'It is the Skin of the Hand that is stuff'd, which has suffer'd by the Spade.' The Sandals [which Stovin later requested comments upon the age of] .. were 'of one Piece of Leather, and Seam at the Heel, with a Thong of the same Leather. See TAB. I. *Fig 2*. and of a raw Hide .., and the Skin of the Lady, were both of one Colour and both had one Tanner; which I presume, is the Moor-Water; which is exactly the Colour of Coffee .. The lady in all probability was overwhelmed by some strong Eddy of Water; for she lay upon one Side bended, with her Head and Feet almost together' (Stovin 1747).

Contemporary remarks upon the footwear included a reasoned scholarly argument presented by George Vertue, who concluded that 'this very Sandal could not well be earlier than *Ed*. I or *Hen*. III.; also, that the cutting the Form, and sewing to form the Heel cleverly, by a stitching behind the Heel with a small Leather Thong, may have been in Use before that of waxed Thread used by Shoe-makers, formerly called Cord-wainers.' (Stovin 1747, *fn* p. 575–6).

Elizabethan 'Several human bodies have been disinterred (from Hatfield Chase), remains of unfortunate persons lost in attempting to cross these moors, faithless as the shifting sands of Arabia. It is to be regretted that a more particular account has not been preserved of the dress in which any of these bodies were enveloped, or of other relics which must one supposes, have been found near them ...' Mention of Stovin's description given above. 'A pair of similar sandals, taken from the feet of a body found in the reign of Elizabeth, formerly hung up in the hall of the Trigotts at South Kirby.' (Hunter 1828).

early 18th century 'In the beginning of the last century the perfect body of a man in the ancient Saxon costume was discovered in the peat at Hatfield Chase.' (Bakewell 1833). This may describe one of the examples given earlier but none are mentioned as clothed, so perhaps it is a separate find.

CLWYD

46   Prestatyn   SJ 07 82   (p. 148)
1924   Skeleton of woman buried in submerged substratum of peat Prestatyn, Flints. Presented F. Gilbert Smith 1924 (*Ann. Rep. Mus. Royal College of Surgeons* 1924).
1984   'The burial was that of an articulated skeleton of a baby, laid on top of a peat deposit. It was surrounded by a stake-built fence, indicated by the preserved tips of pointed wooden stakes. The fence was disturbed on its north side by a 1930's excavation trench, which may have removed some of the baby bones'. (Blockley *pers. comm.*).

DYFED

47   Llyn Mawr Farm, Llandarog   SW 50 16
                                             (p. 148)
1848   In a bog called Commins or Cummins 'between Wenfrith and Llanrynys'. 'In the same year (1848), I found a human skull on the other side of the brook, while opening a drain through the "gorse", or bog, of Llynmawr Farm.' *Arch. Cambr.* 1893, 142.

48   Dolfawr Fair, Gwnnws, Ceredigion   SN 711 670 (approx).   (p. 146)
'Tanning principles in peat bogs. In the year 1811 – when a man was cutting on Dolfawrfair he discovered at 2 ft depth below the sward – a human body consisting only of bones and skin – the muscles &c entirely perished – the bones entirely blacked within and without. The bones in the skin appeared like sticks in a bog – bones soft so as to [be] easily scraped or cut with a knife. The skin fresh, and completely tanned. No head or skull was found – which made it apparent that the person had died a violent death. He was buried in Ystrad Meyrig Chy^d.'

This extract is from the travel diaries of Walter Davies (Gwallter Mechain) of 1813 (Nat. Library of Wales MS 1755B, 15, fols 14 bis –15).
There is still a peatbog at Dolfawr (Gors Dolfawr) which has not been cut for many years. Mr Aeronian Herbert whose family have lived at the farm there for several generations, has never heard of the discovery.

GWYNEDD

49   Maes-y-Pandy, Merionethshire
                                             (pp. 145, 150, 151)
1684   'The coffin was discovered about the year 1684, in a turbary, called Mownog ystratgwyn near Maes y Pandy; it was of wood, and so well preserved, that the gilding remained very fresh: and it is said to have contained an extraordinary large skeleton. This is the only instance I know of burying in such places; and yet they who placed this coffin here might have regard to the perpetual preservation of it, seeing we find, by daily examples of trees found in turbaries, that such bituminous earth preserves beyond all others'. (Gibson 1695, col. 794; 1722, 775).

POWYS

50   Gifron or Gwar-y-Beddau Farm, Nantmel, Radnorshire   SH 92 66   (p. 148)
before 1858   'In the adjoining turbary (to a farm called Gifron or Gwar-y-beddau) there was found some years ago, a human skull, having its full complement of hair; probably the preservation of the hair was owing to the astringency of the peat water.' (Williams 1858, 553).

NOT LOCATED

Several bodies included in the list published by Dieck in 1965 have not been located and no account has been traced. These are; before 1919a Brandon, 1948d Sedge Fen and 1956c Westrow Fen.

Scotland
(16 sites, 36 + individuals)

CENTRAL

51   Stirlingshire   (p. 152)
c. **1830**   'Mr Napier alluded to the discovery of several skeletons in Stirlingshire about 30 years ago, that were buried in peat, and were associated with bronze celts

and other bronze implements. The skulls were long and not those of short-headed individuals'. (Hunt 1866b).

GRAMPIAN
52 Longside, Aberdeenshire NK 03 47
(pp. 151, 152)

before 1845 'In the New Statistical Account for Aberdeenshire (xii, 354) the Rev W. Donald of Peterhead, records the finding in the parish of Longside of two oak coffins or chests in a tumulus of moss. One of them was entire. They had been hollowed out of solid trees and each measured 7 ft by 2 ft. The sides were parallel and the ends rounded and they had projecting knobs to facilitate their carriage. No vestige of bones were found in either coffin. They had been covered over with slabs of wood and lay east to west.' (Abercromby 1905).

HIGHLAND
53 Dava Moor, Cromdale, Morayshire
NA 477 478   (p. 152)

1927 'Woollen clothing and a broad bonnet found on a human skeleton in a peat moss on Dava Moor, Cromdale, Morayshire in July 1927 and a birch stick was found laid on the body.' Bryce reported that the skeleton was short, poorly developed, over 20 years old, sex undetermined. Henshall considers the clothing 16th or more likely 17th century in comparison with the Dungiven find, from Ulster. (*pers. comm.*). (*Proc. Soc. Ant. Scotland* (63) 22; Henshall 1952).

54 Culrain, Ross-shire NH 57 94   (p. 152)
1880 'Pieces of woollen cloth and knitting, and part of a leather shoe taken from some fully clothed skeletons found in a moss in 1880. They are now rather decayed and fragile, all dark brown.' 6 bodies in total (Henshall 1952).

55 Clayton Hill, Keiss, Caithness ND 34 61
(p. 152)

1975 Found during peat digging 3 ft below the surface and immediately below a layer consisting of 5 stone slabs. Partially-preserved skeleton, probably of a male teenager, c. 5 ft 3 ins high, laid on its right side and in a roughly E-W alignment. Left forearm and left side of skull damaged due to pressure from above on the decalcified bone. No hair was found. Cause of death unknown. 'The upper part of the body was clothed in a sleeved woollen jacket (doublet) in the style of the mid 17th century. There was no sign of any clothing for the lower part of the body and the only find was a length of "simmons" (twisted heather rope) in fragmentary condition which lay along the length of the body' (H. Bennett *pers. comm.*) (less than 1½ miles from Quintfall Hill, Barrock find).

56 Quintfall Hill, Barrock, near Wick,
Caithness NO 25 71   (pp. 151, 152)
1920 'In June last, the skeleton of a man, dressed in a complete suit of clothing, was found in a peat moss at Barrock, near Wick, lying with the arms straight along the sides, on its face, at a depth of three feet from the surface. The body was wrapped in a plaid or blanket, and as this was unfolded, the cap and shoes were found above the knees. The hair was long and of reddish colour. Evidently the man had met with a violent death, as the

skull showed the mark of a heavy blow. The clothing was in a wonderful state of preservation and consisted of: A round flat bonnet or cap; an outer jacket or coat of similar shape and material; an outer pair of breeches cut very wide; an inner pair of breeches of similar cut and material; a pair of hose as stockings made of the same cloth as the clothes, a pair of light, low-heeled leather shoes in fragments; a plaid or blanket; and a detached shaped piece of cloth.' In a pocket was a leather purse containing 19 bawbees or sixpenny pieces Scots. All of Charles II except one of William and Mary, struck 1694. (Orr 1921; Henshall 1952).

ORKNEY AND SHETLAND
57 Birsay, Orkney HY 25 27
1881 'Some pieces of extremely worn and patched woollen clothing found about 1881 with the skeleton of a girl in a bog. The find has been included with the 17th century pieces because of the similarity of the single thread colour stripes in piece g) with those from Dava'. (Henshall 1952).

58 Huntsgarth, Harray, Orkney HY 3490 1815
(pp. 151, 152)

1968 'The discovery was made in May 1968 by Mr George Spence whilst digging peats. The peat bank was 3½ ft deep, and the clothing was at the base of the bank. The cloth occupied a small space and a bonnet lay on the top. Further investigation produced no other finds. There was no sign that the peat above the find had been disturbed, although it can hardly be doubted that the cloths represent the burial of a child in a hole dug in the peat bog.' Human hair was found on the cloth 'fair and nonmedullated'. 'Although the presence of a body could not be proved chemically, the subsequent reconstruction of the dress, by reforming every fold and crease and by observing every impression, further emphasises the probability that the clothes had formed a dress which had been buried on a child's body. The child had been laid on its back with the arms across the chest.' The cap and style of clothing suggest an 18th century date and the site lies in a shallow, moorland valley. (Henshall 1969).

59 Bressay, Shetland HU 45 SW   (pp. 151, 152)
1866 Twelve wooden coffins were discovered and excavated from an area about 48 ft by 20 ft in size, all coming from within peat. The coffins were all of roughly sawn Norway Pine and were not orientated in any particular direction. Most appeared to contain no human remains. One had two stones above it, each with a crudely carved symbol, and this coffin contained a fatty substance. Similar substances were found in several boxes, one producing a perfect finger-nail. 'And here it may be interesting to give a few instances of the preservation of the human body in peat, for it becomes of the greatest importance to understand that varieties of peat may so entirely differ in their chemical components, as to have entirely opposite effects. I examined the whole locality for coffins, and the last that could be found was opened in the presence of several friends from Lerwick; it turned out to be the most interesting we had yet discovered. Situated rather lower in the peat than the remainder, when we came on it the top appeared more solid, and we soon found it was filled with water, and we proceeded to make a drain and let the water out from the bottom, so as to

be able carefully to examine the contents of the coffin. Before letting out the water we observed, on taking up the lid, that a body apparently pretty perfect remained for us. I preserved a portion of the water for chemical analysis. In cleaning the skull and the long bones I found considerable difficulty, and also in separating the skin and muscles of the arm from the bone. I had an easy task in scalping the long sought for treasure, and found that with one grip I had a pretty good wig in my hand. When the men who dug up this coffin saw the contents, they could not be got to render any further assistance, and declared the sight and smell had turned their "inside out", this was, however, purely the effect of imagination. It was with some difficulty I could get them to bring some clean water to me, and to deposit it at some yards distant. I had gone to Lerwick for a packing case, and the sailors who brought me over hesitated to take back a skeleton, but an offer of a little extra coin of the realm, quite satisfied their consciences.' On some coffins were pieces of woollen fabric (shrouds?) and in one some wooden buttons. The author did not consider the bodies ancient. (Hunt 1866a).

60   Dunrossness, Shetland   HU 39 15
1847   'Pieces of woollen fabrics found in a moss about 1847: no bones were found.' (Henshall 1952). Dieck (1965) gives it as a bog body.

61   Gunnister, Shetland   HU 328 732
(pp. 151, 152, 155)
1951   Found 12/5/1951 in a peat bank on the side of the Lerwick-Hillswick road. 'The fully clothed body of a man had been laid stretched out on its back in a shallow grave on the uninhabited moor, with its head towards the ESE. It was some 30 in deep in the peat, of which there is a depth of more than 4 ft above rock ... Scarcely anything of the body was left – some curly dark brown hair, with no trace of grey; portions of the skull; some finger and toenails; and very decayed fragments of bone in each sleeve and in one stocking. All the woollen clothing, now of various shades of brown, was well preserved, as were other articles of different materials. The man had worn a long coat, with short, wide-legged breeches of much the same material, a shirt and an outermost ragged jacket, apparently an addition for extra warmth. A leather belt with a brass buckle was round the body. Cold weather was further indicated by a pair of knitted gloves – the right one not on, but lying at the left side. Long knitted stockings came over the knees; the feet of these were reinforced, but the only sign of shoes was a piece of "skin" 6 in long. On the head was a knitted woollen cap with a turned-up brim, another plainer cap, also knitted, was inside the clothing at the right side "as if it had been in a pocket", and was found round a horn spoon. Inside the breeches at the left side, again as if in a pocket, were a small horn and knitted purse containing a folded length of silk ribbon and three late 17th century coins of low value, one Swedish and two Dutch. A stick lay across the legs, and at the feet were a small wooden tub, a wooden knife handle and two tablets of wood. Also near the legs were two lengths of woollen cord.' The coins dated 1681, 1683 and 1690 were not unusual in Scotland. The conclusion was that it was a

traveller who had lost his way in winter, and been buried on the spot. (Henshall and Maxwell 1952).

62   Norsewick, Mainland, Shetland
1849   'The two small pieces of cloth, which are preserved with a lock of hair and a piece of wood, come from 'two tunics' found on a male and female skeleton in a moss in 1849.' (Henshall 1952).

STRATHCLYDE

63   Ards Moss, Ayrshire   (p. 151)
before 1810   'Some bodies were dug up in Ards Moss, in Ayrshire, which had lain for a much longer period, ever since the persecution of the Covenanters in the reign of Charles II.' (Rennie 1810, 520).

64   Greenhead Moss, Cambusnethan,
Lanarkshire   NS 81 55   (pp. 151, 152)
1932   Found 23/3/1932 by a man digging peat. 'Immediately other similar pieces of wood were disclosed and on lifting these, he exposed the body of a man lying full clothed. The place is at the centre of a large flat stretch of peat and marsh, treeless and without dwellings ... The body had been laid in a very shallow grave, the digging of which could not have been occupied more than a few minutes and was outstretched on its back with the head to the west ... Carefully placed just above the body were 5 light pieces of wood of silver birch, set about 6 in apart and all parallel with the body.' The wooden poles were thought to have been used to carry the body across the bog. It was dressed in a woollen cap, a jacket with brass buttons, breeches, shoes and stockings, considered by Eskdale of c. 1680–90. The shoes and cap were cut by sword thrusts. It was suggested that he was a Covenanter, but Henshall (pers. comm.) considers the clothing to be late 18th/early 19th century in date. (Mann 1937).

65   Oban, Argyllshire   (pp. 151, 152)
1879   'The canoe was in peat with an apparent mound over it. The ends of the hollowed out trunk had planks inserted which were kept in place by stakes driven into the bog. Logs were placed on the top and around the structure, a cover of hazel and birch twigs stuffed with moss. There was no sign of bone. The soil in the canoe was unctious and mixed with charcoal. In the canoe, several pieces of birch bark were found, one pierced with a hole'. (Mapleton 1879). Abercromby (1905) considers that this is a wooden coffin burial.

WESTERN ISLES

66   Arnish Moor, Lewis   NB 43 30   (p. 152)
1964   'Clothing, quill pen and a comb in a case, probably of early 18th century date, from the grave of a man at Arnish Moss, Lewis'. (*Proc. Soc. Ant. Scotland* (98) 328).

Ireland
(53 sites, *c.* 60 individuals)
Co. ANTRIM

67   Derrykeighan   (unlocated bog in parish of,
centred on C96 33)   (p. 155)
1861   'In the year 1861 ... at a considerable depth, a skin

cape, 24 inches in length, 36 inches wide at one edge and 50 inches at the other. The material used in the sewings consists of 2 strands twisted together to form one thread, and judging by their length, they are probably the sinews of some large animal. The holes made by the needle are small, the sewing regular, the top and bottom of the cloak backed by a double thong stitched in the most elaborate manner' (McAdam 1861–2; Wood Martin 1902, 109–110). This is possibly the otterskin hood mentioned by McClintock (1950, 109) as having come from Co. Down.

68   Rasharkin Parish   C 97 13   (p. 156)
1827   'The body of a man who had committed suicide in 1776, and had been buried in a bog in the mountain, was found in 1827, without the smallest signs of decomposition' (Lewis 1837, *s.v.* Rasharkin).

Co. ARMAGH

69   Charlemont td., Loughgall Parish   H 85 55
(pp. 146, 155)

1816   'The body of a trooper was discovered in a bog near Charlemont. It was in a complete state of preservation with the clothes and spurs perfect; the dress and armour appeared to be of the reign of Elizabeth' (Lewis 1837, *s.v.* Co. Armagh and Charlemont).

Co. CAVAN

70   Drummacon Bog
before 1857   Two shoes found seventeen spits deep in the bog (Wilde 1857, 289).

71   Lough Shelan
1853   Hair cloth found with a fine woollen band, 14 feet deep in the bog, in 1853. Preserved by Dr Fleming. (*Proc. Roy. Irish Acad.* (6) 19; Wilde 1857, 295).

Co. CLARE

72   Boghill td.
1935   Fragments of ancient dress found in a bog (*Rep. Nat. Mus. Ireland*, 1935–6, 20; NMI 1936; 1775–7).

73   Co Clare   (Unlocated)
before 1935   Skull, found in a bog. Very much distorted and not capable of measurement. Hair well-preserved and dark-red in colour. Preserved in National Museum of Ireland. (Martin 1935, 155; McClintock 1950, 64).

Co. DERRY

Note   Most of the entries for this county derive from the MSS Ordnance Survey Memoirs of the 1830s (abbreviated below to O.S.M.), now housed in the library of the Royal Irish Academy (R.I.A.) in Dublin. The accompanying coded MS numbers are: first, the box number, then parish number, and finally parish section or fascicle; hence O.S.M. 36 = R.I.A. MS box 36. /I = Cumber Parish. (39), = MS section of unedited fair sheets on field information etc. Thomas Fagan = T.F. and John Bleakly = J.B.

74   Ballygroll td., Cumber par.   C 52 15   (p. 156)
1835   'Discovery of a skeleton. In the townland of Ballygroll, in a bog, there was lately discovered the skeleton of a child, coffined. The inside covering was sheets of paper used instead of linen, as a winding sheet. The coffin was made of ruff construction, and sunk several feet down in the moss. The coffin and its contents seemed to be embedded for a long time in the above place, as all appeared in complete decay. T.F. 15th Oct. 1835' (O.S.M. 36/I(39), fol. 31 and condensed version 36/I(28), fol. 15).

75   Ballygudden td., Dungiven par.   C 68 10   (p. 156)
1831   'Extraordinary Discovery of a Female and Infant Bodies. In a bog in the townland of Ballygudden, there were the bodies of a female and an infant child discovered some feet in depth beneath the surface of the bog. The woman's hair seemed to suffer little from change, time or the unnatural tomb in which it was lodged. The body remained in its natural shape with some parts of the flesh in complete cement, this much resembling the fat of an animal. The hair was yellow colour ... The infant's flesh disappeared altogether and round its neck there was a leather strap, with a small buckle attached. This discovery was made in 1831. T.F. 28th Oct. 1834, information from Robert Fleming' (O.S.M. 39/II(11), fol. 89).

76   Boghill td., Coleraine par.   C 8734   (p. 156)
before 1835   'A few years ago, a meather of butter with a few coffin boards was found in this bog. The coffin boards are supposed to have been those of a man named McMurray who committed suicide and was buried in a bed of gravel and moss in the centre of the bog and is called McMurrays Now'. O.S.M. J. Bleakly, 27th Aug. 1835. (O.S.M. 35/II (2)).

77   Camnish td., Bovevagh par.   C 6812
1834   'The grave raised over the remains of the female lately discovered in Cammish and Derryard bogs is 6 feet long, 1 foot high, and well-shaped and a stone placed at the head and foot of the grave, which stands in the interior of the above bog. Thomas Fagan, 28th Nov. 1834'. (O.S.M. 33/I(9), fol. 87).

78   Camus td., Macosquin par.   C 8628
1835   'Intestines got in Bog: There were the entire intestines of either a human being or a beast got 4 feet under the surface of Camus bog, in June last by Samuel McEntire. Parts of the above entrails was in a perfect state of preservation when discovered. They were immediately buried in the place they were found. Thomas Fagan, 13th Aug. 1835, information from Samuel McEntire' (O.S.M. 43/III(3), fol. 13).

79   Drumadreen td., Bovevagh par.   C 6915
(pp. 146, 155, 156)

1813   'Robert Fleming and his wife, formerly residing in the Townland of Drumadreen, discovered in a bog in that townland, several feet beneath the surface, in a pit out of which they were cutting turf, a curious garment or coat. It appeared to have been worn by a female. It is made up as follows. It was open in front with a row of buttons on each side. From the neck or collar to the skirts on each side under the sleeves, there were armholes cut and trimmed, thus seeming as if the wearer had had their arms in the sleeves or armholes at pleasure. From the neck or collar to the skirts on each side under the sleeves there was a row of buttons. On each side of the body and skirt of the garment there were six gores of equal and fixed length. It was altogether curiously but tastefully trimmed, and the buttons covered with cloth the same stuff – a species of grey under the arm and on one side. There was a hole made by some sharp instrument, apparently for the purpose of wounding the wearer to death, as for some inches around the cloth was clotted and stiffened with what had been formerly most probably blood. The garment was found stretched at full length and at the top or neck there were also discovered some locks of hair adhering, in good preservation. The finder did not make a further search, but believes that the body or bones are still near the spot where he found the garment and hair. The coat was purchased at 2/6 and brought to Belfast.' (O.S.M. 33/I(9), fol. 90).

'About the year 1813, *Robert Fleming*, late of Drumadreen, found a tartan or wool garment in a bog in the same townland, and within a short distance of the grave in Jacob Smith's farm. It is described (fol. 17 omitted from this account), and it is believed that the body of the female to which it belonged, as well as a hat of Highland soldier fell, in the troubles of 1641. Information from T.F. 28th Nov. 1834'. (O.S.M. 33/I(17) fols. 25–6).

'Jacob Smith's grave is at present in a dilapidated state. It is altogether composed of turf moss. From the beating of the tempests the grave is partly stripped, and many of the bones are exposed to wind and weather. The long wooden sword (from the same bog) is now lost. A piece of the tartan garment is at present in the possession of Mr Stokes. It is in good preservation and the pattern is plainly visible.' (O.S.M. 33/I(17), fol. 26). This material is not preserved at the National Museum of Ireland.

80   Drumard td., Maghera par.   C 91 07
1833 'Human Skeleton. There was a human skeleton found about 6 feet beneath the surface of a bog in the townland of Drumard, in 1833. It was again buried on the site where found. Thomas Fagan 5th Jan. 1836'. (O.S.M. 44/I(8), fol. 39).

81   close to above   C 93 03   (p. 156)
'Ancient Burial Ground. There is a small island in the flow bog intervening between Drumard and Ballymacpeake, which island has been occupied by burials of young children etc. for centuries back. The ruins of the graves still appear above the surface. Thomas Fagan, 11th Dec. 1836.' (O.S.M. 44/I(8), fol. 24).

82   Drumcroon td., Aghadowey par.   C 84 25
(p. 156)
pre-1835 'A human skeleton in the possession of John Wilson, Esqr, of Drumcroon with a pole at its side and hair still adhering to the scalp.' (O.S.M. 29/I(7), fol. 23).

83   Dunmore bog, Lissan par.   H 76 85   (p. 156)
1881 'Mr John Browne, Drapersfield sent the following note: When in Cookstown on Saturday evening last, the 11th inst., I called at the police station, to have a look at a wooden plate and spoon which had lately been found beside a human skeleton in Dunmore bog. The constable who showed me the plate and spoon mentioned that the skeleton was discovered, about the depth of three spits of turf or so from the surface, in this mountain bog; it was in a space of about three feet in length, and apparently drawn up, or contracted as with cold, and partly

wrapped in blankets; and that there had evidently been two blankets – one coarse and strong, the other finer, and that the plate seemed to have been over the face. Both plate and spoon are very coarsely made, having no trace of either ornament or carving of any description, except an attempt that a W on the handle of the spoon where it joins the bowl.' (*Journ. Roy. Soc. Ants. Ireland* Vol. 5, series 4, 1881, 501–2).

84   Flanders td., Dungiven par.   C 67 11
(pp. 155, 156)
1804 'Most singular discovery of a human body and some deadly weapons in Flanders, Derryard. About the year 1804, there was discovered within a few yards of the ruins of Neil Grooma's house in Flanders, the body of a man in its natural shape. It was found some feet under the surface. The garment worn by the individual at the time of his being murdered and interred in this spot was of home manufacture, a rough woollen coat made of doe leather, and sewed on the cloth with a leather thong. The buttons were sewn on both sides of the garment, from the collar to the lower parts of the skirts, and the back and sleeve buttons were of the same material. The body was stretched at full length when it was found, and covered almost entirely with the long garment. The head was entirely severed from the body. There was also found in the same place, or within a few feet of it, a sort of dagger, and several other deadly weapons, believed to have belonged to the murderous gang of robbers already described. It is the final opinion of the local inhabitants, that the aforesaid body was that of a drover, or some travelling dealer, who had been assassinated or stripped of his money by the robbers, while stopping at Neil Grooma's house, and that after killing him, they buried the maltreated body in Neil's garden, where it lay undiscovered until the above period. This extraordinary discovery caused a great sensation throughout the neighbourhood, and many persons came to the spot to inspect the body and garment. After some deliberation the body and garment was re-interred near the spot where it was found. The inhabitants believe this to be but one out of many who have had a like fate from the aforementioned gang, and who have been put down about the precincts of Neil's dwelling in the same or perhaps in a more disfigured state of brutal butchery. Informants, Archibald and Joseph McSparrin. T. Fagan, 13th Feb. 1835'. (O.S.M. 33/I(9), fol. 193).

85   At 'The Hill' farm   C 677 116   (pp. 154, 155)
1956 On 23 April 1956, following the discovery of clothing and a pair of leather shoes by a labourer, after they had been scattered by drainage machinery, during the removal of a low peat wall, an excavation revealed that these had been lain in what appeared to have been originally a shallow ditch. This was filled with peaty loam. There was no body preserved, though the investigators were fairly sure that one had been originally interred there. The clothing, stained a fairly uniform brown by the peat, comprised a large semi-circular woollen cloak or mantle, and woollen coat or jacket, almost complete except for a part of the right arm, and fragments of a pair of tartan trews. The outfit appeared to have been well mended in antiquity. The clothes were dated upon stylistic grounds to *c.* 1590–1650. (Henshall and Seaby 1961–2).

86   Gortnamoyagh td., Ballinascreen par.
C 80 13   (pp. 146, 155, 156)

1837 'Mr Crofton Croker read a letter which he had received from J. Emerson Tennent, Esq., M.P., stating that about the year 1837–8, some turf cutters, working in a bog at Gort-na-moyagh, near Garvagh, in the county of Derry, found the body of a knight in complete chain armour; beside it were the heads and brazen butts of two spears, but the wooden shaft which connected them had disappeared; and close by, lay one or two trunks which had contained embroidered dresses, for threads of gold and silver could be pulled out of the peat earth which filled the space within the decayed wood of the boxes. The trappings of his horse were likewise found and together with them a pair of stirrups which had been wrought with gold and silver ornaments, like Turkish or Saracenic work. Some fragments of the armour were preserved, and the rings seemed, as it was stated, to indicate that they were of Milanese workmanship, because they were joined inside the ring, instead of outside as the Spanish armour was.' (*Jnl. Roy. Archaeol. Inst.* Vol. 2, 1847, 72).

87   Knocknakeeragh td., Ballinderry par.   C 89 32

1820 'Skeleton got in a bog. John Sterling of Knocknakeeragh got a skeleton of a human body 3 feet under the surface of a bog in the above townland in 1820. Informant, John Sterling. Thomas Fagan, 16th Oct. 1835.' (O.S.M. 30/I(2), fol. 15).

88   Mulkeeragh td., Dungiven par.
C 70 16   (pp. 146, 155, 156)

1753 'In a bog within 200 yards of the road, in the farm of Jacob Smith, and in the townland of Mulkeeragh, a grave of earth 9 feet long, 8 feet broad, and 4 feet high and on the southern end, there is an ordinary stone. This was raised over the remains of a human body discovered at the same spot in a full tartan military uniform dress in or about the year of our Lord 1753. He was discovered by the late Josiah Smith, father of the present Jacob Smith, while in the act of cutting turf in the bog of Mulkeeragh. He found him stretched at full length at about two feet under the surface of a solid bank. He wore over his uniform dress, a long tartan cloak, and both the body and the garments were in an excellent state of preservation and seemed to have suffered little change or decay. Many persons came from all parts of the surrounding neighbourhood to inspect the body of the Highland Soldier. They consulted with each other where he should be re-interred and after some hours of deliberation, they came to the conclusions that there should be an inquest held upon it on the spot, before anything of the kind was done. This was considered the more necessary in consequence of the extraordinary state of preservation of both the body and garments. Agreeable to the wishes of the assembled multitude, the inquest was held in the usual manner, but the result of the coroner's decision is not at present remembered, further than they agreed to bury the body in the same spot in which it was found, with all the tartan dress and as nearly as possible in the order in which they were found. This was immediately done, and the body now lies in its original grave in the manner already described.' (O.S.M. 33/I(17), fol. 24).

89   Terrydremont South td., Balteagh par.
C 69 18   (p. 156)

1832 'Discovery of a skeleton in a bog. James Thompson discovered 3 feet under the surface of a solid bog in the townland of Terrydremont South, in 1832, the skeleton of a female and the shoes worn by her, and a wooden crutch. The colour of the hair was yellow, the bones, hair, shoes and crutch were found in a moderate state of preservation. The crutch was very ingeniously turned on the surface by a wheelwright. There was not a particle of flesh on the bones. The skeleton was disjointed in various parts by the turf spade, before it was discovered to be a human skeleton. After some inspection, the bones and skeleton were collected together and buried very deep in the same place where they were found. Informants James Thompson and others. Thomas Fagan, 6th May 1835.' (O.S.M. 31/II(22), fol. 5).

90   Tintagh td., Lissan par.   H 81 86   (p. 156)

1825 'Discoveries (Body). In 1825 in the townland of Tintagh, in a moss near the limestone quarry in the mountain, 2 feet under the surface of the water, was discovered the body of a full-grown female, covered with a rug or caddy, not quite decayed, by Bryan Lennon of the same townland. J. B. Bleakly, 23rd Sept. 1836.' (O.S.M. 43/I(3), fol. 18).

Co. DONEGAL

91   Carnanmoyle td.   (pp. 155, 156)
1960 Woollen garments were found in 1960 in a bog at a depth of $2\frac{1}{2}$ feet, on the body of a woman 4 ft $6\frac{1}{2}$ in tall, between 45 and 60 years of age, clothed in dress of late Medieval – modern origin (16th–17th century). Cloak, woollen stockings, a bag, woollen tassels and a kerchief are now in National Museum of Ireland (Lucas 1962, 163).

92   Leitrim td.
c. 1870   Textile (nature unknown), found on the body of a man, 8 feet deep in a bog *c.* 1870. National Museum Registers No. 1889:270–1. (R. O'Floinn *pers. comm.*).

93   Meenabradden td.   (pp. 68, 70, 156)
1976 The body of a female in her late twenties, clothed in dress of the 16th–17th centuries. Found in a bog 3 feet deep. The subject of an autopsy in May 1985, it was then conserved at the British Museum. Nat. Mus. Ireland No. 1976: 341a (cloak) and b (body) (R. O'Floinn *pers. comm.*).

Co. DOWN

94   Drumkeeragh td. (1 mile E. of Slieve Croob)   J 33 46   (pp. 146, 155, 156)
1783 The body of a female of unknown age was found beneath a bog only about 1 acre in extent, at a depth of $4\frac{1}{2}$ feet after 5 feet had already been cut off. It was actually lying in gravel, aligned E–W, in what was most probably a grave, marked only by stones about 18 inches square at each end. The bones were re-interred nearby

in the bog. The best of the clothing, which appears to have been extensive in quantity, was taken off by peasants for re-use, though much had been damaged by farmyard animals and children. Lady Moira considered the burial to have been of a famine victim, of Elizabethan date, but she was anxious to inquire further into the nature of the clothing, its material and manufacture. She went to considerable trouble to have fragments recovered and examined them in great detail. It appears some of the cloth was copper impregnated, either through soil conditions, or through proximity to a copper or bronze artifact. The finds included what appears to have been a shroud, a cloak, some form of dress, possibly in a plaid pattern, and hair ornaments together with two plaits of hair. Lady Moira's conjecture as to the date (one in remote antiquity) is difficult to uphold without a detailed reconsideration of the dating of the dress, which may well have been Elizabethan, as she originally conjectured (Moira 1783). Though lost during the earlier part of the 19th century (Wilde 1857, 326) the surviving finds later passed to the Royal Irish Academy Museum (Wilde 1864); Henshall 1951–2, 5; now National Museum of Ireland, R 2028 (hair); R 2029–2035 (cloth fragments).

95   Loughriescouse td., Newtownards par.
J 52 74
1824   'In the bog of Loughriescouse was found in 1824, at a depth of 23 feet below the surface, the body of a Highlander in a good state of preservation; parts of his dress were perfect, but the body crumbled into dust when exposed to the air'. (Lewis 1837, 436).

Co. FERMANAGH

96   Lisnaskea par.
before 1935   A skull found under about 18 feet of peat near Lisnaskea, County Fermanagh. It is stated to have lain very near to the marl below the peat. It was obtained with abundant peat for dating purposes by pollen analysis, but appears not to have been published (Martin 1935, 156).

Co. GALWAY

97   Cloonascurragh td., Barnascurragh Bog, Nr Tuam   (p. 156)
before 1920   'A human head (found in the bog), and not far from it, two primitive leather shoes formed of a single piece of leather...' (Costello 1920, 74).

98   Cloonbenes td., Kilcorsnee par.   (pp. 155, 156)
1936   Fragments of ancient dress were found with human bones in 1936 under a depth of 4½ feet of bog and presented to the National Museum, Ireland, by Sergeant Garda Sisshane, Athenry. The remains are of uncertain date, but appear to be of the 16th–17th centuries. They represent the body of an unsexed individual, possibly of 18–25 years, and an accompanying cloak, now too fragmentary for positive identification. (Rep. Nat. Mus. Ireland, 1935–6, 20: R. O'Floinn *pers. comm.*).

99   Mount Bellew   (p. 154)
before 1935   A skull was found 6 miles north of Mount Bellew on the banks of the River Sliven by the Arterial Drainage Section of the Board of Works. Also fragments of another skull. The first found about 4 or 5 ft below the surface. Specimens of peat were kept for pollen analysis. In the National Museum (Martin 1935, 155–6). Pollen analytical evidence suggested that the find belonged to the transition from Zone VII to Zone VIII (Mitchell 1945, 17).

100   Castle Blakeney, Gallagh par. near Newton Bellew   (pp. 155, 156)
1821   The body of an adult male was found 9 feet deep in a bog 10½ feet deep, in 1821. 'It had all the appearance of recent death when first discovered, excepting that the abdomen was quite collapsed, but on exposure to the atmosphere, it decayed rapidly. The face was that of a young man of handsome features and foreign aspect, and his hair, which was long and black, hung loosely over his shoulders. The head, legs and feet, were without covering, but the body was clothed in a tight dress, covering also the limbs as far as the knees and elbows. The dress was composed of the skin of some animal, laced in front with thongs of the same material, and having the hairy side inwards; and it is not improbable that it might have been that of the Moose-deer. He had no weapon; but near him at each side of the body was found a long staff or pole, which it was supposed he had used near a rivulet; it was further conjectured by the peasantry that the man had met his death accidentally in some such manner.' Petrie goes on to note the frequent discovery of well preserved bodies in bogs and to remark that this one was of particular notice on account of the costume. Petrie believed the dress and body to have been re-buried, but it would seem to have been given to the Royal Dublin Society, where it was displayed for many years before being passed to the Royal Irish Academy on 27 February 1860 (*Proc. Roy. Irish Acad.* VII, 279), to be catalogued by Wilde the following year (1861, 276–8). According to Wood-Martin (1902, I, 110–112), the cloak was of deer skin, laced at the front with leather thongs. The seams were stitched with fine gut, knotted, so that it was almost impossible to rip. The man was partly bearded. After re-burial, the body was dug up on various occasions for inspection by the curious. Stable atmospheric conditions at the Academy have kept the body in good condition (*Pace* Wood-Martin, *loc. cit*; McClintock 1950: see also Petrie 1825; Wilde 1861, 276–8; Wood-Martin 1902, I, 110–112 and Fig. 47).

101   Stoneyisland Bog, Portumna   (pp. 153–4, 156)
before 1931   A complete skeleton found with limbs extended, as if it had fallen into the bog, and it would appear to have sunk so as to be partly in contact with the marl at the bog base. It was suggested that the bog was a lake at the time of interment. The bones were of a male, about 40 years old, 5 feet 2 inches high. They were thought to have been of prehistoric, probably Neolithic date, since pollen analysis showed that the layers of peat in which it was embedded were of the Neolithic period. Preserved in University College Dublin Anatomical Museum (Shea 1931).

Co. KERRY

102   Emlagh td., Cloghane par.   (near Dingle)
(pp. 155, 156)
1950   A clothed body, badly fragmented through contin-

uous peat cutting, was found about one metre deep in
peat in 1950. Examination revealed that the clothes were
on the body at the time of its interment, and had not
been merely wrapped around it. The parts of the skeleton
that survived were in a decalcified condition, and were
identified as having belonged to a child 6–7 years old,
though of indeterminate sex. Osteological observation
suggested male rather than female. A considerable
amount of hair survived, reddish brown in colour, aver-
aging 15 cm in length, and of the anthropological type
wavy I. Examination and experiments with the clothing
have shown that it consists of a long pinafore linen dress,
a possible cloak and several fragments of two other garments. The dress was the only garment which had survived in a reasonably intact condition and it fitted well
on an 8 year old child. Also with the body were a comb
and a leather purse which contained a tuft of flax fibres
and a ball of woollen thread. All the finds are preserved
in the Department of Archaeology, University College,
Cork (Shee and O'Kelly 1966, 81).

Co. KILDARE

103   Co. Kildare   (Unlocated)
before 1935   Two skulls now in the Museum of University College, Dublin. (Martin 1935, 156).

Co. LONGFORD

104   Co. Longford   (Unlocated)   (pp. 152, 156)
1773   'In 1786, (1773) there was found, 17 feet (15) below
the surface of a bog (on a large moor, situated in a valley,
and has been formed by a congeries of leaves, twigs and
branches of different kinds of trees, many of which
remain tolerably sound), a woollen coat of coarse but
even net-work, exactly in the form of what is now called
a spencer. A razor with a wooden handle, some iron heads
of arrows and large wooden bowls, some only half made,
were also found, with the remains of turning tools; these
were obviously the wreck of a workshop, which was probably situated on the borders of a forest. The coat was
presented by me to the Antiquarian Society.' (Edgeworth
1783 and 1812. Soc. Ants. Lond. MS. Mins., 5th June
1783, fols. 76–7. Variations in earlier account brack-
eted).

Co. LOUTH

105   Ardee par.   (p. 156)
1895   'The well-preserved body of a youngish girl, found
in 1845, was presented to the Museum of the Royal College of Surgeons of Ireland'. The body survives in excellent condition. An account of it together with details
of its discovery will be presented elsewhere. (Prof. D.
Holland *pers. comm.*).

Co. MEATH

106   Killarden td.
1978   A clothed undistinguished body was found in a bog
at a depth of 1–2 feet in 1978. The clothing was fragmentary and its identification was not possible. The finds
are now in the National Museum (1978: 148 (body); 1978:
150 (clothing); R. O'Floinn *pers. comm.*).

Co. OFFALY

107   Carne Bog, Coolbanagher par.
1848   Part of a cloak or coarse rug mantle, 1848. Preserved by the Rev. Sir Erasmus Borrowes (Wilde 1857,
325–6).

108   Cloghan Castle
1828   A note in the hand of Sir William Betham accompanying the illustration of an Early Bronze Age dagger
runs: '1828: Found on the estate of Garrett O'More of
Cloghan Castle in the Qu(een's) County, Esq. 40 feet
under the surface of the bog, lying beside the skeleton
of a man. On one of the legs and upon the thigh above
the knee halfway was a leather boot with a brass spur
on the heel. Ex. inf. G. D. Moore Esq.' The bronze dagger
is quite clearly not to be connected with this skeleton,
which may be of post-medieval origin. (Nat. Lib. Ireland
MS 4458; Waddell 1985).

109   Castlewilder
before 1857   'In a dry bog, a shoe of Lucas type 2 (Lucas
1956), Wilde No. 23, early medieval in origin. It is said
that the body from which this curious relic was removed,
was clothed in a woollen garment, had an abundance
of long, black hair on the head, and was decorated with
golden ornaments. From the mystery attending this discovery and the endeavour to conceal the body, the latter
statement is not improbable' (Wilde 1857, 283).

Co. SLIGO

110   Benbulben Mountain
before 1901   The corpse of a 'lady' clad in antique costume, is stated to have been discovered many years ago,
on the summit of Benbulbin (Wood-Martin 1902, I, 113).

111   Killery par.   (pp. 155, 156)
1824   'In 1824, a male body, completely clad in woollen
garments of antique fashion, was found in a bog six feet
beneath the surface, in the parish of Killery, Co. of Sligo.
These articles ... all of which are in an astonishingly
perfect state of preservation, (give) a good idea of our
ancient dress and manufactures of about the 15th and
16th centuries. No weapon was discovered near (it), but
a long staff lay under it, and attached to the hand by
a leather thong was said to have been a small bag of
untanned leather, containing a small ball of knotted
thread and also a small silver coin, which was unfortunately lost. The head-dress which soon fell to pieces, is said
to have been a conical cap of sheepskin, probably the
ancient barread. So perfect was the body when first discovered, that the magistrate was called upon to hold an
inquest on it.' Presented to the Academy by His Grace
the Duke of Northumberland, who purchased them with
the collection of the late R. C. Walker, Esq., Q.C. (Wilde
1857, 291, 326–30; Lucas 1956, 381; dated 16th–17th
centuries; McClintock 1950, 63–4; Wood-Martin 1902,
I, 113).

112   Tawnamore td.   (p. 156)
1969   In 1969 the body of a middle-aged man found completely clothed lying extended on his back on birch twigs

80 cm deep in a bog. The head was in the SSE, the feet facing NNW. The garments were a hat, overcoat, jacket, breeches, a pair of knitted woollen stockings, pair of garters and a pair of shoes. The body was probably of 16th–17th century date. (Lucas 1972).

Co. TIPPERARY

113   Cullen Bog
1763   'In June 1763, in digging for turf, there were found at the bottom of the holes, several skulls of men surprisingly thick and round' (Pownall 1774, 369; Gough, III, 475).

114   Kilcommon td., Gortmahonage   O.S. 6 inch sheet 39
1945   A patched and tattered suit, consisting of cap, mantle, jacket and trews were found in 1945. There were indications that their owner had carried a dirk, and had been a rider. In the National Museum of Ireland, 1946: 359–66, (McClintock 1952, 65).

115   Shinrone td.   (p. 155)
1843   'A dress of coarse woollen cloth, found in the spring of 1843, in a bog near Shinrone procured by Dr Aquilla Smith, for the late R. C. Walker, from whose collection it was purchased by the Duke of Northumberland, it was presented to the Academy' (Wilde 1857, 331; McClintock 1950, 66, Illus. 56; Shee and O'Kelly 1966, 86–7).

116   Co. Tipperary   (Unlocated)

before 1857   The dress of a woman in the costume of some centuries back (Wilde 1858, 327).

Co. TYRONE

117   Gleneely Valley   (general area of)
A woollen garment and a lock of human hair (Armagh Mus. No. 15–60), described in a note addressed to Miss Steele-Nicholson of Falmore House as 'a lock of a man's hair that was found in the bog and a piece of his coat', and from 'Gleniely' Co. Derry. There is no such townland as Gleniely, and Mr D. R. M. Wetherup, who kindly provides this information, suggests that this may have been the Gleneely Valley.

118   Kildress td., and par.   H 77 77   (p. 156)
1900   The body of a man dressed in a coachman's coat with brass buttons was unearthed while rebuilding the churchyard wall in June 1900. The body of a man in a crouched position, who appeared to have been murdered by having his skull split by a blow from a turf spade. The discovery triggered off a murder inquiry, a warrant for the arrest of the would-be assassin, and the eventual disproving of the alleged identity of the body by the documentation of his emigration to Scotland, and a death certificate of his recent demise by a well-respected local schoolmaster (*Mid Ulster Mail*, June 1973; James Brennan *pers. comm.*).

119   Thornhill parish church   (p. 156)
before 1901   At the parish church between Donaghmore and Pomeroy. 'The body of a woman was discovered in the same bog embedded in the peat some feet below the surface. A large fracture in the skull leads one to suppose that this woman was murdered. It seems certain that she had lived some time in the past century' (Latimer 1901, 299).

Co. WICKLOW

120   Co. Wicklow   (Unlocated)
before 1935   Skull only, from a bog in County Wicklow. Royal College of Surgeons Museum No. 4982 (now British Museum Natural History); (Martin 1935, 155).

Bibliography

Chapter 1

Earwaker, J. P., 1877 *East Cheshire: Past and Present*.

Norbury, W. H., 1884 'Lindow Common as a Peat Bog: its age and its people', *Trans. Lancs. and Cheshire Antiq. Soc.* (2) 59–75.

Chapter 2

Cowell, A. P., 1985 'The Lindow Man', *The Photographic Journal* (125) 101–6.

Chapter 3

Ellam, D., 1985 *Wet Bone: The Potential for Freeze-drying* (Unpublished thesis, Institute of Archaeology, London University).

Fischer, C., 1980 'Bog bodies of Denmark', in Cockburn A. and E., (eds), *Mummies, Disease and Ancient Cultures*, 177–93.

Glob, P. V., 1977 *The Bog People*. London.

Lange-Kornbak, G., 1956 'Konservering af en Oldtidsman', *Kuml* (1956) 155–9.

Chapter 5

Andersen, S. H., Constandse-Westermann, T. S., Newell, R. R., Gillespie, R., Gowlett, J. A. J., and Hedges, R. E. M., 1986 'New Radiocarbon dates for two Mesolithic Burials in Denmark', in Gowlett, J. A. J. and Hedges, R. E. M., (eds) *Results and Prospects of Accelerator Dating*. Oxford Committee for Archaeology Monograph Series.

Gillespie, R., Hedges, R. E. M., and Wand, J. O., 1984 'Radiocarbon Dating of Bone by Accelerator Mass Spectrometry', *Journ. Arch. Sci.* (11) 165–70.

Gillespie, R., Gowlett, J. A. J., Hall, E. T., Hedges, R. E. M., and Perry, C., 1985 'Radiocarbon Dates from the Oxford AMS System: Archaeometry Datelist 2', *Archaeometry* (27, 2) 237–46.

Gowlett, J. A. J., Hall, E. T., Hedges, R. E. M., and Perry, C., 1986 'Radiocarbon dates from the Oxford AMS system: Archaeometry Datelist 3', *Archaeometry* (28, 1).

Hedges, R. E. M., and Gowlett, J. A. J., 1986 'Radiocarbon Dating by Accelerator Mass of Spectrometry', *Scientific American* (254, 1) 100–7.

Jacobi, R. M., Gowlett, J. A. J., Hedges, R. E. M., and Gillespie, R., 1986 'Accelerator Mass Spectrometry Dating of Upper Palaeolithic finds with the Poulton elk as an example', in Roe, D. A., (ed) *Studies in the Upper Palaeolithic of Britain and Northwest Europe*. Oxford, BAR International Series (forthcoming).

Klein, J., Lerman, J. C., Damon, P. E., and Ralph, E. K., 1982 'Calibration of radiocarbon dates: tables based on the consensus data of the Workshop on Calibrating the Radiocarbon Time Scale' *Radiocarbon* (24) 103–50.

Pearson, G. W., and Baillie, M. G. L., 1983 'High Precision 14C Measurement of Irish Oaks to show the Natural Atmospheric 14C Variations of the AD Time Period', *Radiocarbon* (25, 2) 187–96.

Stead, I. and Turner, R. C., 1985 'Lindow Man', *Antiquity* (59) 25–9.

Stuiver, M., 1982 'A High-Precision Calibration of the AD Radiocarbon Time Scale', *Radiocarbon* (24, 1) 1–26.

Tauber, H., 1979 'Kulstoff-14 datering af moselig', *Kuml* (1979) 73–8.

Chapter 6

Barker, H., Burleigh, R., and Meeks, N., 1969 'British Museum Natural Radiocarbon Measurements VI', *Radiocarbon* (11) 278–94.

Gupta, S. K., and Polach, H. A., 1985 *Radiocarbon Dating Practices at ANU*, Handbook, Radiocarbon Laboratory, Research School of Pacific Studies, ANU, Canberra.

Chapter 7

Otlet, R. L., 1979 'An Assessment of Laboratory Errors in Liquid Scintillation Methods of 14C Dating', in Berger, Rainer, and Suess, H. E., (eds) *Internat. Radiocarbon Conf., IXth. Proc.*, 256–67. University of California Press.

Otlet, R. L., and Warchal, R. M., 1978 'Liquid Scintillation Counting of Low-Level 14C', in Crook, M. A., and Johnson, P., (eds) *Liquid Scintillation Counting* (5) 210–18. Heyden, London.

Otlet, R. L., Sanderson, D. C. W., and Walker, A. J., in press 'Comments on Miniature Gas Counter Dating Techniques based on Two Years of Operating Experience', in *Internat. Archaeometry Conf., XXIVth, Proc.* Washington.

Otlet, R. L., Walker, A. J., Hewson, A. D., and Burleigh, R., 1980 '14C Interlaboratory Comparison in the UK: experiment design, preparation and preliminary results', in Stuiver, Minze, and Kra, Renee, S., (eds) Internat. Radiocarbon Conf., Xth, Proc. *Radiocarbon* (22, 3) 936–46.

Otlet, R. L., Huxtable, George, Evans, G. V., Humphreys, D. G., Short, T. D., and Conchie, S. J., 1983 'Development and Operation of the Harwell Small Counter Facility for the Measurement of 14C in Very Small Samples', in Stuiver, Minze, and Kra, Renee, S., (eds) Internat. Radiocarbon Conf., XIth, Proc. *Radiocarbon* (25, 2) 565–75.

Pearson, G. W., Pilcher, J. R., Baillie, M. G., and Corbett, D. M., in press 'High Precision 14C Measurement of Irish Oaks to show the Natural 14C Variations from 5000 BC to 1840 AD', in *Internat. Radiocarbon Conf., XIth, Proc.* Trondheim (June 1985).

Stuiver, Minze, 1982 'A High Precision Calibration of the AD Radiocarbon Time Scale', *Radiocarbon* (24, 1) 1–26.

Chapter 11

Gerasimov, M., 1971 *The Face Finder* (1st ed), 52–61. London.

Kenyon, K. M., 1979 *Archaeology in the Holy Land* (4th ed), 35–9. London, New York.

Kollman, J., and Büchly, W., 1898 'Die Persistenz der Rassen und die Rekonstruktion per Physiognomier Prähistorischer Schädel', *Archiv für Anthropologie* (25).

Krogman, N. M., 1962 *The Human Skeleton in Forensic Medicine*, 244–76. Illinois.

Neave, R. A. H., 1979a 'The Reconstruction of the Heads of Three Ancient Egyptian Mummies', *Journ. Audiovisual Media in Medicine* (2) 156–64.

Neave, R. A. H., 1979b 'The
Reconstruction of the Heads and Faces
of Three Ancient Egyptian Mummies',
in David, A. R., (ed) *The Manchester
Museum Mummy Project*, 149–57.
Manchester.

Neave, R. A. H., in press 'Skull
Reconstruction', *Journ. Audiovisual
Media in Medicine*.

Prag, A. J. N., Musgrave, J. H., and
Neave, R. A. H., 1984 'The Skull from
Tomb II at Vergina: King Phillip of
Macedon', *Journ. Hellenic Studies* (104)
65–8.

Rhine, J. S., and Elliott Moore, C. E., 1982
Maxwell Museum Technical Series (1).

Snow, C. C., Gatliff, B. P., and Williams,
S. K. R., 1982 'Reconstruction of the
Facial Features of the Skull. An
Evaluation of its Usefulness in Forensic
Anthropology', *American Journ.
Physical Anthropology* (33) 221–8.

Chapter 15
Fischer, C., 1983 'Bog Bodies of Denmark',
in Cockburn, A. and E., (eds) *Mummies,
Disease, and Ancient Cultures*, 177–93.

Lewin, P. K., and Harwood-Nash, D. C.,
1977 'X-ray Computed Axial
Tomography of an Ancient Egyptian
Brain', *I.R.C.S. Med. Sci.* (5) 78.

Sutton David (ed) 1980 In *A Textbook of
Radiology and Imaging*, 3rd Edition,
Churchill Livingstone, 1134.

Yahey, T., and Brown, D., 1984 'Comely
Wenuhotep: Computed Tomography in
Egyptian Mummy', *Journ. Comp.
Assist. Tomogr.* (8, 5) 992–7.

Chapter 18
Connolly, R. C., 1969 'Microdetermination
of Blood Group Substances in Ancient
Human Tissue', *Nature* (224) 325.

Embery, G., 1976 'Glycosamino glycans of
Human Dental Pulp', *Journ. Biol.
Buccale* (4) 229–36.

Evershed, R. P., Jerman, K., and Eglinton,
G., 1985 'Pine Wood Origin for Pitch
from "Mary Rose"', *Nature* (314) 528–30.

Harrison, R. G., Connolly, R. C., and
Abdalla, A., 1969 'Kinship of
Smenkhare and Tutankhamen
Demonstrated Serologically', *Nature*
(224) 325–6.

Jeffreys, A. J., 1984 'Palaeomolecular
Biology: Raising the dead and buried',
Nature (312) 198.

Matson, G. A., 1936 'A Procedure for the
Serological Determination of Blood-
Relationships of Ancient and Modern
Peoples with special reference to
American Indians. II Blood Grouping of
Mummies', *Journ. Immunol.* (30)
459–70.

Sandison, A. T., 1955 'The Histological
Examination of Mummified Tissue',
Stain Technology (30) 277–83.

Svante, P., 1985 'Molecular Cloning of
Ancient Egyptian Mummy DNA',
Nature (314) 644–5.

Chapter 20
Appleby, P. G., Nolan, P. J., Gifford, D. W.,
Godfrey, M. J., Oldfield, F., Anderson,
N. J., and Battarbee, R. W., in press
'210Pb dating by Low Background
Gamma Counting', *Hydrobiologia*.

Godwin, H., 1975 *History of the British
Flora* (2nd ed). Cambridge University
Press.

Oldfield, F., 1963 'Pollen-Analysis and
Man's Role in the Ecological History of
the South-east Lake District',
Geografiska Annaler (45) 23–49.

Oldfield, F., and Statham, D. C., 1963
'Pollen-Analytical Data from Urswick
Tarn and Ellerside Moss, North
Lancashire', *New Phytologist* (62) 53–66.

Oldfield, F., and Statham, D. C., 1965
'Stratigraphy and Pollen-Analysis on
Cockerham and Pilling Mosses, North
Lancashire', *Memoirs and Proceedings
of the Manchester Literary and
Philosophical Society* (107) 1–16.

Tolonen, K., 1966 'Stratigraphic and
Rhizopod Analyses on an Old Raised
Bog, Varrasuo, in Hollola, South
Finland', *Annales Botanici Fennici* (3)
147–66.

Tolonen, K., 1979 'Rhizopod Analysis', in
Berglund, B. E., (ed) *Palaeohydrological
Changes in the Temperate Zone in the
last 15000 years* Vol. II. *Specific Methods*
(IGCP Project, 158) 271–90.

Chapter 21
Aaby, B., 1976 'Cyclic Climatic Variations
in Climate over the last 5,500 Years
Reflected in Raised Bogs', *Nature* (263)
281–4.

Barber, K. E., 1981 *Peat Stratigraphy and
Climatic Change: a palaeoecological test
of the theory of cyclic peat bog
regeneration*. Balkema, Rotterdam.

Barber, K. E., 1982 'Peat-bog Stratigraphy
as a Proxy Climate Record', in Harding,
A. F., (ed) *Climatic Change in Later
Prehistory*, 103–13. Edinburgh
University Press.

Barber, K. E., 1985 'Peat Stratigraphy and
Climatic Changes: Some Speculations',
in Tooley, M. J., and Sheail, G. M., (eds)
*The Climatic Scene: essays in honour of
Gordon Manley*, 175–85. Allen and
Unwin, London.

Birks, H. J. B., 1965 'Pollen Analytical
Investigations at Holcroft Moss,
Lancashire, and Lindow Moss,
Cheshire', *Journ. Ecol.* (53) 299–314.

Boatman, D. J., 1983 'The Silver Flowe
National Nature Reserve, Galloway,
Scotland', *Journ. Biogeog.* (10) 163–274.

Boatman, D. J., and Tomlinson, R. W.,
1977 'The Silver Flowe II: Features of
the Vegetation and Stratigraphy of
Brishie Bog and their Bearing on Pool
Formation', *Journ. Ecol.* (65) 531–46.

Clymo, R. S., 1983 'Peat', in Gore, A. J.
P., (ed) *Ecosystems of the World: 4A:
Mires: Swamp, Fen, Bog and Moor*,
159–224. Elsevier, Amsterdam.

Clymo, R. S., 1984 'The Limits to Peat Bog
Growth', *Phil. Trans. R. Soc. Lond. B*
(303) 605–54.

Davies, E. G., 1944 'Figyn Blaeu Brefi, a
Welsh Upland Bog', *Journ. Ecol.* (32)
147–66.

Dickson, J. H., 1973 *Bryophytes of the
Pleistocene*. Cambridge University
Press.

Geel, B. van, 1978 'A Palaeoecological
Study of Holocene Peat Bog Sections in
Germany and the Netherlands, Based
on the Analysis of Pollen, Spores and
Macro- and Microscopic Remains of
Fungi, Algae, Cormophytes and
Animals', *Review of Palaeobotany and
Palynology* (25) 1–120.

Godwin, H., 1954 'Recurrence Surfaces',
Danm. Geol. Unders. (II R 80) 22–30.

Godwin, H., 1981 *The Archives of the Peat
Bogs*. Cambridge University Press.

Godwin, H., and Switsur, V. R., 1966
'Cambridge University Natural
Radiocarbon Measurements VIII',
Radiocarbon (8) 390–400.

Grosse-Brauckmann, G., 1963 'Zur
Artenzusammensetzung von Torfen',
Ber. Deutsch. bot. Gesell. (76) 22–35.

Grosse-Brauckmann, G., 1982 'Vegetative
Plant Macrofossils', in Berglund, B. E.
(ed) *Palaeohydrological changes in the
Temperate Zone in the Last 15,000
Years: Subproject B: Lake and Mire
Environments. Project Guide Volume
III: Specific Methods* 111–30.

Ingram, H. A. P., 1982 'Size and Shape in
Raised Mire Ecosystems: a Geophysical
Model', *Nature* (297) 300–3.

Lamb, H. H., 1982 *Climate, History and
the Modern World*. Methuen, London.

Ratcliffe, D. A., and Walker, D., 1958 'The
Silver Flowe, Galloway, Scotland',
Journ. Ecol. (46) 407–45.

Turner, J., 1981 'The Iron Age', in
Simmons, I. G., and Tooley, M. J., (eds)
The Environment in British Prehistory,
250–61. Duckworth, London.

Walker, D., 1970 'Direction and rate in
some British post-glacial hydroseres', in
Walker, D., and West, D. G., (eds)
*Studies in the vegetational history of the
British Isles*, 117–39. Cambridge
University Press.

Chapter 22
Balfour-Browne, W. A. F., 1940 *British
Water Beetles* (3). Ray Society, London.

Britton, E. B., 1956 'Scarabaeoidea',
*Handbooks for the Identification of
British Insects* (5, 2). Royal
Entomological Society, London.

Crowson, R. A., 1981 *The Biology of the
Coleoptera*. Academic Press, London.

Fowler, W. W., 1890 *The Coleoptera of the
British Islands* (4). Reeve, London.

Guignot, F., 1931–3 *Hydrocanthes de
France*. Douladoure, Toulouse.

Hoffmann, A., 1950 'Coléoptères
Curculionides', *Faune de France* (59).
Lechevalier, Paris.

Horion, A., 1957 *Lamellicornia. Faunstik der Mitteleuropaischen Käfer* (6). Bodensee, Uberlingen.

Joy, N. H., 1932 *A Practical Handbook of British Beetles* (1 and 2). Witherby, Edinburgh.

Pope, R. D., 1977 'A Check List of British Insects, Coleoptera and Strepsiptera', *Handbooks for the Identification of British Insects* (11, 3). Royal Entomological Society, London.

Reitter, E., 1916 *Fauna Germanica, Die Käfer des Deutschen Reiches* (4). Lutz, Stuttgart.

Chapter 23

Mégnin, P., 1894 *La faune des cadavres. Application de l'entomologie à la medicine légale.* Paris.

Chapter 24

Battarbee, R. W., and Renberg, I., 1985 'Royal Society Surface Water Acidification Project Palaeolimnological Programme', Working Paper no. 12. Palaeoecological Research Unit, Dept. Geography, University College, London.

Brundin, L., 1949 *Chironomiden und andere Bodentiere der Sudschwedischen Urgebirgseen* (32) 32–42. Inst. Freshwater Res. Drottningholm Rep.

Brundin, L., 1956 *Die Bodenfaunischer Seetypen und ihre Anwenbarkeit auf die Sudhalbkugel. Zugleich eine Theorie der produktions-biologischer Bedeutung der glazialen Erosion* (37) 186–235. Inst. Freshwater Res. Drottningholm Rep.

Brundin, L., 1958 'The Bottom Faunistical Type System and its Application to the Southern Hemisphere. Moreover a Theory of Glacial Erosion as a Factor of Productivity in Lakes and Oceans', *Verh. Int. Ver. Limnol.* (13) 288–97.

De Costa, J. J., 1964 'Latitudinal Distribution of the Chydorid Cladocera in the Mississippi Valley, Based on their Remains in Surficial Lake Sediments', *Invest. Indiana Lakes and Streams* (6) 65–101.

Deevey, E. S., Jr, 1942 'The Biostratonomy of Linsley Pond', *Amer. Journ. Sci.* (240) 233–64, 313–24.

Deevey, E. S., Jr, 1955 'Paleolimnology of the Upper Swamp Deposit, Pyramid Valley', *Rec. Canterbury Museum* (New Zealand) (6) 291–344.

Fittkau, E. J., and Reiss, F., 1978 'Chironomidae', in Illies, J., (ed) *Limnofauna Europaea* (2nd ed), 404–40.

Frey, D. G., 1955 'Langsee: a History of Meromixis', *Mem. Ist Ital. Idrobiol.* (suppl. 8) 141–64.

Frey, D. G., 1958 'The Late-Glacial Cladoceran Fauna of a Small Lake', *Arch. Hydrobiol.* (54) 209–75.

Frey, D. G., 1959 'The Taxonomic and Phylogenetic Significance of the Head Pores of the Chydoridae (Cladocera)', *Int. Rev. ges. Hydrobiol.* (44) 27–50.

Frey, D. G., 1960 'The Ecological Significance of Cladoceran Remains in Lake Sediments', *Ecology* (41) 684–99.

Frey, D. G., 1961 'Developmental History of Scleinsee', *Verh. Internat. Ver. Limnol.* (14) 271–8.

Frey, D. G., 1962 'Cladocera from the Eemian Interglacial of Denmark', *Journ. Palaeontology* (36) 1133–54.

Frey, D. G., 1965 'Differentiation of *Alona costata* Sars from two related species (Cladocera, Chydoridae)', *Crustaceana* (8) 159–73.

Fryer, G., 1968 'Evolution and Adaptive Radiation in the Chydoridae (Crustacea: Cladocera): a Study in Comparative Functional Morphology and Ecology', *Phil. Trans. R. Soc. B* (254) 221–385.

Fryer, G., 1985 'Crustacean Diversity in Relation to the Size of Water Bodies: Some Facts and Problems', *Freshwater Biology* (15) 347–61.

Goulden, C. E., 1964 'The History of the Cladoceran Fauna of Esthwaite Water (England) and its Limnological Significance', *Arch. Hydrobiol.* (60) 1–52.

Harmsworth, R. V., 1968 'The Developmental History of Blelham Tarn (England) as shown by Animal Microfossils, with Special Reference to the Cladocera', *Ecol. Monographs* (38) 334–41.

Kansanen, P. H., Aho, J., and Paasivirta, L., 1984 'Testing the Benthic Lake Type Concept Based on Chironomid Associations in some Finnish Lakes using Multivariate Statistical Methods', *Ann. Zool. Fennici* (21) 55–76.

Megard, R. O., 1967 'Late-Quaternary Cladocera of Lake Zeribar, Western Iran', *Ecology* (48) 179–89.

Mesyatsev, I. I., 1924 'The fossil fauna of the Kossino lakes', *Trud. Kosinsk. Biolog. Stanz. Mosk.* (1) 16–27.

Mueller, W. P., 1964 'The Distribution of Cladocera Remains in Surficial Sediments from Three Northern Indiana Lakes', *Invest. Ind. Lakes and Streams* (6) 1–64.

Rossolimo, L., 1927 *Atlas tierischer Uberreste in Torf und Sapropel*, Volkskommissariat für Landwirtschaft R.S.F.S.R., Zentrale Torfstation Moscow (27–48).

Scourfield, D. J., and Harding, J. P., 1966 'A Key to the British Freshwater Cladocera with Notes on their Ecology', *Freshwater Biological Association Sci. Publication* 5(3rd edition).

Sendstad, E., Solem, J. O. and Aagaard, K., 1977 'Studies of Terrestrial Chironomids (Diptera) from Spitsbergen', *Norw. Jour. Entomol.* (24, 2) 91–8.

Stahl, J. B., 1959 'The Developmental History of the Chironomid and *Chaoborus* Faunas of Myers Lake', *Invest. Indiana Lakes and Streams* (5) 47–102.

Stahl, J. B., 1969 'The Uses of Chironomids and other Midges in Interpreting Lake Histories', *Mitt. Internat. Ver. Limnol.* (17) 111–25.

Warwick, W. F., 1975 'The Impact of Man on the Bay of Quinte, Lake Ontario, as Shown by the Subfossil Chironomid Succession (Chironomidae, Diptera)', *Verh. Int. Ver. Limnol.* (19) 3134–41.

Wiederholm, T., (ed), 1984 'Chironomidae of the Holarctic. Part I. Larvae', *Entomol. Scand. Suppl.* (19)

Chapter 25

Atterberg, A., 1899 'Die Varietäten und Formen der Gerste', *Journ. für Landwirtschaft* (47) 1–68.

Baegert, J., 1864–65 'Account of the aboriginal indians of the California Peninsula'. Edited and translated by C. Rau. a) *Smithsonian Institution Ann. Report for 1863*, 351–69. b) *Smithsonian Institution Ann. Report for 1864*, 387–99.

Bakels, C. C., 1980 'Een Sittardse beerput en mestvalt', *Archaeologie in Limburg* (9) 2–3. (As cited by Greig 1983.)

Beck, H., Denecke, D., and Jankuhn, H., (eds) 1984 *Untersuchungen zur eisenzeitlichen und frühmittelalterlichen Flur in Mitteleuropa und ihrer Nutzung.* Abhandlung der Akadamie der Wissenschaft in Göttingen (116). Vanderhoeck und Ruprecht, Göttingen.

Behre, K-E., 1983 'Ernährung und Umwelt der wikingerzeitlichen Siedlung Haitabu', *Die Ausgrabungen in Haitabu*, (8) Wachholz, Neumunster.

Behre, K-E., 1984 'Zur mittelalterlichen Plaggenwirtschaft in N. W. Deutschland und angrezenden Gebieten nach botanischen Untersuchungen', in Beck, *et al*, 30–44.

Bingham, S., 1978 *Dictionary of Nutrition.* Corgi Paperback, London.

Brandt, J., 1950 'Plant remains in an early Iron Age Body', *Aarbog for Nordisk Oldkyndig og Historie* (1950) 347–51.

Brothwell, D. R., and Brothwell, P., 1969 *Food in Antiquity*. Thames and Hudson, London.

Bryant, V. M. Jnr, 1969 *Late Fullglacial and Postglacial Pollen Analysis of Texas Sediments*. PhD dissertation on file at the University of Texas at Austin Library. (As cited in Bryant, 1974c.)

Bryant, V. M. Jnr, 1974a 'Prehistoric Diet in Southwest Texas: the coprolite evidence', *American Antiquity* (39) 407–20.

Bryant, V. M. Jnr, 1974b 'Pollen Analysis of Prehistoric Human Faeces from Mammoth Cave', in *Archaeology of the Mammoth Cave area*. Academic Press, New York and London.

Bryant, V. M. Jnr, 1974c 'The Role of Coprolite Analysis in Archaeology', *Bull. Texas Archaeological Soc.* (45) 1–28.

Bryant, V. M. Jnr, 1979 *Prehistoric Diets.* College Station, Texas; University lecture series of the Texas A & M University.

Bryant, V. M. Jnr, and Williams-Dean, G., 1975 'The Coprolites of Man', *Scientific American* (232, 1) 100–9.

Callen, E. O., 1965 'Food Habits of some Pre-Columbian Mexican indians', *Economic Botany* (19) 335–43.

Callen, E. O., 1967 'Analysis of the Tehuacán Coprolites', in Byers, D. S., (ed) *The prehistory of the Tehuacán valley* (1) 261–89.

Callen, E. O., 1968 'Plants, Diet and Early Agriculture of some Cave-Dwelling Pre-Columbian Indians', *Actas et Memorias del XXXVII Congreso Internacional de Americanistas* (2) 641–56.

Callen, E. O., 1969 'Diet as Revealed by Coprolites', in Brothwell, D. R., and Higgs, E. S., (eds) *Science in Archaeology*. Thames and Hudson, London.

Callen, E. O., and Martin, P. S., 1969 'Plant Remains in some Coprolites from Utah', *American Antiquity* (34) 329–30.

Charles, M. P., 1984 'Introductory Remarks on the Cereals', *Bulletin on Sumerian Agriculture* (1) 17–31.

Colledge, S. M., forthcoming *SEM Investigation of the Surface Cell-Patterns of the Grains of some Wild Wheats and Ryes: methods and problems*. Paper to be presented at the 'SEM in Archaeology' conference, London, April 1986 and thereafter published in the conference proceedings.

Davies, M. S., and Hillman, G. C., forthcoming *The Waterlogging Tolerance of a Primitive form of Emmer Wheat (Triticum diococcum) from the Pontus Mountains of Turkey*. (Place of publication still undecided.)

Dennell, R. W., 1970 'Seeds from a medieval sewer at Woolster Street, Plymouth', *Economic Botany* (24) 151–4.

Evans, E. Estyn, 1957 *Irish Folkways*, 39–58. Routledge and Kegan Paul, London.

Evans, J., and Hill, A. G., 1982 'Dietetic information from chemical analysis of Danish neolithic sherds', *Proc. 22nd Symp. on Archaeometry and Archaeological Prospecting*. Bradford.

Evans, J., and Merrilddes, R. S., 1980 'An essay in provenance: the Late Minoan pottery from Egypt', *Berytus* (28) 1–45.

Evans, J., and Needham, S., in press 'Honey and pork fat in the Neolithic', *Antiquity*.

Farnsworth, P., Brady, J. E., DeNiro, M. J., and MacNeish, R. S., 1985 'A Re-evaluation of the Isotopic and Archaeological Reconstructions of Diet in the Tehuacán valley', *American Antiquity* (50, 1) 102–16.

Fenton, A., 1978a *The Island Blackhouse*. HMSO, Edinburgh.

Fenton, A., 1978b *The Northern Isles: Orkney and Shetland*. J. Donald, Edinburgh.

Forsyth, A. A., 1968 'British Poisonous Plants', *Ministry of Agriculture, Fisheries and Foods Bulletin* (161) HMSO, London (1977 reprint).

Fry, G. F., 1968 *Prehistoric diet at Danger Cave, Utah, as determined by analysis of coprolites*. MA thesis in Department of Anthropology, University of Utah. (As cited by Heizer and Napton, 1970.)

Fry, G. F., 1970a *Prehistoric Human Ecology in Utah: based on the analysis of coprolites*. PhD dissertation, Department of Anthropology, University of Utah, Salt Lake City.

Fry, G. F., 1970b 'Preliminary Analyses of the Hogup Cave Coprolites', in Aiken, C. M., *et al* (eds) *Hogup Cave*. University of Utah Anthropological papers (93), Salt Lake City. (As cited by Heizer and Napton, 1970.)

Fry, G. F., 1980 'Analysis of Human Coprolites from Frightful Cave', in Taylor, W. W., *et al. Contributions to Coahuila Prehistory*. Ethnology Monographs. (As cited by Stock 1983.)

Fry, G. F., 1985 'The analysis of faecal material', in Gilbert, R. I., and Miekle, J. I., (eds) *The analysis of prehistoric diet*. Academic Press, New York.

Galen *Claudii Galeni Opera Omnia VI*. Ed. C. G. Kuhn. Leipzig 1823, reprinted 1965, Georg Olms, Hildesheim.

Girling, M., 1979 'Calcium Carbonate Replaced Arthropods', *Journ. Arch. Sci.* (6) 309–20.

Gott, B., 1983 'Murnong – *Microseris scapigera*: a study of a staple food of Victorian Aborigines', *Australian Aboriginal Studies* (2) 2–18.

Grant, I. F., 1961 *Highland Folk Ways*. Routledge and Kegan Paul, London.

Green, F. J., 1979 'Phosphatic Mineralisation of Seeds from Archaeological Sites', *Journ. Arch. Sci.* (6) 279–84.

Greig, J. R., 1976 'The Plant Remains', in Buckland, P. C.,'The Environmental Evidence from the Church Street Roman Sewer System', in Addyman, P. V., (ed) *The Archaeology of York* (14, 1) 23–8. Council for British Archaeology, London.

Greig, J. R., 1981 'The Investigation of a Medieval Barrel-Latrine from Worcester', *Journ. Arch. Sci.* (8) 265–82.

Greig, J. R., 1982 'Garderobes, Sewers, Cesspits and Latrines', *Current Archaeology* (85) 49–52.

Greig, J. R., 1983 'Plant Foods in the Past: a review of evidence from northern Europe', *Journ. Plant Foods* (5) 179–214. (Arguably the best review ever compiled on the subject.)

Greig, J. R., 1984 'The Palaeoecology of some British Hay Meadow Types', in Zeist, W. van, and Casparie, W. C., *Plants and Ancient Man*. Balkema, Rotterdam.

Gunda, B., 1983 'Cultural Ecology of Old Cultivated Plants in the Carpathian Area', *Ethnologia Europaea* (13, 2) 146–79.

Hall, A. R., Jones, A. K., and Kenward, H. K., 1983 'Cereal Bran and Human Faecal Remains from Archaeological Deposits – some preliminary observations', in Proudfoot, B., (ed) *Site, environment and economy*, British Arch. Reports International Series (173) 85–104. Oxford.

Hall, A. R., Kenward, H. K., Wiliams, D., and Greig, J. R., 1983 'Environment and Living Conditions at two Anglo-Scandinavian Sites', in Addyman, P. V., (ed) *The Archaeology of York* (14, 4). Council for British Archaeology, London.

Hall, A. R., and Tomlinson, P. R., 1984 'Dye Plants from Viking York', *Antiquity* (222) 58–60.

Hall, H. J., 1977 'A Paleoscatological Study of Diet and Disease at Dirty Shame Rockshelter, Southeast Oregon', *Tebiwa* (8) 1–15. (As cited by Stock 1983).

Harlan, 1918 'The Identification of the Varieties of Barley', *Bull. U.S. Dept. Agric.* (622) 1–32.

Hastorf, C. A., and DeNiro, M. J., 1985 'Reconstruction of Prehistoric Plant Production and Cooking Practices by a New Isotopic Method', *Nature* (315) 589–91.

Hatt, G., 1943 *Jydsk bondeliv i ældre Jernalder*. København. (As cited by Brandt 1950)

Hendrick, U. P., (ed) 1919 'Sturtevant's Notes on Edible Plants', *State of New York, Dept. of Agriculture: Annual Report* (27, 2, part 2). Lyon, Albany.

Heizer, R. F., 1967 'Analysis of Human Coprolites from a Dry Nevada cave', *Reports of the University of California Archaeological Survey* (70) 1–20. Univ. of California Arch. Research Facility, Berkeley.

Heizer, R. F., 1969 'Anthropology of Great Basin Coprolites', in Brothwell, D. R., and Higgs, E. S., (eds) *Science and Archaeology*. Thames and Hudson, London.

Heizer, R. F., and Napton, L. K., 1970 *Archaeology and the Prehistoric Great Basin Lacustrine Subsistence Regime as seen from Lovelock Cave, Nevada*. Contributions of the University of California Archaeological Research Facility (10). Berkeley.

Helbaek, H., 1950 'Tollundmandens sidste måltid. Botanical study of the stomach of Tollund Man', *Årbøger for Nordisk Oldkyndighed og Historie* (1950) 329–41.

Helbaek, H., 1954 'Prehistoric Food Plants and Weeds in Denmark: a survey of archaeobotanical research 1923–54', *Dansk Geologische Undersuchungen* (2) 250–61.

Helbaek, H., 1958 'Grauballemandens sidste måltid. The last meal of Grauballe Man: an analysis of food remains in the stomach', *Kuml* (1958) 83–116.

Helbaek, H., 1960 'Comment on *Cheonpodium* as a Food Plant in Prehistory', *Berichte der geobotanischen Forschunginstitut Rubel Zürich* (31) 16–19.

Hillman, G. C., 1973 'Crop Husbandry and Food Production: modern models for the interpretation of plant remains', *Anatolian Studies* (23) 241–4.

Hillman, G. C., 1981 'Reconstructing Crop Husbandry Practices from Charred Remains of Crops', in Mercer, R., (ed) *Farming practice in British prehistory*, 123–62. Edinburgh University Press.

Hillman, G. C., 1984a 'Interpretation of Archaeological Plant Remains: the Application of Ethnographic Models from Turkey', in Zeist, W. van, and Casparie, W. A., (eds) *Plants and Ancient Man*. Balkema, Rotterdam.

Hillman, G. C., 1984b 'Traditional Husbandry and Processing of Archaeic Cereals in Recent Times: the operations, products and equipment which might feature in Sumerian texts. Part I: The Glume wheats', *Bull. on Sumerian Agric.* (1) 114–52.

Hillman, G. C., 1985 'Traditional Husbandry and Processing of Archaeic Cereals in Recent Times: the operations, products and equipment which might feature in Sumerian texts. Part II: The Free-Threshing Cereals', *Bull. on Sumerian Agric.* (2) 1–28.

Hillman, G. C., in press 'Crop Husbandry in the Late Iron Age at Breiddin Hillfort', in Musson, C. R., Britnell, W. J., and Smith, A. G., (eds) The Breiddin Hillfort, Powys: excavations 1969–76, *Cambrian Archaeological Monographs* 7. (Includes substantial appendix on criteria for identifying chaff remains of glume wheats.)

Hillman, G. C., forthcoming a 'Distinguishing Rachis Remains of Tetraploid and Hexaploid Free-Threshing Wheats', paper presented in 1983 to the International Work-Group for Palaeoethnobotany, Groningen. To be submitted to *Journ. Arch. Sci.*

Hillman, G. C., forthcoming b 'Criteria for Distinguishing Chaff Remains of Diploid and Tetraploid Glume Wheats: examples from Mycenae Granary', completed 1974. Yet to be submitted to *Journ. Arch. Sci.*

Hillman, G. C., undated 'Some Poorly Digested Medieval Meals: mineralised plant remains from a latrine at Usk (Wales)', report submitted in 1977 for publication in impending volume of Manning, W., (ed) *Excavations at Usk, Gwent*.

Hillman, G. C., Colledge, S. M., Harris, D. R., and Vaughan, M-D., forthcoming 'Pre-Agrarian Exploitation of Plant Foods in Near Eastern Steppe and Euphrates Valley', paper shortly to be submitted to *Science*.

Hillman, G. C., and Madeyska, E., in press 'Wild Plant Foods used in the Nile Valley during the Late Palaeolithic: the charred remains of plants and palaeofaeces from Wadi Kubbaniya', in Wendorf, F., *et al* (eds) title unknown.

Hillman, G. C., Robins, G. V., Oduwole, D., Sales, K. D., and McNeil, D. A. C., 1983 'Determination of Thermal Histories of Archaeological Cereal Grains with Electron Spin Resonance Spectroscopy', *Science* (222) 1235–6.

Hillman, G. C., Robins, G. V., Oduwole, D., Sales, K. D., and McNeil, D. A. C., 1985 'The use of Electron Spin Resonance Spectroscopy to Determine Thermal Histories of Cereal Grains', *Journ. Arch. Sci.* (12) 49–58.

Hjelmqvist, H., 1984? 'Botanische analyse einiger Brote', in *Birka II: 1, Systematische Analysen der Gräberfunde*. (Incomplete details of publication given on offprint.)

Holden, T., in prep. 'The Identification of Cereal Bran Fragments from Waterlogged Archaeological Deposits', to be submitted to *Journ. Arch. Sci.*

Hütteroth, W-D., 1959 *Bergnomaden und Yaylabauern in mittleren kurdischen Taurus*. Marburg, Geographische Schriften 11. Selbstverlag des Geographischen Inst. der Universitat, Marburg.

Jankuhn, H., 1984 'Agrarisches Brauchtum in vor und frühgeschichtlicher Zeit nach archäologischen Befunden', in Beck *et al*, 1984, 354–60.

Jessen, K., 1933 'Planterester fra den aldre Jernalder i Thy', *Botanisk Tidsskrift* (42, 3). With German Summary. (As cited by Brandt 1950.)

Jones, C. E. R., in press 'Chromatographic Identification of Organic Residues in Ground Stone Tools from Late Palaeolithic Wadi Kubbaniya', in Wendorf *et al* (eds) title as yet unknown.

Jones, G. E. M., 1981 'Crop Processing at Assiros Toumba – a taphonomic study', *Zeitschrift für Archäologie* 15: 105–11.

Jones, G. E. M., 1984a 'Interpretation of Archaeological Plant Remains: ethnographic models from Greece', in Zeist, W. van, and Casparie, W. C., (eds) *Plants and Ancient Man: studies in palaeoethnobotany*, 43–61. Balkema, Rotterdam.

Jones, G. E. M., 1984b *Ethnographic and Ecological Models in the Interpretation of Archaeological Plant Remains*. PhD thesis in the University of Cambridge.

Jones, M. K., 1985 *The Archaeological and Ecological Implications of Selected Arable Plant Assemblages in Britain*. PhD thesis at the Botany Department, University of Oxford.

Jørgensen, G., 1980 'Onkostvaner i det middelalderlige Svendborg', *Naturens Verden* (1980) 203–9. (As cited by Greig 1983.)

Knights, B. A., Dickson, C. A., Dickson, J. H., and Breeze, D. J., 1983 'Evidence Concerning Roman Military Diet at Beardsden, Scotland, in the 2nd Century AD', *Journ. Arch. Sci.* (10) 139–52.

Knörzer, K-H., 1970 'Römerzeitliche Pflanzenfunde aus Neuss', *Novaesium* (4). Berlin.

Knörzer, K-H., 1975 'Mittelalterliche und jüngere Pflanzenfunde aus Neuss am Rhein', *Zeitschrift für Archäologie des Mittelalters* (3) 129–81.

Knörzer, K-H., 1979 'Spatmittelalterliche Pflanzenreste aus der Burg Bruggen, Kr. Viersen', *Bonner Jahrbücher* (179) 595–611.

Knörzer, K-H., 1981 'Römerzeitliche Pflanzenfunde aus Xanten', *Archaeo-Physica* (11) 1–176.

Knörzer, K-H., 1984a 'Aussagemöglichkeiten palaeoethnobotanische Latrinen-untersuchungen', in Zeist, W. van, and Casparie, W. S., 1984, 331–8.

Knörzer, K-H., 1984b 'Pflanzensoziologische Untersuchung von subfossilen Pflanzenresten aus anthropogener Vegetation', in Knapp, R., (ed) *Sampling methods and taxon analysis in vegetation science*. Junk, The Hague.

Knörzer, K-H., and Müller, G., 1968 'Mittelalterliche Fäkalian Fassgrube mit Pflanzenresten aus Neuss', *Rheinische Ausgrabungen* (28) 131–69.

Körber-Grohne, U., 1964 'Bestimmungsschlüssel für subfossile Juncus-Samen und Gramineen-Früchte', Band 7 of Haarnagel, W., (ed) *Probleme der Küstenforschung im südlichen Nordseegebiet*. August Lax, Hildesheim.

Körber-Grohne, U., 1967 *Geobotanische Untersuchungen auf der Fedderesen Wierde*, 2 volumes. Steiner Verlag, Wiesbaden.

Körber-Grohne, U., 1981 'Distinguishing Prehistoric Grains of *Triticum* and *Secale* on the Basis of their Surface Patterns Using Scanning Electron Microscopy', *Journ. Arch. Sci.* (8) 197–204.

Kowalski, K., Malinowski, T., and Wasilokowa, K., 1976 'Coprolites from a castrum of a Lusatian culture in Komorowo, Poznán District', *Folia Quatanaria* (48) 1–13.

Kroll, H., 1983 'Die Pflanzenfunde von Kastanas', in Hansel, B., (ed) *Prähistorische Archäologie in Südosteuropa*, II. Speiss, Berlin. See pp. 158–60 for details of ergot finds.

Krzywinski, K., 1979 'Preliminaer undersøkelse av planterester i latrine', *Arkeo* (1979) 31–3. Bergen. (As cited by Greig 1983.)

Kühn, F., 1970 'Ausklingen der Emmerkultur in der Tschechoslowakei, *Acta. Univ. Agric. Brno*, Ser. A (18) 587–94.

Lee, D., 1959 *Freedom and Culture*, 163–4. Prentice Hall, New Jersey. (As cited by McLuhan 1971.)

Legge, A. J., and Rowley-Conwy, P., forthcoming 'Steppe Hunters and the Rise of Domestication: the evidence from Tell Abu Hureyra', paper submitted to *Scientific American*.

Lynch, A., and Paap, N. A., 1982 'Untersuchungen an botanischen Funden aus der Lübecker Innenstadt: ein Vorbericht', *Lübecker Schriften zur Archäologie und Kulturgeschichte* (6) 339–60.

Maier, U., 1983 'Nahrungspflanzen des späten Mittelalters aus Heidelberg und Ladenburg aus einer Fäkaliengrube und einem Brunnen des 15–16 Jahrunderts', *Forschungen und Berichte der Archäologie des Mittelalters in Baden-Württemberg* (8) 139–83. (As cited by Grieg 1983.)

Maurizio, A., 1927 *Die Geschichte unserer Pflanzennahrung von den Urzeiten bis zur Gegenwart*. Parey, Berlin.

McLuhan, T. C., 1971 *Touch the Earth: a self-portrait of Indian existence*. Sphere Books (Abacus paperback edition), London. Reprint 1982. Particularly pp. 6, 15 and 179.

Metropolitan Police Forensic Science Laboratory, 1978 *Biology Methods Manual*. Commissioner of Metropolitan Police, London.

Milles, A., 1984 *The Problems of Applying Ethnographic Interpretive Models to Assemblages of Charred Plant Remains both Lacking in Glume Wheats and Poor in Weed Seeds*. MSc dissertation, Department of Plant Science, University College of South Wales, Cardiff.

Moeschling, S., 1980 *Klinik und Therapie der Vergiftung* (6th ed). Georg Thieme Verlag, Stuttgart.

Moreau, C., and Moff, M., 1979 *Moulds, Toxins and Food*. Wiley, New York.

Moritz, L. A., 1958 *Grain Mills and Flour in Classical Antiquity*. Oxford University Press.

Musil, A., 1928 *The Manners and Customs of the Rwala Bedouins*. American Geographical Society, New York.

Netolitzky, F., 1906 *Die Vegetabilien in den Faeces: ein mikroscopisch-forensische Studie*. Wien.

Netolitzky, F., 1931 'Speisereste in einer Moorleiche', *Forschungen und Fortschritte* (12) 269–70.

O'Crohan, T., 1978 *The Islandman* (English translation from the Irish Gaelic original). Oxford University Press.

Orlov, A. A., and Aberg, E., 1941 'The Classification of Subspecies and Varieties of *Hordeum sativum* Jessen', *Feddes Repertorium* (50) 1–18.

Paap, N. A., 1976 'Coprolites: preliminary results of the investigation of prehistoric faeces from Westfriesland (province of North Holland, the Netherlands)', *Berichten van de Rijksdienst voor het Oudheitkundig Bodemonderzoek* (26) 127–32.

Paap, N. A., 1983 'Economic plants in Amsterdam: qualitative and quantitative analysis', in Jones, M. K. (ed.) *Integrating the Subsistence Economy*, British Archaeological Report, International Series (181).

Paap, N. A., 1984 'Botanical Investigations in Amsterdam', in Zeist, W. van, and Casparie, W. S., 1984, 339–44.

Pierpoint Johnson, C., 1862 *The Useful Plants of Great Britain*. W. Kent, London.

Reynolds, P., 1981 'Deadstock and Livestock', in Mercer, R., (ed) *Farming Practice in British Prehistory*, 97–122. Edinburgh University Press.

Riskind, D. H., 1970 'Pollen Analysis of Human Coprolites from Parida Cave', in Alexander, R., (ed) *Archaeological investigations at Parida Cave, Val Verde County, Texas*. University of Texas Press, Austin. Papers in the Texas Archaeological Salvage Project (19). (As cited by Stock 1983)

Robins, G. V., 1980 *Food Science in catering*. Heinemann, London.

Robins, G. V., 1983 'Analysis of Archaeo-Organic Residues', *Analytical Proceedings of the Royal Society of Chemistry* (1983) 379–81.

Robins, G. V., 1984 'The Study of Heated and Charred Archaeological Materials with Electron Spin Resonance Spectroscopy', *Journ. Analyt. and Appl. Pyrolysis* (6) 31–43.

Robins, G. V., and Gutteridge, C., in press 'Pyrolysis Mass Spectrometry in the Analysis of Archaeological Materials', *European Spectroscopy News*.

Roust, N. L., 1967 'Preliminary Examination of Prehistoric Human Coprolites from Four Western Nevada Caves', *Reports of the University of California Archaeological Survey* (70) 47–88. Berkeley: Univ. Calif. Arch. Res. Facility.

Rowley-Conwy, P., forthcoming *Desiccated Plant Remains from Qasr Ibrim in Nubia*. Paper to be presented to the 1986 meeting of the International Workgroup for Palaeoethnobotany.

Rymer, L., 1976 'The History and Ethnobotany of Bracken', *Bot. Journ. Linn. Soc.* (73) 151–76.

Sabine, E. L., 1934 'Latrines and Cesspools of Medieval London', *Speculum* (9) 303–21. (As cited by Greig 1983.)

Sahlins, M. D., 1968 *Stone age economics*. Aldine Atherton, Chicago and New York.

Sales, K. D., Oduwole, A. D., Robins, G. V., and Olsen, S., in press 'The Radiation and Thermal Dependence of ESR Signals in Ancient and Modern Bones', *Nuclear Tracks*.

Schiemann, E., 1948 *Weizen, Roggen, Gerste: Systematik, Geschichte und Verwendug*. Gustav Fischer, Jena.

Schwanitz, G., 1939 *Die Vorgeschichte Schleswig-Hosteins (Stein und Bronzezeit)* Band I. Wachholz, Neumunster. See in particular pp. 146–51.

Shay, C. T., 1984 'A Preliminary Report on Archaeobotany and History at Upper Fort Garry, Manitoba, 1946–82', in Zeist, W. van, and Casparie, W. S., 1984, 123–9.

Sigaut, F., 1978 'Identification des techniques de récolte des grains alimentaires', *Journ. d'Agric. Trad. et de Bot. Appl.* (24) 145–61.

Smith, H. H., 1923 'Ethnobotany of the Menomini Indians', *Bull. Public Museum of City of Milwaukee* (4, 1) 1–175.

Smith, H. H., 1932 'Ethnobotany of the Ojibwe Indians', *Bull. Public Museum of City of Milwaukee* (4, 3) 327–525.

Standing Bear, Chief Luther, 1933 *Land of the Spotted Eagle*, 192–7. Houghton Mifflin, New York. (As cited by McLuhan 1971.)

Stock, J. A., 1983 *The Prehistoric Diet of Hinds Cave, Val Verde County, Texas: the coprolite evidence*. MA thesis in Texas A & M University, Department of Anthropology.

Strabo *Geography*, English translation by Jones, H. L., 1923. Heinemann, Loeb Classical Library, London.

Sturtevant, 1919 See Hendrick.

Tannahill, R., 1975 *Food in History*. Paladin paperbacks, St Albans (UK).

Thomas, D. H., 1984 'Three Generations of Archaeology at Hidden Cave, Nevada', *Archaeology* (37) 40–7.

Tauber, H., 1981 '13C Evidence of Dietary Habits of Prehistoric Man in Denmark', *Nature* (292) 332–3.

Vanderborgh, N. E., Fletcher, M.A., and Jones, C. E. R., 1979 'Laser Pyrolysis of Carbonaceous Rocks', *Journ. Analyt. and Appl. Pyrolysis* (1) 177–86.

Vaughan, M-D., in prep 'Charred Remains of Plants from PPNB Levels at El Koum II in Syria', probably to appear in *Cahiers de l'Euphrat* (Lyon) (5).

Warren, S. H., 1911 'On a Prehistoric Interment near Walton-on-the-Naze', *Essex Naturalist* (16) 198–208.

Wasylikowa, K., 1981 'The Role of Fossil Weeds for the Study of Former Agriculture', *Zeitschrift für Archäologie* (15) 11–23.

Watson, E. V., 1963 *British Mosses and Liverworts*. Cambridge University Press.

Watson, P. J., 1969 *The Prehistory of Salts Cave, Kentucky*, Reports of Investigations (16). Illinois State Museum.

Williams-Dean, G., 1978 *Ethnobotany and Cultural Ecology of Prehistoric Man in Southwest Texas*. PhD dissertation, Department of Biology, Texas A & M University, College Station, Texas.

Williams-Dean, G., and Bryant, V. M.,
Jnr, 1975 'Pollen Analysis of Human
Coprolites from Antelope House', *The
Kiva* (41) 97–111.

Wilson, D. G., 1975 'Plant Foods and
Poisons from Medieval Chester', *Journ.
Chester Arch. Soc.* (58) 57–67.

Wilson, D. G., 1979 'Horse Dung from
Roman Lancaster: a botanical report',
Archaeo-Physica (8) 331–49.

Yarnell, R. A., 1969 'Contents of Human
Palaeofaeces', in Watson, P. J., 1969,
41–64.

Zeist, W. van, and Casparie, W. A., (eds)
1984 *Plants and Ancient Man: studies in
palaeoethnobotany*. Balkema,
Rotterdam.

Zeist, W. van, Hoorn, J. C. van, Bottema,
S., *et al*, 1976 and 1981 'An Agricultural
Experiment in Unprotected Salt-
Marsh', *Palaeohistoria* (18) 111–53 and
(22) 128–40.

Chapter 26

Brandt, J., 1950 'Planterester fra et
Moselig fra Aeldre Jernalder;
Borremose (Plant Remains in the Body
of an Early Iron Age Man from Borre
Fen)' *Arboger for Nordisk Oldkyndighed
og Historie* 348–350.

Clapham, A. R., Tutin, T. G. and Warburg,
E. F., 1962 *Flora of the British Isles*.
Cambridge: University Press.

Dickson, C. A., forthcoming 'A Paper
Outlining the Method of Preparing
Modern Reference Material such that it
Resembles Ancient Waterlogged
Material – special reference to cereals',
due to appear in *Circaea*.

Hall, A. R., Jones, A. K. G., and Kenwood,
H. K., 1983 'Cereal Bran and Human
Faecal Remains from Archaeological
Deposits – Some Preliminary
Observations', in Proudfoot, B., (ed) *Site,
Environment and Economy* 85–103.
B.A.R. International Series (173).

Helbaek, H., 1950 'Tollundmandens Sidste
Maltid' (The Tollund Man's Last Meal),
*Arboger for Nordisk Oldkyndighed og
Historie*, 328–41.

Helbaek, H., 1958 'Grauballemandens
Sidste Maltid' (The Grauballe Man's
Last Meal), *Kuml*, 111–16.

Hillman, G. C., 1981 'Crop Husbandry
Practice in British Prehistory:
Reconstructions from Charred Remains
of Crops', in Mercer, R. J., (ed) *Farming
Practice in British Prehistory*, 123–62.
Edinburgh University Press.

Hillman, G. C., in press 'Emmer
Cultivation at Breidden Hill Fort', in
Smith, A. G., Musson, C., and Britnell,
W., (eds) *Excavations at Breidden,
Wales*. Cambrian Archaeological
Association, Monographs and
Collection, Cardiff.

Jones, M., 1978 'The Plant Remains', in
*The Excavation of an Iron Age Hill
Settlement, Bronze Age Ring Ditches
and Roman Features at Ashville

Trading Estate, Abingdon (Oxon)*,
C.B.A. Research Report (25) 93–110.
London.

Körber-Grohne, U., 1981 'Distinguishing
Prehistoric Cereal Grains of Triticum
and Secale on the Basis of their Surface
Patterns Using the Scanning Electron
Microscope', *Journ. Arch. Sci.* (8)
197–204.

Körber-Grohne, U., and Piening, U., 1980
'Microstructure of the Surfaces of
Carbonised and Non-Carbonised Grains
of Cereals as Observed in Scanning
Electron and Light Microscopes as an
Aid in Determining Prehistoric
Findings', *Flora* (170) 189–228.

Percival, J., 1921 *The Wheat Plant*.
Duckworth and Co., London.

Schel, J. H. N., Stasse-Wolthuis, M.,
Katan, M. B., and Willemse, M. T. M.,
1980 'Structural Changes of Wheat
Bran after Human Digestion',
*Mededelingen Landbouwhogeschool
Wageningen* (80–14) 1–9.

Tauber, H., 1979 'Kulstof-14 Datering af
Moselig' (Carbon-14 Dating of Peat
Bodies), *Kuml*, 73–8.

Vaughan, M. D., 1982 *The Charred Plant
Remains from Hanbury Street,
Droitwich*. Unpublished MSc.
Dissertation, Dept. of Human
Environment, Institute of Archaeology,
University of London.

Winton, A. L., and Winton, K. B., 1932
The Structure and Composition of Foods
1. John Wiley and Sons, New York.

Chapter 27

Bryant, V., 1969 *Late Full-Glacial and
Post-Glacial Pollen Analysis of Texas
Sediments*. Unpublished Ph.D.
dissertation, University of Chicago.
Reference taken from Bryant 1974a.

Bryant, V. M., 1974a 'Prehistoric Diet in
Southwest Texas: The Coprolite
Evidence', *American Antiquity*, (39)
407–20.

Bryant, V. M., 1974b 'Pollen Analysis of
Prehistoric Faeces from Mammoth
Cave', in Watson, P. J., (ed) *Archaeology
of the Mammoth Cave Area*, 203–9.
Academic Press, New York.

Bryant, V. M., 1974c 'The Role of Coprolite
Analysis in Archaeology', *Bull. Texas
Arch. Soc.* (45) 1–28.

Bryant, V. M., 1975 'Pollen as an Indicator
of Prehistoric Diets in Coahuila,
Mexico', *Bull. Texas Arch. Soc.* (46)
87–106.

Bryant, V. M., 1977 'Late quaternary
Pollen Records from the East-Central
Periphery of the Chihuahuan Desert', in
'The Chihuahuan Desert, United States
and Mexico' National Park Service
Trans. and Proc. Series 3: 3–21.
(Reference taken from Stock 1983.)

Bryant, V. M., 1979 'Prehistoric Diets',
University Lecture Series. Texas A & M
University, November 28, 1979.

Bryant, V., and Lasen, D. A., 1968 'Pollen

Analysis of the Devil's Mouth Site, the
Third Season, 1967 by William M.
Sorrow', *Papers of the Texas Arch.
Salvage Project*. (14) 57–70. Austin.

Bryant, V. M., and Williams-Dean, G.,
1975 'The Coprolites of Man', *Scientific
American* (232, 1) 100–9.

Callan, E. O., 1967 'Analysis of Tehuacan
Coprolites', in *The prehistory of the
Tehuacan Valley: Volume 1.
Environment and Subsistence*, 261–89.
University of Texas Press, Austin.

Callan, E. O., 1969 'Diet as Revealed by
Coprolites', in Brothwell, D. R., and
Higgs, E. H., *Science in Archaeology*
(2nd ed), 186–94. Thames and Hudson,
London.

Callan, E. O., 1969 'Les coprolithes de la
Cabane Acheuleene du Lazaret', in
Lumley, H. de, (ed) 'Une Cabane
Acheuleene dans la Grotte du Lazaret',
*Mémoires de la Société Préhistorique
Française* (7) 123–4. Nice.

Callan, E. O., and Cameron, T. W. M.,
1960 'A Prehistoric Diet Revealed in
Coprolites', *The New Scientist* (8, 190)
35–40.

Callan, E. O., and Martin, P. S., 1969
'Plant Remains in some Coprolites from
Utah', *American Antiquity* (35, 3)
329–31.

Culpeper, N. *Culpeper's Complete Herbal:
consisting of a comprehensive
description of nearly all herbs with their
medicinal properties and directions for
compounding the medicines extracted
from them'*. Numerous editions; this one
Foulsham, W., London.

de Lumley, H., 1966 'Les fouilles de Terra
Amata à Nice', *Bulletin de Musée
d'Anthropologie Préhistorique de
Monaco* (13) 29–51.

de Lumley, H., 1969 'Les coprolithes de la
Cabane Acheuleene du Lazaret. II –
Analyse et diagnostic', in de Lumley, H.,
(ed) 'Une Cabane Acheuleene dans la
Grotte du Lazaret (Nice)', *Mémoires de
la Société Préhistorique Française* (7)
123–4.

Dickson, J. H., 1978 'Bronze Age Mead',
Antiquity (205) 108–13.

Dimbleby, G. W., 1968 'Ivinghoe Beacon
Excavations 1963–1965', in Cotton, M.
A., and Frere, S. S., *Records for
Buckinghamshire* (19, 3) 187–260.

Dimbleby, G. W., 1978 *Plants and
Archaeology* (2nd ed). John Baker, London.

Farrand, W. R., 1961 'Frozen Mammoths
and Modern Geology', *Science* (133)
729–35.

Greig, J. R. A., 1981 'The Investigation of
a Medieval Barrel-Latrine from
Worcester', *Journ. Arch. Sci.* (8) 265–82.

Greig, J. R. A., 1982 'The Interpretation
of Pollen Spectra from Urban
Archaeological Deposits', in Hall, A. R.,
and Kenward, H. K., (eds)
*Environmental Archaeology in the
Urban Context*, Council of British
Archaeology (43) 47–65.

Harshenberger, J. W., 1896 'The Purpose of Ethnobotany', *American Antiquarian* (17, 2) 73–81.

Hall, A. R., Jones, A. K. G., and Kenward, H. K., 1983 'Cereal Bran and Human Faecal Remains From Archaeological Deposits – Some Preliminary Observations', in Proudfoot, B., (ed) *Site, Environment and Economy (Symposia of Assoc. for Environmental Archaeology No. 3)* B.A.R. International Series (173) 85–104.

Heizer, R. F., 1969 'The Anthropology of Prehistoric Great Basin Human Coprolites', in Brothwell, D. R., and Higgs, E. S., *Science in Archaeology* (2nd ed), 244–50. Thames and Hudson, London.

Heizer, R. F., and Napton, L. K., 1969 'Biological and Cultural Evidence from Prehistoric Human Coprolites', *Science* (165) 563–8.

Helbaek, H., 1950 'Tollundmandens sidste måltid. Botanical study of the Stomach of the Tollund Man', *Årboger for Nordisk Oldkyndighed og Historie*, 329–41.

Helbaek, H., 1954 'Prehistoric Food Plants and Weeds in Denmark: a Survey of Archaeobotanical Research 1923–54', *Danske Geologiske Undersøgelser* (2) 250–61.

Helbaek, H., 1958 'Grauballemandens sidste måltid. The Last Meal of Grauballe Man: an Analysis of Food Remains in the Stomach', *Kuml* (1958) 83–116. Århus.

Iversen, J., 1944 '*Viscum, Hedera* and *Ilex* as climatic indicators', *Geol. För. Stock. Föhr.* (66) 463–83.

Jones, A. K. G., 1983 'A Coprolite from 6–8 Pavement', in Hall, A. R., Kenward, H. K., Williams, D., and Greig, J. R. A., *Environment and living conditions at two Anglo-Scandinavian sites* (The Archaeology of York. 14/4) 225–9. Published by Council for British Archaeology for the York Archaeological Trust.

Jones, V., 1936 'The Vegetal Remains of Knewt Kash Hollow Shelter', in Webb, W. S., and Funkhouser, J. W., 'Rock Shelters in Menifee Country, Kentucky', *University of Kentucky Reports in Archaeology and Anthropology* (3, 4).

Knights, B. A., Dickson, C. A., Dickson, J. H., and Breeze, D. J., 1983 'Evidence Concerning the Roman Military Diet at Bearsden, Scotland, in the 2nd Century AD', *Journ. Arch. Sci.* (10) 139–52.

Krausel, R., 1922 'Die Nahrung von Trachodon', *Palaeontol. Zeitschr.* (4) 80.

Krwzinski, K., 1979 'Preliminar underskelse av planterester i latrine', *Arkeo* (1) 31–3.

Krwzinski, K., Fjelldal, S., and Soltvedt, E., 1983 'Recent Palaeoethnobotanical Work at the Medieval Excavations at Bryggen, Bergen, Norway', in

Proudfoot, B., (ed) '*Site, Environment and Economy*' (*Symposia of Assoc. for Environmental Archaeology No. 3*) B.A.R. International Series (173) 145–69.

Laudermilk, J. D., and Munz, P. A., 1938 'Plants in the Dung of Nothrotherium from Rampart and Muave Caves, Arizona', *Carnegie Institution of Washington, Publication* (487) 271–81. Washington.

Leakey, M. D., 1971 *Excavations in Beds I and II Olduvai Gorge* 3: 1960–1963. Cambridge University Press.

Loud, L. L., and Harrington, M. R., 1929 'Lovelock Cave', *University of California Publications in American Archaeology and Ethnology* (25, 1).

Martin, P. S., Bruno, E. S., and Shutler, R. Jnr, 1961 'Rampart Cave Coprolite and Ecology of the Shasta Ground Sloth', *American Journ. Sci.* (259) 102–27.

Martin, P. S., and Sharrock, F. W., 1964 'Pollen Analysis of Prehistoric Human Faeces: a New Approach to Ethnobotany', *American Antiquity* (30, 2) 168–80.

Moore, P. D., and Webb, J. A., 1978 *An Illustrated Guide to Pollen Analysis.* Hodder and Stoughton, London.

Napton, L. K., and Kelso, G., 1969 'Preliminary Analysis of Lovelock Cave Coprolites. Archaeological and Palaeobiological Investigations in Lovelock Cave, Nevada', *Kroeber Anthropological Society Papers. Special Publications* (2) 19–27. Berkeley University of California Press.

Oldfield, F., Richardson, N., and Yates, G., 1985 'Lindow Man', in Stead, I., and Turner, R. C., *Antiquity* (59) 25–9.

Ostrom, J. H., 1964 'A Reconstruction of the Palaeoecology of Hadrosaurian Dinosaurs', *American Journ. Sci.* (262) 975–97.

Perring, F., 1973 'Mistletoe', in Green, P. S. (ed) *Plants Wild and Cultivated.* B.S.B.I. Conference Report (13).

Robinson, M., and Hubbard, R. N. L. B., 1977 'The Transport of pollen in the Bracts of Hulled Cereals', *Journ. Arch. Sci.* (4) 197–9.

Riskind, D. H., 1970 'Pollen Analysis of Human Coprolites from Parida Cave, Val Verde County, Texas', *Papers of the Texas Archaeological Salvage Project* (19) 89–101.

Scaife, R. G., in press 'Analysis of a Canine Coprolite from Ditches, North Cerney, Gloucestershire', in Trow, S., *Excavations at a Romano-British site, Ditches, Gloucestershire.*

Scaife, R. G., 1979 'Pollen Analytical Investigation of Broad Sanctuary, Westminster, London', *Ancient Monuments Laboratory Report* No. 3070.

Scaife, R. G., 1982 'Pollen Analysis', in Mills, P., 'Excavations at Broad Sanctuary, Westminster', *Transactions*

of the London and Middlesex Archaeological Society (33) 345–65.

Shoenwetter, J., 1974 'Pollen Analysis of Prehistoric Human Faeces from Salts Cave Kentucky', in *The Archaeology of the Mammoth Cave area.* Academic Press. (As cited by Bryant, V. M., 1974c.)

Stock, J. A., 1983 *The Prehistoric Diet of Hinds Cave (41 VV 456), Val Verde County, Texas: The Coprolite Evidence.* Department of Anthropology, Texas A & M University.

Trevor-Deutsch, B., and Bryant, V. M., 1978 'Analysis of Suspected Human Coprolites from Terra Amata, Nice, France', *Journ. Arch. Sci.* (5) 387–90.

Voorhies, M. R., and Thomasson, J. R., 1979 'Fossil Grass Anthoecia within Miocene Rhinoceras Skeletons: Diet in Extinct Species', *Science* (206) 331–3.

Williams-Dean, G., and Bryant, V. M., 1975 'Pollen Analysis of Human Coprolites from Antelope House', *The Kiva* (41) 97–111.

Wren, R. C., 1941 *Potter's Cyclopaedia of Botanical Drugs and Preparations* (5th ed). Potter and Clarke, London.

Young, B. H., 1910 *The Prehistoric Men of Kentucky.* Filson Club publication No. 25. Louisville.

Chapter 28

Beer, R. J. S., 1976 'The Relationship Between *Trichuris trichiura* (Linnaeus 1758) of Man and *Trichuris suis* (Schrank 1788) of Pig', *Research in Veterinary Science* (20) 47–54.

Feachem, R. G., Bradley, D. J., Garelick, H., and Mara, D. D., 1983 *Sanitation and Disease*, World Bank Studies in Water Supply and Sanitation (3). John Wiley, Chichester.

Hall, A. R., Jones, A. K. G., and Kenward, H. K., 1983 'Cereal Bran and Human Faecal Remains from Archaeological Deposits – Some Preliminary Observations', in Proudfoot, B., (ed) *Site, Environment and Economy.* British Archaeological Reports International Series (173), 85–104.

Helbaek, H., 1958 'Grauballemandens sidste måltid', *Kuml* (1958) 83–116 (with extended English summary).

Jones, A. K. G., 1983 'A coprolite from 6–8 Pavement' in Hall, A. R., Kenward, H. K., Williams, D., and Greig, J. R. A., *Environment and living conditions at two Anglo-Scandinavian Sites* (The Archaeology of York, 14/4) 225–9.

Jones, A. K. G., 1984 'Recent Finds of Intestinal Parasite Ova at York, England', in Haneveld, G. T., and Perizonius, W. R. K., (eds) *Proceedings of the Paleopathology Association Fourth European Meeting*, 229–33.

Jones, A. K. G., forthcoming 'Intestinal Parasites from 'Sondrefelt', Oslo.'

Ministry of Agriculture, Fisheries and Food, 1977 *Manual of Veterinary Parasitological Laboratory Techniques* (Technical Bulletin No. 18). Her Majesty's Stationery Office, London.

Spencer, F. M., and Monroe, L. S., 1975 *The Color Atlas of Intestinal Parasites.* Charles Thomas, Springfield, Illinois.

Szidat, L., 1944 'Uber die Erhaltungsfähigkeit von Helmintheiern in Vor- und Frühgeschichtlichen Moorleichen', *Zeitschrift für Parasitenkunde* (13) 265–74.

Chapter 29

Hillman, G. C., Robins, G. V., Oduwole, D., Sales, K. D., and McNeil, D.A.C., 1985 'The Use of ESR Spectroscopy to Determine the Thermal History of Cereal Grains', *Journ. Arch. Sci.* (12) 49–58.

Robins, G. V., Sales, K. D., and McNeil, D. A. C., 1984 'Ancient Spins', *Chemistry in Britain*, 894–9.

Stahl, A. B., 1984 'Homonid dietary selection before fire', *Current Anthropology* (25) 151–68.

Chapter 30 (including Appendix)

Abercromby, J., 1905 'Report on Excavations at Fethaland and Trowie Krowe, Shetland; and of the Exploration of a Cairn on Dumglow, one of the Cleish Hills, Kinrossshire', *Proc. Soc. Ant. Scotland* (39) 181.

Alexander, R. W., Coxon, P., and Thorn, R. H., 1985 'Bog Flows in South-East Sligo and South-West Leitrim', in Thorn, R. H., (ed) *Sligo and West Leitrim Field Guide* 8 (Irish Association for Quaternary Studies).

Andrews, J., 1975 *A Paper Landscape: the Ordnance Survey in nineteenth-century Ireland.* Oxford.

Baines, E.,1868 *The History of the County Palatine and Duchy of Lancaster* (2nd ed) 1.

Bakewell, R., 1833 *An Introduction to Geology.* London.

Balguy, C., 1734 'An Account of the Dead Bodies of a Man and Woman which were preserved 49 years in the Moors in Derbyshire', *Phil. Trans. Roy. Soc.* (38) no. 434, 413–15.

Bateman, T., 1855 *The Bateman Catalogue of Antiquities.*

Boate, 1726. *Ireland's Natural Historie* (2nd ed.) Dublin.

Bradley, J., 1985 'Planned Anglo-Norman Towns in Ireland', in Clarke, H. B., and Simms, A., (eds) *The Comparative History of Urban Origins in Non-Roman Europe*, Brit. Archaeol. Rep. Internat. Ser. (255) 411–67.

Briggs, C. S., *in press* 'Buckets and Cauldrons in the Late Bronze Age of North-West Europe, a Review', *Proc. 20ième Coll. de la Soc. Préhist de France 1984.*

Buckland, P. C., and Kenward, H. K., 1973

'Thorne Moor: a palaeoecological study of a Bronze Age site', *Nature* (241) 405–6.

Busk, G., 1866 'An Account of the Discovery of a Human Skeleton Beneath a Bed of Peat on the Coast of Cheshire', *Trans. Ethnol. Soc.* (4) 101-4.

Busk, G., 1874 'Human Skull and Fragments of Bones of the Red Deer, etc., found at Birkdale, near Southport, Lancashire', *Journ. Anth. Inst.* (3) 104–5.

Charlesworth, J. K., 1953 *The Geology of Ireland.* Edinburgh and London.

Clark, G., 1933 'Report on an Early Bronze Age Site in the South-Eastern Fens', *Antiq. Journ.* (13) 278–9.

Clarke, R. R., 1960 *East Anglia.* London.

Clarke, R. R., 1971 *East Anglia* (2nd ed). London.

Costello, T. B., 1919–20 'Cauldron from Barnascurragh Bog, Tuam', *Journ. Galway Archaeol. and Hist. Soc.* (11) 72–5.

Cotton, M. A., 1960 'Preservation in Iron Age Bog Burials', *The Archaeological News Letter*, 247–51.

Cust, E., 1864 'The Prehistoric Man of Cheshire', *Trans. Hist. Soc. Lancs. and Ches.* (4) 193–201.

Davies, G. L. Herries, 1983 *Sheets of many Colours; The Mapping of Ireland's rocks, 1750–1840* (Roy. Dublin Soc.).

de la Pryme, A., 1694 and 1746 'Of Trees Underground in Hatfield Chase', *Phil. Trans. Roy. Soc.* No. 275, and *Abridged Phil. Trans. Roy. Soc.* (4, 2) 212–8.

Denny, H., 1871 'Notice of the Discovery of a Pair of Ancient Shoes and a Human Skeleton in the Peat Moss on Austwick Common, near Clapham, Yorkshire', *Proc. Geol. and Polytech. Soc., West Riding of Yorks* (5) 162–78.

Dieck, A., 1958 'Zur Geschichte der Moorleicherforschung und Moorleichendeutung', *Jahresschrift für Mitteldeutsche Vorgeschichte* (41–2).

Dieck, A., 1963 'Zum Problem der Hominidenmoorfunde', *Neue Ausgrabungen und Forshungen in Niedersachsen*, 105–112.

Dieck, A., 1965 *Die europäischen Moorleichenfunde.* Neümunster.

Dieck, A., 1972 'Stand und Aufgaben der Moorleichenforschung', *Archäologisches Korrespondenzblatt* (2) 365–8.

Dieck, A., 1983 'Die Moorleiche von Obenaltendorf bei Stade', *Stader Jahrbuch* (1983) 7–56.

Duckworth, W. L. H., and Shore, L. R., 1911 'Report on Human Crania from Peat Deposits in England', *Man* (11) 134–40.

Dunbar, J. T., 1949 'Early Tartans', in McClintock 1950, 63–79.

Edgeworth, R. L., 1783 'A further Account of Discoveries in the Turf Bogs of Ireland', *Archaeol.* (7) 111–12.

Edgeworth, R. L., 1812 'Appendix to Report No. II', in *Report to the*

Commissioners for improving the bogs of Ireland (Dublin), 174.

Edwards, B. J. N., 1969 'Lancashire Archaeological Notes', *Trans. Hist. Soc. Lancs. and Ches.* (121) 101–3.

Edwards, B. J. N., 1973 'A Canoe Burial near Lancaster', *Antiquity* (43) 298–301.

Elgee, F., 1930 *Early Man in North-East Yorkshire.* Gloucester.

Evans, J., 1956 *A History of the Society of Antiquaries.* Oxford.

Fischer, C., 1979 'Moseligene fra Bjaeldskovdal', *Kuml* (1979) 7–44.

Flower, W. H., 1907 *Catalogue of the Specimens Illustrating Osteology and Dentition of Vertebrated Animals, Recent and Extinct, Contained in the Museum of the RCS of England. Part I, Man* (2nd ed).

Fox, C., 1923 *The Archaeology of the Cambridge Region.* Cambridge.

Ganno, G. D., 1975 'The artificial nature of the River Don north of Thorne, Yorkshire', *Yorks Arch. Journ.* (47) 15–22.

Gibson, E., 1695 *Camden's Britannia* (1st ed). London.

Gibson, E., 1722 *Camden's Britannia* (2nd ed). London.

Gilpin, 1786 *Observations on the Mountains and Lakes of Cumberland and Westmorland.* London.

Glob, P. V., 1969 *The Bog People.* London.

Gough, R., 1789 *Camden's Britannia.* London.

Grainge, W., 1892 *Ripon Millenary*, preface to part II. Ripon.

Green, C., and Wells, C., 1961 'A Human Skull from Runham, Norfolk', *Norfolk Arch.* (32) 311–5.

Gunn, J., 1883 *White's History, Gazetteer and Directory of Norfolk* (4th ed).

Hammond, R. F., 1981 *The Peatlands of Ireland.* Dublin.

Haughton, J. I., n.d. 'Soil and Vegetation', in Meally, V., (ed) *Encyclopaedia of Ireland* (Dublin), 45–6.

Henshall, A. S., 1952 'Early Textiles found in Scotland: Part 1 (locally made)', *Proc. Soc. Ant. Scotland* (86) 1–30.

Henshall, A. S., 1969 'Clothing found at Huntsgarth, Harray, Orkney', *Proc. Soc. Ant. Scotland* (101) 150–9.

Henshall, A. S., and Maxwell, S., 1952 'Clothing and Other Articles from a Late 17th Century Grave at Gunnister, Shetland', *Proc. Soc. Ant. Scotland* (86) 30–42.

Henshall, A. S., and Seaby, W. A., 1961–2 'The Dungiven Costume', *Ulster Journ. Arch.* (24–5) 119–42.

Hughes, T. Mck., 1916 *Notes on the Fenland with a description of the Shippea Hill Man.* Cambridge.

Hume, A., 1863 *Ancient Meols: or some account of the Antiquities found near Dove Point on the Sea-Coast of Cheshire.* London.

Hunt, J., 1866a 'On the Influence of some kinds of Peat in Destroying the Human Body, as shown by the Discovery of Human Remains buried in Peat in the Zetland Islands', *Mems of the Anth. Soc. of London* (2) 364–72.

Hunt, J., 1866b 'Observations on the Influence of Peat in Destroying the Human Body, as shown by the Discovery of Human Remains buried in Peat in the Zetland Islands', *The Anth. Rev.* (4) ccvi–ccix.

Hunter, J., 1828 *South Yorkshire: the History and Topography of the Deanery of Doncaster in the Diocese and the County of York*. London.

Kane, R., 1845 *The Industrial Resources of Ireland* (2nd ed). Dublin.

King, W., 1685 'Of the Bogs and Loughs of Ireland', *Phil. Trans. Roy. Soc.* (15) 948–60.

Latimer, W. T., 1901 'Discovery of Relics in County Tyrone', *Journ. Roy. Soc. Antiq. Ireland* (31) 288–9.

Leigh, C., 1700 *The Natural History of Lancashire, Cheshire and the Peak of Derbyshire*. Oxford.

Lewis, S., 1837 *A Topographical Dictionary of Ireland*. London.

Low, G., 1773 'Extract of a letter from the Reverend Mr George Low, to Mr Paton, of Edinburgh. Communicated by Mr Gough', *Archaeol.* (3) 276–8.

Lucas, A T., 1956 'Footwear in Ireland'. *Co. Louth Arch. Journ.* (13) 309–94.

Lucas, A. T., 1962 'National Museum of Ireland. Archaeological Acquisitions in the year 1960', *Journ. Roy. Soc. Antiq. Ireland* (92) 139–73.

Lucas, A. T., 1972 'National Museum of Ireland Acquisitions in the year 1969', *Journ. Roy. Soc. Antiq. Ireland* (102) 181–223.

Lyell, C., 1838 *The Principles of Geology* London.

Mann, L. Mc L., 1937 'Notes on the Discovery of a Body in a Peat Moss at Cambusnethan', *Trans. Glasgow Arch. Soc.* (9) 44–55.

Macadam, R., 1861–2 'Ancient Leather Cloak', *Ulster Journ. Archaeol.* (9) 294–300.

Mapleton, J., 1879 'Notice on the Discovery of an old canoe in a Peat Bog at Oban', *Proc. Soc. Ant. Scotland* (13) 336–8.

Martin, C. P., 1935 *Prehistoric Man in Ireland*. London.

Mason, E. J. and D., 1951 'Report on Human Remains and Material Recovered from Wookey Hole from October 1947 to January 1949', *Proc. Som. Arch. and Nat. Hist. Soc.* (95) 238–43.

Maughan, J., 1873 'A Runic Inscription on Hessilgil Crags: Murchie's Cairn', *Trans. Cumberland and West. Ant. and Arch. Soc.* (1) 320–1.

McClintock, H. F., 1950 *Old Irish and Highland Dress* (2nd ed). Dundalk.

Mitchell, G. F., 1945 'The Relative Ages of Archaeological Objects recently found in bogs in Ireland', *Proc. Roy. Irish Acad.* (50C) 1–19.

Mitchell, G. F., 1951 'Studies in Irish Quaternary Deposits: No. 7', *Proc. Roy. Irish Acad.* (53B) 111–206.

Moira, Countess of, 1783 'Particulars relative to a human skeleton, and the garments that were found thereon, when dug out of a bog at the foot of Drumkeeragh, a mountain in the County of Down, and Barony of Kinalearty, on Lord Moira's estate, in the autumn of 1780. In a letter to the Hon. John Theophilus Rawdon, by the Countess of Moira; communicated by Mr Barrington', *Archaeol.* (7) 90–110.

Molyneux, W., 1697 'Account of a moving Bog in Ireland' and 'A true development of the Bog of Kapanihane . . .', *Phil. Trans. Roy. Soc.*, 714–5.

Morris, 1906. Untitled contribution to *Jnl. Co. Louth Arch. Soc.*

Norbury, W. H., 1884 'Lindow Common as a Peat Bog: its age and its people', *Trans. Lancs. and Ches. Antiq. Soc.* (2) 59–75.

Orr, S., 1921 'Clothing found on a Skeleton Discovered at Quintfall Hill, Barrock Estate, near Wick', *Proc. Soc. Ant. Scotland* (55) 213–21.

Owen, D. M., 1982 'The Minute Books of the Spalding Gentleman's Society 1712–55', *Lincoln Rec. Soc.* (73).

Petrie, G., 1825 'Account of a human body in a singular costume, found in a high state of preservation in a bog on the lands of Gallagh, in the county of Galway', *Dublin Phil. Journ. and Sci. Rev.* (1) 433–5.

Piggott, S., 1953 'Three metal-work hoards of the Roman period from Southern Scotland', *Proc. Soc. Ant. Scotland* (87) 1–51.

Piggott, S., 1965 *Ancient Europe*. Edinburgh.

Pownall, T., 1774 'An account of some Irish antiquities', *Archaeol.* (3) 355–70.

Pugh, R. B., and Crittall, E., 1909 *A History of Wiltshire* (1, 1). VCH London.

Raftery, J., 1959 'A Travelling Man's View of Christian Times', *Proc. Rov. Irish Acad.* (60C) 1–8.

Reade, T. M., 1883 'The Human Skull found near Southport', *Geological Mag.* (10) 547–8.

Rennie, R., 1810 *Essay on the Natural History and Origin of Peat-Moss*. Edinburgh.

Ross, A., *Pagan Celtic Britain*. London, New York.

Shea, 1931 'Report on the Human Skeleton found in Stoney Island Bog, Portumna', *Journ. Galway Archaeol. and Hist. Soc.* (15) 73–9.

Shee, E. A., and O'Kelly, M. J., 1966 'A Clothes Burial from Emlagh, near Dingle, County Kerry', *Journ. Cork Archaeol. and Hist. Soc.* (71) 81–91.

Stovin, G., 1747 'A Letter from Mr T. G.

Stovin, to his Son, concerning the Body of a Woman, and an Antique Shoe, found in a Morass in the Isle of Axholme in Lincolnshire', *Phil. Trans. Roy. Soc.* (44) 571–6.

Stukeley, W., 1776 *Itinerarium Curiosum* (2nd ed) 2.

Tauber, H., 1979 'Kulstof-14 Datering of Moselig', *Kuml* (1979) 73–8.

Tinsley, H. M., 1974 'A Record of preserved Human Remains from Blanket Peat in West Yorkshire', *The Naturalist* (931) 134.

Tooley, M., 1978 'The History of Hartlepool Bay', *Int. Journ. of Naut. Arch. and Underwater Exploration* (7, 1) 71–87.

Torbrügge, W., 1972 'Vor und frühgeschichliche Flussfunde zur Ordnung und Bestimmung einer Denkmälergruppe', *Ber. RGK* (51–2) 1–146.

Travis, C. B., 1913 'Geological Notes on Recent Dock Excavations at Liverpool and Birkenhead', *Proc. Liverpool Geol. Soc.* (11) 273.

Tupper, A. C., 1866 Untitled note about exhibits, *The Anthropological Review* (4) 128–9.

Waddell, J., 1985 'Bronzes and Bones', *Journ. Irish Archaeol.* (2) 71–2.

Whimster, R., 1981 'Burial Practices in Iron Age Britain', *B.A.R. British Series* (90, 1).

Wilde, W. R., 1863 *A Descriptive Catalogue of the Antiquities in the Museum of Royal Irish Academy* 1. Dublin 1857 (1863).

Wilde, W. R., 1864 'On the Antiquities and Human Remains found in the County of Down, in 1780, and described by the Countess of Moira, in the *Archaeologia* vol. VII', *Proc. Roy. Irish Acad.* (9) 101–4.

Williams, J., 1858 'History of Radnorshire: Hundred of Knighton', *Arch. Cambr.* (12) 469–614.

Wood-Martin, W. G., 1902 *Traces of the Elder Faiths of Ireland* (1).

Chapter 31

Carmichael, A., 1928 *Carmina Gadelica* (1). Oliver & Boyd.

Carmichael, A., 1954 *Carmina Gadelica* (5), Matheson, A., (ed). Oliver & Boyd.

Close-Brooks, J., 1984 'Some objects from peat bogs', *Proc. Soc. Ant. Scotland* (114) 578–81.

Danaher, K., 1972 *The Year in Ireland*. Cork.

Jackson, K., 1940 'The Motive of the Threefold Death in the Story of Suibhne Geilt', in Ryan, J., (ed) *Essays and Studies presented to Professor Eoin MacNeill*, 535–50. Dublin.

Kendrick, T. D., 1927 *The Druids*. Methuen.

Martin, M., 1703 *A Description of the Western Islands of Scotland*. London. (republished, Stirling, 1934).

Ross, A., 1957 'The Human Head in Insular Pagan Celtic Religion', *Proc. Soc. Ant. Scotland* (91) 10–43.

Ross, A., 1962 'Severed Heads in Wells: an Aspect of the Well Cult', *Scottish Studies* (6) 31–48.

Ross, A., 1966 'A Stone Head from Muirton, Blairgowrie', *Trans. and Proc. Perths. Soc. Nat. Science* (11) 31–7, and note in *Journ. Roman Studies* (56) 198.

Ross, A., 1967a 'A Celtic Three-faced Head from Wiltshire', *Antiquity* (41) 53–6.

Ross, A., 1967b *Pagan Celtic Britain.* Routledge & Kegan Paul.

Ross, A., 1969 'A Romano-British Cult Object from Boldre, Hampshire', *Proc. Hants. Field Club* (26) 57–9.

Ross, A., 1970a 'Two Celtic Heads from Bron y Garth', *Arch. Cambrensis* (119) 64–7.

Ross, A., 1970b *Everyday Life of the Pagan Celts.* Batsford, (paperback, Carousel, 1972).

Ross, A., 1973 'Some New Thoughts on Old Heads', *Arch. Aeliana* (5s, 1) 1–9.

Ross, A., 1974 'A Pagan Celtic Tricephalos from Netherton, Lanarkshire', *Glasgow Arch. Journ.* (3) 26–33.

Ross, A., 1975 *Grotesques and Gargoyles.* David and Charles: text illustrated by and book published under name of Ronald Sheridan.

Ross, A., 1981 'A Pagan Celtic Shrine at Wall, Staffordshire; *Trans. Lichfield and S. Staffs. Arch. Soc.* (22) 3–11.

Ross, A., 1984 'Heads Baleful and Benign', in Burgess, C., and Miket, R., (eds) *Between and Beyond the Walls,* 338–52. J. Donald.

Chapter 32

Baring-Gould, S., 1913 *A Book of Folklore.* London.

Briggs, K., 1977 *A Dictionary of Fairies.* Penguin.

Burrow, J. A., 1965 *A Reading of Sir Gawain and the Green Knight.* London.

Cawley, A. C., 1962 *Pearl and Sir Gawain and the Green Knight,* introduction. Everyman.

Crossley-Holland, K., 1984 *The Anglo-Saxon World.* Oxford.

David, C., 1971 *St Winefride's Well: a history and guide.*

Farmer, D. H., 1978 *The Oxford Dictionary of Saints.* Oxford.

Gantz, J., 1976 *The Mabinogion.* Penguin.

Glob, P. V., 1969 *The Bog People.* London.

Gutch, and Peacock, M., 1908 'Folklore concerning Lincolnshire', *County Folklore* (5) (Folklore Soc.).

Henderson, G., 1899 *The Feast of Brictiv* (Irish Text Soc., 2).

Kendrick, T. D., 1927 *The Druids: a study in Keltic Prehistory.* London.

Killip, M., 1975 *The Folklore of the Isle of Man.* London.

Palmer, G., and Lloyd, N., 1972 *A Year of the Festivals.* London.

Piggott, S., 1968 *The Druids.* London.

Ross, A., 1967. *Pagan Celtic Britain.* London.

Savory, H. N., 1976 *Guide Catalogue of the Early Iron Age Collections.* Cardiff.

Scarfe, N., 1970 'The Body of St Edmund: an essay in Necrobiography', *Proc. Suffolk Inst. of Arch.* (31) 303–17.

Tolkien, J. R. R., 1975 *Sir Gawain and the Green Knight with Pearl and Orfeo.* London.

Whitelock, D., 1970 'Fact and Fiction in the Legend of St Edmund', *Proc. Suffolk Inst. of Arch.* (31) 217–33.

Wright, A. R., 1938 *British Calendar Customs: England* (2). London.

Chapter 33

Connolly, R. C., 1985 'Lindow Man: Britain's Prehistoric Bog Body', *Anthropology Today* (1, 5) 15–17.

Cuming, H. Syer, 1857 'On the Discovery of Celtic Crania in the Vicinity of London', *Journ. Brit. Arch. Ass.* (13) 237–9.

de Navarro, J. M., 1972 *The finds from the site of La Tène, 1, Scabbards and the Swords found in them.* London.

Fischer, C., 1980 'Bog bodies of Denmark', in Cockburn, A. and E., (eds) *Mummies, Disease, and Ancient Cultures.* Cambridge.

Fox, Sir Cyril, 1946 *A Find of the Early Iron Age from Llyn Cerrig Bach, Anglesey.* Cardiff.

Glob, P. V., 1969 *The Bog People.* London.

Hammond, N. G. L., and Scullard, H. H., 1970 *The Oxford Classical Dictionary* (2nd ed). Oxford.

Munksgaard, E., 1984 'Bog Bodies – a brief survey of interpretations', *Journ. Danish Arch.* (3) 120–3.

Parker Pearson, M., 1986 'Lindow Man and the Danish Connection – further light on the mystery of the Bogman', *Anthropology Today* (2, 1) 15–18.

Piggott, S., 1968 *The Druids.* London.

Tauber, H., 1979 'Kulstof-14 datering af maselig', *Kuml* (1979) 73–8.

Appendix

(See Bibliography for Chapter 30).

Index